The Minister's Annual Manual

for Preaching and Worship Planning
2003–2004

Compiled by
Sharilyn A. Figueroa

Edited by
Rebecca H. Grothe

Logos Productions Inc.
6160 Carmen Avenue East
Inver Grove Heights, MN 55076-4422

First Edition
Seventeenth Annual Volume

This book has been published by Logos Productions Inc.
Printed by Bethany Press International
Minneapolis, Minnesota

The Hymn of the Day for each week has been prepared by Donald Schmidt who has served congregations in both Canada and the U.S. in several denominations. He is currently editor of congregational life resources for *Seasons of the Spirit,* and serves a church in Lahaina, Hawaii.

Children's Time sermons were prepared by Gillian Wallace who has worked as a Christian education director in churches in Ottawa, Canada, for five years and has written Sunday school curriculum for the *Whole People of God.* She has her Ph.D. in religious studies and is currently a freelance writer.

ISBN: 1-885361-49-1
ISSN: 0894-3966

Contents

Children's Time

Appendices

How to Use This Book

This book is intended for use from August 2003 through July 2004. Because many ministers prefer to plan an entire year of preaching and worship during the summer, this manual is designed to assist in summer-to-summer planning.

Every minister develops his or her own style of preaching and worship planning. Methods, planning, study, writing, and delivery are all unique. Preaching practice comes from experiences over the years; therefore, use this book in whatever ways will benefit your worship and sermon preparation most fully. Its usefulness is determined by your own style and manner of preparation. Included in this book are helpful suggestions to guide your worship planning for each Sunday, as well as for several special worship occasions.

Many ministers prefer to spend time several weeks in advance of a specific Sunday reviewing the texts for that day. The materials in this book will be most helpful for that task. Please read David H. Schmidt's "Resources for Preparing to Preach" on page 437. A variety of resource materials, commentaries, and translations are listed to help you in your exegeses.

For each worship experience, the writer has prepared brief explanatory notes for the lessons, notes that you can use to get a feel for the texts. You can also use these notes in your Sunday bulletins to help your congregation grasp the central idea in the lessons for the day.

As your worship plans develop for a particular Sunday, please note the variety of prayers and calls to worship suggested by our writers to fit in with the theme for the day. You may use these in any way appropriate to your planning.

The children's time can be especially useful for those pastors who have difficulty developing ideas and presentations for this important ministry to children.

The sermon materials may be used as thought-starters for your own sermon preparation. In past years we included a "text" for each sermon heading. Many pastors have informed us that they preach on the whole lectionary passage, not just one specific verse. The text references have, therefore, been omitted from the sermon materials.

Not all preachers use the lectionary lessons on a regular basis. If you don't use these texts for your preaching, the materials in this book can still be useful in providing sermon ideas and illustrations on specific texts appropriate for the time of year. On the other hand, if you are accustomed to using the lectionary lessons, you will find these materials especially suited to your preaching needs.

A large majority of denominations now follow the Revised Common Lectionary. Therefore, we are using the Revised Common Lectionary so that *Minister's Annual Manual* will be helpful to more people. You should have no difficulty adapting these materials to your own church calendar. The Consultation on Common Texts asks that we indicate the following:

"For the Sundays following Pentecost, the Revised Common Lectionary provides two distinct patterns for readings from the Old Testament. One pattern offers a series of semi-continuous Old Testament readings over the course of these Sundays. The other pattern offers paired readings in which the Old Testament and gospel reading for each Sunday are closely related. In adopting the Revised Common Lectionary, the Presbyterian Church U.S.A., United Church of Christ, and United Methodist Church elected to use the pattern of semi-continuous Old Testament readings. The other pattern of paired readings is found in the Revised Common Lectionary (Nashville: Abingdon Press, 1992)." (The Revised Common Lectionary, 1992, Consultation on Common Texts [CCT].)

The following materials are included for each worship experience:

Lessons, assigned for liturgical preaching.
Introduction to the Lessons, a brief explanation of all texts.
Theme of the day's materials.
Thought for the Day to help set the tone for preaching.
Call to Worship for the beginning of the service.
Pastoral Prayer for the beginning of worship.
Prayer of Confession, asking for forgiveness and pardon.

Prayer of Dedication of Gifts and Self at the offering.
Sermon Summary for the day.
Hymn of the Day suggestions.
Children's Time for conversation with children.
The Sermon, including **Hymns,** and **Scripture.**

Hymn of the Day selections were chosen from the following hymnals:

The United Methodist Hymnal, Nashville, TN: United Methodist Publishing House, 1989.

With One Voice: A Lutheran Resource for Worship, Minneapolis, MN: Augsburg Fortress, 1995.

Presbyterian Hymnal, Louisville, KY: Westminster John Knox Press, 1990.

Voices United: The Hymn and Worship Book of the United Church of Canada, Toronto: United Church Publishing House, 1996.

Common Ground: A Song Book for all the Churches, Edinburgh, UK: Saint Andrew Press, 1998.

The Faith We Sing, Nashville, TN: Abingdon Press, 2000.

New Century Hymnal, Cleveland, OH: Pilgrim Press, 1995.

This Far by Faith: An African American Resource for Worship, Minneapolis: Augsburg Fortress, 1999.

Many of the hymns suggested are available for congregational use through *LicenSing: Copyright Cleared Music for Churches.*™

Names and addresses for all of the writers who have prepared these materials are listed in the appendices, should you wish to write to any of them.

To assist in your planning, a four-year church year calendar is included in the appendices, as well as calendars for the years 2003 and 2004.

For even more worship planning helps, you may wish to use the 2003 May/June planning issue or the regular monthly issues of *The Clergy Journal.* These resources include additional sermons and hymn selections. The planning issue also includes more children's time ideas.

Preachers who use this *Minister's Annual Manual 2003–2004* and also subscribe to *The Clergy Journal* will have valuable resources for worship planning that include:

1) Three complete sets of sermons for every Sunday of the year: this book, the annual planning issue, plus "Preaching on the Lessons" in each issue of *The Clergy Journal.* (The sermon materials in all three publications have been cross-referenced so you will know at a glance which publication to use for a particular passage.)
2) Two sets of children's time ideas.
3) Almost three dozen additional sermons.
4) Hymn selections to match the lectionary texts.
5) Prayers and calls to worship.

Both the *Minister's Annual Manual 2003–2004* and the 2003 May/June planning issue of *The Clergy Journal* will make excellent additions to your library.

– *Rebecca H. Grothe*
Spring 2003

August 3, 2003

8th Sunday after Pentecost (Proper 13)

RC/Pres: 18th Sunday in Ordinary Time

Lessons

RCL	2 Sam 11:26–12:13a	Eph 4:1-16	Jn 6:24-35
Roman Catholic	Ex 16:2-4, 12-15	Eph 4:17, 20-24	Jn 6:24-35
Episcopal (BCP)	Ex 16:2-4, 9-15	Eph 4:17-25	Jn 6:24-35
Lutheran	Ex 16:2-4, 9-15	Eph 4:1-16	Jn 6:24-35

Introduction to the Lessons

Lesson 1

(1) ***2 Samuel 11:26–12:13a*** **(RCL)**

After the death of Uriah the Hittite, the prophet Nathan confronts King David with his sin in coveting and taking Uriah's wife, Bathsheba. Nathan's confrontation is in the form of a parable about the theft of a poor man's only ewe lamb.

(2) ***Exodus 16:2-4, 12-15*** **(RC);** ***Exodus 16:2-4, 9-15*** **(Epis/Luth)**

The Israelites, wandering through the wilderness, complain to Moses and Aaron about the lack of food. In response, God sends bread (manna) and meat (quails) – along with specific instructions for their use – as both gift and test.

Lesson 2

(1) ***Ephesians 4:1-16*** **(RCL/Luth)**

The author of Ephesians appeals for unity in Christ amid outward diversity, using the gifts Christ has given to each member of the body of Christ to further the work of ministry on earth.

(2) ***Ephesians 4:17, 20-24*** **(RC);** ***Ephesians 4:17-25*** **(Epis)**

Exhorting the Ephesians to live in Christ, and not as the Gentiles do, the author reminds them that true righteousness and holiness are shown in their actions toward others.

Gospel

John 6:24-35 **(RCL/RC/Epis/Luth)**

The crowds find Jesus on "the other side" of the Sea of Galilee, expecting him to repeat the miracle of the feeding of the multitudes that they experienced the previous day. Jesus tells them that God is the source of the bread of heaven that gives life to the world.

Theme

Jesus is the bread of life.

Thought for the Day

The knowledge of God is very far from the love of Him.

– Blaise Pascal, quoted in *The Viking Book of Aphorisms,* W. H. Auden and Louis Kronenberger, eds., New York: Viking, 1993, p. 77

Call to Worship

Leader: Let us worship God, who nourished our ancestors with manna.

People: Let us worship God, who sustained God's people's wilderness journey.

Leader: Let us worship God, who opened the doors of heaven.

People: Let us worship God, who guides and guards our lives.

– Based on Psalm 78:23-29

Pastoral Prayer

Holy and compassionate God, you created us to be your children. When our ancestors in faith wandered the wilderness after you released them from captivity in Egypt, you sent manna, bread from heaven, food to sustain their lives. At the acceptable time, you sent your Son Jesus to be for the world your bread of life, so that whoever comes to him may never hunger. For your ongoing providence, your presence and care, we offer our thanks and praise.

You know your children's needs before the words to name those needs take shape. We entreat your sustaining care for all who suffer: for the sick and the dying, and all who minister to their bodies and spirits; for those whose expected miracles never come; for those who feel abandoned by others, or even by you; for those without homes, without work, without food, without hope; for those whose lives are shattered by war or violence or substance abuse. Be present to each and all, offering the hope that as you fed the multitudes, so you continue to nourish us with the bread of heaven, your life-giving Son, in whose name we pray. Amen.

Prayer of Confession

You have called us, O God, to be your church. You have sent your Son among us, that we might be one body in the unity of one Spirit. We confess that we have not followed the way of life you have offered us. We have promoted ourselves when we should have practiced humility. We have tolerated violence, not gentleness, to achieve national power. We have not been patient, but want our desires instantly gratified. We try to stand alone, dependent on no one, when you have challenged us to bear one another in love. We have not spoken the truth in love. Have mercy on us, we pray. Help us to recognize in one another the gifts that bind us together, that we may seek to build up your body here on earth, constantly under your mercy and protection, made real in Jesus Christ our Lord. Amen.

Prayer of Dedication of Gifts and Self

Your gifts to us are without number, merciful God. You have ordered your church, that some might be apostles, prophets, evangelists, pastors, teachers, and those who equip the saints for the work of ministry, to build up your body, the church, here on earth. Out of what you have given us, we return these offerings in grateful thanks to you, asking you to use both gifts and givers to establish love within the body of Christ. We pray in the name of your Son, Jesus Christ our Lord. Amen.

Sermon Summary

To those who return to Jesus, expecting the miracle of the feeding of the multitudes the previous day to be repeated, Jesus offers instead his self-understanding that he is the bread of life, sent from heaven.

Hymn of the Day

"Forgive Us, Lord" *("Perdón, Señor")*

More a prayer of confession than a hymn, this simple piece is based on Psalm 51, which is today's psalm. The song by Jorge Lockwood can be sung in call/response style, with either a leader or choir singing the petitions and the congregation responding with "Forgive us, Lord." Without too much difficulty, one could add other petitions. Indeed, people could be invited in advance of worship to prepare simple petitions based on issues they are facing in their own lives and, while the choir sings or simply hums the main line, people could silently offer their own verses.

Children's Time

Food for Life

Once upon a time there was a girl who loved the icing on cake. When she graduated from high school, went off to university, and moved into an apartment, do you know what she did? She made a big bowl of icing and ate all of it with a spoon.

How do think she felt? Happy? Full? Sadly, the only thing she felt was sick to her stomach.

Food is funny stuff. When we eat small amounts, almost any food is good for us. When we eat way too much, almost any food can be bad.

Jesus was talking to a crowd of people one day about food because he'd fed them bread and fish the day before. Now, the people wanted more bread and fish. Jesus told the crowd that God sent him to give them what their hearts – their souls and their spirits – needed. Jesus said that his love was bread for their hearts. Jesus explained that only God can give this bread of life for our hearts. We can ask Jesus for as much of this heavenly bread as we want. It will always be good for us.

The Sermon

Living Bread: Food That Endures

Hymns

Beginning of Worship: "This Is a Day of New Beginnings"
Sermon Hymn: "Christ Was the Word Who Spoke It"
Closing Hymn: "Grace Greater Than Our Sin"

Scripture

John 6:24-35 (For additional sermon materials on this passage, see the April 2003 and the 2003 May/June planning issue of *The Clergy Journal.*)

"Expect miracles." These words spoke to passers-by, both friends and strangers, from the bulletin board in front of the United Methodist Church in Newport, New Hampshire. That summer of 1978, the church building did not appear to be a place destined for birthing the miraculous. It was, and still is, a white clapboard structure, standing on the eastern side of the village green, just down from the more substantial-looking brick post office and the gray stone Episcopal church. "Typical New England," was my first assessment. Not ostentatious; certainly not presumptuous enough to tout itself as a place where one might "expect miracles."
That chance encounter with the church bulletin board, a quarter-century ago, has been part of my mental landscape ever since. Over the intervening years, as I have tried to come to terms with a variety of personal and pastoral issues, I have wondered, with some frequency, what about the miracles we might expect, but that just don't happen?

"When they found [Jesus] on the other side of the sea, they said to him, 'Rabbi, when did you come here?' Jesus answered them, 'Very truly, I tell you, you are looking for me, not because you saw signs, but because you ate your fill of the loaves. Do not work for the food that perishes, but for the food that endures for eternal life, which the Son of Man will give you. For it is on him that God the Father has set his seal' " (Jn 6:25-27).

In the opening section of John 6, a large crowd of people went to see Jesus, expecting to hear him teach. Instead of teaching with words, Jesus taught through a sign, providing bread and fish for the hungry multitudes. The lesson today tells us what happened the day after the multitudes were fed. The crowd returns to Jesus, expecting miracles.

As we might anticipate, news of the miraculous feeding has spread far and wide. Hoping to escape the crowds, Jesus and his disciples cross to the opposite side of the Sea of Galilee, not inconsequentially encountering a violent storm on the way. The people, driven by desperation, finally locate Jesus in Capernaum. They come, believing Jesus will repeat the miracle. Jesus knows this and tells them, "You are back, not because you believed what I told you, but because your stomachs were filled."

Why do the crowds return? Because they are greedy? Because they look at Jesus as a useful curiosity, who makes endless quantities of food appear out of nowhere?

I suspect that some of the returnees come for both reasons. But many probably come back precisely because Jesus has fed them. The issue for these people is survival – sheer physical survival. They are not the wealthy, for whom obtaining food is no problem. They are the ones who live on the edge of subsistence, for whom a whole day's manual labor brings just enough money for one day's food, and no more. Jesus' feeding miracle has relieved them of the constant struggle of seeking food, if only for a day. This is no small accomplishment. It has obviously made a big impression on those who return. Can we blame them for expecting another miracle?

Jesus has something else in mind. He has given them the gift of bread, but he finds it difficult to convince the people that it is God's power, and not his own, that made the miraculous feeding possible. Now, Jesus wants to teach them that the "bread of life" – that is, Jesus himself – is given by God as well, and that this bread is the one that should be their ultimate concern. The previous day, those present experienced only the bread that alleviated their bodily hunger. Even when Jesus explains what the miracle signifies, the people confuse the giving of physical food with God's gift of Jesus to humankind. On the day after, the people are truly disappointed. Their hopes and anticipations about Jesus are not fulfilled. The miracle that they expect – indeed, that they have gone searching for – does not come. The multitudes are fed one day, but go home with empty stomachs the day after.

The day before, the people "were about to come and take [Jesus] by force to make him king" (Jn 6:15). Perhaps if Jesus had repeated the miracle of the loaves and fishes, the people would persist in this quest. In an action akin to refusing the devil's temptation to "turn stones into bread" (Mt 4:3), Jesus does not follow the easy way of gaining popular support. The people's stomachs, gnawing and empty though they may be, cannot control or define who Jesus is or his ministry.

"Then Jesus said to them, 'It is my Father who gives you the true bread from heaven. For the bread of God is that which comes down from heaven and gives life for the world.' They said to him, 'Sir, give us this bread always.' Jesus said to them, 'I am the bread of life. Whoever comes to me will never be hungry, and whoever believes in me will never be thirsty' " (vv. 32b-35).

We can certainly identify with the folks who return to Jesus the day after the miraculous feeding. We really *do* expect that our faith will lead to miracles. We expect that if we pray hard enough, or believe strongly enough, we can barter with God for the healing of friends or family who are critically ill. We expect that our churches will be full of people whose contributions will sustain our ambitious programs. We expect that our buildings, when we need to fix them, can be expeditiously repaired without going into debt. Sometimes, our expectations are indeed met, but sometimes they are not.

Our "day after" thinking does not guarantee the results we desire. People become ill and die; all our prayers, and all our faith, cannot prevent their suffering. Our church attendance and contributions are easily altered by changes in the economic climate. Even the most carefully maintained church buildings suddenly need expensive repairs, for which no money is set aside in the church budget. The world in general seems to be in a steady downward spiral. We become angry with God when God does not act as we expect God to act.

As I read it, this passage from John 6 tells us that not only must we rejoice in the faith that leads to miracles; we must also accept that miracles cannot be bidden or controlled. Miracles do happen: people regain health, churches grow, ministries expand. When these things happen, they are God's gifts, not results that follow automatically because we "expect miracles."

Here, as in many places in the gospel witness, there is a discernable tension: a tension between loaves of bread and living bread; a tension between what we can see and what is hidden from us; a tension between what we control and what God controls. These tensions need to be recognized. We must realize that ultimately, all that happens is within the providence of God, who has created and is creating, whose presence and care never fails, whose love for humankind is shown in the gift of Jesus, the living bread that endures.

Sometimes, our lives of faith will include miracles. Sometimes, they will not. No matter what happens, we are called to believe in God's continuing work in our lives, to set our sights on things beyond ourselves, and to keep on seeking out God's new age, made real in God's living bread.

Thanks be to God.

– Nancy E. Topolewski
Vestal Center United Methodist Church
Vestal, New York

August 10, 2003

9th Sunday after Pentecost (Proper 14)

RC/Pres: 19th Sunday in Ordinary Time

Lessons

RCL	2 Sam 18:5-9, 15, 31-33	Eph 4:24–5:2	Jn 6:35, 41-51
Roman Catholic	1 Kgs 19:4-8	Eph 4:30–5:2	Jn 6:41-51
Episcopal (BCP)	Deut 8:1-10	Eph 4:(25-29) 30–5:2	Jn 6:37-51
Lutheran	1 Kgs 19:4-8	Eph 4:25–5:2	Jn 6:35, 41-51

Introduction to the Lessons

Lesson 1

(1) ***2 Samuel 11:5-9, 15, 31-33*** **(RCL)**

King David's possession of Bathsheba, wife of Uriah the Hittite, results in her pregnancy. David, to cover his sin, sends Uriah into battle, where he is killed.

(2) ***1 Kings 19:4-8*** **(RC/Luth)**

The prophet Elijah flees from the wrath of Queen Jezebel after winning the contest with the prophets of Baal on Mount Carmel. God sustains Elijah on his way to hide at Mount Horeb.

(3) ***Deuteronomy 8:1-10*** **(Epis)**

As the Israelites prepare to enter the Promised Land, Moses warns them against the arrogance of forgetting their utter dependence on God, who has brought them out of Egypt and sustained them in their wanderings.

Lesson 2

Ephesians 4:24–5:2 **(RCL/RC/Luth);**
Ephesians 4:(25-29) 30–5:2 **(Epis)**

The author appeals to those who read this letter to the Ephesians to change the ways in which they relate with others – to be imitators of the sacrificial and forgiving actions of God and Christ.

Gospel

***John 6:35, 41-51* (RCL/Luth); *John 6:41-51* (RC); *John 6:37-51* (Epis)**

The day after he fed the multitudes, Jesus tells the crowd that he is the bread of life, giving God's sustenance through eternity. Using distinctively Eucharistic language, Jesus tells them that the bread he will give for the life of the world is his flesh.

Theme

God's salvation is in Jesus, the bread of heaven.

Thought for the Day

God usually answers our prayers so much more according to the measure of his own magnificence than of our asking that we do not know his boons to be those for which we besought him.

– Coventry Patmore, from *The Rod, the Root, and the Flower*,
quoted in Charles Williams' *The New Christian Year*,
London: Oxford University Press, 1941, p. 179

Call to Worship

Leader: Let us worship God by constantly blessing God's name.
People: Let us worship God by speaking God's praise.
Leader: Let our souls make their boast in the Lord.
People: Let the humble hear, and be glad.
Leader: Let us worship God by magnifying God's name.
People: Let us exalt God's name forever.

– Based on Psalm 34:1-3

Pastoral Prayer

O You who have made all that exists, in the ongoing mystery of creation, we your creatures long to know you as our God. Even as we seek you, we find that you have already come to us in the person of your Son, who gives us glimpses of your infinite care. For this magnificent and costly gift of God-with-us, we offer you our grateful thanks.

Our gratitude is joined by supplications, because none of us is without need. You know the suffering of individuals and communities within your creation. Our hope is in you. We entreat your compassion and love for all that seems most hopeless in our world: the persistence of violence; the fear in which so many of your children live; the sickness of body or mind that clouds your shining world with uncertainty. Be with us, we pray, in all that we do, and all that we are, keeping us ever in the love that never abandons us, shown so clearly in your Son, Jesus Christ our Lord. Amen.

Prayer of Confession

God of us all, you have called us as your church to imitate you, living in the love which Christ showed so clearly in his self-offering on the cross. We confess that we have not grasped the complexity of following you in this very confusing world. We have harbored anger against others. We have not guarded the words we speak, allowing malice and jealousy to overcome us. We have nurtured bitterness about the past. We have not been kind; we have missed opportunities to demonstrate our words of faith in thoughtful action. Forgive us, we pray. Guide us to grow daily to be more faithful disciples, constantly under your mercy and protection, made real in Jesus Christ our Lord. Amen.

Prayer of Dedication of Gifts and Self

Gracious God, in Jesus Christ you have accepted us as we are, and you have freely offered us salvation through your "living bread." As we return thanks for the gift and gratitude for the Giver, we offer you ourselves and our substance, out of the bounty you have provided, following the example of him who gave his life that we might live, Jesus Christ our Lord. Amen.

Sermon Summary

While we may complain to Jesus about his message and may be tempted to see people in terms of extremes – all good or all evil – Jesus' witness and mission is to offer salvation freely to whomever believes in him.

Hymn of the Day

"Let Us Talents and Tongues Employ"

First sung at the World Council of Churches Assembly in Nairobi, Kenya, in 1975, this hymn has found its way into the hymnals of most mainline denominations. The catchy Jamaican folk tune (adapted by Doreen Potter) inspired Frederick Herman Kaan to write words that help us remember that the sacrament of communion is a celebration.

The refrain is sung twice after each verse, once softly and then with more volume. Handclapping, drums, or simply rhythm instruments can add to the flavor. Be sure to keep the hymn moving at a lively pace, taking advantage of the syncopation to keep things moving.

Children's Time

The Bread of Life

(Bring in a flat round of pita bread and an unsliced regular loaf of bread. Break pieces from the regular loaf and give a piece to each child to eat, being aware of possible food allergies.)

Ask them if they feel hungry after eating it. Tell them that Jesus talked about bread, saying: "I am the bread of life. Whoever comes to me will never be hungry, and whoever believes in me will never be thirsty" (Jn 6:35).

Bread was an important part of the daily diet back when Jesus lived. Bread was eaten at most meals. Their bread was not the kind you just ate, but more like this pita bread. *(Hand out pieces of the pita for the children to try.)*

When do you eat bread? What kind of bread do you like? What do you like to eat with your bread?

Bread is important to us.

So, when Jesus talked about himself as the living bread, everyone could understand what he was saying. Everyone knew what bread was and how important it was. We know that Jesus is important for us, too. Jesus is the essential "bread" for our hearts. Jesus is our food for faith.

The Sermon

Living Bread: Offered to All

Hymns

Beginning of Worship: "All Praise to Our Redeeming Lord"
Sermon Hymn: "Come, and Let Us Sweetly Join"
Closing Hymn: "Become to Us the Living Bread"

Scripture

John 6:35, 41-51 (For additional sermon materials on this passage, see the April 2003 issue of *The Clergy Journal* and on Ephesians 4:25–5:2, see the 2003 May/June planning issue of *The Clergy Journal.*)

An aspect of the history of Christian thought that has always fascinated me concerns the various heresies that arose during Christianity's early centuries. A *heresy* is an opinion or doctrine that is contrary to the orthodox doctrine (that is, doctrine considered authoritatively correct) of the church. Before there were creeds in place, before the church had systematically decided what it believed about such issues as whether Christ was human, or divine, or both, there were many ideas floating around that claimed to be true Christian beliefs.

Most of the early heresies have disappeared and are of little interest, except to historians. However, one of the heresies of the third century of the Common Era continues to influence our thinking in the twenty-first century. It is called the *Manichean Heresy.*

As the eminent church historian Henry Chadwick points out in his classic text, *The Early Church*, Manicheanism represented the thought of a Babylonian named Mani, who lived in what is now Iran from about 216 to 276 C.E. Basically a syncretist, Mani took elements of three existing religions – Buddhism, Christianity, and a popular Persian religion called Zoroastrianism – and tried to form a single religion that might attract a wider following than any of its component parts had done. Manicheans believed that a great conflict between darkness and light had occurred in the primeval world. This conflict, in turn, made the world of contemporary experience into a mixture of good and evil. Manicheans taught that things, influences, and people are either good or bad, part of the light or part of the darkness, with nothing in between. They divided persons and individuals into those who are "from God" and those who are "from the devil." Their worldview was sharply exclusivistic and oversimplified. Interestingly, it was not this aspect of the Manicheans' beliefs that led to their condemnation as heretics, but rather, their secretive, magical rituals. That, however, is another story.

Elements of the Manichean worldview remain very near the surface of our consciousness. Whether we look at the concept of the "axis of evil," at the perpetual conflict between Israelis and Palestinians, or at the shadowy world of international drug cartels, it is an easy jump of thought to believe in a clear division between good and evil. In so doing, do we not usually cast ourselves in the role of champions of the good, and not as perpetrators of evil?

If we look back on the gospel witness, however, we find that boundaries between good and evil, faith and unbelief, are not so readily drawn. According to the gospels, Jesus acknowledged that human behavior is exceedingly complex. Because all of humankind has fallen into sin, all human beings are capable of both good and ill. All of God's children, irrespective of gender, social status, age, or racial background, stand in need of redemption. We need go no further than the many instances when Jesus eats with "sinners," to see how acutely Jesus is aware of the constant coexistence of good and evil among the people he encounters. More to the point are Jesus' words from the cross, spoken on behalf of those who have crucified him: "Father, forgive them; for they do not know what they are doing" (Lk 23:34). Perhaps some of his opponents can divide people into two groups – "clearly and solely good" and "obviously and singularly evil." Jesus does not do so.

We need only to listen to the news to realize that good and evil are inextricably intertwined. Especially in times of tragedy, when the incursion of darkness into our lives seems irrevocable, do we not, as people of faith, look for something, *anything*, to remind us that chaos will not ultimately triumph? Don't we cling to stories in the news, which remind us that even amid catastrophic destruction beyond their control and outside their volition, ordinary people reached out to one another to show compassion and love.

In today's gospel , Jesus makes these straightforward declarations in verse 51, which tell something about him and something about us. "I am the living bread that came down from heaven," tells us who Jesus is. "Whoever eats of this bread will live forever," places a clear choice before us, to change our focus from food for the body to food for the soul. "The bread that I will give for the life of the world is my flesh," places the irrefutable seal of promise on Jesus' side of the transaction. Part of what we do when we worship together, especially when we celebrate communion, is to show our willingness to be sustained by the Living Bread.

But let's get real. We all know that we fall terribly short of the way of life that we are called to live. The gift of "living bread" has been offered, but we have not yet fully reconciled ourselves to the claim placed upon us by Jesus' saving presence. That blessing, which signifies God's providential care for us, is difficult to discern – especially when we find ourselves asking, along with the Jews in today's lesson, "Is not this Jesus, the son of Joseph, whose father and mother we know?" (v. 42).

The attitude that some people are good (or chosen) and others are evil (or damned) also concerns the writer of Ephesians in today's second lesson: "Put away from you all bitterness and wrath, and anger and wrangling and slander, together with all malice, and be kind to one another, tender-hearted, forgiving one another, as God in Christ has forgiven you. Therefore be imitators of God, as beloved children, and live in love, as Christ loved us and gave himself up for us, a fragrant offering and sacrifice to God" (Eph 4:31–5:2).

The admonitions are not for a select few; they are directed to each one of us. Forgiveness is a powerful tool to aid our work of understanding the confusion of good and evil that we encounter every day. Jesus went a step further than simple forgiveness. He offered his own body in opposition to the greatest evil of all, the bondage of sin and death. As we recognize God's forgiveness as life affirming, we can work to eradicate vestiges of the Manichean heresy from our consciousness, acknowledging that each of us is *simultaneously* good and evil, noble and ignoble. Evaluating anyone as all and only good, or all and only evil, flies in the face of the gospel witness.

Jesus offers a golden opportunity: "Very truly, I tell you, whoever believes has eternal life" (Jn 6:47). *Whoever* is all-inclusive. Jesus invites, as well as promises: "I am the living bread that came down from heaven. Whoever eats of this bread will live forever; and the bread that I will give for the life of the world is my flesh" (v. 51).

Thanks be to God.

– Nancy E. Topolewski
Vestal Center United Methodist Church
Vestal, New York

August 17, 2003

10th Sunday after Pentecost (Proper 15)

RC/Pres: 20th Sunday in Ordinary Time

Lessons

RCL	1 Kgs 2:10-12; 3:3-14	Eph 5:15-20	Jn 6:51-58
Roman Catholic	Prov 9:1-6	Eph 5:15-20	Jn 6:51-58
Episcopal (BCP)	Prov 9:1-6	Eph 5:15-20	Jn 6:53-59
Lutheran	Prov 9:1-6	Eph 5:15-20	Jn 6:51-58

Introduction to the Lessons

Lesson 1

(1) ***1 Kings 2:10-12; 3:3-14*** **(RCL)**

Solomon becomes king of Israel after the death of his father, David. At Gibeon, where he has gone to make a sacrifice, God asks him in a dream what gift he desires. Solomon asks for wisdom and understanding, a request that pleases God.

(2) ***Proverbs 9:1-6*** **(RC/Epis/Luth)**

Wisdom, personified as a woman, invites all, including those who are simple or immature, to her banquet, so that they may learn from her.

Lesson 2

Ephesians 5:15-20 **(RCL/RC/Epis/Luth)**

Continuing to provide exhortations for daily living, the author admonishes the readers of this letter to the Ephesians to live each day in thanks to God the Father, in the name of the Lord Jesus Christ.

Gospel

John 6:51-58 **(RCL/RC/Luth);** ***John 6:53-59*** **(Epis)**

In language that points to the Eucharist, Jesus teaches that those who eat his flesh and drink his blood will have eternal life.

Theme

Jesus, the living bread, provides eternal life.

Thought for the Day

[T]he fully Christian life is a Eucharistic life: that is, [one] conformed to the pattern of Jesus, given in its wholeness to God, laid on His altar as a sacrifice of love, and consecrated, transformed by His inpouring life, to be used to give life and food to other souls.

– Evelyn Underhill, *The Mystery of Sacrifice: A Meditation on the Liturgy,* London: Longmans, Green, and Company, 1938, p. xiv

Call to Worship

Leader: Let us worship the Lord, for whom our soul waits.
People: Let us worship God, our help and shield.
Leader: Our hearts are glad in God,
People: For we trust God's holy name.
Leader: Let your steadfast love be upon us, O God,
People: Even as we hope in you.

Pastoral Prayer

All-wise, all-creating God, we see your wisdom and power at work in the wonders of the world around us. The wisdom you gave to our ancestors, to judges and prophets, apostles and martyrs, and the wisdom that you continue to give to us, your children, fits us to offer our lives in praise to you. For this great and wonderful blessing, we offer you our thanks and praise.

Grant us, O God, the wisdom to discern how best to use the gifts and graces you provide in service to those of particular need: to those whose lives have been entangled in violence or abuse; to those who suffer diseases of mind or body; to those no longer able to live on their own; to those who feel no purpose in living. Remind us constantly that your Son came to us as living bread, bread offered for the life of the world, to open the gates of eternal life to all who believe in him; for it is in Christ's holy name that we pray. Amen.

Prayer of Confession

We confess our sins to you, O God, in a spirit of deep contrition. We have not been the people you would have us be as your beloved sons and daughters. You give us wisdom and discernment, but we fail to use these gifts in service to others. We waste precious time on trivial pursuits, assuming we will never die. We pass by the homeless, the hopeless, and the helpless in a hurry to get to nowhere important. We neglect the things of the Spirit in our headlong rush to gratify physical desires. Forgive us, we pray. Teach us again to trust and to follow the ways your wisdom leads us, constantly under your mercy and protection, made real to us in Jesus Christ our Lord. Amen.

Prayer of Dedication of Gifts and Self

In word and deed, most gracious God, your only Son showed us the way to live and to give. In his self-offering as living bread, he has opened for us the way to eternal life. In these offerings we present, we seek to follow Jesus' example, giving of our time, our talent, our substance, and our service, in gratitude for your gifts to us. Bless these, our gifts, and us as givers, for the work of your church in the world; we ask in Jesus' name. Amen.

Sermon Summary

In words with strong connections to the language of the Eucharist, Jesus offers himself as "living bread," in both the present and the future, for the life of the world.

Hymn of the Day

"O God of Matchless Glory"

Professor and hymn writer Ruth C. Duck has been at the forefront of the movement to expand our understanding of God and the church in hymnody and worship, having created a number of books of hymns and worship resources using inclusive language and imagery.

This hymn of praise (set to music by Ruth Watson Henderson) employs a number of biblical references to remind us of God's work in creation, and the care and compassion God continues to lavish on that creation. It fits well with today's gospel, wherein Jesus speaks of the bread of eternal life, and also next week, wherein the disciples asks rhetorically "To whom shall we go? You have the words of eternal life."

Children's Time

Abide in Me

(Bring in something that helps you to feel comforted: a picture of a loved one, a book, or an article of clothing. Arrange to have the congregation sing the first verse of "Abide with Me" at the place indicated below.)

What do like to have when you're sick? Do you like to have your mother read you stories? Does your father make you chicken noodle soup? Do you curl up in bed with a favorite stuffed animal? What comforts you when you're feeling down or unhappy? This is what helps me. *(Share what you brought.)*

Jesus told a crowd of people that he was the living bread and that everyone who had this living bread in their lives would live forever. Jesus says that he will abide in whoever takes in this living bread.

Now *abide* is a very old-fashioned, but beautiful word. It means to rest in, remain faithful to, sustain, and support. There's a lovely old hymn that many people find comforting when they're going through a hard time. Let's have the congregation sing us the first verse.

It's comforting to know that Jesus, the living bread, has promised to abide in us forever. Because God loves us, we have Jesus, the Bread of Life. We have life with Jesus forever.

The Sermon

Living Bread: For the Life of the World

Hymns

Beginning of Worship: "O Spirit of the Living God"
Sermon Hymn: "Deck Thyself, My Soul, with Gladness"
Closing Hymn: "Jesus, Lord, We Look to Thee"

Scripture

John 6:51-58 (For additional sermon materials on this passage, see the April 2003 issue of *The Clergy Journal* and on Ephesians 5:15-20, see the 2003 May/June planning issue of *The Clergy Journal.*)

In August of 2000, my husband and I attended the Passion Play in the village of Oberammergau, in southern Germany. It is an experience that neither of us will ever forget. The play has its origins in the Thirty Years' War in the 17th century, a religious war that by 1630 had smothered most of Europe. As if the desolation of constant warfare was not enough, the war brought with it the plague, the Black Death, the same disease that in the 14th century had killed half the population of Europe. The plague swept into Oberammergau in 1632–1633, claiming many lives. People believed the Black Death had come because God sent it from heaven to punish the villagers for their sins. They believed they had to pacify God's obvious fury. So, in 1633, the people of Oberammergau pledged to perform a Passion Play as a sign of their remorse and repentance.

The first Passion Play was staged in 1634. With only two exceptions – in 1770 (when passion plays were outlawed) and in 1940 (during World War II) – the play has been offered every 10 years, usually in the first year of each decade. In 2000, 1,600 adults and 550 children, about half the population of the village, were involved in some aspect of the Passion Play.

The story, of course, is familiar. Even though the entire performance is given in German, the action is not difficult to follow. As one might imagine, the Passion Play has changed since 1634; however, a common thread unites all performances. In all times this play is a simple, yet profound interpretation of the passion of Jesus, showing his love for and absolute devotion to his Father and to humankind. The director of the 2000 presentation called the Passion Play, "a school of love."

A curious process is at work in the re-presentation of Christ's passion. The story itself does not change. Yet neither the text of the play nor the music and costumes that accompany each scene is a museum, something frozen in time. In a museum, time stops. But the story of the passion gives life to each generation, as do the scriptures themselves, in the living, breathing present. Text and music, costumes and action confront the viewers with the need to decide what effect the passion of Jesus Christ will have on the fluid living of a life in faith. At no time is this element of decision more apparent than when the thieves being crucified with Jesus begin to scream, as the nails are driven into their flesh.

"I am the living bread that came down from heaven. Whoever eats this of bread will live forever; and the bread that I will give for the life of the world is my flesh" (Jn 6:51).

Over a number of weeks, we have been exploring the sixth chapter of the Gospel of John, learning about the relationship between Jesus and bread. Early in the chapter, Jesus feeds a multitude from an offering of loaves and fish from a nameless boy. The next day, the crowds return, hoping to be fed again. Jesus has to tell them that feeding with bread is different from Jesus himself, the "living bread." In today's lesson, Jesus speaks of himself as the bread given for the life of the world.

The words deliberately point us toward the communion service. In a relationship that is both physical and mystical, Jesus becomes the "living bread" and prefigures his own atoning death. Notice that the verbs are present tense, and then future tense: "Whoever eats (present tense) of this bread will live (future tense) forever" (v. 51). The "living bread" is eaten within our time. The "living bread" gives us life in the future, in God's time.

Each of us must decide: Shall we eat the manna our ancestors ate in the wilderness? Shall we go back into the past, to something long ago, in the hope that it will suffice for us? Or shall we eat the "living bread," the body of Jesus, the bread of heaven, something radically different from everything that has come before?

"I am the living bread that came down from heaven. Whoever eats this bread will live forever; and the bread that I will give for the life of the world is my flesh" (v. 51).

For us, who encounter these words many centuries later, the miracle is not that the words are frozen in time. The miracle is that the words call us to a life unlike any we have ever known, to a reliance on God's gift of Jesus

Christ for the life-giving redemption of the world, and to the realization that Christ's passion continues to give life this very day. Oberammergau's Passion Play of 2000 was different from those of 1634, 1710, 1850, and 1960; it could not help but reflect changes in the world. The underlying message, however, remains. Time and time again, at the moment of humanity's greatest need, God has graciously intervened to give healing and salvation. In the midst of most dire catastrophe, when our suffering plumbs the depths of hell, God continues to love and to save us.

Each generation has tried to tell Jesus' story in a fashion comprehensible to its own experience, relevant to its own audiences. The Passion Play, as we saw it in 2000, tells the story of a faithful Jew who set out to recover what he thought the people had lost: justice, compassion, and faith; who held contempt for all who wore their piety like festive costumes; who was ready to be stripped naked, maltreated, and mocked before howling crowds on behalf of his God; who stayed steadily on his path to its final consequence: his execution on the cross.

> Living Bread, bread of life, bread of heaven:
> life of the world,
> life of the world to come,
> life of love,
> bread of love;
> love of God, known in the breaking of bread,
> in a criminal's shameful death on the cross,
> in the discovery of an empty tomb.

John's account of Jesus' teaching about bread, and the theology of Oberammergau's Passion Play both remind us that faith is not a frozen museum. Faith is a decision, a way of life, that must be affirmed each day in the heart of each believer, not removed from the rest of the world, but in the midst of it, to the greater glory of God.

"I am the living bread that came down from heaven. Whoever eats this bread will live forever; and the bread that I will give for the life of the world is my flesh" (v. 51).

– Nancy E. Topolewski
Vestal Center United Methodist Church
Vestal, New York

August 24, 2003

11th Sunday after Pentecost (Proper 16)

RC/Pres: 21st Sunday in Ordinary Time

Lessons

RCL	1 Kgs 8:(1, 6, 10-11) 22-30, 41-43	Eph 6:10-20	Jn 6:56-69
Roman Catholic	Josh 24:1-2, 15-17, 18	Eph 5:21-32	Jn 6:60-69
Episcopal (BCP)	Josh 24:1-2a, 14-25	Eph 5:21-33	Jn 6:60-69
Lutheran	Josh 24:1-2a, 14-18	Eph 6:10-20	Jn 6:56-69

Introduction to the Lessons

Lesson 1

(1) ***1 Kings 8:(1, 6, 10-11) 22-30, 41-43*** **(RCL)**

Solomon has the ark of the covenant brought to the newly-completed temple in Jerusalem, where in the cloud of God's presence, Solomon prays for God to continue the covenant with God's people through this more permanent location – a covenant of prayer now extended to foreigners, as well.

(2) ***Joshua 24:1-2, 15-17, 18*** **(RC);** ***Joshua 24:1-2a, 14-25*** **(Epis);** ***Joshua 24:1-2a, 14-18*** **(Luth)**

Joshua gathers the tribes of Israel at Shechem and asks them to choose to serve the Lord or to follow other gods, thus reformalizing and ratifying Israel's covenant with the God who brought them out of Egypt.

Lesson 2

(1) ***Ephesians 6:10-20*** **(RCL/Luth)**

The author exhorts his audience to prepare for spiritual battles that lie ahead, by putting on God's armor and by being constant in prayer.

(2) ***Ephesians 5:21-32*** **(RC);** ***Ephesians 5:21-33*** **(Epis)**

In a series of admonitions, the author details the hierarchy of relationships expected within marriage between husbands and wives, as mirrored in the relationship of Christ with his church.

Gospel

***John 6:56-69* (RCL/Luth); *John 6:60-69* (RC/Epis)**

When many of his would-be disciples find the teaching about eating his flesh as the bread of life to be difficult, they leave Jesus. The Twelve, however, remain, for they realize Jesus has the "words of eternal life."

Theme

Jesus' message is not a comfortable teaching.

Thought for the Day

If God lived on earth, people would break his windows.

– Yiddish Proverb, in *The Viking Book of Aphorisms*,
W. H. Auden and Louis Kronenberger, eds.,
New York: Viking, 1993, p. 79

Call to Worship

Leader: How lovely is your dwelling place, O Lord of hosts!
People: Our souls long to enter your courts.
Leader: We worship you, O God, whose care extends even to the sparrows.
People: Those who live in your house ever sing your praise.

Pastoral Prayer

Loving God, you have shown your faithfulness by making covenants with your people. To Noah, your rainbow promised you would never again destroy the earth by water. From Abraham and Sarah, you made a great nation of descendants, a blessing to all peoples of the earth. You gave your law to Moses, instructing your people how to live. To David, you pledged a dynasty of royal leaders. For your covenant faithfulness, we give you our thanks and praise.

Through the new covenant, your Son Jesus Christ, you have assured us of your ongoing care. Hear us as we offer our petitions: for all who suffer from any need or trouble; for the aged and the dying; for those who have lost their way; for those who seek you, but have not yet come to know you; for our own needs, spoken in the silence of our hearts.

In your providence, you continue to create us anew. For all your blessings, we raise our hearts in grateful praise, in the name of Jesus Christ our Lord. Amen.

Prayer of Confession

In your loving creativity, O God, you made us male and female in your own image, and called us "good." But the goodness of your first creation was soon tainted by human sin; your image became distorted. You sent your Son to us to begin to restore that faulty image. We confess that in many ways, we have continued to move away from your goodness and from the people your Son has called us to be by setting up distinctions among people by gender, age, race, ability, and nationality, as if in believing ourselves superior to others, we are ensuring your favor toward us. Forgive our arrogance and pride. Remind us that it is only in your love that we find forgiveness and peace, constantly under your mercy and protection, made real in Jesus Christ our Lord. Amen.

Prayer of Dedication of Gifts and Self

For all your blessings; for all your gifts; for all your goodness; for all your love; and for feeding us with your living bread we praise your name, O God. Accept in these our offerings, and in our act of giving, our hope that you will use all for your coming realm, a kingdom promised to us in the person of your Son, Jesus Christ our Lord. Amen.

Sermon Summary

The popularity of Jesus' early ministry is called into question by many would-be disciples, who are offended by his teaching about "living bread," leading Jesus to teach that belief in him is not a comfortable process.

Hymn of the Day

"God of Grace and God of Glory"

Celebrated preacher Harry Emerson Fosdick wrote this hymn for the opening of Riverside Church in New York City where he served as pastor for 20 years. The stirring words are at the same time praising God, pleading for God's wisdom and courage, and exhorting the church to passionate Christian discipleship.

This tune is most commonly sung to the Welsh tune "Cwm Rhondda" (also used for "Guide Me, O Thou Great Jehovah"), although it is said that Fosdick despised this tune. The tune he originally had in mind for the text was "Regent Square," which is associated with "Angels from the Realms of Glory." It also appears at times with the Welsh tune "Rhyddlan."

Children's Time

Tough Stuff

Do you sometimes find it hard to understand what you're taught in church or Sunday school? You're not alone. Jesus' disciples sometimes found it hard to understand, too.

At first, large groups of disciples followed Jesus around from place to place, watching him heal people and listening as he taught, and sometimes they just couldn't understand what he was saying. In today's reading, the disciples heard what Jesus had to say, and then they exclaimed: "This teaching is difficult!" (Jn 6:60). They thought Jesus' words were complicated to understand and hard to believe. Some disciples even stopped following Jesus because they just didn't understand. They gave up.

It's okay to struggle with questions. To doubt and wonder.

Peter, one of Jesus' disciples, struggled with what Jesus was teaching but when Jesus asked him if he wished to leave, too, Peter said, "No. Where else could I go?" Peter knew that even if he didn't fully understand them, Jesus' words offered hope and life in a way that nothing else did. He also knew that Jesus himself was the "Holy One of God" (v. 69). Even if Peter didn't always understand what Jesus was saying, Peter knew that he could trust Jesus' promises.

And that's true for us, too. When it's hard to understand something about God or Jesus, it's all right. We can trust God to stick with us, even when we have questions.

The Sermon

Living Bread: Afflicting the Comfortable

Hymns

Beginning of Worship: "Jesus, Thine All-Victorious Love"
Sermon Hymn: "Wonderful Words of Life"
Closing Hymn: "Blest Be the Dear Uniting Love"

Scripture

John 6:56-69 (For additional sermon materials on this passage, see the April 2003 and the 2003 May/June planning issue of *The Clergy Journal.*)

Jesus enjoyed great success early in his ministry. From the stories told in the gospels, we get the impression that Jesus' teaching and healing attracted people to him in droves throughout the region of Galilee. In spite of his success with ordinary people – or perhaps, because of that success – there were people who viewed him with envy and suspicion, people identified by the gospel writers as "scribes," "Pharisees," "Saduccees," and "the Jews."

Those who heard and believed came to Jesus for many reasons. First, perhaps, they came out of curiosity, to see for themselves what they have heard other people discussing. Maybe they didn't recognize it, but a deep spiritual hunger was driving them to the fields, hillsides, and lakeshore spots where Jesus met the crowds. They came to him; they listened and watched; they came again and kept coming back. They followed Jesus, as we are told in the sixth chapter of John.

They followed Jesus, expecting miracles. They brought their sick to him, desperate for his healing touch. They gave him little rest, pursuing him from one village to the next. They remained faithful to him, because of what they had seen him do and heard him say, until the final moments of his life. This is why these verses, from the concluding section of John 6, are so arresting:

"When many of his disciples heard it, they said, 'This teaching is difficult; who can accept it?' . . . Because of this many of his disciples turned back and no longer went about with him" (Jn 6:60, 66).

At this point in the story, some people apparently are beginning to have doubts. This experience rings true for me. Jesus has amassed a great following, sought out by many who crave his words. Now, he has spoken words that are unsettling, disturbing, seemingly out of character, and those disciples go away. The only ones left are those from the inner circle, the Twelve. Trying to find out how these disciples feel, Jesus asks them, "Do you also wish to go away?" (v. 67). It is a painful moment that cries out for truth telling.

What causes people to turn away from Jesus? Is it his refusal to repeat the miracle, to alleviate the hunger of the crowds again the next day? Is it the reference to himself as "bread of heaven"? Or is it the graphic language of eating his flesh and drinking his blood?

I suspect it is a combination of all three of these factors. Jesus has pressed people too far off from the familiar territory of their ancestral faith, toward a kind of change that is difficult for them. Then, there is also the matter of grace – God's unmerited favor. Jesus has said, "I am the living bread that came down from heaven. Whoever eats of this bread will live forever; and the bread that I will give for the life of the world is my flesh" (v. 51). Has the core offense been reminding them of their inability to save themselves, of their ultimate dependence on God's grace?

There is plenty in the teaching of Jesus that offends people, a scandal that is sometimes mirrored in the lives of those who seek faithfully to be his disciples. Every once in a while, such people come into our lives, and we are forever changed. I knew a person like this. His name was Jule Ayers.

Jule Ayers died at the age of 83, in 1994; he had been retired for more than a decade, and in failing health. Yet, there remained a spark that was reminiscent of the fire that burned throughout his ministry.

Before he was anything else, Jule Ayers was a man of faith. He had gone to Union Theological Seminary in New York City in the late 1930s, during the heyday of such giants of the modern church as Harry Emerson Fosdick and Reinhold Niebuhr. He had learned, both from his experience and his education, that ministry is primarily this: to comfort the afflicted, and to afflict the comfortable. He came to First Presbyterian Church in Wilkes-Barre, Pennsylvania, in 1944. In the 38 years of his ministry there, Jule Ayers spoke out on virtually every issue of importance: racism, labor relations, fair housing, justice for the downtrodden, equal opportunities for all, the inhumanity of war. I have vivid memories of sitting in the choir loft on some occasions, and seeing one or more of the saints of the church walk out during the sermon because his words caused offense. Dr. Ayers, however, refused to alter his stance, no matter how much individuals in the congregation or the community might disagree with him.

He earned the respect of his own flock, and of countless others in northeastern Pennsylvania, because he was a man of action as well as words. He was not content to only preach about racism or fair labor relations; he marched in civil rights demonstrations and stood with union members on picket lines. He did not just talk about holding politicians accountable; he wrote letters and visited the corridors of power to make his thoughts known. He did not simply tell others that fair housing was a good idea; he helped to create an interfaith nonprofit housing authority. He did not only give voice to the idea that ecumenism was a good thing;

his commitment to God's children led him to churches and synagogues throughout the community.

Above all else, however, Jule Ayers was a pastor. He visited the hospitals every day. He spent countless hours in nursing homes and prisons. He made endless telephone calls and wrote thousands of personal notes. If something catastrophic happened in a family, Jule Ayers was likely to be at the door early in the morning or late at night, to bring the love of God. He was my pastor for 22 years, and I loved him.

Jesus Christ was a reality for Dr. Ayers. I remember his saying that if we thought Jesus was just a nice guy, we hadn't really been listening to what Jesus said. Jule Ayers' ministry reflected the ministry of Christ: he comforted the afflicted, and afflicted the comfortable. Along with many others, I have been blessed by Christ's presence in his life.

Have we been comforted, as were the multitudes Jesus fed, as were the individuals whose bodies and spirits Jesus healed?

Have we been afflicted, as were the wavering disciples in today's lesson?

Having been both comforted and afflicted, as were the people who were closest to Jesus, where are we to go if not to Jesus? In all your life, have you ever found such a life as the life offered in the Bread of Heaven? Among all the people you have known, have you ever found a person who was willing to give up her or his life for the sins of the whole world?

Some went away from Jesus. But to whom shall we go?

We come to Jesus and we remain with him, because there is nowhere else, and no one else in all creation, in whom we can find such life as we have found in him.

Thanks be to God.

– Nancy E. Topolewski
Vestal Center United Methodist Church
Vestal, New York

August 31, 2003

12th Sunday after Pentecost (Proper 17)

RC/Pres: 22nd Sunday in Ordinary Time

Lessons

RCL	Song 2:8-13	Jas 1:17-27	Mk 7:1-8, 14-15, 21-23
Roman Catholic	Deut 4:1-2, 6-8	Jas 1:17-18, 21-22, 27	Mk 7:1-8, 14-15
Episcopal (BCP)	Deut 4:1-9	Eph 6:10-20	Mk 7:1-8, 14-15, 21-23
Lutheran	Deut 4:1-2, 6-9	Jas 1:17-27	Mk 7:1-8, 14-15, 21-23

Introduction to the Lessons

Lesson 1

(1) ***Song of Solomon 2:8-13*** **(RCL)**

These are alluring words of courtship and attraction as the birth of spring brings out a demonstration of passion and desire in two people who are in love with one another.

(2) ***Deuteronomy 4:1-2, 6-8*** **(RC);** ***Deuteronomy 4:1-9*** **(Epis);** ***Deuteronomy 4:1-2, 6-9*** **(Luth)**

Moses commands the people to pay strict attention to the laws and statutes that God has given to them. He warns that their well-being, individually as well as in the community, depends upon their adherence to the laws, and Moses implores them to pass understanding and devotion to the law to succeeding generations

Lesson 2

(1) ***James 1:17-27*** **(RCL/Luth);** ***James 1:17-18, 21-22, 27*** **(RC)**

This is the familiar passage in which James admonishes us to "be doers of the word, and not merely hearers." These words come in the larger context of James' counsel to curb our tendency to speak carelessly. We are called to commit ourselves to doing acts of kindness and care.

(2) ***Ephesians 6:10-20*** **(Epis)**
This stirring passage utilizes the imagery of armor to illustrate the readiness and dedication required to overcome spiritual evil. The reader is urged to put on the belt of truth, the breastplate of righteousness, the shoes of peace, the shield of faith, the helmet of salvation, and the sword of the Spirit.

Gospel
Mark 7:1-8, 14-15, 21-23 **(RCL/Epis/Luth);**
Mark 7:1-8, 14-15 **(RC)**
Jesus argues with the Pharisees and scribes over what it means to be "unclean." Jesus declares that cleanliness is rooted in neither hygiene nor ceremony, but rather is fundamentally a spiritual condition.

Theme

Even our good deeds need to arise out of a purity of intent.

Thought for the Day

Sometimes, we construe the opening chapters of Genesis to mean that work is a curse put on us by an angry God. The whole of scripture, however, suggests that God does not look favorably upon idleness or laziness. Work is part of the intended order for creation, and for the cycle of work and Sabbath to have meaning, we need to be worthy of our rest.

Call to Worship

"Come to me, all you that are weary and are carrying heavy burdens, and I will give you rest" (Mt 11:28). Let us come and worship the one who has given us life, filled it with possibilities, and who continues to receive and renew us.

Pastoral Prayer

O God, who was the first worker in all of creation and who has given us dominion over all things on this earth, we pray for all who exercise that dominion in their daily work. We pray for teachers who offer the next generation a glimpse at the wonder of the world; for the doctors and nurses who restore health and wholeness to those who suffer and hurt; for the factory workers who produce goods by the strength of their hands and the sweat of their brows; for politicians and leaders of governments who spend their days as servants for their constituents; for farmers who work the fields and raise the crops that feed us all; and for artists who fill the world with the beauty of music, images, and drama. We pray for those whose work is for the sake of justice and peace.

As we pray for workers, dear God, we pray for those who want work but are unable to find it, and we pray for those who have work but find it unfulfilling. We pray for the underemployed who engage in work fairly and with determination but who find at the end of the day, it has not provided enough. We pray for those whose work keeps them from other duties they face.

We give thanks, dear God, that you have made us partners in your continuing acts of creation. So use our work that this world may be more clearly touched by your holiness. Amen.

Prayer of Confession

Could it be, our Creator, that we have not labored enough or worked toward the right ends? You have shown us a vision of what your world can be and have called us to work with you in making that vision a reality, but we have been easily distracted and drawn to lesser ideals. If we have invested too much of ourselves in pursuits that enrich us, and neglected the gospel which you have called us to serve, then forgive us, dear God. Renew a sense of vocation and calling within us and restore our direction to the ways of your service. In the name of Christ, whose time of labor on this earth was brief, but worthy beyond all measure, we pray. Amen.

Prayer of Dedication of Gifts and Self

We bring before you, Giver of all good things, a portion of the fruits of our labors. Forbid that what we have accumulated should sit idly by or be put only to serving our needs and desires, for what could cheapen our work more than such selfishness? Receive this portion of what we have earned and put it to use with the tithes and offerings of those who form this community. Use these treasures as you use our time and talents, to enrich the lives of many of your children. Amen.

Sermon Summary

Both grace and law are intended to transform not just our behavior, but also our inner spirits. Our actions are intended to be derivative of our love, and both freedom and obligation are to work toward that end.

Hymn of the Day

"Come My Way, My Truth, My Life"

This hymn was written as a poem by George Herbert in 1633 when hymn-singing was not permitted in the Church of England.

While the first line echoes Jesus' self-description from John 14:6, the remaining two stanzas each begin with three other images for Christ, expading on them in the lines that follow. On this one Sunday in the three-year cycle of the lectionary when we read from the Song of Solomon, an unabashed poetic celebration of love, it seems fitting to sing this hymn, which amounts to a delightful love song to our Savior.

Children's Time

Traditions

What traditions do you have in your family? Maybe it's a tradition that you go to your grandparents' house for Christmas each year, or that Dad walks you to school on the first day each fall. Maybe on Thanksgiving, you take turns saying something you are grateful for. Even spending time together like this during worship is a tradition in our church.

Traditions are very important to us. We'd be sad if they stopped. Our traditions have meaning because of the love that lies behind them. We go to our grandparents' house because we know they love us; we have birthday traditions because our parents are so happy that we are their children; on Thanksgiving, we get a chance to say thanks because of all the love that God shows us. Without love, traditions don't mean much.

One day, Jesus was talking to some Pharisees, the religious leaders. He was worried because the Pharisees were following their traditions without paying attention to God's love. Worse yet, they were teaching other people to do the same. God wants us always to put love first in our hearts and in our actions. That way, our traditions will continue to be full of meaning.

August 31, 2003
12th Sunday after Pentecost (Proper 17)
RC/Pres: 22nd Sunday in Ordinary Time

The Sermon

The Motives Behind Our Work

Hymns

Beginning of Worship: "Spirit of the Living God"
Sermon Hymn: "Restless Weaver"
Closing Hymn: "Spirit"

Scripture

Mark 7:1-8, 14-15, 21-23 (For additional sermon materials on this passage, see the April 2003 and the 2003 May/June planning issue of *The Clergy Journal.*)

Labor Day – it's that day when we celebrate our work by taking a break from it. You have to admit, it doesn't make a great deal of sense. But we will do it. We'll be grateful for the day of rest and relaxation, and perhaps even return to our labor with some renewed sense of invigoration. This morning, I suggest that we hitch our wagon to this holiday, which is rather secular in its conception. (After all, the world has not been reluctant to seize our religious holidays for its purposes.) This morning, we will take the occasion of Labor Day to think about work and labor and our doing – at least our doing in a religious sense.

We begin with a curious, even harsh, encounter between Jesus and the Pharisees. A group of Pharisees, who were extremely observant students of Jewish law, noticed that some of Jesus' disciples were not following some of the fine points of the law. To the point, they observed that some of these disciples were eating without having performed the prescribed rituals of cleanliness. They were sitting at the dinner table without having washed their hands in the proper way. The Pharisees challenge the rabbi on the matter. Jesus takes exception to their barbs and offers a defense that exposes the emptiness of their legalistic practices. While they may have demonstrated absolute allegiance to the Law, Jesus points out that this is not the same thing as honoring those principles that the Law had been created to uphold.

You see, laws can restrict human behavior, but laws cannot, in and of themselves, create devotion. For example, there is a law that says that it is not lawful to drive a car more than 20 miles per hour in a school zone, but that law cannot guarantee that each driver will be careful in the presence of pedestrian children, and this is, of course, the desire behind the law. Also, the person who is driving a few miles above the speed limit may actually be exercising more caution than the person driving below the posted speed while talking on a cell phone and drinking a cup of coffee. Now, I cannot speak about what was in the hearts of any of these Pharisees, but apparently Jesus knew them well enough to suggest that some of them, while meticulous in their behavior legally speaking, had not embraced the spirit of these laws.

While this passage serves as our text for the day, the lectionary includes additional readings, one from the epistle of James that is instructive because of its seeming contradictions to what we are hearing from the mouth of Jesus. This letter serves as almost a solo New Testament voice speaking as a counterpoint to the promise of grace. "What about our works?" asks James. "You will know the tree by the fruit it bears. It isn't enough to just talk the talk; we have to walk the walk . . ." Well, you get the point. In grasping for some sense of what James meant, it is helpful to recall that he wasn't writing to people who were advocating an abuse of grace that permitted hedonism and libertarian behavior – you know, do whatever you want and let God's grace clean up after you. Rather, he seems to have been locked in debate with some folks who had decided that it wasn't important to do anything at all except trust in the Lord.

We are left wondering what to do, or more to the point, whether doing has any significance. Jesus chews on the Pharisees for their excessive preoccupation with exercising the fine points of the law. James chimes in to say, "be doers of the word and not hearers only" (Jas 1:22). What are we supposed to make of this?

The obvious solution, of course, is to try to preserve the value of each position, and indeed, that is where we often find truth – not at one extreme or another, but in a lively tension between two contrasting points of view. In this case, it is not difficult to see that there can be a value in what we do; there is something to be produced in the work of our faith. We also know how easy it is to be working so hard that we lose God in all of the sweat. On the other hand, it is easy to see how self-righteous religious people can become, while at the same time understanding how helpful structure ("law") can be to maintain a community's or an individual's focus.

If we can see how, in this case, truth is to be found more in the tension than in the absolute positions, we are left to ponder what it means with respect to the work of our congregation. As for how you personally fit into this matter, I leave it for you to work out. What I will say is that when I look around this place, I see both Pharisees and slackers.

Some of us have a propensity to become obsessive about the agenda of the church. For us, the lines sometimes get blurred between deep, transforming faith and committee meetings. We are the ones who can be so aligned to the past that we define the community of faith only one way – by what we have always known. We are the ones who can become so caught up in structure and the work of the church, that if the Spirit were pounding on the door, we would not hear.

Then there are those of us for whom church becomes a peripheral thing in our lives. We give it lip service. For us, faith has been reduced to a mostly nebulous and fuzzy sense that we ought to be nice. We find ourselves investing far more time, thought, and energy in other areas of our lives and leave the work of church to others. We produce little in terms of faith, and there are times that, if we are honest, we wonder why our faith means so little to us.

Where do you fit in this tension between Jesus' and James' words? I trust that somewhere in this constellation of texts there is a word for you. And maybe all of this is something to ponder as we begin a new year of work here at Heights Christian Church. Perhaps we can see afresh that the church is a gift entrusted to us – a gift we violate if we hold it to be of ultimate importance, and a gift that we cheapen if we do not take it seriously.

The Pharisees among us need to be challenged in their allegiance to form over function, to know that it is not contrary to God's laws to do something different this time around. The liberal disciples among us need to be reminded that the work of the church is not empty, to know that if we are going to hand a cup of coffee to a visitor, someone is going to have to make the coffee and clean up the pot.

So, how do we put all this together? In the end, I think that Jesus was not attacking the passion of doing, but rather, he was exposing the potential nothingness in the doing out of obligation rather than passion. And I don't think that James was negating the primacy of God's grace, but rather, he was pointing out that authentic faith is intended to lead to something with the power to transform us. In the end, does it strike you that both Jesus and James are steering us from obligation to love?

– Gary L. Walling
Heights Christian Church
Shaker Heights, Ohio

September 7, 2003

13th Sunday after Pentecost (Proper 18)

RC/Pres: 23rd Sunday in Ordinary Time

Lessons

RCL	Prov 22:1-2, 8-9, 22-23	Jas 2:1-10 (11-13), 14-17	Mk 7:24-37
Roman Catholic	Isa 35:4-7	Jas 2:1-5	Mk 7:31-37
Episcopal (BCP)	Isa 35:4-7a	Jas 1:17-27	Mk 7:31-37
Lutheran	Isa 35:4-7a	Jas 2:1-10 (11-13), 14-17	Mk 7:24-37

Introduction to the Lessons

Lesson 1

(1) *Proverbs 22:1-2, 8-9, 22-23* (RCL)

Inequity in dealing with others is addressed. First, there is the conviction that reputation is of more value than wealth, but those who do have riches are commanded to be generous and kind.

(2) *Isaiah 35:4-7* (RC); *Isaiah 35:4-7a* (Epis/Luth)

Those who are frightened are given assurance that God is coming and will save the righteous and destroy the wicked. The world will be transformed and all things will be set right.

Lesson 2

(1) *James 2:1-10 (11-13), 14-17* (RCL/Luth); *James 2:1-5* (RC)

The passage is a warning against showing partiality to those who are wealthy or hold positions of honor over against those who are poor and in need. The text progresses to remind the reader that a transgression of any portion of the law makes one as needful of mercy as any other sinner.

(2) *James 1:17-27* (Epis)

This is the familiar passage in which James admonishes us to "be doers of the word, and not merely hearers." These words come in the larger context of James' counsel to curb our tendency to speak carelessly. We are called to commit ourselves to doing acts of kindness and care.

Gospel

***Mark 7:24-37* (RCL/Luth); *Mark 7:31-37* (RC/Epis)**

Jesus heals the daughter of a Gentile woman after her plea that even dogs get to have the crumbs spilled by children. Jesus then heals a deaf man, and admonishes those who witness the healing to tell no one, but the people spread the word anyway.

Theme

The gospel has no limitations.

Thought for the Day

One of my college professors was fond of saying that "God has hit many a lick with a crooked stick." Not only is every person of value in God's sight, each of us has some unique contribution to make in building God's realm.

Call to Worship

Say to those who live in fear, be strong and do not fear, for your God reigns. In trust, let us stand and worship our protector and redeemer.

Pastoral Prayer

O God, you have created all things and done so with a boundless imagination. We praise all that you have created: the peacock and the ant, the radish and the oak, the rain and the stars.

This day we especially give thanks for the people who surround and fill our lives, and we marvel at your attention to detail. You have made no one to be a copy of any other person, and you love each person as if he or she were your only child. We give thanks for our differences – for the diversity that makes life interesting and new. We find ourselves appreciating the varied hues of skin color which give different races and ethnic groups their distinctive loveliness; the charming array of accents which roll off different tongues and charm our ears; and the assorted personalities and temperaments out of which people respond to life.

Let us never lose the sense of wonder about the beauty of those who surround us, and let each of us never fail to appreciate the unique gifts of one another. Amen.

Prayer of Confession

We can be suspicious, dear God. Confronted with the diversity of your family on earth, we have shown a capacity to be wary and distrustful. We confess that we have chosen time and time again to stick with our own – to be with those who are most like us. Moreover, in rejecting the uniqueness of others, we have found ourselves rejecting our own individuality. We have yielded to the pressure to fit in and be like everyone else, often showing a reticence to offer our unique gifts and perspectives.

Help us to learn anew that there is only beauty in the breadth and depth of your family. Then give us the additional courage to be fully who you intend us to be. Remind us that you desire that we will give authentically of ourselves. In the name of the one who came to embrace life in all of its fullness, Jesus Christ our Lord. Amen.

Prayer of Dedication of Gifts and Self

We offer these gifts as an expression of who we are. Responding to your invitation to share of ourselves, we offer a portion of our treasure as we offer also portions of our time and talent to your service. We offer these gifts with every confidence that you will receive them joyously. And so, dear God, give these tithes and offerings a place in the grand scheme of your loving and healing work, even as you have called each one of us to share in Christ's ministry. Amen.

Sermon Summary

We are called to offer Christ's gospel to all people, but before that can be done, we must live the gospel before all people.

Hymn of the Day

"When the Church of Jesus"

Prolific English hymn writer Fred Pratt Green wrote this challenging hymn in 1968 for a stewardship campaign. Similar to today's reading from James, from which the text is drawn, this hymn challenges the church to examine its actions, its practices, and its appearance.

No words are minced as Green invites us to remember that, while worship is important and vital to the church, we must never let it be a substitute for Christian living. "Lest our hymns should drug us to forget [the world's] needs, forge our Christian worship into Christian deeds."

Children's Time

Quiet Time

When have you heard good news? Perhaps you heard that your mom got a promotion at work or that your grandpa was coming to visit. When you hear good news, what do you do? I usually call out "Hurray!" then go find someone to tell.

Imagine what you would do if you lived when Jesus did. One day, Jesus comes and heals your brother, who couldn't hear. Would you keep quiet about it? Within one day, how many people do you think would know that Jesus healed your brother?

Well, one day Jesus healed a man; then he asked the people who were there not to tell anyone! Why do you think he did that? I'm not sure, but on that day, Jesus had gone into a house to get away from the crowds, just to have some quiet time for prayer. Maybe Jesus didn't want anyone else to know he was in town.

Now, this man and his family were very excited about the healing. What do you think they did?

Sometimes we want to share the good news that Jesus loves us and sometimes we want to sit quietly with God. Both are important.

The Sermon

Dog Food

Hymns

Beginning of Worship: "O for a Thousand Tongues to Sing"
Sermon Hymn: "All Creatures of Our God and King"
Closing Hymn: "In Christ There Is No East or West"

Scripture

Mark 7:24-37 (For additional sermon materials on this passage, see the April 2003 and the 2003 May/June planning issues of *The Clergy Journal.*)

At first glance, this is a very troubling story. At first glance, it may well do some damage to the picture you have put together of just who Jesus was. That is, if you have in your mind that Jesus was a kind and compassionate person who moved about the countryside doing good and extending kindness to people who were otherwise rejected by society, then here you must wrestle with an image of Jesus that seems to show him as a bit cold and unfeeling.

Run back over the story again. Jesus is up in the northern part of Galilee and he leaves the area. That is, he crosses the border and goes further north into the area of Tyre and Sidon – into lands that would have been part of ancient Phoenicia and what would have been Syria in that day. There Jesus encounters a woman who is described as a Syrophoenician – a description that indicates she was from Palestine, but was not a Jew. She was a Gentile with terrible problems. Her daughter was possessed by a demon. As in other gospel stories, we do not know what was wrong with the girl, except to say that she was living with some mental or physical handicap. This mother sought out Jesus, which took a great deal of courage. She was a woman, not Jewish, and a sinner, following the accepted assumption that cases of demon possession resulted from the sins of parents.

This woman asks for help and Jesus makes no answer. She continues to follow and plead her case. The disciples ask Jesus to get rid of her, leading him to say that he was sent to the lost sheep of Israel. Still, the woman persists, being bold enough to run in front of Jesus and throw herself down at his feet. In response to this final plea, Jesus makes a statement that is ice-cold. He tells her that it is not right to take bread from children so that it can be thrown to dogs. It is hard to imagine how such an insult could have failed to get rid of this woman, but her love for her child drove her on. She told Jesus that she (like a dog) would be content to lap up the scraps that fell off the children's plates. Jesus lets go of his argument with her and heals her daughter.

Does Jesus as we meet him in this encounter seem like the Jesus that you have pictured all of your life? Does this sound like the Jesus who said, "Let the little children come to me; do not stop them; for it is to such as these that the kingdom of God belongs" (Mk 13:14)? Does this sound like the Jesus who said, "Jerusalem, Jerusalem. How often have I desired to gather your children together as a hen gathers her brood under her wings, and you were not willing" (Lk 13:34)? Does this sound like the Jesus through whom we come to know the Father, the Jesus who is Savior over all the earth? Or does this sound like an Israelite bigot?

September 7, 2003
13th Sunday after Pentecost (Proper 18)
RC/Pres: 23rd Sunday in Ordinary Time

This is a difficult story and one that I am not entirely sure about. This much I do suspect. It was not intended to be a story about Jesus' personality. If we start asking questions about Jesus' temperament, then we are likely off base. To make very much of this snapshot of Jesus as insensitive and insulting would run counter to everything else we might believe about him from the gospels. We must search elsewhere for a meaning. Even the excuses that have been offered over time on his behalf – he was testing her or bringing her to a point of humility or using her as an example of faith for his followers – sound lame.

What then? Well, I suspect that the real point of the story has less to do with how Jesus behaved and more to do with the direction of the church's mission. After Jesus' death, the church's mission was a hot topic. In fact, the first church convention was held to consider the question of whether there would be a mission to the Gentiles and if so whether they would have to become Jewish in order to become Christian. It was a difficult question, and in reflecting upon the ministry and example of Jesus, what the early church folks saw was a mission to the house of Israel. Any push for a broader mission – such as the Great Commission commanded – was pretty scarce indeed. Scarce, but perhaps strong enough.

Mark offers this little isolated incident, which is full of honest struggle and turmoil on the part of Jesus. Surely during Jesus' lifetime the question surfaced: should I be going out to other lands as well; are not all people to be touched by my work? And it would seem that Jesus resisted the temptation to engage in such a broader ministry. Time was limited, and perhaps that was the factor, which led him to restrict his mission – a decision that may well have tortured him. Could that be the turmoil we see in the story: whether to heal the daughter of a foreigner – whether to heal and minister to all of the foreigners who needed God's touch, whether to reach out to all of God's children?

Could this story be Mark's reminder that while Jesus primarily served among the Jews, he did not reject a mission to the non-Jewish world? Far from being about the heartlessness of Jesus, the story is a reminder about Jesus' love for people outside the nation of Israel. Jesus had taken time and opportunities within his lifetime to reach beyond those boundaries when need arose.

As if to reinforce this idea, Mark portrays the Caananite woman as being a perceptive and persistent disciple. In contrast to the 12 men that

Jesus chose as intimates, the woman comes off quite favorably. Immediately before our story, Jesus tells a parable and the disciples ask what it means prompting Jesus to scold, "Then do you also fail to understand" (Mk 7:18)? And immediately after our text, Jesus feeds a crowd of four thousand men, but later when his disciples still worry about provisions so that Jesus asks with irritation, "Do you not yet understand?" (Mk 8:17). And sandwiched in the middle of these reminders of the faithlessness and lack of understanding of his disciples – men from the nation of Israel – there is this story about the faithfulness and insight of a foreign woman. She knows that Jesus has the power to do the thing she asks. We find ourselves asking, just who is the real disciple?

In the end as in the beginning, it is a troubling little story – at least from our point of view. This seems a harsh little story of Jesus which surely must have been intended as a lesson about the faithfulness that can come from persons whom we least expect. It is surely meant to be a reminder that we are called to minister across boundaries that we might not wish to cross.

– Gary L. Walling
Heights Christian Church
Shaker Heights, Ohio

September 14, 2003

14th Sunday after Pentecost (Proper 19)
RC/Pres: 24th Sunday in Ordinary Time

Lessons

RCL	Prov 1:20-33	Jas 3:1-12	Mk 8:27-38
Roman Catholic	Isa 50:4-9	Jas 2:14-18	Mk 8:27-35
Episcopal (BCP)	Isa 50:4-9	Jas 2:1-5, 8-10, 14-18	Mk 8:27-38 or Mk 9:14-29
Lutheran	Isa 50:4-9a	Jas 3:1-12	Mk 8:27-38

Introduction to the Lessons

Lesson 1

(1) *Proverbs 1:20-33* (RCL)

Wisdom is personified as one who is chastising those who have ignored her and refused to take her counsel. She promises to laugh at the disaster that will strike those who have been so foolish as to ignore wisdom.

(2) *Isaiah 50:4-9* (RC/Epis); *Isaiah 50:4-9a* (Luth)

The prophet is certain that his humiliation will be reversed and that his devotion to God will be rewarded when God enters to punish those who have oppressed him.

Lesson 2

(1) *James 3:1-12* (RCL/Luth)

James uses some wonderful imagery to make his point that words can be extremely damaging. The tongue is compared to the small bit that controls a horse's behavior, a little rudder that directs a ship, and a tiny fire that can set a forest ablaze.

(2) *James 2:14-18* (RC); *James 2:1-5, 8-10, 14-18* (Epis)

The passage is a warning against showing partiality to those who are wealthy or hold positions of honor. The text progresses to remind the reader that a transgression of any portion of the law makes one as needful of mercy as any other sinner.

Gospel

***Mark 8:27-38* (RCL/Epis/Luth); *Mark 8:27-35* (RC)**

Jesus asks Peter who he thinks Jesus is, and Peter declares him to be the Messiah. However, when Jesus announces that his way will be the way of the cross, Peter scolds Jesus, prompting Jesus to scold Peter, saying that life is ultimately preserved as it is given away.

Theme

Following Christ requires a willingness to take on the burdens Jesus accepted.

Thought for the Day

The Christian faith is ultimately discovered in the deepest contradictions of the Spirit. Otherwise, what can it mean to suggest that life is found only in our dying?

Call to Worship

You are the salt of the earth, the light of the world, a city built upon a hill. You are claimed and treasured by God, so come into the divine presence, that you may come to see yourselves for who you have been created to be.

Pastoral Prayer

We give thanks for those in our company who so freely give of themselves, that the lives of others may be blessed:

those who have left lucrative careers to defend and heal the impoverished;

those who give time to work in the shelters and pantries;

those who have donated organs in order that others' lives may continue;

those who have traveled to far lands for the sake of the gospel;

those who are quick to smile, to listen, and to slow down;

those who are mindful of others so as to include them in their prayers.

In the spirits of these and others of like heart, we have caught a glimpse of Christ, alive and among us. We have found ourselves yearning to join that company of friends whose touch seems always to grace life and restore its wholeness. So, dear God, as you have blessed us with the love of others, use our lives also, that our love may become a blessing to others. In Christ's name we pray. Amen.

Prayer of Confession

How we have perverted our faith, dear God! We have seized the cross and substituted a crown. We have chosen the easy path instead of the more difficult way. We have deluded ourselves that sacrificial loving was simply Jesus' way of following your will. Renew our faith, that we may have a touch of the ardor and passion of those saints through time who have held Jesus above everything, and who have been willing to follow any road down which he has led them. Help us understand that we have been called not to a path of pleasure and ease, but to a journey that requires our all. Amen.

Prayer of Dedication of Gifts and Self

Have we examined our wealth and concluded that the things we have are evidence of our faith, O Giver, when we should be letting our faith ask questions about our possessions? Too often we have twisted our prayers into requests for privileges and blessings. So, dear God, let us understand that if we have much, we dare not conclude that we are loved above others, nor think that if we find ourselves in want, that we are loved less. Instead, let each one of us know that we are given so that we may be transformed into givers. Accept our gifts, large and small, and use them in every way that pleases you. Amen.

Sermon Summary

The power of the cross ought not to be anesthetized by Christians. When the cross became the central image of our faith, it was a scandalous image. To understand that we are called to take up our crosses is to grasp that we are called to a very different way of living.

Hymn of the Day

"Wisdom's Table"

While inspired by the images in Proverbs 9 wherein Wisdom invites the people to a feast – a text not included in the lectionary – this new hymn by Doug Gay from Scotland fits well with any of the passages that talk about Wisdom.

The playful text and simple tune evoke a sense of dancing and celebration, which is appropriate (this is the same wisdom who delighted to play for God at the time of creation). Furthermore, the connection of Wisdom and table reminds us of biblical references to Jesus as the Wisdom (logos) of God.

Children's Time

Who Am I?

(Ask several members of the congregation to dress in their work or volunteer uniforms. Invite them to stand at the front with the children. As you introduce each person, ask children to guess who he or she is in the community.)

It's not always easy to tell what someone does by looking at them. Would you guess the special things that these people do if you didn't see them in uniform? How do you get to know other people? It could be by talking to them, asking others about them, or maybe reading about them in the newspaper. Sometimes you learn about a person quickly and sometimes it takes a long time.

One day, Jesus was walking with some of his followers and he asked them who people thought Jesus was. Some disciples said that people thought Jesus was John the Baptist; others thought that he was a prophet. A prophet is someone who speaks God's word, so that was a pretty good guess. But Peter, who was one of Jesus' disciples, said that he thought Jesus was the Messiah, which means the one that God sent to save others.

Who do you think Jesus is?

September 14, 2003
14th Sunday after Pentecost (Proper 19)
RC/Pres: 24th Sunday in Ordinary Time

The Sermon

Choosing a Crossroad

Hymns

Beginning of Worship: "Lead On, O King Eternal"

Sermon Hymn: "To Us All, to Every Nation" ("Once to Every Man and Nation")

Closing Hymn: "Take My Life, that I May Be"

Scripture

Mark 8:27-38 (For additional sermon materials on this passage, see the 2003 May/June planning and July 2003 issues of *The Clergy Journal.*)

Jesus said, "The Son of Man must undergo great suffering, and be rejected by the elders, the chief priests, and the scribes, and be killed" (Mk 8:31).

Peter said, "Absolutely not! People are getting excited about your message, and when they hear you speak, they catch a glimpse of the possibilities that their lives hold; so let's lose this cross message."

Jesus said, "The Son of Man must undergo great suffering, and be rejected by the elders, the chief priests, and the scribes, and be killed."

And I said, "I hope you're speaking metaphorically, because while I believe in sacrifice as much as the next person, I do have a wife and two children who need me, alive and in one piece. Truth be told, I hope you're not even speaking metaphorically, because I have a good church and a good life, and I really don't need to be stepping on too many toes. I understand that there are lots of things that are wrong in this community, and in this country for that matter, but I think it is best to work within the system. I know that things are not progressing as fast as any of us would like, but I cannot see the point in any of us becoming martyrs here."

Jesus said, "The Son of Man must undergo great suffering, and be rejected by the elders, the chief priests, and the scribes, and be killed."

And the two presidential candidates said, "It doesn't have to be that way – this is the big leagues, and we have to be prepared to go negative if that is what it takes. We got in this race to win, and by God, that is what we intend to do."

Jesus said, "The Son of Man must undergo great suffering, and be rejected by the elders, the chief priests, and the scribes, and be killed."

And Bill Gates said, "I am not saying we ought to crush everyone else – you never heard me say that – but are we really under any obligation to limit our own ability to compete? Why must we give a hand to our competitors? Let them work harder; that's what we do! I don't see why we should be less than what we can be."

The way of the cross? Who believes in such a way anymore? The way that many Christians have dealt with Jesus' challenging words in this passage is to make the cross into a symbol rather than a reality; we have robbed it of its power by turning it into a decoration. It no longer offends. Think about it; does the cross have the same effect on you as if we had brought an electric chair into this sanctuary? Does looking at it unsettle you as much, as say, you had to look at a hangman's noose hanging up there? Would a gurney with straps and an IV hookup bother you more than that decorative cross that we have put up there?

The cross once was an offensive object, and properly used as a symbol of faith, it ought to convey that offensiveness today. The cross is about loss and death and sacrifice.

And yet, why is Peter's encounter in this story told at all, if not to make the point that it is not only the powers and principalities of the world that have difficulty accepting the way of Jesus? It is, first and foremost, Jesus' own followers who reject his way.

Consider Peter, fresh from making his confession that Jesus is the Christ. Peter hears Jesus describe his mission: "the Son of Man must undergo great suffering, and be rejected by the elders, the chief priests, and the scribes, and be killed." Peter cannot take this grim view of the future, so he takes Jesus aside and he rebukes him. Now this is not a word that we often use today, but whatever its precise meaning, it is clear that to rebuke someone is to exercise power over him or her. One rebukes children, not parents; employees, not a boss; students, not teachers. So, for Peter to rebuke is clearly to assume the superior position in the relationship. Peter is the one at the head of the parade – teaching, defining, patronizing.

From our perspective, this portrait of Peter is hardly flattering. Scripture then is engaging in a similar pointless exercise – commanding us to do what we would never dream of doing. If that is the function of Peter's part in the larger story being played out here, then there ought to be a shiver running up and down our spines when Jesus turns the rebuke around and says to Peter: "Get behind me Satan" (v. 33). It is enough to make us ask whether we have sought to teach, define, and patronize Jesus, or for that matter, whether we have told the truth about who Jesus is and what he has come among us to be and to do.

There is a story about Clarence Jordan that makes my point. Perhaps best known for his cotton patch version of the New Testament, a translation that he wrote in the colloquial style of the American South, Jordan was also the founder of an interracial, pacifist, self-sufficient, Christian community in Americus, Georgia, called Koinonia. The people who live there are great advocates for the causes of justice. The story is told that Jordan once had occasion to visit another minister's church, and he was given the grand tour of the magnificent new facilities. His host pointed out the splendid wood pews and the beautiful decorations, but he made the biggest fuss over a large cross that adorned the top of a tall steeple. Lighted by an impressive spotlight, the minister boasted that the cross alone had cost more than ten thousand dollars. This prompted Jordan to comment, "Well, you got cheated. Times were when Christians could get crosses for free."

Jesus said, "The Son of Man must undergo great suffering, and be rejected by the elders, the chief priests, and the scribes, and be killed."

And you said . . .

– Gary L. Walling
Heights Christian Church
Shaker Heights, Ohio

September 21, 2003

15th Sunday after Pentecost (Proper 20)

RC/Pres: 25th Sunday in Ordinary Time

Lessons

RCL	Prov 31:10-31	Jas 3:13–4:3, 7-8a	Mk 9:30-37
Roman Catholic	Wis 2:12, 17-20	Jas 3:16–4:3	Mk 9:30-37
Episcopal (BCP)	Wis 1:16–2:1 (6-11), 12-22	Jas 3:16–4:6	Mk 9:30-37
Lutheran	Jer 11:18-20 or Wis 1:16–2:1, 12-22	Jas 3:13–4:3, 7-8a	Mk 9:30-37

Introduction to the Lessons

Lesson 1

(1) *Proverbs 31:10-31* (RCL)

This closing portion of Proverbs is a poem that praises the woman who is a good wife. Her industry, righteousness, and devotion are examined and praised.

(2) *Wisdom 2:12, 17-20* (RC)

Evildoers conspire to set a trap for a just person, proposing to destroy the one who is righteous that can only be saved by God.

(3) *Wisdom 1:16–2:1 (6-11), 12-22* (Epis)

A worldly philosophy is espoused which suggests that only what is held in this life really matters. This cynical view arises from the notion that God has made people mortal and thereby limited the meaning of their existence.

(4) *Jeremiah 11:18-20* (Luth)

Jeremiah uses the dual imagery of a lamb led to slaughter and a tree destroyed with its fruit to describe the threat against his life by those who oppose his prophecy.

Lesson 2

***James 3:13–4:3, 7-8a* (RCL/Luth); *James 3:16–4:3* (RC); *James 3:16–4:6* (Epis)**

A contrast is made between what is heavenly and what is earthly, first in setting the wisdom from above over against the wisdom of this world, and then by arguing that a person cannot take up a friendship with this world without sacrificing a relationship with the world beyond.

Gospel

***Mark 9:30-37* (RCL/RC/Epis/Luth)**

Jesus predicts his suffering and death a second time, which prompts his disciples to begin arguing about which one of them is the greatest. Jesus sets a child in their presence and says that whoever aspires to be first must become a servant.

Theme

Great disciples are those who welcome and serve each person in Jesus' name.

Thought for the Day

There is no coercion in the Christian faith. The choice is put before us, and we are free to follow or to turn away; but if we choose to follow, the demands are great.

Call to Worship

Grace to you and peace from God our Creator and Jesus of Nazareth and the Spirit of Holiness. Come and worship, and in worshiping the Holy One, let us open our lives for transformation.

Pastoral Prayer

We would give anything to see the face of Jesus – to stand before him, to hear him speak, and to take our measure of him. We would go to the far reaches of the world to sit at his feet and to be in his holy presence.

So, dear God, teach us that we do not have to travel far at all to see Jesus' face. Unveil our eyes, that we may see him in the faces of those he loves. May we see him in the faces of children who revel in the gift of life. May we see him in the need of the world – in the hunger and the hurting. May we see him in the countless acts of courage and self-giving in which people put their own interests aside for the sake of others. May we see him in the confidence of those who live and risk as though death can never have the final word.

Let us seize each day and see in it the opportunity for welcoming and serving all in Jesus' name, and let us be assured that at day's end, we will have seen his face. Amen.

Prayer of Confession

We are an ambitious and hard-driving people, dear God. We are accustomed to scoring at the high end of the scale and achieving what we have desired. We work long hours and have high aspirations. We know what we want and we go after it, and we hold these traits to be admirable qualities. Though we do not want to think of ourselves as like those disciples who argued about who was the greatest, we can see ourselves in them. We are taken aback by the gentleness and humility of Jesus, and we feel shame over our striving and our self-promotion. Forgive us, and give us something of the mind and heart that was in Jesus, so that we might lose our need to be the best in the eyes of others and thereby find ourselves in you. Amen.

Prayer of Dedication of Gifts and Self

What gift could we give that would delight you any more than a gift of ourselves – not a gift of something we have held for a moment, but rather a gift that truly reveals a loving heart and a passionate spirit? We bring our gifts before you now, O God, and pray that the joy you demonstrate in receiving these gifts will be matched by our joy in giving. Bless these and all the gifts we give, and let your joy be our added blessing. Amen.

Sermon Summary

Our stature as disciples comes from welcoming and serving others. To choose to follow Jesus is to understand how that choice will open our eyes to the needs of others.

Hymn of the Day

"Make Me a Channel of Your Peace"

"When peacemakers plant seeds of peace, they will harvest justice" (Jas 3:18, CEV). While the Prayer of Saint Francis is highly popular and has been sung on many occasions since being set to music by Sebastian Temple in 1967, this hymn does not appear in many hymnals. And yet its message is timeless. The selfless Christian living exemplified by Francis of Assisi shines through in these words, which in turn are well served by Temple's simple tune.

Children's Time

Greatest of All

Who do you think is the most important person in our church? *(Invite children to state their choices and their reasons for choosing that person.)*

Jesus' disciples talked about this question one day as they were walking with Jesus to a house in Capernaum, where Jesus was going to teach them. Actually, the disciples argued with each other about which one of them was the greatest disciple.

Jesus knew they were arguing and he asked them about it. As you can imagine, the disciples were embarrassed and ashamed to admit what they'd been arguing about. Jesus sat down, looked at them, and said something very unexpected. He told them that whoever wanted to be a great disciple had to love and serve others.

Then Jesus took a little child in his arms and he told his disciples that whoever welcomes a little child welcomes him. Jesus told the disciples that whenever they welcome each person and make each person feel important, it's the same as loving and welcoming God. So, who do you think is the most important person in our church? *(Allow a moment for responses.)* Each one of us is important. Each one of us can be Jesus' disciple, loving and welcoming others.

The Sermon

Servant of All

Hymns

Beginning of Worship: "God of Grace and God of Glory"
Sermon Hymn: "The Church of Christ, in Every Age"
Closing Hymn: "I Am Thine, O Lord"

Scripture

Mark 9:30-37 (For additional sermon materials on this passage, see the 2003 May/June planning issue of *The Clergy Journal* and on James 3:13–4:3, 7-8a, see the July 2003 issue of *The Clergy Journal.*)

I departed for my trip to the Holy Land with a healthy dose of skepticism about some of the geographic traditions and claims that are part and parcel of touring the Holy Land. And now, having heard the various claims that have been made for this site and that point, my doubts are even stronger. For example, I saw the 14th station of the cross, said to be the traditional site of Jesus' burial, now under the care of the Roman Catholic Church in the Church of the Holy Sepulchre. Behind this shrine, however, a Coptic priest was calling out for people to see the marker under his care, also reported to be the site of Jesus' grave. Sunday morning, we worshiped perhaps a quarter of a mile away – at the garden tomb staffed by Protestants who were caring for Jesus' grave.

Some of the geographic sites, of course, were accurate – the Sea of Galilee has not moved in the course of two millennia. Masada is Masada. But while we can say with a level of certitude, "This is the Jordan River," I think we must leave a little more wiggle room when we declare, "This is the spot on the Jordan where Jesus was baptized." I toured many places that may not have been accurate in the strictest historical sense – the site of Peter's house in Capernaum, the spot where Jesus preached the Sermon on the Mount, the place where the angel made his divine announcement to Mary, and so on – but I discovered that it is possible to put aside academic skepticism. There is a different sense of accuracy in marking some of these spots. One has a sense of "if not here, then a place like this." In this way, it is possible to mark the essence of the setting of an event.

I think I have a better understanding of the need that people of faith over the centuries have had to attach the gospel accounts of Jesus' activities to places. I felt this on the Mount of Olives in a grove of olive trees known then and now as Gethsemane. Looking across the Kidron Valley, I could see the walls of Jerusalem and the Golden Gate. It is a view not all that different than what Jesus would have seen. Sitting on the steps of the temple, I could say, "These are the steps that Jesus would have climbed to enter the temple."

Walking along the road to Capernaum, one can imagine the hushed, yet strident voices of the disciples. "I'm the greatest because Jesus called me first." "I'm the greatest because I am most faithful in prayer." "I'm the greatest because I have preached in the most towns."

It's equally easy to imagine them gathered in that house in Capernaum, perhaps wishing they were still on the road when Jesus asks, "What were you arguing about on the way?" (Mk 9:33). So, the text nudges us in a vital direction for our reflection on the life of discipleship. Jesus teaches, "Whoever wants to be first must be last of all and servant of all" (v. 35).

We can imagine the puzzled looks that the disciples exchange. We can picture Jesus picking up a small child – a child that the disciples did not even notice on their way in – and proclaiming, "Whoever welcomes one such child in my name welcomes me, and whoever welcomes me welcomes not me but the one who sent me" (v. 37). It's as if Jesus calls them to open their eyes to their surroundings and listen for the needs that are expressed there. Jesus challenges them to find greatness in discipleship by noticing the people around them and seeking to serve them.

Before the walk to Capernaum, Jesus told the disciples, "The Son of Man is to be betrayed into human hands, and they will kill him" (vs. 31). The disciples were confused and upset. Perhaps this explains why they chose to focus on themselves rather than on striving to understand and follow their teacher. Jesus went on to Jerusalem as the servant of these disciples and the servant of you and me. Along the way, he served the needs of those whom he met. To choose to follow Jesus is to have Jesus open our eyes to the needs of others along the paths that our lives take.

So, when you picture the disciples walking away from Capernaum, what do you imagine their conversation to be? As you walk away from this building this morning, what will your conversation be?

– Gary L. Walling
Heights Christian Church
Shaker Heights, Ohio

September 28, 2003

16th Sunday after Pentecost (Proper 21)

RC/Pres: 26th Sunday in Ordinary Time

Lessons

RCL	Esth 7:1-6, 9-10; 9:20-22	Jas 5:13-20	Mk 9:38-50
Roman Catholic	Num 11:25-29	Jas 5:1-6	Mk 9:38-43, 45, 47-48
Episcopal (BCP)	Num 11:4-6, 10-16, 24-29	Jas 4:7-12 (13–5:6)	Mk 9:38-43, 45, 47-48
Lutheran	Num 11:4-6, 10-16 24-29	Jas 5:13-20	Mk 9:38-50

Introduction to the Lessons

Lesson 1

(1) *Esther 7:1-6, 9-10; 9:20-22* (RCL)

This portion of the book includes the fall of Haman and the institution of the Jewish festival of Purim.

(2) *Numbers 11:25-29* (RC);
***Numbers 11:4-6, 10-16, 24-29* (Epis/Luth)**

In the longer reading, the people are complaining of their situation yet again and Moses is distraught. God advises him to gather a group of 70 elders to advise him. God then touches these people with the Spirit.

Lesson 2

(1) *James 5:13-20* (RCL/Luth)

The conclusion of the letter of James implores readers to turn to prayer for healing and spiritual renewal.

(2) *James 5:1-6* (RC)

Here is a statement about the folly of placing one's hope in wealth and material possessions.

(3) ***James 4:7-12 (13–5:6)*** **(Epis)**
This longer version of the reading above contains further injunctions to the readers to live humbly in the fear of God.

Gospel
Mark 9:38-50 **(RCL/Luth);**
Mark 9:38-43, 45, 47-48 **(RC/Epis)**
Jesus invites the disciples to see that all those who act in God's name and with godly love are true children of God. He also notes that self-righteousness will lead to the sin of creating stumbling blocks for others.

Theme

When God invites us – no, *urges* us – to be salted with fire, why are we content to be temperate?

Thought for the Day

Lot's wife is remembered as a tragic figure. . . . But it is rather amazing that she wasn't thrown out and trampled underfoot as the story moved on. Now she stands forever in the text: white-hot light on the breast of a hill while the cities are burning.

– Barbara K. Lundblad,
"Taking Off the Armor of God,"
Sermon preached at The Festival of Homiletics,
Chicago, May 2002

Call to Worship

Leader: We come to learn strength
People: so that we may lift up those who are burdened.
Leader: We come to learn generosity
People: so that we may welcome those who are outcast.
Leader: We come to learn patience
People: so that we may soothe those who are angry.
Leader: We come to learn love
People: so that we may reveal God's presence here and now.

Pastoral Prayer

Salty God, you are the stinging in our wounds that makes us aware that we *have* wounds, when we would prefer to believe that we are whole. You are the sharp bite of the gospel message on our tongues, which challenges bland complacency. You are the health-ensuring preservative that protects our souls from perishing into eternal death.

Salty God, grant us the wisdom to welcome your saltiness in every aspect of our lives. And grant us the grace to reflect your image by being salt for others. Amen.

Prayer of Confession

Forgiving God, forgive us for thinking we need to protect your universe from your power! Forgive us for our self-righteousness in judging others unworthy if they worship you with different rituals, or call you by a different name, or offer a welcome to those who don't fit our ideas of appropriate companions for our journey.

Forgiving God, forgive us for using our hands to slam doors shut rather than open them wide. Forgive us for using our feet to escape responsibility rather than to walk beside a lonely or wounded sister or brother. Forgive us for turning our eyes aside from injustice and pain rather than using them to see with clarity and vision.

Forgiving God, forgive us these sins of commission and omission in the name of the one who showed us the true way of the servant, Jesus, our Christ. Amen.

Prayer of Dedication of Gifts and Self

Generous God, you invite us to be a lively presence in the world, bringing spice to all things through our whole-hearted and zesty participation. Receive and bless these gifts, that they may do more than make life merely palatable. Bless them, that they may carry the rich and abundant flavor of your realm to those who have known nothing but bland existence. And, Generous God, bless us, that we may savor every opportunity to share the sweetness you have poured into our lives. Amen.

Sermon Summary

Discipleship demands a risky engagement with the power of the Holy Spirit, which is wildly unsafe, burning and tempering the human soul, preparing it for radical and unconditional love.

Hymn of the Day

"This Is My Song"

The first two stanzas were written by poet Lloyd Stone while he was teaching at the University of Hawaii in the period between the two world wars. They are a profound patriotic celebration of homeland, while recognizing that the patriotism, hopes, and dreams of those of other nations is no less valid. Accordingly, the hymn works well with today's gospel wherein Jesus affirms the work of all who do God's will, regardless of their identity. A third verse by Methodist theologican Georgia Harkness quotes the Lord's Prayer as it exhorts Christian unity. The tune is Finlandia by Finnish composer Jean Sibelius.

Children's Time

Salt Is Good

(Preparation: Bring unsalted and salted tortilla chips or popcorn, enough for each child to have a taste of each.)

Hand out the unsalted food and ask the children to eat it, being aware of possible food allergies. Then give them the salty version to eat and ask them to describe the difference. Which tastes better? Why?

Salt has been used for a long time to flavor food. It can make something bland taste really good. In Jesus' day, salt was valuable also because it kept food from spoiling. Because it was so valuable, salt was used like money. Sometimes salt was even used to pay salaries to workers. Can you imagine if your moms or dads got salt instead of money for doing their jobs?

Jesus told his disciples to "have salt" in themselves and be at peace with each other. The first bit sounds a little odd to us until we remember how valuable salt was in their world. Jesus told his disciples to add good things to life, and to work at making peaceful things happen in the world. Jesus tells us the same thing. Be salty! Help good and peaceful things happen. When we care for each other, we are being salty Christians.

The Sermon

Salted with Fire

Hymns

Beginning of Worship: "Spirit Divine, Attend Our Prayers"
Sermon Hymn: "You Are Salt for the Earth"
Closing Hymn: "Renew Your Church"

Scripture

Mark 9:38-50 (For additional sermon materials on this passage, see the 2003 May/June planning issue and July 2003 issue of *The Clergy Journal.*)

When I was a little girl, I can remember my grandmother describing a friend of hers as "the salt of the earth." I heard that expression frequently as I was growing up. Often it was applied to those stalwart and tireless women who ran church suppers, knit mittens by the dozens for church fairs, served lunches after the funerals of church members, and sent their husbands out in the fall to rake the church lawn. These women, in other words, did what needed to be done to keep the church going. As I got older, the expression seemed to vanish – right along with the generation of churchwomen of whom it was such an apt description.

As a pastor, I have had many occasions to lament the loss of down-to-earth women and men who seemed to personify these familiar words of Jesus and the sturdy quality of character he seemed to be trying to evoke in his disciples. I was startled, therefore, to notice that Mark does not use the expression "salt of the earth" in this passage. Instead, he uses a more startling and less comfortable phrase. Mark says, "For everyone will be salted with fire" (Mk 8:49). Everyone will be salted with fire! With fire!

That is not the solid, friendly image of the faithful churchwoman! "Salted with fire" conjures the wild and reckless picture of disciples in an upper room as the wind of the Spirit roars and tongues of flame burn restlessly above each head. Gone is the idea that disciples are to grow into a comfortable maturity, nurtured by comfortable traditions and staid familiarity. Instead, this picture of discipleship suggests being goaded and set within a tempest. It summons unsettling images of witness in the face of violence and injustice, of people of faith arrested at peace vigils and jailed for contempt of law, of chaplains praying with medical personnel over the bodies of bombing victims. "Everyone will be salted with fire."

There is no disrespect intended in the comparison; the church of my youth was a church for its time. In a world recovering from the Great Depression and World War II, the "salt of the earth" parishioners were building stability out of turmoil and a vision of normalcy in place of the horrors of the Blitz, the Nazi death camps, the fire bombing of Dresden, and the atomic destruction of Nagasaki and Hiroshima. Those faithful "salt of the earth" women and men created the environment in which I learned the great hymns and creeds and prayers of the Christian tradition. The "child-sized" Bible stories I learned defined the Christian culture of the 1950s and early 1960s. It was a church for the time when being a good Christian and being a good American were considered the same thing for 95 percent of the people in the United States.

The miracle of the Bible is that it speaks good news in every age. The challenge of discipleship is to hear the good news that is the word for the particular age in which we find ourselves. The generation who came to adulthood in the 1930s and 1940s were called to be "the salt of the earth," but I believe that we, in this age, are being called to be "salted with fire" and the Holy Spirit. We are being invited to let the Spirit touch us deeply enough to burn us, to set us afire with passion and compassion, with love and justice and mercy.

Pierre Teilhard de Chardin said, "Someday, after mastering the winds, the waves, the tides and gravity, we shall harness for God the energies of love, and then, for a second time in the history of the world, [we] will have discovered fire."

We who call ourselves followers of Christ are being tested and challenged in new ways. We are being called, in a world where the difference between rich and poor has never been wider, to hold all things in common in new and radically demanding ways. We are being called to share the resources of the earth and the resources entrusted to us through our labor not only with our fellow Christians, but with Buddhists, Jews, Muslims, Shintoists, Zoroastrians, and others too numerous to mention. We are being called to comprehend and honor social and cultural norms and structures that we regard as bizarre or alien in the extreme, remembering that Jesus said, "I have other sheep that do not belong to this fold" (Jn 10:16). We are being called to work beside, heal beside, build beside, and learn beside women and men and children of ethnic and religious and national backgrounds, which, only two decades ago, were mere abstractions to us. We are being called to understand justice and mercy in completely new ways. We are being called to share the table with those who sing, pray, eat, preach, and worship in styles that we have never seen before.

We are being salted with fire, with *fire!* The dross – the peripheral, the superficial, the nonessential – must be burned away lest we mistake the inconsequential for the imperative. Our parents and grandparents were called to a different discipleship, but to each era comes its own call. We are being invited to yield to the tempestuous winds and the roaring flame of the uncontrolled and uncontrollable Spirit. The Spirit pours down, wrenching open the closed doors and windows of the soul, consuming all the unnecessary stuff (the rules, the safety nets, the material excess, the worldly agendas), turning it to ash, then swirling it away on the commanding breath of the Holy One.

Earlier in this passage, Jesus warns against putting stumbling blocks in the way of the innocent. We are being called, in these early years of the third millennium after Jesus, to submit ourselves – mind, body, heart, and soul – to a trial by fire. We are called to a tempering and a purging that will eliminate from our very beings every thought or word or choice of action that might be a stumbling block for another soul. We are being called to harness the energies of love for God so that the fire we unleash will not be the fire of nuclear destruction, but the living flame of the Spirit made manifest among the nations. Let it be so. Let it be so.

– Andrea La Sonde Anastos
Intentional Interim Minister
Greenfield, Massachusetts

October 5, 2003

17th Sunday after Pentecost (Proper 22)
RC/Pres: 27th Sunday in Ordinary Time

Lessons

RCL	Job 1:1; 2:1-10	Heb 1:1-4; 2:5-12	Mk 10:2-16
Roman Catholic	Gen 2:18-24	Heb 2:9-11	Mk 10:2-16 or 10:2-12
Episcopal (BCP)	Gen 2:18-24	Heb 2:(1-8) 9-18	Mk 10:2-9
Lutheran	Gen 2:18-24	Heb 1:1-4; 2:5-12	Mk 10:2-16

Introduction to the Lessons

Lesson 1

(1) ***Job 1:1; 2:1-10*** **(RCL)**

This prologue contains the first half of the original story of Job, which brackets the later development of the story. It describes Job as a righteous man and tells what happened to him and his family.

(2) ***Genesis 2:18-24*** **(RC/Epis/Luth)**

These verses are the conclusion of the second creation story in which Havva (Eve) is created from one of Adham's ribs, and marriage is established.

Lesson 2

(1) ***Hebrews 1:1-4; 2:5-12*** **(RCL/Luth)**

Jesus is described as the one through whom God created the whole world and to whose care the world has been entrusted.

(2) ***Hebrews 2:9-11*** **(RC);** ***Hebrews 2:(1-8) 9-18*** **(Epis)**

Christ shared our full humanity to show us how to attain God's glory.

Gospel

Mark 10:2-16 **(RCL/RC/Luth);** ***Mark 10:2-9*** **(Epis)**

The longer reading contains two distinct pericopes – a discussion of divorce and the account of Jesus receiving the children.

Theme

The core question that Jesus asks is why we look for ways to avoid abiding commitment and the challenging task of loving with our whole hearts.

Thought for the Day

We are not sufficient unto ourselves – I am not; my husband, my family, my friends give me my meaning and, in a sense, my being, so that I know that I am ontological: essential: real.

– Madeleine L'Engle, *A Circle of Quiet,*
San Francisco: Harper SanFrancisco, 1986

Call to Worship

Leader: We come in joy, remembering we are created in your image, Holy One.
People: We come in joy, remembering that together we are your body, O God.
Leader: We come in joy, celebrating your presence in our sisters and brothers.
People: We come in joy, celebrating your presence throughout creation.
Leader: We come in joy!
People: Alleluia! Amen!

Pastoral Prayer

Most Perfect Love, the floodtide of your love swirls around us like undertow, tugging us into your enfolding presence, even as we try to wash our hands of any dependence on our sisters and brothers. Your rain of compassion pours over us in an everflowing stream of mercy, trying relentlessly to soften our parched hearts into fruitful receptiveness, preparing us to receive the tender seeds of each other's love.

Catch us up and sweep us together into a dancing whirlpool of connection where alienation is no longer possible and we recognize that separation is death. Amen.

Prayer of Confession

Embracing God, we confess that too often we look for ways to justify superficial love, rather than seeking the strength to live challenging love. We confess that we look for the emotional and spiritual loopholes that grant us permission to put our personal desires before the needs of others. We confess that we look for ways to toughen our hearts against hurt, rather than seeking the courage to soften our hearts into compassion.

Embracing God, forgive us and draw us into your heart, into the perfect love that casts out all fear, apathy, and alienation. Fold our brokenness into your wholeness until we know that, only in connection with others, are we able to be your living presence on earth. Amen.

Prayer of Dedication of Gifts and Self

Generous God, you have loved us so that we might have the love to care for others as true sisters and brothers. You have entrusted us with unmeasured wealth so that no one need go hungry, naked, or unsheltered. Receive what we have brought this day from the bounty you have given, and bless us with such generosity of spirit that even the stranger will see your power at work in us – opening our hands and our hearts to meet every need. Amen.

Sermon Summary

God did not create us for separation, for alienation, or for "divorce" from one another, but for connection and companionship, to be truly and forever one flesh.

Hymn of the Day

"Enter in the Realm of God"

Lavon Bayler, a writer of both hymns and worship resources, wrote this hymn for the *New Century Hymnal.* The hymn speaks of the intriguing dynamics of God's reign – "it has come, and yet will be. It is known, and yet unknown." It also reminds us of our part in making God's realm a reality in our world.

The tune is an arrangement of a Pilipino folk melody, incorporating the harmonies and rhythm common to Asian music. While perhaps unusual to the Western ear, the tune is not difficult – playing it through once will help singers learn it.

Children's Time

Blessed by Jesus

When crowds of people were gathering around Jesus, who do you think was allowed to talk personally with Jesus? *(Allow a moment for responses.)* It seems likely to us that Jesus should have been spending his time with important teachers and leaders.

This is exactly what Jesus' followers thought one day. At the end of that long day of teaching and traveling, the disciples were tired and they probably thought that Jesus was tired, too. Some people brought their children to see Jesus. The disciples scolded these people and told them to take their children away.

But when Jesus saw what was going on, he was upset with his disciples. Can you imagine why? *(Allow a moment for responses.)* Jesus told the disciples to let the children come to him. Jesus loved children and they were always welcome. Jesus knew that children also have faith in God. In fact, Jesus told the disciples that it is good for adults to have faith that is like the faith of a child.

Jesus touched the children and blessed them. Let's bless each other in Jesus' name. *(Lead a blessing of laying a hand on a neighbor's shoulder, saying, "God bless you.")*

October 5, 2003
17th Sunday after Pentecost (Proper 22)
RC/Pres: 27th Sunday in Ordinary Time

The Sermon

A Softer Heart

Hymns

Beginning of Worship: "Our God, Creation's Loving Source"
Sermon Hymn: "Though I May Speak"
Closing Hymn: "Bless Now, O God the Journey"

Scripture

Mark 10:2-16 (For additional sermon materials on this passage, see the 2003 May/June planning issue and July 2003 issue of *The Clergy Journal.*)

"Therefore, what God has joined together, let no one separate" (Mk 10:9).

This text is a teaching about marriage, divorce, and adultery. For those of us who are married or are preparing for marriage, or for those who are divorced and recovering from that pain, or for those who are in broken marriages and thinking about or actually engaged in adultery, these verses cut very close to the bone. However, if we hear Jesus' teaching as applying only to those who have experienced or are experiencing a committed relationship with a single partner – whether straight, gay, or lesbian – we are missing the deepest level of Christ's message. We imperil more than the institution of marriage when we look only at the surface of God's call, rather than plumbing its depths.

In the text from Genesis 2 that Jesus quotes, God creates Eve in response to Adam's need for companionship. The text tells us that Adam did not discover a partner, a companion, among all the cattle and the birds of the air; therefore, God separated the earth-being (the *adham*) into two parts and the two parts were companions and helpers for one another. This story tells us about community; it reminds us that we need other people, not just other living beings. The story also hints at something important about God – that God understands and participates in the need to know one's self in relation to another.

Returning to the gospel passage, we see a pattern that is familiar in the gospels. Jesus is asked a question; he answers; his disciples request more information; he offers further teaching; the disciples lapse into silence. In this instance, having already told the Pharisees that the allowance for divorce was given to them only because Moses and God recognized their (*our*) hard hearts, Jesus briskly disposes of all legal grounds for divorce by stating simply that to put aside one's partner is to commit adultery.

If we think about it for more than a moment, it is obvious that Jesus is addressing much more than the narrow, technical definition of adultery as sexual betrayal. Jesus is speaking about adultery as a way of being, an unholy desire to seek alienation from another, a way of shutting someone else formally out of our lives and our circles of commitment. We cannot read this teaching about marriage, divorce, and adultery as if it stands alone; it doesn't. It is consistent with every other word Jesus speaks about our relationship as people of God with each other.

"Therefore, what God has joined together, let no one separate."

We are joined in one flesh with all humanity because we came of one flesh – all of us. We all came from the single earth-being that God created from dust, spit, and breath. God did not create us as couples, each with a single partner, each couple separate from all others. God created every person who ever was and ever will be from one flesh. We don't need to read the story from Genesis literally; it is a story that tells us a truth about how God wants us to be in community. We are to recognize our abiding connection to every other person around us. We are not to look for legal loopholes so that we can "divorce" ourselves from the needs of others. We were not created to be continually dividing the world into "us" (the people to whom we owe allegiance and for whom we are responsible) and "them" (everyone else). We are created to be people of soft hearts. We are created to be unseparated.

God has joined us together.

It is frightening how much time we spend looking for ways to escape our interconnectedness as a human species. It is frightening how many of the ills which beset humanity and, therefore, the other species that share this planet, are a direct result of the hard hearts that try to justify detachment rather than integration.

Our hard hearts can always justify drawing the circle of inclusion smaller and smaller, so that we build connections only with those of our religion, or our denomination within that religion, or our sect within that denomination. Everyone else is damned. Or we unite only with those who share our nationality, or our political party within our national borders, or the part of our political party (right, left, center) that narrowly defines our values. We work to silence one another rather than to find common ground and a common voice.

Wars are fought not because individual people have behaved aggressively toward one another, but because "they" – an ethnic group, a religious group, a political group – have attacked "us." Our enemies become a faceless mob from whom we can legitimately divorce ourselves rather than human beings like ourselves who happen to hold different opinions or believe in a different form of government or use a different name for God. People go hungry or naked or unsheltered because they are not "our flesh." We label these others as "the lazy poor," or "someone else's concern," or "terrorists," or "Iraqis."

"Therefore, what God has joined together, let no one separate."

Jesus asks us to see life through a different lens. Jesus calls us to see all flesh as one flesh – to see all humanity as inextricably bound together by the love of God. Whether we are married or not, we are bound to others by a covenant as strong as any wedding vow. Moses, knowing our stony hearts, gave us laws to allow us to break our vows. But God, seeing God's deepest desire within our bone and blood, gave us a different law, a law of hope – you shall love your neighbor as yourself.

May it be so, starting in this place, this day. Amen and amen.

– Andrea La Sonde Anastos
Intentional Interim Minister
Greenfield, Massachusetts

October 12, 2003

18th Sunday after Pentecost (Proper 23)

RC/Pres: 28th Sunday in Ordinary Time

Lessons

RCL	Job 23:1-9, 16-17	Heb 4:12-16	Mk 10:17-31
Roman Catholic	Wis 7:7-11	Heb 4:12-13	Mk 10:17-30 or 10:17-27
Episcopal (BCP)	Amos 5:6-7, 10-15	Heb 3:1-6	Mk 10:17-27 (28-31)
Lutheran	Amos 5:6-7, 10-15	Heb 4:12-16	Mk 10:17-31

Introduction to the Lessons

Lesson 1

(1) ***Job 23:1-9, 16-17*** **(RCL)**

Job longs for God's presence, convinced that God will respond to ("give heed to") Job's desire for an explanation of his suffering.

(2) ***Wisdom 7:7-11*** **(RC)**

The writer speaks of wisdom as the most precious of possessions, with value beyond gold and silver.

(3) ***Amos 5:6-7, 10-15*** **(Epis/Luth)**

The prophet warns the people of the cost of their unrighteousness and pleads with them to turn from their sin and live with justice and mercy.

Lesson 2

(1) ***Hebrews 4:12-16*** **(RCL/Luth);** ***Hebrews 4:12-13*** **(RC)**

We stand, revealed in our grace and in our sin, before the word of God to render account. The longer reading continues that our faith in the Lord allows us to approach this account with boldness.

(2) ***Hebrews 3:1-6*** **(Epis)**

The writer compares the faithfulness of Moses (a servant of God) to Jesus (the Son of God), and reminds us that we are of the house of Jesus.

Gospel

***Mark 10:17-31* (RCL/Luth); *Mark 10:17-30* (RC);**
***Mark 10:17-27 (28-31)* (Epis)**

These verses include the story of the meeting between the rich man and Jesus, and Jesus' teaching to the disciples about the very human attachment to material possessions and wealth.

Theme

For most of us, in this day and age, it is more challenging to receive than it is to give.

Thought for the Day

The test of love is not feeling, but obedience.

– William Ullathorne

Call to Worship

Leader: Holy Wisdom, teach us to honor each moment of our lives
People: that we may renounce entitlement and grow in wisdom.
Leader: Holy Love, teach us to trust in your compassion
People: that we may renounce fear and grow in love.
Leader: Holy Creator, teach us to respond to your call
People: that we may renounce apathy and grow in service.

Pastoral Prayer

Gentle God, you invite us to discard our burdens so that our buoyant spirit can pass through the eye of the needle into your presence. You invite us to lay down the duties and rituals, the rules and regulations, and the expectations that tie us to old visions and responsibilities long over.

Gentle God, encourage us to grieve the old so that we can let it go. Then invite us with new words to take up your new hope, and journey down new paths where, with new eyes, we will discover you revealed in plain sight in the radiant company of your disciples. Amen.

Prayer of Confession

God of the lilies and the sparrows, we confess that we do not live a trusting life. We confess that we grasp and hoard the temporal things of this world until we are so burdened and weighed down with stuff that we can't move, much less follow you. We confess that we would rather earn our place in your realm than receive it as a gift because then we can claim the credit for it, and feel self-righteous.

God of the lilies and the sparrows, give us the courage to trust you rather than ourselves and the humility to accept your power in us rather than the puny power granted by worldly success. Grant us the grace to learn the lesson of the sparrow: that we can never fly until we let go of our material possessions. Grant us the grace to learn the lesson of the lilies: that we cannot dance while we are shackled to things. Amen.

Prayer of Dedication of Gifts and Self

Abundant God, you entrust all our gifts and all our possessions into our hands so that we may learn to reflect you in our generosity. Receive these offerings we bring today and bless us with eyes to see their smallness, so that we may be inspired to risk more and more until, in exuberant joy, we sell all we have and follow. Amen.

Sermon Summary

When we are willing to give up the self that needs to earn God's love, we are able to give up everything that keeps us from following God's call.

Hymn of the Day

"Pass Me Not, O Gentle Savior"

Fanny Crosby was one of the most prolific hymn writers of all time, producing over 8,000 hymns before her death at the age of 94. She wrote this one in 1868 in response to a cry she heard from a prisoner in a jail in New York City.

The rather joyful tune by William H. Doane (who frequently collaborated with Crosby) is in hopeful contrast to the lament of the text, and thus the hymn provides a good musical response to Psalm 22, a lament that gives way to praise.

Children's Time

Eye of the Needle

Preparation: Bring a large toy camel, a darning needle, and a spool of thread.

Once there was a rich man who asked Jesus what he needed to do so that he could live with God and Jesus forever. Jesus loved this man. Jesus told him to follow the commandments and sell his possessions and give the money to the poor.

The rich man was shocked! He was sad and went away. You see, he owned a lot of stuff and he loved his stuff! Jesus told his disciples that it is hard for rich people to live in God's way. The disciples didn't understand. So Jesus gave them an example, "It is easier for a camel to go through the eye of a needle than for someone who is rich to enter God's world."

When we love our money or our stuff more than we love God, it's hard to live in God's way. We become like this camel, trying to get through the eye of the needle. When we love God and share the gifts that God has given us, then we're like this thread: we fit into God's world easily. This sounds impossible, doesn't it? The good news is that God will help us as we try!

The Sermon

For Sale: One Self

Hymns

Beginning of Worship: "O Jesus, I Have Promised"
Sermon Hymn: "Will You Come and Follow Me?"
Closing Hymn: "O Christ, in Thee My Soul"

Scripture

Mark 10:17-31 (For additional sermon materials on this passage, see the 2003 May/June planning issue and the July 2003 issue of *The Clergy Journal.*)

Far too often, clergy approach this lesson as an indictment against wealth and far too many sermons make the unjustified assumption that simply because the rich man went away shocked and grieving, he didn't sell all that he had to follow Jesus. This allows both clergy and parishioners to skim along the surface of the passage without noticing any deep criticism of our own selves or our own choices. It allows us to shrug our mental shoulders and say, "Oh, well, not everyone can be a follower in the same way as Peter or Andrew. And Jesus still loved the rich man – it says so in the Bible. Besides, I am not really all that wealthy anyway, so these verses don't have much to do with me."

Perhaps it would be more fruitful for all of us if we stopped seeing this as a passage about wealth and saw it as a passage about enslavement. It is true that we can be enslaved to wealth and possessions, but it is equally true that we can be enslaved to many other things that prevent us from "passing through the eye of the needle." For the vast majority of the working classes at the beginning of the third millennium in the United States, there are two different motivations – two different aspects of our lives – that we allow to stand in the way of answering the call to follow. The first is societal pressures and the second is behavioral habits.

Under the first category, societal pressures, we can put such things as the cultural encouragement to be upwardly mobile – progressively increasing our net worth so that we can provide a steadily higher standard of living for our children or partner or spouse. We respond to societal pressure by accumulating "things," because our culture functions most profitably if it can persuade us that material goods have the power to make us safe and secure.

Under the second category, behavioral habits, we are confronted by such things as the habit of being overstressed, the habit of being unhappy, and the habit of believing that we live in scarcity rather than abundance. Our behavioral habits enslave us not only to the literal "stuff" that needs to be dusted, picked up, filed, sorted, and packed when we move. We are equally enslaved by the energy-sapping emotional "stuff" that fills our date books: the boards or committees we sit on, the teams our children play on, the classes we take or they take, and the business functions we "must" attend.

So, we turn our backs on God's invitation to be spontaneous ("Sell all you have, and follow"), and we walk away because we believe that we have no time to accept this gift. We walk away because every waking moment of our days is scheduled! We reject the offer to be free of our burdens and shackles; we walk away because we are uncertain about our own values and which of those values have priority. It seems easier to bow to the pressure to want it all than to sit down and sort through what we really need. We walk away because we have come to depend on our "stuff" – whether physical or emotional – to define us. Giving up the stuff seems to mean giving up our identities.

Barbara Brown Taylor says about this passage, "The [man in the story doesn't seem to comprehend that the] opposite of rich might not be poor, but free." Millard Fuller, CEO of Habitat for Humanity, and his wife are two people who have ordered their lives so that they can respond to God's invitation to freedom, spontaneity, and abundance. They are not poor. Fuller draws a decent, although not excessive, salary. They have prepared reasonably for retirement, but they have also chosen to live in a modest home where they can walk to work. They have made choices so that they will have spaces in their lives that are not filled with stuff. This creates time in their lives that is not devoted to caring for stuff – neither the physical stuff nor the images they might need to uphold. The Fullers know that they need some material things to live, but they want to own those things, not be owned by them. They also choose modesty and simplicity so that they can say no to the societal pressures and behavioral habits that would drain their time and energy. They are not poor, but they are well on their way to being free.

The Fullers see clearly what most of us have trouble noticing in this passage. Jesus isn't asking for something, he is offering something: liberation, freedom, and exuberant abundance. What makes receiving Jesus' gift a challenge is that to receive, we need to stand still and open our hands – which may mean dropping some of that stuff we are holding onto! We have been taught that it is more blessed to give than to receive, and while I am positive that everyone in this sanctuary today could be more generous, I would also note that giving increases our sense of self-worth because it makes us feel mature and self-sufficient. Receiving, on the other hand, increases our sense of dependence and puts us in a place where the only proper response is gratitude.

Jesus invites the rich man and invites us to lay down the burden of self-sufficiency, the burden of earning God's love. Yes, we respond to God by doing good things – just like the rich man – but they count for little if they enslave us rather than freeing us to live into God's image of spacious generosity, of heartfelt thanksgiving, of abundant joy. Jesus invites the rich man to sell all that he has. Everything, including his own self that is all tied up in knots trying to be worthy of God's attention, compassion, and mercy.

This morning, I invite you to hear again the call of God through Jesus. I invite you to sell everything that enslaves you – rules and rituals, wealth and possessions, worldly success, societal expectations, fear, power, habits of attachment, and the wounded self that believes it needs to buy a place in God's presence. I invite you to wrap yourself in the bright beauty of God's freely offered gift of a self defined not by your hard work, but by God's divine image in you, that image which clothes you to live in God's commonwealth here on earth, as you will in heaven. Amen and amen.

– Andrea La Sonde Anastos
Intentional Interim Minister
Greenfield, Massachusetts

October 19, 2003

19th Sunday after Pentecost (Proper 24)

RC/Pres: 29th Sunday in Ordinary Time

Lessons

RCL	Job 38:1-7 (34-41)	Heb 5:1-10	Mk 10:35-45
Roman Catholic	Isa 53:10-11	Heb 4:14-16	Mk 10:35-45 or 10:42-45
Episcopal (BCP)	Isa 53:4-12	Heb 4:12-16	Mk 10:35-45
Lutheran	Isa 53:4-12	Heb 5:1-10	Mk 10:35-45

Introduction to the Lessons

Lesson 1

(1) *Job 38:1-7 (34-41)* (RCL)

God speaks to Job out of the whirlwind, inviting Job to know God more deeply rather than merely seeking an explanation for his suffering.

(2) *Isaiah 53:10-11* (RC); *Isaiah 53:4-12* (Epis/Luth)

Both readings come from the Fourth Servant Song, reminding the people that the servant community willingly suffers even on behalf of the unjust and the unrighteous.

Lesson 2

(1) *Hebrews 5:1-10* (RCL/Luth)

Jesus became our high priest in the same manner as those who were high priests in the temple: receiving that appointment from God and carrying out its responsibilities with humility.

(2) *Hebrews 4:14-16* (RC); *Hebrews 4:12-16* (Epis)

We stand revealed, in our grace and in our sin, before the word of God to render account, yet our faith in the Lord allows us to approach this account with boldness.

Gospel

Mark 10:35-45 (RCL/RC/Epis/Luth)

James and John, still misunderstanding the cost of discipleship, seek to share in Jesus' glory. In response, Jesus speaks to all the disciples about servanthood.

Theme

When push comes to shove, we don't want the grace to endure; we really want the approval to remain just as we are.

Thought for the Day

Our chief want in life is someone to make us do what we can.

– Ralph Waldo Emerson

Call to Worship

Leader: When we rest in God, dwelling close to the Most High,
People: evil has no power over our souls.
Leader: When we choose shelter under God's wings,
People: we live in safety because the angels of the Holy One uphold us.
Leader: No trials or troubles can overcome our spirit
People: because God's love transforms all despair and fear.

– Based on Psalm 91

Pastoral Prayer

Ransoming God, our hearts overflow with gratitude, that you ransomed our mothers and fathers from slavery in Egypt. We rejoice that you redeemed them and brought them back from exile in alien lands. We sing our thanksgiving that you invited us to freedom from sin through the life, ministry, death, and resurrection of our brother, Jesus of Nazareth.

Ransoming God, fill our hearts not only with appreciation for all that was done for us in the past, but also with the grace to accept the liberation you offer this very day, so that we may live as a whole and holy people, as your living body in creation. Amen.

Prayer of Confession

Holy God, forgive us the pride that welcomes rights while rejecting responsibilities. Forgive us the vanity that wants success without any sacrifice. Forgive us for the sense of entitlement that accepts the life of Jesus, poured out for us, as nothing more than our due.

Holy God, break open hearts that are so consumed with self-interest that we are always grasping for more: more power, more possessions, more attention. Break open our hearts, and soften our spirits, that we may see the magnitude of all we have been given and live in deep and abiding gratitude. Amen.

Prayer of Dedication of Gifts and Self

As we have received, let us give, O God. We have received the gift of your very self, offered for us so that we might live in whole-hearted trust. Receive and bless these portions of our selves, offered to you so that all people may live in dignity. Amen.

Sermon Summary

Jesus ransomed (released) our lives from slavery to worldly agendas. The gospel is clear; true disciples accept that liberation so that we can continue to take up the covenant vocation of chosen, servant people.

Hymn of the Day

"Jesu, Jesu, Fill Us with Your Love"

Thomas Colvin of Scotland served as a missionary in Africa and wrote this hymn while serving in northern Ghana. He adapted a local folk tune to suit the text, naming the tune Chereponi in honor of a church in the community of Chereponi, Ghana. The hymn fits well with today's gospel about humble service.

The first word should be pronouned "zha-SOO," which is the standard pronunciation of Christ's name in most African languages. Drums, handclapping, and swaying enhance the singing.

Children's Time

Upside Down

(Preparation: Bring a crown, an apron, a fancy chair, and a plain cushion.)

Ask for a volunteer to play the role of an important person. Ask the group which seat they think the person should sit in, and if they should wear the crown or the apron. Dress and seat them accordingly.

When we imagine what an important person looks like, we might think of things like fancy cars and clothes. We might imagine that they have servants to look after them.

Jesus looked at things in a very different way. Some might say almost an upside-down way. Two of his disciples, brothers named James and John, went to him one day and said that in heaven, they wanted to be seated like important people, right on either side of Jesus. The other disciples were very upset about their request.

Jesus taught all the disciples that the important people aren't the great rulers or leaders who treat others in mean or uncaring ways. Instead, Jesus says that the truly great people in the world are the ones who serve others, just as Jesus did. How can you be a great person this week? *(Allow a moment for responses.)*

The Sermon

A Life in Ransom

Hymns

Beginning of Worship: "The Church of Christ in Every Age"
Sermon Hymn: "In Suffering Love"
Closing Hymn: "As a Fire Is Meant for Burning"

Scripture

Mark 10:35-45 (For additional sermon materials on this passage, see the 2003 May/June planning issue and the July 2003 issue of *The Clergy Journal*.)

Picture the gospel scene. Jesus is on his way to Jerusalem, aware that he is going to a confrontation that will likely end in his death. His disciples, James and John, press forward, coming close to him to speak. Did Jesus hope for some understanding? Some wise and steadying words of support in this hour before the trial began? Or did he know, even before they asked, that this was simply going to be one more example of people missing the whole point of what he had come to teach?

As a Christian disciple at the beginning of the third millennia after Jesus taught and died, I would have to say that I am, that most of us are, still missing the point of what he came to teach. Far too often I am aware – both in myself and in those with whom I minister – that we expect special consideration, special praise, and special recognition, simply because we belong to churches that have crosses on the steeples or above the communion tables. Far too often I am aware that my colleagues and I, as well as the lay leaders of the churches with whom we work, are playing a numbers-and-prestige game. How many attend worship on Sunday? (More is better.) How fancy is the facility? (Fancier is better.) How upscale is the congregation or the town? (More wealth is better.)

It is the rare pastor who moves by choice from a large, wealthy church to a small, poor, deteriorating one. It is the rare parishioner who by choice would take her or his substantial pledge and go to a poor, inner-city congregation if there were an upwardly mobile, suburban parish available. Yet, as Christian disciples, we are called to serve those in need and to build up the body of Christ. We are not called to be served by the programs and professionals at the most comfortably endowed local community of worship. As Christian disciples we are followers of the one who chose to live among the outcasts of his own society – indeed, among those who were not even considered "faithful people" – rather than among the elite of the religious establishment.

Jesus was quite clear about how the world's values were to be regarded by his followers. In response to the request from James and John, he tells all the disciples, "whoever wishes to be first among you must be slave of all. For the Son of Man came not to be served, but to serve, and to give his life as a ransom for many" (Mk 10: 44-45). Jesus came to be a ransom for many, not for the elite few whose clothes, possessions, and behavior meet the world's standards for success, but for the many. Jesus gave his life as ransom for us – to release us from slavery to clothes, possessions, power, success, and even to religious rules and regulations. By Jesus' willingness to accept death rather than compromise what he knew to be the desire and hope of God, he showed us how to be free of every prison, every shackle, and every self-proclaimed tyrant.

When we turn our backs on that priceless self-offering and cling instead to the material things and the expectations of this life to define us, Jesus' death was in vain. Yes, my brothers and sisters, we who call ourselves disciples need to face into that hard reality – when we choose, by our own volition, to remain slaves to all the idols of this life, we are betraying Christ all over again. We need to accept that we cannot point the finger of blame at anyone else. No one else chooses for us. We choose. We choose whether to live a ransomed life – released, liberated – or to be co-opted by values we know to be unworthy of a chosen, servant people.

This choice is possible for all of us. There are no excuses. We can all live more simply, in keeping with the pattern of life shown us by Jesus. Not one of us needs to live beyond our means, to accumulate debt so that we can accumulate things, and, therefore, be unable to be generous with those who are suffering. Every one of us can give up a single cup of coffee so that we can put that dollar or more into the Salvation Army kettle or the street person's cup. Every single one of us can give up two pieces of clothing from our closet, or a pair of shoes, or a coat, so that someone else can be warm. Every one of us can choose not to buy another book, another pint of ice cream, another television, another car, or another house so that those resources can go to Habitat for Humanity, Heifer Project, the United Way, C.A.R.E., or Physicians without Borders.

I preach these things not because I have attained the self-giving generosity of Mother Teresa, Albert Schweitzer, or Father Damien. I haven't. I preach this good news because the gospel is clear. I may claim to be confused when I want to do something that I know in my heart is buying into the comfortable values of the world, but I am only playing mind games because the gospel is not confusing at all; it is absolutely clear.

Ralph Waldo Emerson once said, "Our chief want [lack] in life is someone to make us do what we can." But Christians are not, in fact, lacking that "someone." Jesus ransomed us and Jesus released us, so that we can be that someone. God does not make us do anything; God invites us to live a liberated life. Jesus does not make us do anything; Jesus invites us to live a liberated life. Only we can make ourselves do what we know we can. Only I can make myself do those generous, loving, compassionate things that lead to God's commonwealth of shalom. Only you can make yourself reveal God's image in every word and deed of your life. Only I, only you, only we, can choose individually to accept the gift of a ransomed life from the one who ransomed it – and thereby give Jesus' act of ransom ultimate meaning.

I pray that we may each have the courage to live the baptism to which we have been baptized, and drink the cup which Christ first drank, so that God's realm may blossom among us as the divine fulfillment of his love. Amen.

– Andrea La Sonde Anastos
Intentional Interim Minister
Greenfield, Massachusetts

October 26, 2003

20th Sunday after Pentecost (Proper 25)

RC/Pres: 30th Sunday in Ordinary Time

Lessons

RCL	Job 42:1-6, 10-17	Heb 7:23-28	Mk 10:46-52
Roman Catholic	Jer 31:7-9	Heb 5:1-6	Mk 10:46-52
Episcopal (BCP)	Isa 59:(1-4) 9-19	Heb 5:12–6:1, 9-12	Mk 10:46-52
Lutheran	Jer 31:7-9	Heb 7:23-28	Mk 10:46-52

Introduction to the Lessons

Lesson 1

(1) *Job 42:1-6, 10-17* (RCL)

At the end of a legendary book about faithful endurance amid repeated calamities, Job's material fortunes double and the Lord blesses him with a large family and a long life.

(2) *Jeremiah 31:7-9* (RC/Luth)

Among the preeminent of prophetic voices at the beginning of the 6th-century (BCE) exile, Jeremiah foretells a great return of the remnant of Israel from all corners of the earth.

(3) *Isaiah 59:(1-4) 9-19*

In a book that looks forward to the establishment of God's justice, especially through the restoration of Jerusalem, this passage speaks of human sin as something that separates us from God and from God's justice, thereby causing human beings' blindness.

Lesson 2

(1) *Hebrews 7:23-28* (RCL/Luth)

In comparison to the Levitical priesthood of the Jewish temple, Christ, our high priest, has no need to offer sacrifices for the sins of humanity; they have already been satisfied through his death.

(2) *Hebrews 5:1-6* (RC)
One of the primary points of this book is to show Jesus as the culmination of the priestly system that conducted sacrifices in the Jewish temple. The author makes clear in this passage that Jesus' authority in this role comes not from himself, but from God.

(3) *Hebrews 5:12–6:1, 9-12* (Epis)
While encouraging people to grow in faith, the writer of Hebrews commends readers to persevere in doing works that favor God and that serve saints in need.

Gospel

***Mark 10:46-52* (RCL/RC/Epis/Luth)**

In calling upon Jesus as "Son of David," the blind beggar Bartimaeus demonstrated that he did indeed see who Jesus was. Meanwhile Jesus' own disciples struggled to have this same insight.

Theme

Believers see with the eyes of faith.

Thought for the Day

There is no one so blind as the one who will not see.

Call to Worship

Leader: On that day the deaf shall hear the words of a scroll,
People: And out of their gloom and darkness the eyes of the blind shall see.

Pastoral Prayer

O God, you bring light to those who are blind and sound to those who are deaf. Illumine us through the words of your holy scriptures, that we might see you as you are and follow you more completely. Through your sacrifice on the cross at Calvary, you have destroyed the power of sin forever and have given eternal life for those who believe in you. Help us to avoid the allure of other would-be saviors, that we might trust in your power alone in our lives. May those who see you anew – and who serve you with the zeal of the newly converted – help to transform those of us who have lost the freshness of our faith. Give us faith to trust in your power even in confusing and bewildering times. May we learn to see signs of your presence everywhere. In Jesus' name, we pray. Amen.

Prayer of Confession

O God, your light shines throughout the world, illuminating the dark corners of our lives. Yet we often seek the darkness in order to plan selfish schemes and to deny your will for a just society. We confess that we have chosen to do things that thwart your will for us. Give us faith to see the ways in which we have resisted your love for all people. Help us realize that nothing we do will be kept from your sight. Convert us to your will for us so that all of our actions may give witness to your righteous rule. Lead us to serve in places where many of the world's authorities refuse to look, but where there is much misery and pain. May our actions be ways that others might glimpse your eternal glory. We ask this, in Jesus' name. Amen.

Prayer of Dedication of Gifts and Self

Light of the world, you have opened our eyes to your life in our midst. We thank you for the abundance of your creation, and for the gifts each of us are privileged to enjoy. Receive these offerings that we have brought today, that they may serve to further the spread of your good news to those who have not yet received it. Inspire us to use the gifts that you have given us, that your name may be glorified by all that we do. In the name of Christ, we pray. Amen.

Sermon Summary

Even those who follow Jesus do not always fully understand who he really is. It often takes someone from the sidelines to point us in the right direction.

Hymn of the Day

"All Who Hunger"

This communion text by Canadian hymn writer Sylvia G. Dunstan takes as its refrain the familiar line from Psalm 34, "taste and see that God is good." The wonderful invitation to communion celebrates that all are welcome at Christ's table, the table of grace.

The tune "Holy Manna" by William Moore was written for shape-note singing, a style popular in the southern United States in the 19th century. Shape-note takes its name from the different shapes afforded to notes making it easier for those who did not read music to learn new tunes.

Children's Time

Determination

Only two months until Christmas! Have you already started asking your parents for things? Only kidding. But there are times when all of us see something that we want and try to get it. It's all we talk about, all we dream about. Sometimes it's a visit from a favorite aunt or a trip to see a friend who has moved. There are times when we are determined to have something.

Once there was a man who was utterly determined to talk to Jesus. This man was blind and he was certain that Jesus could heal him. One day Jesus and a large crowd of people were walking through his town. This man kept calling out – yelling louder and louder – asking Jesus to have mercy on him. The people in the crowd shushed him. But still, he called out for Jesus.

Jesus stopped. He asked the man what he could do for him. The blind man told Jesus that he wanted to see again. Jesus said, "Go; your faith has made you well." That's all it took. Because of his determination and his faith, the man found a way to talk to Jesus. When we are determined to talk to Jesus, what can we do?

The Sermon

Believing Is Seeing

Hymns

Beginning of Worship: "Open My Eyes That I May See"
Sermon Hymn: "Amazing Grace"
Closing Hymn: "Guide Me, O Thou Great Jehovah"

October 26, 2003
20th Sunday after Pentecost (Proper 25)
RC/Pres: 30th Sunday in Ordinary Time

Scripture

Mark 10:46-52 (For additional sermon materials on this passage, see the 2003 May/June planning issue and the July 2003 issue of *The Clergy Journal.*)

The central section of Mark's gospel has been the source of our gospel readings during these last several weeks. It is here where the author traces Jesus' journey with his disciples from Caesarea Philippi in Galilee down to Jericho, at the outskirts of Jerusalem. While traveling on this route, Jesus prepared his disciples for what was to happen after their arrival in Jerusalem. As a result we gain deeper insight into who Jesus is and what it means to follow him.

Mark has placed a frame around the whole central section of the book, since it opens with the healing of a blind man, and it closes with the healing of another blind man, as told in our gospel reading today. We could also say that along the entire trip from Galilee to Jerusalem, Jesus opened the eyes of his disciples.

According to Mark, what does Jesus want the disciples to see? Three times in these central chapters Jesus repeats that he is going to Jerusalem to suffer, to die, and to be raised again. In this section there is great emphasis on Jesus' suffering. He will be rejected, delivered up into the hands of the authorities, tortured, and killed. Jesus did not spare his disciples a thing – he told them plainly about what they were going to see. And so it would seem that by the time the disciples got to Jerusalem with Jesus, they would have been prepared for what would happen. Yet, they appeared to remain blind to it all.

At first Peter called Jesus the Messiah. We found out that the disciples' notion of who the Messiah would be was in conflict with Jesus' understanding of his role. The Messiah in Jewish thought was the one who would conquer all the enemies of God by force. But Jesus rejected this understanding of Messiah flat out.

No doubt the disciples saw Jesus as a kind of miracle worker – someone who could redeem God's people through the use of remarkable healing powers. Yet this wasn't a full description of everything that Jesus came to do either.

Then, as we may remember from last week's reading, James and John argued about who would be first in the kingdom of God. They were looking forward to seeing Jesus take his seat of power. But Jesus reprimanded them, saying that his kingdom was a lot different from the one that they had in mind.

So we know that many times the disciples saw what Jesus was doing, but they failed to understand him. They didn't really see him. The gospel reading for today illustrates this clearly. The crowds tried to keep the blind beggar Bartimaeus away from Jesus. Yet this unlikely character in the story called Jesus, "Son of David." No one else had yet used this name for Jesus in the Gospel of Mark.

When asked what he wanted Jesus to do for him, Bartimaeus responded, "My teacher, let me see again" (Mk 10:51). This stands in sharp contrast to the previous passage in which James and John argued about which of them would be first in Jesus' kingdom. With Bartimaeus we find an outsider who has a greater insight into who Jesus is than do any of his closest followers.

In this episode, Jesus praised the blind man's faith. Bartimaeus' faith demonstrated that he was open to God's saving power. Yet in contrast, the disciples' eyes remain clouded, because they came to Jesus filled with their own importance and their desire to sit in high places with him.

Like the plot of a quick-paced drama, all of this is going to change soon. Soon after Jesus enters Jerusalem, the authorities are after him, Peter denies him, and Jesus suffers death on the cross. Only through this defeat and death will the true peace that the Messiah has come to bring begin to flower.

When we read the Gospel of Mark closely, we may discover that it communicates something very disturbing. It is possible for the people who are closest to Jesus, and claim to know him best of all, to be farthest from the truth.

We often confuse what it means to be a disciple with what it means to be a good church member. Being a loyal, supportive member of the church should not be an end in itself. The goal of following Jesus is to deny self, to serve others, and to suffer willingly for others. Sometimes such a radical form of following Jesus may not seem to fit the picture of what is appropriate behavior for a good church member. A loyal disciple may need at times to step away from family, community, and even the fellowship of the church in order to be able to see things as they really are.

October 26, 2003
20th Sunday after Pentecost (Proper 25)
RC/Pres: 30th Sunday in Ordinary Time

In her book, *Pilgrim at Tinker Creek*, Annie Dillard offers some classic observations on what it means to see. She describes the confusion, wonder, and delight experienced by patients blind from birth, who are granted sight by surgery. For some people the new way of seeing is not a gift, but a frightening burden. Dillard offers in the book a picture of one newly sighted young woman who

> carefully shuts her eyes whenever she comes to a staircase, and . . . is never happier or more at ease when, by closing her eyelids, she relapses into her former state of total blindness. (Annie Dillard, *Pilgrim at Tinker Creek* [New York: Harper's Magazine Press], p. 28.)

Gaining new vision, new knowledge, or a new capacity for understanding can be a frightening thing for us, just as it was with the disciples. Our old ways of seeing and imagining things are replaced. Having stumbled onto something new and unsettling, we may yearn for a simpler and less challenging time.

Critics of the Christian faith have said that our religion is a way for us to deny the realities of life – to deny the brutalities of suffering and even of death. But whoever makes those claims cannot be familiar with the Gospel of Mark. Mark deals extensively with Jesus' suffering and death. That is reality.

The Bartimaeus story is an example of meeting the realities of life head-on. There is no reward without toil and pain, and there is no success without suffering which precedes it. When we listen to Jesus in the Gospel of Mark, we hear quite plainly that there is also no life without death, and that there is no Easter without a crucifixion.

Being a Christian means following Jesus on the way – drinking the cup of suffering and being concerned with the salvation of others – before we give a thought to our own comfort or rewards. When we understand that, then we can say that we have seen Jesus with the eyes of faith.

– Dennis Bushkofsky
Interim Pastor
Metropolitan Chicago Synod of the
Evangelical Lutheran Church in America

October 31, 2003

Reformation

Lessons

Lutheran	Jer 31:31-34	Rom 3:19-28	Jn 8:31-36

Introduction to the Lessons

Lesson 1

Jeremiah 31:31-34

Though the people of Israel have often forgotten God, the prophet Jeremiah speaks about a day in which the law to know the Lord will not be necessary, since all of God's people will know the Lord in their hearts.

Lesson 2

Romans 3:19-28

A central point in the book of Romans, and indeed for the apostle Paul's theology in general, is that while still sinners, God brought redemption to all people through Christ Jesus. Salvation is obtained through faith, not through keeping the law perfectly. This news is meant to unite Jews and Gentiles alike.

Gospel

John 8:31-36

In speaking both to the Jewish leaders and to the Jewish people in general, Jesus speaks about knowing the truth that will bring freedom and salvation. Such truth comes through the word of God, particularly as Jesus himself announces it.

Theme

God's salvation comes to us as a free gift.

Thought for the Day

God finds lost sinners, saves, and redeems them.

Call to Worship

Leader: God is our refuge and strength,
People: A very present help in trouble.
Leader: Therefore we will not fear, though the earth should change, though the mountains shake in the heart of the sea;
People: Though its waters roar and foam, though the mountains tremble with its tumult.
Leader: The Lord of hosts is with us;
People: The God of Jacob is our refuge.

Pastoral Prayer

O God, you are indeed our refuge and sanctuary. Throughout all of time you have guided and sustained your people, and have been a blessing to those without a strong footing amid life's uncertainties. We give you thanks for your word, and for those who boldly witness to its power and to its radical truth. We need your anchoring each day. Teach us to be your faithful disciples.

Write on our minds and hearts such love for you that we will be glad to practice the disciplines of our faith: prayer, continued study of your word, and giving of ourselves to serve those unjustly oppressed. Lift up all whose courage falters, and bring us to our eternal home with you where we shall live safely and securely. In Jesus' name, we pray. Amen.

Prayer of Confession

O God, we confess that we have often gone seeking after worldly riches, rather than depending solely on your gracious gifts to us. We have trusted more in our own merit, rather than in your mercy. How frequently we have sought to advance our own selves, rather than serving you and those in need. Challenge us to hear anew your gospel of grace this day. Gather us together with all sinful humanity before your righteous throne where we may receive your pardon and redemption. Lead us always to drink from the freely flowing streams of your word and sacraments, and to invite others to join us without reserve. In the name of Christ, we pray. Amen.

Prayer of Dedication of Gifts and Self

Everything we are and everything we have comes from you, most gracious Creator. You formed us in your image and have deemed us worthy of your grace. Enable us to praise you not only with our lips, but also with our deeds of love and mercy to strengthen those in need. We dedicate these gifts and our whole lives to proclaim your gracious saving love for the whole world. These things we ask, through Christ our Lord. Amen.

Sermon Summary

The paramount Christian teaching rediscovered during the Reformation of the 16th century is that God finds lost sinners, saves, and redeems them. While this news is always true, we run the risk of forgetting it if we do not also practice the discipline of continuing in God's word.

Hymn of the Day

"Praised Be the Rock"

On this "most Lutheran of days" it seems appropriate to choose a hymn from within that tradition, and so we turn to Howard Olson, a Lutheran theologian in Tanzania whose translations and arrangements of serveral East African hymns have found their way to the West.

This hymn, set to a traditional tune, arranged by A. Louise Anderson Olson, celebrates salvation through grace offered to all humanity in Jesus Christ. The tune is easy to learn, and the words echo the traditional texts for this day, including Psalm 46, the inspiration for Luther's classic "A Mighty Fortress Is Our God."

Children's Time

No Charge

If you were at the check-out line at the store and the clerk said, "No charge," what would that mean? *(Allow a moment for responses.)*

Today is Reformation Day. About 500 years ago, there was a teacher named Martin Luther. He taught people to trust in God's word – to trust God's promise that God will always love us and forgive us because of Jesus. Luther reminded people that God's love and forgiveness are free gifts. No charge.

Some other church leaders in Luther's day were teaching that people should pay money for God's forgiveness and love. Luther spoke up. He told how God's word in the Bible says that God gives us love and forgiveness at no charge because of Jesus. Many people agreed with Luther and together they made some changes in what the church was doing. To change something is to reform it; that is where the name Reformation Day comes from.

If anyone ever tells you that you must look a certain way or act a certain way or go to a certain church in order for God to love you, trust in God's word. Tell everyone that God gives us love and forgiveness because of Jesus. No charge.

The Sermon

How Are You Saved?

Hymns

Beginning of Worship: "To God Be the Glory"
Sermon Hymn: "Standing on the Promises"
Closing Hymn: "A Mighty Fortress"

Scripture

Romans 3:19-28 (For sermon materials on John 8:31-36, see the 2003 May/June planning issue of *The Clergy Journal* and on Jeremiah 31:31-34, see the August 2003 issue of *The Clergy Journal.*)

With a few swings of the hammer, the Protestant Reformation began 486 years ago. Certainly Martin Luther did not intend for the document he posted on October 31, 1517 to cause a major schism in the church of his day. More likely his intent in posting the *95 Theses* on the door of Wittenberg Church was to begin an academic debate over some abuses that he saw in the church. The *95 Theses,* though, struck a chord with many other people, inside and outside of his academic community of Wittenberg.

When you read the *95 Theses*, you discover that Luther had one major gripe against the church of his day and against the pope. He was mad that a practice known as the selling of indulgences had become a common means of raising money, mainly to build St. Peter's Basilica in Rome. Now, churches have had a variety of fundraising methods over the years, but I think we would have to agree that the practice of giving indulgences was one of the more flagrant abuses of fear in encouraging people to contribute.

In Luther's time, people were quite concerned about their eternal salvation. They were fearful of what would happen to them if they died and did not go to heaven. Unfortunately, there were people who were unscrupulous operators during this time, people who capitalized upon the fears that many people had regarding their own salvation or the salvation of others who were close to them. So in came the practice of indulgences.

One master of this practice was a man by the name of John Tetzel. He was one of the pope's best traders in indulgences for building St. Peter's in Rome. He got people to contribute by selling off little certificates that amounted to what Monopoly game players would call a "get-out-of-jail-free card." The more indulgences you bought, the more certain you could be of your soul not having to be tormented by going to hell or purgatory. (This at least was the thought of the day.)

Well, the match of a fear-based piety with an aggressive army of fundraisers – such as the pope had in northern Germany during the 16th century – ensured that indulgences would be a big business. And Luther, who had struggled considerably over the matter of his own salvation, was annoyed to the point of anger over this practice. Since Luther saw the main beneficiary to be the pope in Rome, he vehemently addressed his complaint to the pope and to anyone who came to the pope's assistance. This is basically what the document known as the *95 Theses* was all about. It is fundamentally the reason why there is Reformation Sunday at the end of October each year.

Luther had been troubled over the matter of just how he could be counted among God's righteous people. Luther spent years trying to do everything that he possibly could do to be assured of God's grace and favor. But the problem was that he never reached the point where he felt satisfied that he had done enough. He had not reached that point where he felt at peace with God. Then, he stumbled across words like those in Paul's letter to the Romans which said, "since all have sinned and fall short of the glory of God; they are now justified by his grace as a gift, through the redemption that is in Christ Jesus" (Rom 3:23-24).

The proverbial light bulb switched on when Luther discovered in God's word that salvation cannot be purchased or earned. No, it is a gift from God – given to those who believe or have faith in Jesus Christ the Son of God. Certainly in the gospel assigned for today, Luther and the other reformers read that they were not to be in bondage to any system or practice apart from Christ himself. "If you continue in my word, you are truly my disciples" and, "if the Son makes you free, you will be free indeed" (Jn 8:31, 36).

It is easy to see how the practice of indulgences could have enslaved so many people. It exploited people's faith and fear of death for the welfare and commercial gain of a privileged few within the church. The liberating power of the grace of God is not something to which a price tag can be attached. One can only hear that word and believe in it. To put a price tag on God's grace cheapens it. Christ's death on the cross in payment for the sins of the world is a priceless treasure.

So where does that leave us today? The church of today is in a different place than it was during Luther's time. While some congregations may practice forms of fundraising that seem questionable, it's hard to imagine that there is anything like the sale of indulgences that existed in the 16th century.

We have the scriptures available to us. We can read quite plainly that God's love is a free gift – one without strings attached. We have only to believe in it in order to be saved for eternity. There are few Christians of any denomination who would dispute that claim today. So we may think that the agenda of the Reformation has run its course, that there is nothing that we need to do now in order to reform the church.

However, the church, like any human institution, is always in need of reforming and renewing itself. We need to examine all of those corners of our lives that bear little resemblance to Christ and his teaching for us. One of the places where we might begin is in an area that today's gospel mentions. "If you continue in my word," Jesus says, "you are truly my disciples" (Jn 8:31). In this passage, Jesus tells us that we cannot receive the freedom that he offers us without also continuing in his word – without also hearing what he has to say to us.

Do we live by the words of scripture, or do we give greater value to other authorities in our lives? What books do we read? What television shows do we watch? We may say that we are a people formed by the good news of God in Jesus Christ, and yet many times our lives are more filled by bad news or by a message that simply is not Christ's message at all.

How many times do we go through a complete day without hearing a word of encouragement or a word of hope that comes from a life anchored in the scriptures or in prayer? Without continuing in God's word in some fashion during each day of our lives, how can we possibly know whether or not we are one of Christ's disciples? If we are always listening to other advisers, in the form of news commentators, self-help books, or a whole host of authorities on this or that, how do we know what squares with our faith? In short, we don't know. And so it's up to us, as disciples, to continue the discipline of being in God's word each day, and also to be a part of the Christian assembly of believers each week.

These are the things we have to help us understand the freedom that only Christ can give. It is ironic that many of us are not any better off than people were at the outset of the Reformation. We may not have the practice of indulgences to separate us from the knowledge of God's love and forgiveness freely offered, yet we don't avail ourselves of that message often. How can we continue to stay in the word, so that our identity as Christ's disciples is assured?

– Dennis Bushkofsky
Interim Pastor
Metropolitan Chicago Synod of the
Evangelical Lutheran Church in America

November 1, 2003

All Saints' Day

Lessons

RCL	Wis 3:1-9 or Isa 25:6-9	Rev 21:1-6a	Jn 11:32-44
Roman Catholic	Rev 7:2-4, 9-14	1 Jn 3:1-3	Mt 5:1-12
Episcopal (BCP)	Sir 44:1-10, 13-14	Rev 7:2-4, 9-17	Mt 5:1-12
Lutheran	Isa 25:6-9 or Wis 3:1-9	Rev 21:1-6a	Jn 11:32-44

Introduction to the Lessons

Lesson 1

(1) *Wisdom 3:1-9* (RCL)

In a book written to encourage *diaspora* Jews living outside of Israel, this passage speaks about the lasting peace for all righteous people. Though they may appear to have faced punishment, they will receive eternal life.

(2) *Revelation 7:2-4, 9-14* (RC)

In the midst of an entire book, where the chief message is that Christian believers will be spared in the face of great persecution, this chapter speaks of the great multitude that will be victorious.

(3) *Sirach 44:1-10, 13-14* (Epis)

This passage recalls and praises Israel's ancestors in the faith, beginning with the covenant that God made with the patriarchs. All of these great ancestors in the faith will be remembered and their offspring will live on.

(4) *Isaiah 25:6-9* (Luth)

The significance of a messianic banquet on a mountaintop is closely linked to the meeting of the elders on the top of Mt. Sinai in Exodus 24. The coming banquet will be celebrated on Mt. Zion. In addition to being a great feast, God's people will be vindicated and death will be destroyed.

Lesson 2

(1) *Revelation 21:1-6a* (RCL/Luth)

New Jerusalem will entail a complete and utter transformation of all people and creatures. In New Jerusalem, death will be destroyed and God will live forever with humankind. The vision of Jerusalem being adorned as a bride contrasts with the image of Rome (and its leaders) being adorned as a harlot.

(2) *1 John 3:1-3* (RC)

Christians are God's children and have become holy in the same way that Christ is holy.

(3) *Revelation 7:2-4, 9-17* (Epis)
(See Lesson 1, #2)

Gospel

(1) *John 11:32-44* (RCL/Luth)

The raising of Lazarus is the paramount sign about Christ's impending death and resurrection. In this chapter, resurrection is not only a symbol of future reward and salvation, but also a present reality for those who believe.

(2) *Matthew 5:1-12* (RC/Epis)

In the pronouncement of these nine beatitudes, Jesus speaks about the desirable characteristics of the faithful community. Not only are people who do the things mentioned here blessed in their current lives, but they are to be blessed in the world to come.

Theme

The joy of the resurrection gives hope to all who face death.

Thought for the Day

God works in our lives, putting to death those things that rob us of life and raising to life those things that help us live more fully.

Call to Worship

Leader: There was a great multitude that no one could count, from every nation, from all tribes and peoples and languages, standing before the throne and before the Lamb, robed in white, with palm branches in their hands. They cried out in a loud voice, saying:

People: Salvation belongs to our God who is seated on the throne, and to the Lamb!

– Based on Revelation 7:9-10

Pastoral Prayer

God of eternity, we give thanks for all your faithful people who have lived in your truth. For apostles and saints of every age who have born witness to you, we give thanks. For all who have faithfully served you, witnessed bravely, and died in faith, we give thanks. For those who are still remembered for their faithful and dedicated witness to you, we give thanks. For those who are no longer remembered, but who earnestly sought you in their time and who held their faith through trial and temptation, we give thanks.

For those who have been dear to us, and who by their lives of faith and hope have born witness to the same spirit that was in Christ Jesus, we give thanks. May we, like them, be eager to follow in the way of Christ. Bring us at last to share with all your faithful people in the joys that are eternal; through Jesus Christ the pioneer of our faith, who lives and reigns with you forever and ever. Amen.

Prayer of Confession

Most gracious and eternal God, we confess that we have not always been true to the faith you have given us. In the face of difficult challenges to your will and purposes for us, we have often been silent, shunning opportunities to stand up against the sins of oppression, violence, and murder. Unlike the many saints and martyrs who have witnessed boldly to you, without fear for their own lives, we have been timid in our practice of the faith. Give us courage to confess you not only when events are in our favor, but also when evil hunts us down and stares us in the face. In the name of Christ, we pray. Amen.

Prayer of Dedication of Gifts and Self

O God, we return to you what you have first given us: our talents, our material blessings, and our whole beings. May we, as your blessed saints of dear memory, strive to live faithfully in our own day, and be willing to use our resources to proclaim your gospel to all who have not yet heard the saving power of your love. In Jesus' name, we pray. Amen.

Sermon Summary

As Jesus testified to the power of his defeat over death through the raising of Lazarus, God is also at work in our own lives, putting to death the powers that rob us of life, and helping us to live more fully.

Hymn of the Day

"O Lord, You Gave Your Servant John"

The Irish tune "St. Patrick's Breastplate" takes its name from its use as the tune for the ancient hymn attributed to St. Patrick, which celebrates the presence of God in one's life in many ways.

Here, the tune has been given new life with a fresh text by Joy F. Patterson. Beginning with a paraphrase of Revelation's stirring vision of the New Jerusalem (today's epistle reading), the hymn moves through a description of life in modern cities, so starkly contrasted with the biblical vision. The third stanza implores God, working through us, to bring in that great vision.

Children's Time

Saints Alive

Jesus had three very good friends: Mary, Martha, and Lazarus. One day, Lazarus fell ill while Jesus was far away and his sisters sent a message to him. Before Jesus could get there, Lazarus died. You can imagine how Mary and Martha felt! They wept and wept. When Jesus finally arrived, he cried too. People usually cry when people who they love die.

Jesus told Martha and Mary that God had sent him for a special reason. He told them that he is the "resurrection and the life" and that people who believe in him will live with God and Jesus forever, even after their bodies die.

Today is a good day to tell the story of Mary and Martha and Lazarus, since today is All Saints' Day. Today in church we remember those who have died and are now living with God forever.

It's always very sad when someone we love dies. We miss them so much! When we are feeling so sad that we can hardly stand it, it's good to remember Jesus' promise. Because of Jesus, we will live with God forever.

The Sermon

Jesus Destroys Death

Hymns

Beginning of Worship: "For All the Saints"
Sermon Hymn: "Sing with All the Saints in Glory"
Closing Hymn: "Rejoice in God's Saints"

Scripture

John 11:32-44 (For additional sermon materials on this passage, see the 2003 May/June planning issue and the August 2003 issue of *The Clergy Journal.*)

A number of years ago I had the opportunity to attend an open meeting of Alcoholics Anonymous in order to come to a better appreciation of people who live with alcoholism and how they might best be supported in their recovery process.

The meeting that I attended was on a Friday night in March. It seemed rather unusual going to a church basement on a Friday night, but I soon learned how vital that particular A.A. meeting was for people who were struggling to stay sober amid the great societal pressure to drink at the end of a long workweek.

At the meeting people stood up one by one to tell stories about how their lives had been nearly ruined when they were under the control of alcohol. One woman talked about how her family and friends had almost given her up as dead. She rarely left the house, and when people would call, she claimed that she had the flu, or was coming down with some other kind of illness. It didn't take long for people to discover that her sickness wasn't ever what she claimed it was. Her sickness was the bottle.

In the atmosphere of the night, which almost resembled a spiritual revival meeting, this woman, along with several others, gave testimonies of how helpless they were before they got support from A.A. They talked about how important it was to have someone they could call up in the middle of the night when they felt a need to drink. A.A. had given these people another chance in life. Recovering alcoholics sometimes use words like *miracle* and *healing* to describe the difference between their drinking days and their newfound state of sobriety. It is as if their old selves had died, giving life to a new person.

Our readings today speak about those possibilities as well. The reading from Isaiah 25 imagines a great celebration on a mountain where God will feast with humankind and when death will be destroyed. Revelation 21 speaks of a similar hope, a time and place where "death will be no more." Of course the story of Lazarus from our gospel for the day also tells of new life coming from death. In the verses just before today's story, Jesus received news that "the one you love is sick" (Jn 11:3). Jesus responded by staying where he was for two more days. By the time Jesus got to Lazarus, he had been dead for four days.

In Jewish belief of that time, the spirit hovered around a dead body for three days. So when we read that Lazarus had been dead for four days, we get the idea that he was *really dead* when Jesus arrives. Finally, when Jesus got to Bethany, Martha said, "Lord, if you had been here my brother would never have died, and even now I am sure that God will give you whatever you ask" (vv. 21-22).

Jesus used this experience to reveal himself as the gift of life and to give readers of the gospel a different perspective on life. Martha's firm belief in Jesus redirects our attention not to some kind of great miracle, but to the very giver of life himself. Jesus himself is the resurrection and the life. Life in the Lord Jesus is not a matter of living in the past, or merely hoping for some kind of future in the great by and by. Life in Jesus is living now.

Like Lazarus' sister Martha, we live in a world that is filled with death. We understand how Martha must have felt at the death of her brother. Death is painful. But in Christ, our gaze is redirected. We are given faith to trust in the one who goes with us not only to the grave but through it.

Often we may recall these and other stories about life after death in order to speak about the hope for someone within our midst who has just died. But our scriptures also breath hope into the many other crises and calamities in our lives that have driven us to despair and hopelessness. Economic downturns and employment difficulties don't usually last forever. New friends and acquaintances can be made. There are reasons for hope, even in the face of the most discouraging of times. Of course we can't have the old days back. God didn't promise to turn back the hands of time – just to restore life. We aren't promised our old friends, our old job, our old neighborhood (nor the old-time religion for that matter). But God will be able to do something with that which remains. We haven't lost our futures. Something will one day grow in the place where now all we may be able to see is emptiness and death.

We gather today as a community of faith – indeed as God's community of saints – that believes in life through death. We cling to Christ's life as we feed on God's word. We cling to that life as we receive the bread and wine of heaven in our outstretched hands and thirsting mouths. In all of these ways, we receive the new life offered to us by our Lord. In the midst of the frailty, death, and the lifeless moments of our lives, Christ comes to us offering us new life: something beyond the grave. And like a once-barren field, our lives become green again.

God does not abandon us in death, but calls out our names and breathes into us a resurrecting Spirit: "I am the resurrection and the life; all who believe in me, even though they die, will live, and everyone who lives and believes in me will never die. Do you believe this?" (vv. 25-26). And we respond with Martha and with all the faithful who have ever lived, "Yes, Lord, I have come to believe that you are the Christ, the Son of God, the one who is coming into the world" (vs. 27).

– Dennis Bushkofsky
Interim Pastor
Metropolitan Chicago Synod of the
Evangelical Lutheran Church in America

November 2, 2003

21st Sunday after Pentecost (Proper 26)

RC/Pres: 31st Sunday in Ordinary Time

Lessons

RCL	Ruth 1:1-8	Heb 9:11-14	Mk 12:28-34
Roman Catholic	Deut 6:2-6	Heb 7:23-28	Mk 12:28-34
Episcopal (BCP)	Deut 6:1-9	Heb 7:23-28	Mk 12:28-34
Lutheran	Deut 6:1-9	Heb 9:11-14	Mk 12:28-34

Introduction to the Lessons

Lesson 1

(1) ***Ruth 1:1-8*** **(RCL)**

By going with Naomi to live in Bethlehem, Ruth went beyond what was required of her in order to be with her Israelite mother-in-law, and placed herself in the situation of living in a strange land.

(2) ***Deuteronomy 6:2-6*** **(RC);** ***Deuteronomy 6:1-9*** **(Epis/Luth)**

As the people of Israel enter the promised land, they are charged with the responsibility of keeping the law for future generations. This passage contains the Shema (vv. 4-5), an important aspect of daily prayer for Jewish people.

Lesson 2

(1) ***Hebrews 9:11-14*** **(RCL/Luth)**

In Jewish practice, the Day of Atonement symbolizes the annual ritual cleansing of the people. However, in Christ's sacrificial death on the cross, the cultic sacrifices of the Jewish temple have been satisfied once for all.

(2) ***Hebrews 7:23-28*** **(RC/Epis)**

The Israelite priesthood was imperfect because it was composed of mortal beings, while in Christ's eternal and perfect priesthood, no one else is needed to perform what he alone is able to do.

Gospel

Mark 12:28-34 **(RCL/RC/Epis/Luth)**

A scribe asked Jesus which commandment was first of all. Jesus responded that love of God and love of neighbor are both important commandments, and together they describe the ethical behavior of human beings in the realm of God.

Theme

More than just an emotion, love is the central action that binds us to God and to one another.

Thought for the Day

Jesus' commandments to love God and our neighbor form a code of ethics for all the situations that we face in life.

Call to Worship

Leader: Happy are those whose way is blameless, who walk in the law of the Lord.

People: Happy are those who keep God's decrees, who seek God with their whole heart.

– Based on Psalm 119:1-2

Pastoral Prayer

Holy God, your word teaches us that loving you and loving others are to be highest among our priorities. We acknowledge that all your law and prophetic witness point to the desirability of relationships based on love. Though we often place our own selfish ambitions before our praise of you and our service to others, your love for us never falters. You have blessed us richly through the gifts of your creation. We give thanks for your forgiveness when we fail to measure up to your will for us. Help us to recognize your will for the relationships we have with others, that we might be stewards of your undying love for all creatures in this world. May we also recognize the big and small opportunities that we have every day to proclaim your love. In Christ's name, we pray. Amen.

Prayer of Confession

Have mercy on us, O God, according to your steadfast love. According to your abundant mercy, blot out our transgressions. Wash us thoroughly and cleanse us from our sin. For we know our transgressions, and our sin is ever before us. We have sinned against you and done what is evil in your sight. Wash us, and we shall be clean. Hide your face from our sins and blot out all our iniquities. Create in us clean hearts, O God, and put a right spirit within us. Amen.

– Based on Psalm 51:1-5, 10, 11

Prayer of Dedication of Gifts and Self

Generous God, as your love reaches out to the corners of this world, so your love has enriched us with blessings too numerous to name. We give thanks for all that you have made us to be and for all the gifts that we have received from your bounty. As we return a portion of the wealth that you have entrusted to us, may we be dedicated once again to serving you and to serving others who are most in need of a word of grace in their lives. These things we ask in the name of Jesus, our Lord. Amen.

Sermon Summary

Jesus teaches that the two greatest commandments are to love God and to love one's neighbors. This is a summary of the Ten Commandments. Rather than providing simply a minimalist interpretation of Jewish tradition, though, Jesus provides guidance for ethical behavior in nearly any situation.

Hymn of the Day

"Where Charity and Love Prevail"

This 9th-century Latin hymn was, prior to the Second Vatican Council in the 1960s, required to be sung at Maundy Thursday footwashing services. Yet, while appropriate to such worship, its lyrics, translated by Omer Westendorf in 1961, fit well with this week's gospel text about the greatest commandment.

The hymn appears with various tunes in a number of hymnals.

Children's Time

Love

Preparation: Print the two commandments from Mark 12:29-31 on separate strips of construction paper.

Have you heard of the Ten Commandments? What are some of these commandments? *(Invite responses; provide help as needed.)* Which commandment do you think is the most important?

One day, a man asked Jesus this very question. Jesus didn't answer with one of the Ten Commandments. Jesus told the man, "The first is, 'You shall love the Lord your God with all your heart, and with all your soul, and with all your mind, and with all your strength.' The second is this, 'You shall love your neighbor as yourself.' "

At first, it might seem odd that Jesus didn't answer with one of the Ten Commandments. Let's take a look at these two. *(Hold up the paper strips and read them.)* These two commandments sum up the other ten very well! If we love God, then we're not going to worship any other gods or take God's name in vain. And if we love each other, then we won't hurt each other in any way.

Love. That's the important word in Jesus' lesson for us today. Let's practice some words to help us remember Jesus' commandments. "Love God. Love one another." *(Repeat several times as a cheer.)*

The Sermon

All You Need Is Love

Hymns

Beginning of Worship: "Love Divine, All Love's Excelling"
Sermon Hymn: "Blest Be the Tie That Binds"
Closing Hymn: "Lord, Whose Love in Humble Service"

Scripture

Mark 12:28-34 (For additional sermon materials on this passage, see the 2003 May/June planning issue and the August 2003 issue of *The Clergy Journal.*)

No doubt *Fiddler on the Roof* is a perennially popular musical because its central message is about keeping one's core identity in the midst of bewildering change – something that speaks to people of any time and place. The action of *Fiddler on the Roof* takes place in the poor Russian village of Anatevka. The town was made up mostly of Jewish families during a time when Russia was ruled by a czar. The people in Anatevka were faithful to God and lived simple lives close to the land. They didn't hear much news from the outside world, and they didn't have much time for it, really, because their lives were governed by age-old traditions of farming the land and centuries of Jewish custom.

As the curtain rises on the first act, the center of the stage has a backdrop of a barn, and on the thatched roof of the barn a fiddler is playing a tune on his violin. When the lights come up, Tevye the dairyman appears and speaks to the importance of traditions in his life and the lives of others in his community. He talks of honoring tradition as a way of maintaining one's balance. Without traditions, Tevye says, "our lives would be as shaky as a fiddler on the roof!"

Like Tevye, the scribes in today's gospel were concerned with tradition. They knew that without observing Israel's traditional commandments, life would be shaky indeed. They thought they knew all about God and what God expected of them. They knew the commandments and laws that were written in the holy book called the Torah.

So it is out of concern for that tradition that the scribes asked Jesus in today's gospel, "Which commandment is the first of all?" (Mk 12:28). The scribes wanted to know whether Jesus stood within the traditional teachings of Israel or whether he opposed them.

The scene is really a set-up. We can see that the scribes were poised and ready to attack Jesus' answer as a seriously flawed position. The scene has all of the characteristics of a good legal debate. But Jesus rises above their little game by going to the heart of their tradition – and his own. "The first is, 'Hear, O Israel: the Lord our God, the Lord is one; you shall love the Lord your God with all your heart, and with all your soul, and with all your mind, and with all your strength' " (v. 30).

Every scribe with Jesus that day, and every faithful Jew who had lived before them, knew those words. They are central in Jewish piety. The book of Deuteronomy was the source of Jesus' reply. A devout Jew says these words in the morning and in the evening. These words are to be taught to children. And they are to be recited just before the moment of death. So Jesus' words were hardly a surprise to his hearers.

Jesus went on, of course. He quoted a section of the Law in Leviticus dealing with the proper conduct towards a neighbor. "You shall love your neighbor as yourself" (v. 31). When Jesus highlighted these two commandments, he was challenging the scribes who were intent on knowing all of the laws and commandments that governed every action of their lives.

Jesus wasn't championing some kind of religious minimalism. Rather, he was challenging a whole way of life by saying that it was more important to act out of love, rather than out of concern for what would look good, or to get hung up on trying to obey every little rule. Every thought, every action, every word can be governed by the commandments to show love to God and to one's neighbor.

As much as we may claim that we do not like a lot of rules and regulations, many people really do want specific directions in life. A certain number of rules and traditions seem to be necessary for us to function in the midst of a world that is often chaotic. We need some order to make sense of things.

Many of us may have observed that conservative churches, which often place a great number of restrictions upon their members, have grown considerably in recent years. Some people seem to be attracted to these churches that place a great number of expectations upon their members. When you have rules, at least you know where you stand. You know exactly what is or is not acceptable behavior. There is no ambiguity. Many people find this concrete guidance quite appealing.

It is without question more difficult to love others unconditionally than it is to love only those who have obeyed all of the rules of society. It is easier for us to have rules that clearly define who is good and who is not. Of course, the problem is that the people in our community and in our world don't wear black hats or white hats like the characters in the old Western movies did. We can't tell the good guys from the bad guys because there is good and bad in every person; each of us is both saint and sinner. Jesus challenges us to love all our neighbors, even when it may be difficult to do so.

Rule-bound forms of religion tell us that if we do things "right," everything will work out. But of course we don't always do things right.

In this day and age we should understand that there is no one set of customs or rules which will serve us in every situation. We live in an increasingly complex world where the tried and true traditions and customs that we have learned don't always work.

But there is hope for us. There is something that makes sense out of our shaky and confused times. If all of our actions are based upon Jesus' commandments to love God and to love our neighbors, we will be challenged to make our actions fit the needs of the moment. We are given the opportunity to bear witness to a God of love, who has already chosen to act kindly and graciously on our behalf.

Sometimes we are like Tevye in *Fiddler on the Roof.* We might agree that a community that puts a greater emphasis on loving people rather than applying stern discipline is as shaky as a fiddler on a roof. And like the scribes, we might want a more "law and order" kind of society, where justice is more easily prescribed.

But we must remember that the bottom line for all of the commandments is to love God and to love our neighbor. If all of our actions are based on love, then the rest of the commandments will take care of themselves.

– Dennis Bushkofsky
Interim Pastor
Metropolitan Chicago Synod of the
Evangelical Lutheran Church in America

November 9, 2003

22nd Sunday after Pentecost (Proper 27)

RC/Pres: 32nd Sunday in Ordinary Time

Lessons

RCL	Ruth 3:1-5; 4:13-17	Heb 9:24-28	Mk 12:38-44
Roman Catholic	1 Kgs 17:10-16	Heb 9:24-28	Mk 12:38-44 or 12:41-44
Episcopal (BCP)	1 Kgs 17:8-16	Heb 9:24-28	Mk 12:38-44
Lutheran	1 Kgs 17:8-16	Heb 9:24-28	Mk 12:38-44

Introduction to the Lessons

Lesson 1

(1) ***Ruth 3:1-5; 4:13-17*** **(RCL)**

Ruth comes to Naomi to support her in her grief for the death of Naomi's husband and sons. Naomi demonstrates the reciprocal nature of her love for Ruth by arranging for her marriage to a wealthy relative.

(2) ***1 Kings 17:10-16*** **(RC);** ***1 Kings 17:8-16*** **(Epis/Luth)**

In a book that demonstrates God's control over life's events, as opposed to the power that people have ascribed to other deities, these verses proclaim God's unique power in the midst of a devastating drought and famine.

Lesson 2

Hebrews 9:24-28 **(RCL/RC/Epis/Luth)**

Christ's sacrificial death on the cross has been a final satisfaction of the cultic sacrificial practices in the Jewish temple. Christ does not die again and again each year. He is forever alive with God.

Gospel

Mark 12:38-44 **(RCL/RC/Epis/Luth)**

After several incidents of speaking with the religious authorities in the temple, Jesus raises up the example of a poor widow who gives all that she has.

Theme

In the midst of our troubling times, those whose faith rests in Christ have reason to hope for the future. God has a place for us now, and in the world to come that will be without end.

Thought for the Day

The Lord will keep your going out and your coming in from this time on and forevermore.

– Psalm 121:8

Call to Worship

Leader: Christ has died, Christ is risen, Christ will come again.
People: Come, let us worship and give thanks.

Pastoral Prayer

Everlasting God, we praise you that through Jesus' death at Calvary you have redeemed us from sin's destruction. As our high priest before you day and night, Christ continually intercedes for us, giving us access to your divine nature. Help us to recognize and honor this remarkable gift, that we might not take your love for granted. This day we come to you with our concerns for those who are in need of your help: those who are sick, those who are homeless, those who lack the necessary resources for daily living, and those who mourn. Provide for their needs and comfort them with your presence. Make us your messengers and servants, that people throughout the world might know the power of your love through our witness. As we only glimpse your eternal power, sustain us in our longing for the day when Christ shall come to reign more completely. These things we ask in the name of Jesus Christ our Lord. Amen.

Prayer of Confession

O God, you have given us a priceless treasure through Christ's saving death and resurrection. We confess that we do not always value this gift as we ought. Relying on the certainty of your love and forgiveness, we confess that we have too often forgotten your will for us, and have been careless in our use of the precious resources you have placed in our hands. Help us appreciate your love more fully, that we might not squander it, but do everything in our power to enlarge the circle of those who may become aware of your awesome deeds of mercy. In the name of Christ, we pray. Amen.

Prayer of Dedication of Gifts and Self

O God, your blessings are beyond our imagining. Though we often forget the wonders of your creation, we acknowledge today that everything we are and everything we have comes from your gracious hand. As we return a portion of what you have first given us, may we serve those who have needs greater than our own. Once again we dedicate ourselves to your mission of peace and goodwill for all creation. May we forever be joined to the community of all who seek to see your face. In the most precious name of Jesus Christ, we pray. Amen.

Sermon Summary

For many people, the thought of Jesus' second coming brings fear and dread, yet for the believer in Christ this will be a happy day. It is a day that we can only glimpse in a partial way now through God's word, the sacraments, and the community of saints.

Hymn of the Day

"Cuando El Pobre"

Written by Spanish priests J. A. Olivar and Miguel Manzano, this hymn is variously translated "When the Poor Ones" or "When a Poor One." It reflects the vision of the last judgment in Matthew 25, as well as celebrating the presence of God whenever the poor, the oppressed, or the mistreated are served. Accordingly, it fits well with the story of the widow's mite.

Tambourines and other rhythm instruments on the first two notes of each measure help carry the rhythm.

Children's Time

Heavenly

Preparation: Bring some silver and gold Christmas garland, a white robe, an angel figurine, and anything else that is part of your image of heaven.

What do you think heaven might be like? What might you see there? What might you hear there? Who do you think is there? *(Show the props you brought to help stimulate discussion.)*

The Bible tells us that Jesus has gone to heaven to be with God. Jesus has promised that he is preparing a place for each and every one of us in heaven, so that when we die we can live with God and Jesus forever. It will probably be a long, long time before most of us go to heaven with God and Jesus, but isn't it good to know that Jesus is there for us already?

Actually, we don't really know what heaven will be like, and that's okay. We can use our imaginations to think about what it is like. We know for certain that it will be a wonderful place because we can trust Jesus' promises.

The Sermon

The Second Time Around

Hymns

Beginning of Worship: "Blessed Assurance, Jesus Is Mine"
Sermon Hymn: "Oh, Happy Day When We Shall Stand"
Closing Hymn: "How Great Thou Art"

Scripture

Hebrews 9:24-28 (For additional sermon materials on this passage, see the August 2003 issue of *The Clergy Journal* and on Mark 12:38-44, see the 2003 May/June planning issue of *The Clergy Journal*.)

There is an old story about three demons who were arguing over the best way to destroy the Christian mission in the world. The first demon says, "Let's tell all the Christians there is no heaven. Take away the reward incentive and the mission will collapse." The second demon says, "Let's tell all the Christians there is no hell. Take away the fear of punishment and the mission will collapse." The third demon says, "There is a better way.

Let's tell all the Christians that there is no hurry." The three demons agreed immediately. "That's it! All we have to do is tell them there's no hurry and the whole Christian enterprise will collapse."

A fan of the San Francisco 49ers, who was at Candlestick Park when an earthquake hit there in 1989, recalled later the flood of questions that poured into his mind as he looked up at the massive concrete overhang being supported by a shaking support post. He wondered: "If it falls, will I die?" "If I die, will I see God?" "Is my faith in Christ strong enough?" "Is it true?" "What will happen to my family?" "If I'm not killed, will I be maimed?" "If I don't die, will I be a coward and run for my life or will I stay and help?" The whole experience reminded this particular fan of the transitory nature of this life. One can't depend on a whole lot – except God.

Today's reading from chapter 9 of Hebrews speaks of Christ's coming again as a time when Christ will save all who are eagerly waiting for him. We may well ask ourselves today, "How shall we be prepared for this second coming of Christ?"

The writer of Hebrews proclaims that the sins of the world have already been born completely by Jesus Christ. Christ's second coming, then, should be a joyous time for those who wait in faith. This announcement in Hebrews is not one of terror and judgment for us. It is a word of reassurance and hope. Our sins have been forgiven. Christ will come again to save those who wait for him.

How do we prepare ourselves for Christ's second coming? The obvious answer is that we must live in constant readiness and preparation for God's coming. Faith and faithful action are not matters to be delayed. The time for living lives of faith is now.

All who are already in Christ have nothing to fear. In a very real sense, those whose lives have been transformed by faith in Jesus Christ will have nothing new to look forward to with Christ's second coming, except that Christ's presence will be even more intensely felt than it is now. Through baptism, through reading and hearing the scriptures, through regular participation in the Lord's Supper, and through our serving with others in the community of faith, we are already united with Christ. We are continually made one body with all the saints.

As we prepare to eat the bread and drink from the cup [this day], we share in God's kingdom that is both present among us now and yet to come. We cry out, "Amen. Come, Lord Jesus." We wait for Christ's return and for the creation of a new heaven and a new earth. We long for the final victory, when all creation will be new. We cry out, "Christ has died. Christ is risen. Christ will come again."

In this meal [today], we give thanks for Jesus' sacrificial death on the cross and for the salvation that has already been given to us. We pray that we may continue to receive Jesus Christ through word and sacrament and the communion with other believers. Living in faith now is how we prepare to meet Jesus for eternity.

We are called to live in faith each day of our lives, to live in such a way that every day we are prepared to meet and receive the Lord when Christ comes again. We are called each day to meet God in the faces of those who are homeless and hungry. We are called each day to meet God through our interactions with family members and coworkers.

Our gospel for the day provides yet another glimpse into the way in which we may be prepared to meet Christ on the day of the second coming. The beauty of what the poor widow did in today's gospel is that in giving everything she had, she was placing herself totally in God's care. Through her gratitude she demonstrated how she was living utterly dependent on God. It's a reminder to us that the more we are focused on needs of others, the more ready we will be when Christ comes again.

Would our Sunday celebrations be any different if we fully expected Christ to appear before us every week? Would our serving suddenly take on a greater meaning and urgency? Would this meal in which we receive the body and blood of Christ take on even more importance in our daily lives?

These are the questions. How we respond may indicate our readiness for Christ's second coming one day in the future. No doubt it will be a time of great surprise. But may each of us anticipate it as a day of great joy – one in which we are fully prepared to meet our Lord, Jesus Christ, face to face. Amen.

– Dennis Bushkofsky
Interim Pastor
Metropolitan Chicago Synod of the
Evangelical Lutheran Church in America

November 16, 2003

23rd Sunday after Pentecost (Proper 28)
RC/Pres: 33rd Sunday in Ordinary Time

Lessons

RCL	1 Sam 1:4-20	Heb 10:11-14 (15-18), 19-25	Mk 13:1-8
Roman Catholic	Dan 12:1-3	Heb 10:11-14, 18	Mk 13:24-32
Episcopal (BCP)	Dan 12:1-4a (5-13)	Heb 10:31-39	Mk 13:14-23
Lutheran	Dan 12:1-3	Heb 10:11-14 (15-18), 19-25	Mk 13:1-8

Introduction to the Lessons
Lesson 1

(1) *1 Samuel 1:4-20* (RCL)

Hannah cried out, asking God to rescue her from her sorrow by granting her a son. Eli, the temple priest, blessed her prayerful petition and in due time God gave her a son.

(2) *Daniel 12:1-3* (RC/Luth); *Daniel 12:1-4a (5-13)* (Epis)

Daniel, the prophet of God, prophesies to his people who are languishing in Babylonian captivity. He says that one day, God will rescue God's people from their woeful plight and visit judgment on the wicked.

Lesson 2

**(1) *Hebrews 10:11-14 (15-18), 19-25* (RCL/Luth);
Hebrews 10:11-14, 18 (RC)**

We are trapped by the guilt of our sin, but our high priest, Jesus Christ, has made the once-and-for-all-time sacrifice for sin, giving us the privilege and freedom of communion with God.

(2) *Hebrews 10:31-39* (Epis)

It is a dreadful thing to let God down by turning our back on God. Our divine calling is to pay the price, if necessary, for being faithful. God will reward those who remain faithful.

Gospel

(1) *Mark 13:1-8* (RCL/Luth)

In the end times there will be great upheaval in the world, nation against nation, family member against family member. Believers will be persecuted unmercifully for their testimony. But in the end God will deliver them to safety.

(2) *Mark 13:24-32* (RC)

In the last days there will be great and global turmoil, but Jesus will rescue those who belong to him. No one can know when this will take place. Our challenge as believers is to be ready for Christ's coming at all times.

(3) *Mark 13:14-23* (Epis)

When the end of the world approaches, there will be widespread and terrifying upheaval. Our summons as believers is to be ready, filled with anticipation for the second coming of Jesus Christ, the true Deliverer.

Theme

Things may get tough for believers, but God will deliver them to eternal safety in God's time.

Thought for the Day

May the storms of life drive us into the shelter of God's rock-solid arms.

Call to Worship

Leader: We lift up our eyes to the hills – where does our help come from?

People: Our help comes from the Lord, the maker of heaven and earth.

Leader: The Lord watches over us.

People: God will keep us from all harm, now and forevermore

– Based on Psalm 121

Pastoral Prayer

O Lord, life is indeed difficult and sometimes we find ourselves in predicaments that take us far beyond our own capacities to manage. Sometimes we bring these situations on ourselves. Sometimes others place them on us. And sometimes they just seem to happen. Whatever the cause, in those moments we feel helpless and alone, as if the whole world were on our shoulders. Such situations intimidate us, O God, and threaten to unravel our trust in you. Yet, deep down we know you are there. We know you are deeply invested in our well-being. And we know that when all is said and done you will keep us safe in your eternal care. We thank you and praise you for this confidence. Fill us, we humbly ask, with a strength that goes beyond earthly measure, so that we may remain faithful to you even when some come unglued. Make us into living testimonies of your power so others may see your sustaining Spirit at work in us and be drawn to you in faith. Amen.

Prayer of Confession

Gracious and loving God, we enter your holy presence aware that we have fallen short of your expectations in thought, word, and behavior. And we confess the sinful error of our ways. It grieves us to see just how weak-spirited we are and how quickly we let go of Christ-like principles when it is uncomfortable for us to be true to you and all you represent. Forgive us for our failings. Please don't measure the depth of our love for you by the weakness of our character. Instead, we humbly pray, look at the deepest longing of our hearts and see that our failings are not a representation of what we truly want; namely, to be faithful to you as you have been faithful to us. We offer this prayer, trusting in the saving power of Jesus Christ. Amen.

Prayer of Dedication of Gifts and Self

We offer these gifts now, O Lord, mindful of the fact that you own all that we are and all that we possess. Touch these gifts miraculously, we ask, as Jesus touched the loaves and the fish. Multiply them and transform them into tangible blessings for countless others whose lives will be uplifted by our ministries. Help us to fulfill our role as Christ's hands, eyes, ears, and feet. Take all that we have and all that we are and use it for your glory. Amen.

Sermon Summary

Sin is real and ruinous, affecting us all. And in the eyes of God it demands a once-and-for-all-time sacrifice which Christ, our high priest, has made for us. Christ has built a bridge between God and us. We share this good news while we wait for our final and triumphant deliverance.

Hymn of the Day

"My Heart Is Overflowing"

Medical Mission Sister Miram Therese Winter wrote this hymn based on the song of Hannah (1 Sam 2:1-10) for the *New Century Hymnal* where it appears set to a tune by Paulette Tollefson. Winter has captured well the sense of praise, joy, wonder, and transformation inherent in the biblical text.

Another of Winter's best-known hymns if "My Soul Gives Glory to My God," based on the Magnificat or Song of Mary, which, in turn, has echoes of Hannah's song. While traditionally sung in Advent, it would also be appropriate on this Sunday.

Children's Time

Snowball Effect

Show me how to make a snowman. *(Allow a moment for responses and demonstration.)* Isn't it amazing how you can start with a small snowball in your hand, then roll it in the snow, so that it gathers more and more snow with each roll?

This morning, I want you to imagine how doing kind things for other people can be a lot like making a snowman. One person starts by doing one small act of kindness, and that inspires another person to do a good deed, and that inspires another person and before long, there is a big ball of kindness rolling throughout the community.

But it always needs someone to start the ball rolling. Someone needs to do the first good deed, the first kind thing that inspires someone else. Jesus wants us to encourage each other to do kind things for each other. Jesus calls us to encourage each other to get the ball of kindness rolling. In worship we can be reminded of Jesus' love for us and pray for strength to share that love.

So, what can you do this week to get the ball of kindness rolling around your family and your school and our town?

The Sermon

Doing for Us What We Can't Do for Ourselves

Hymns

Beginning of Worship: "O God Our Help in Ages Past"
Sermon Hymn: "Grace Greater than Our Sin"
Closing Hymn: "Amazing Grace"

Scripture

Hebrews 109:11-14 (15-18), 19-25 (For additional sermons on this passage, see the 2003 May/June planning issue and the August 2003 issue of *The Clergy Journal.*)

German theologian Hans Küng once wrote,

> As a theologian and a Christian, I am firmly on the side of Karl Barth, the great Protestant theologian, who once told me that he would not point at the end to his collected writings for justification, or even mention his good intentions. In his view, the only suitable words that he could say in the presence of his judge were: "God have mercy on me a sinner." (Hans Küng, *Why I Am Still A Christian* [Nashville: Abingdon Press, 1987], page 86.)

Coming from someone of the stature of Karl Barth, whose systematic theology represents a monumental contribution to sophisticated Christian thinking, that's a provocative statement. If we could question Barth on why he made this statement, how would he respond? Perhaps he would direct us to a passage like today's text from Hebrews, suggesting that we read the message for ourselves.

Clearly, this text in Hebrews implies that no matter how vigorously we may try to sweep it under the rug of denial, sin is real and it stands between us and a holy God. That's the underlying truth of today's passage. Sin, this soul-level malady of all encompassing self-centeredness, is real. And it has contaminated even the noblest motives behind our expressions of love. Even worse, it is infinitely beyond our capacity to manage. We need a savior, or as the Hebrews writer expresses it to his Jewish Christian readers, a great high priest. We need someone who is without sin, whose spiritual coattails we can ride into the heavenlies because his sacrificial death on the cross has miraculously and mysteriously opened the door of that possibility. The writer puts it like this, "We have confidence to enter the sanctuary by the blood of Jesus, by the new and living way that he opened for us through the curtain (that is, through his flesh)" (Heb 10:19, 20).

These words may sound confusing. Sanctuary, holy place, blood of Jesus, curtain – strange images that cause one to wonder what in the world the writer of Hebrews is talking about. But to those who are truly passionate about getting close to God, what is being said, strangely enough, makes complete sense. We have tried to get it right with God on our own. We have sacrificed ourselves on the altar of good works again and again only to discover that after all was said and done, the chasm between God and us is no narrower than it was when we first began. We comprehend that sin is not just something we do or say, but a condition we're in – an inescapable condition, a condition of self-centered preoccupation so entrenched that it stiff arms the Lord every time he tries to bond his Spirit with ours. It's no wonder Paul lamented, in the face of this reality, "Wretched man that I am! Who will rescue me from this body of death?" (Rom 7:24).

Who will rescue us? Christ will rescue us. This is the gospel's good news. We have a high priest, a Savior, a bridge-builder between God and us. His name is Jesus.

The story is told about Al Smith who, as governor of New York a few generations ago, was invited to give a talk before a group of salespeople. The majority were already inebriated when he got up to speak, an annoyance made worse by the casual, even flippant, introduction given to him by the toastmaster. It climaxed with the impertinent words, "And now boys I present to you a great guy, Al Smith." On this occasion Smith sensed an almost irreverent affront to his office. He made his comments brief and terse.

They went something like this, "Gentlemen, when I was a little boy on the East Side my father once took me to see a great parade. I held his hand tightly as bands played and the military marched. And then suddenly my father stiffened and said, 'Son, take off your hat, the governor of New York is passing by.' " Smith then looked at his audience and after a moment of silence said, "Gentlemen, the governor of New York bids you good night."

I dare say that many today harbor a similar downgrading attitude toward Jesus – a great moral teacher, a great prophet, and when all is said and done, certainly a great guy. But what an affront this attitude represents! Christ would be justified in saying to all who harbor such an attitude, "Ladies and gentlemen, the savior of the world bids you good night." Jesus has done for us what we cannot do for ourselves no matter how hard we try. He has made intimate friendship with the holy, loving, and eternal God possible by paying the price for our sin.

Living in such knowledge inspires response. This passage in Hebrews tells us there are certain things we ought to be doing out of gratitude.

First of all, "let us approach [God] with a true heart in full assurance of faith" (v. 22). What an invitation! Some might say, "So what?" To which we respond, "So everything!" What our souls long for more than anything else in this world of change and death is to be close to the eternal God. It was St. Augustine who wrote, "Thou hast made us for Thyself, O Lord, and our hearts are restless until they find their rest in Thee." This is now possible, made so by the bridge-building work of the great high priest, Jesus Christ.

Next, "Let us hold fast to the confession of our hope without wavering, for he who has promised is faithful" (v. 23). The writer of Hebrews feared that his readers would, in the face of persecution, turn around and walk back over the bridge Christ had built to God, relinquishing their only hope for freedom from sin's consequences. He knew that the only thing we take from this life is our soul. We are not a body indwelled by a soul. We are a soul temporarily indwelling a body. Therefore, protecting the safety and well-being of the body at the expense of the soul's eternal connection to God is a tragic mistake.

Next, "Let us consider how to provoke one another to love and good deeds, not neglecting to meet together, as is the habit of some, but encouraging one another" (vv. 24-25). The word translated *provoke* comes from a word that usually has a meaning like "irritation" or "exasperation." It is unusual to have it used in a positive sense, which makes its use all the more striking in this passage. What is the writer telling us? That we ought to be each other's cheerleaders. Like a bystander yelling encouragement to a passing runner, we ought to be speaking words of motivation to each other, spurring each other on to acts of selfless love, the kind Christ demonstrated to us. These acts are the antithesis of the self-centeredness that permeates our lifestyle apart from the Lord.

Furthermore, the readers are implored to not give up meeting together. The implication is obvious. Flying solo as a follower of Christ is hazardous to our spiritual health and witness. No matter how blessed we are by Christ as our high priest, we run a great risk in thinking that we can stay close to God without the mutual support of our faith family. The intimacy of these relationships provides us with a stimulating earthly preview of what heavenly closeness to God will be like.

Finally, "let us encourage one another." We are to be sons and daughters of encouragement – men and women who press courage into one another and do not extract courage from each another. Sadly, our church and our society has more than its share of people whose constant criticism and negative spirit sap courage from the souls of others, leaving them drained and defensive. We ought not to be numbered among them.

Will you trust Christ's once-and-for-all-time sacrifice for your sin? And will you then join freely in the community of men and women who share this soul-level liberation? It is the only way we can persevere as Christians in our sin-ridden world until the time of Christ's final deliverance.

– David Wesley Reid
First Baptist Church
Reading, Massachusetts

November 23, 2003

Reign of Christ/Christ the King

Lessons

RCL	2 Sam 23:1-7	Rev 1:4b-8	Jn 18:33-37
Roman Catholic	Dan 7:13-14	Rev 1:5-8	Jn 18:33-37
Episcopal (BCP)	Dan 7:9-14	Rev 1:1-8	Jn 18:33-37 or Mk 13:14-23
Lutheran	Dan 7:9-10, 13-14	Rev 1:4b-8	Jn 18:33-37

Introduction to the Lessons

Lesson 1

(1) *2 Samuel 23:1-7* (RCL)

David prophesies about the eternal anointed one of God who will one day rule over all the earth, saving those who are righteous and bringing judgment upon those who are evil.

(2) *Daniel 7:13-14* (RC); *Daniel 7:9-14* (Epis); *Daniel 7:9-10, 13-14* (Luth)

Daniel has a prophetic vision in which he sees the ancient one on a throne, surrounded by glory and witnessed by thousands upon thousands. One like a human being appears suddenly and is granted righteous authority over all peoples and all places for all time.

Lesson 2

***Revelation 1:4b-8* (RCL/Luth); *Revelation 1:5-8* (RC); *Revelation 1:1-8* (Epis)**

John writes to the seven churches in Asia and proclaims the coming of Christ in glory. Every eye will see Christ, the Alpha and the Omega of history.

Gospel

***John 18:33-37* (RCL/RC/Epis/Luth)**

Jesus appears before Pilate and Pilate asks if he is the king of the Jews. Jesus replies that his is an eternal kingdom and that his purpose is to testify to the eternal truth.

Theme

Christ is king over all creation and Christ's triumphal reign will last for eternity.

Thought for the Day

As we listen in on Jesus informing Pilate that his kingdom is not of this world, we are led to ask, "In what kingdom are we most invested?"

Call to Worship

Leader: Do not be afraid; the Alpha and the Omega comes to us.
People: Christ is the living one; the one who was dead is now alive forever and ever!
Leader: Do not be afraid; Christ comes as King.
People: Thanks be to God.

– Based on Revelation 1

Pastoral Prayer

Gracious God, our heavenly Father, we come into your presence now, privileged to do so through Jesus Christ, our Savior, our Lord, and our eternal king – the one to whom we look for our daily guidance and for our eternal hope. How grateful we are, Lord, that you loved us enough to send Jesus into this earthly mix of sin and death. How grateful we are that Jesus' sacrifice on the cross opened for us a door of access into your presence, a door that will never again be closed. Lord, more than anything else, we want to place ourselves on the side of Jesus in this world. Help us to do exactly that – to be bold for your truth, courageous for your purposes, demonstrative of your love. We covenant with you now to work for Jesus until he comes again. We pray all this in Jesus' precious name. Amen.

Prayer of Confession

God, we humbly enter into your presence now, mindful of the horrible gap that exists between what we profess and how we live. We wish we were stronger, Lord. We wish that our flesh were as mighty as our spiritual aspirations. Please forgive us each time we fail you and help us to get back on our feet, dust ourselves off, and throw ourselves headlong into the sacred task of serving you by serving others. We know Jesus is the king of kings, that one day every knee will bow to him and every tongue confess that he is sovereign over all. We draw strength from that knowledge, Lord, and look forward to the time when in love Christ will lift us out of our world of broken promises, into the heavens, where sin and sorrow will never again wear us down. Amen.

Prayer of Dedication of Gifts and Self

We thank you, O God, for all that you have given us from your unlimited reservoir of love. Your blessings are not just spiritual, they are material and sometimes that amazes us. We know Jesus taught that we should not worry about our material needs, that you will provide for them as they arise, but we are still amazed that all of creation is at your fingertips and that you care for us as a loving parent cares for a child. Such knowledge is too wonderful for us. Now, O God, we place our resources at your disposal. Use them and us, we pray, as you see best. And may the name of Jesus be praised. Amen.

Sermon Summary

Jesus informs Pilate that his kingdom is not of this world, a declaration that should lead us to ask, "In what kingdom are we most invested?" A self-inventory is in order. How do we do it? By using the Sermon on the Mount as a self-evaluative tool.

Hymn of the Day

"Crown Him with Many Crowns"

The familiarity of this hymn and its triumphant tune "Diademata" may hide the incredible sense of irony in the text. A combination of texts by Canadian ministers Matthew Bridges and Godfrey Thring, the hymn celebrates many aspects of the risen Christ. On this Reign of Christ Sunday, when the lectionary texts invite us to ponder just what kind of king Jesus is, we do well to sing of a lamb on a throne, a resurrected savior, and a ruler whose power lies not in might but in the ability to bring peace.

Children's Time

A King Is Born

A king is going to be born soon! Where do you think he will be born? What kind of clothes do you think he will wear? Do you think they will make a little crown for him? Who will come to visit him? Do you think that when this king grows up, he'll sit on a throne and rule a country?

Surprise! This king is different. The king we honor today is Jesus Christ. Jesus is a king like no other. He didn't want a crown or fancy robes. Instead, he walked around in sandals or bare feet, and wore clothes that looked just like everyone else's. He didn't even own a house – instead, he always stayed with friends and followers, wherever he went.

When a leader asked Jesus if he was a king, Jesus told him that he was a king with a difference. Jesus didn't come to earth to rule people or tax them, or to tell them what to do and where to live. Instead, Jesus came to tell the good news of God's love for everybody. What a great king that God has given us. This is a good kind of king to follow.

The Sermon

Inverted Believers

Hymns

Beginning of Worship: "All Glory Laud and Honor"
Sermon Hymn: "Rejoice, the Lord Is King"
Closing Hymn: "Jesus Shall Reign"

Scripture

John 18:33-37 (For additional sermon materials on this passage, see the 2003 May/June planning issue of *The Clergy Journal* and on Revelation 1:4b-8, see the August 2003 issue of *The Clergy Journal.*)

In his book, *The Divine Conspiracy*, Dallas Willard suggests that we Christians need to understand and buy into what he calls "the great inversion." (SanFrancisco: Harper, 1998.) While the Pilates of this world throw themselves headlong into the pursuit of power and possessions, we

Christ followers are to do just the opposite. We are called to invest in the kingdom of heaven, not the kingdoms of this earth. Jesus reminds us of this with his words, "For what will it profit them if they gain the whole world but forfeit their life?" (Mt 16:26).

In today's text, we observe Jesus in a painful dialogue with Pilate, governor of Judea, on the eve of his crucifixion. Things are obviously heating up. Jesus is in deep trouble. The Jews are screaming for his head and looking for governmental sanction on his condemnation. Pilate is hearing them out, but is unsure about what Jesus may have done to warrant such a harsh treatment.

"Are you king of the Jews?" Pilate asks Jesus, "Your own nation and the chief priests have handed you over to me. What have you done?" (Jn 18:33, 35).

But in response to Pilate's question, Jesus says something that must have seemed cryptic, confusing, maybe even a little crazy. "My kingdom is not of this world" (v. 36). For those of us who deeply care about Christ, that declaration doesn't sound crazy at all. We know exactly what Jesus is talking about. Yet we should never take what he declares for granted. His assertion to Pilate should routinely compel us, as men and women of Christ-like integrity, to inventory our lives, asking ourselves, "I say I'm a Christian, but does my lifestyle suggest that I'm clustering my convictions, values, and choices around Christ's kingdom that is not of this world? How much of my time, talent, and personal resources am I spending on the kingdoms of this world? Am I living an 'inverted' lifestyle?"

These are provocative questions, but ones that we must ask if we're serious about testifying with Jesus to the truth.

Perhaps you're thinking to yourself at this point, "And how do we go about this self-inventory? What standard do we use?"

Probably the best tool for self-evaluation in the New Testament is the Sermon on the Mount, recorded in chapters 5 through 7of Matthew's gospel. There Jesus provides a synopsis of what the "inverted" Christian life looks like.

We see, first of all, that a man or woman whose life is "inverted" is going through a character makeover. This character makeover is an ongoing and lifelong process. In his most recent and stunning book, *Renovation of the Heart,* Dallas Willard writes about the makeover in this way:

Pthe greatest need you and I have – the greatest need of collective humanity – is renovation of our heart. . . . Indeed, the only hope of humanity lies in the fact that, as our spiritual dimension has been formed, so it also can be transformed. Now and throughout the ages this has been acknowledged by everyone who has thought deeply about our condition . . . we, very rightly, continually preach this possibility and necessity from our pulpits. (Dallas Willard, *Renovation of the Heart* [Colorado Springs: Navpress, 2002], page 14.)

Every so often on television, one of the afternoon talk shows will feature a "makeover" theme. Usually a woman will submit to a re-do of hair, makeup, and clothing that leaves the audience gasping with the before and after contrast. If the average person were able to peer into the character of a true believer they, like the television audience, would gasp over the inner makeover that is taking place as a result of Christ's work.

For example, in the Beatitudes we see that "made over" or "inverted" Christians display a humble attitude, a hunger for righteousness, and a merciful spirit. What's more, we're bent on seeking peace, not conflict, in relationships and are so deeply convinced of the eternal truth of all this that we're willing to endure the ridicule of others for being different.

Continue on in the Sermon on the Mount and we discover something else, that an "inverted" Christian has a clear sense of life purpose. God intends for believers to live as salt and light in the world. That is to say, our God-given purpose on earth is to flavor with Christ-like selfless love, the bland lives of those who don't know him. Or, as Jesus also suggests, we are to bring light; that is, our main mission, task, and objective as Christians is to shine the light of the gospel on the shadows of human need.

"Inverted" believers clearly understand that our good behavior as salt-and-light-driven-people does not earn brownie points with God. We have a healthy dependence on Christ, whose goodness is miraculously and mysteriously credited to us by God through our simple but sincere faith.

Our self-inventory continues as we stand our overall lifestyle up against the lifestyle Jesus describes through the Sermon on the Mount. What more do we learn? That an "inverted" Christian does not nurse resentments, does not use others sexually for reasons of selfish indulgence, is faithful in marriage, and is a person whose word is bond. The "inverted" believer has a forgiving spirit, even toward personal adversaries. The "inverted" believer is generous with money, and spiritually disciplined. The "inverted" believer trusts God completely.

Jesus says to Pilate, "My kingdom is not of this world" and we nod in agreement. In our soul we may even shout a hearty "amen." But that doesn't end the matter. We receive these simple words as a clarion call, summoning us to an upside-down lifestyle, at least as the world perceives it.

The story is told about a minister who, a generation or so ago, visited a diamond market in Brussels, Belgium. He was shown into a room where hundreds and hundreds of uncut diamonds were spread out on a table in front of an assessor whose job was to assess the value of each diamond and then send them on to the merchants. The minister watched him for several minutes and then said to the assessor, "If I were looking at all these stones, hour after hour, I would begin to lose my perspective on the value of one as compared to another. How can you make an intelligent and accurate decision about the value of each one?" The diamond assessor turned quietly in response to this question and held up his hand, on which was a ring that featured a magnificent diamond. "This is the perfect diamond," he said, "and when I look at all these uncut gems, every couple of minutes I stop and stare at this one. From this I recalibrate my perspective. I measure all these against this one perfect stone."

Jesus is the perfect diamond by which we calibrate or self-inventory our life. What he preached in the Sermon on the Mount, he practiced in real life. His kingdom was not of this world and his "inverted" lifestyle reflected it. Now, we who claim his name need to ask ourselves, "What does our lifestyle reveal? Are we with him or are we, like Pilate and his countless facsimiles in history, given over to the preoccupations of this world?"

As Jesus neared the end of his Sermon on the Mount, he confronted the disciples with these penetrating words, "Not everyone who says to me, 'Lord, Lord,' will enter the kingdom of heaven, but only the one who does the will of my Father in heaven" (Mt 7:21).

In which kingdom are you most invested?

– David Wesley Reid
First Baptist Church
Reading, Massachusetts

November 27, 2003

Thanksgiving

Lessons

RCL	Joel 2:21-27	1 Tim 2:1-7	Mt 6:25-33
Roman Catholic	Sir 50:22-24	1 Cor 1:3-9	Lk 17:11-19
Episcopal (BCP)	Deut 8:1-3, 6-10 (17-20)	Jas 1:17-18, 21-27	Mt 6:25-33

Introduction to the Lessons

Lesson 1

(1) *Joel 2:21-27* (RCL)

If the people of Israel repent, not only will God's promise of rest and restoration come to them, but they will be freed to experience God's great consolation, a life free of fear.

(2) *Sirach 50:22-24* (RC)

Praise and thanksgiving are given to God for God's glorious works and a blessing is invoked on all men and women that they may enjoy peace and gladness of heart in the abiding goodness of the Most High.

(3) *Deuteronomy 8:1-3, 6-10 (17-20)* (Epis)

If the people of Israel live in a way that is faithful, God will provide them with the gift of a land that is overflowing with blessings. It is God who will provide this land, not the efforts of the people.

Lesson 2

(1) *1 Timothy 2:1-7* (RCL)

God wants to bless us with salvation through knowledge of the truth. We have an obligation to pray and give thanks for all persons, including those who are in positions of civil authority. This is the way to a peaceful life.

(2) ***1 Corinthians 1:3-9*** **(RC)**
The Corinthian church has been richly blessed by God in speech, knowledge and in spiritual giftedness. What's more, God is faithful and will continue to bless them with strength and purity until Christ returns.

(3) ***James 1:17-18, 21-27***
God blesses us with new birth, and this blessing entails certain obligations for us. We are to live lives consistent with God's word, reflected in such things as how we bridle our tongues and care for others.

Gospel
(1) ***Matthew 6:24-33*** **(RCL/Epis)**
Why worry about our material well-being when we have God looking out for us? God will provide for us. We live by faith in this promise.

(2) ***Luke 17:11-19*** **(RC)**
Jesus heals 10 lepers on his way to Jerusalem, and only one returns to thank and praise God. Jesus affirms the faith of the one who returns.

Theme
God desires to provide for all our needs. Can we trust God to make that provision?

Thought for the Day
God will provide.

Call to Worship
Leader: Lord, you have been our dwelling place in all generations.
People: From everlasting to everlasting you are God.
Leader: So teach us to count our days that we may gain a wise heart.
People: Let the favor of the Lord our God be upon us, and prosper the work of our hands – O prosper the work of our hands!

Pastoral Prayer

Almighty and everlasting God, we enter into your holy presence, praising you for your love that is far beyond anything we can measure. It amazes us that you, who made the universe, would be personally invested in each one of us as if each one of us were the only one on earth to love. How can we thank you? We know, O God, as the Bible says, that you provide for us specifically, tangibly, in this world and the world to come. Jesus told us that you feed the birds and that you will feed us. What's more, you clothe the lilies of the field and you will clothe us. Help us, we pray, to trust you more completely, growing each day in our awareness and appreciation of your blessings. Amen.

Prayer of Confession

Merciful God, we ought to count our blessings every day and be surprised at what you have done for us. Forgive us for not doing that. Instead, we have complained about our lot, feeling self-pity when things have not gone in the manner we have prescribed for ourselves. How shallow and selfish we are. Gracious and forgiving God, please help us to turn over a new leaf, to see that no matter how unfavorable our circumstances may seem to us, they pale when compared to your goodness, a goodness that is not limited to this earthly time and space, but extends beyond the grave. We offer this prayer of confession now in the name of our Lord and Savior, Jesus Christ, in whom and through whom we have life eternal. Amen.

Prayer of Dedication of Gifts and Self

God in heaven, giver of all things, we present these material blessings to you now, recognizing that we are simply returning to you what is already yours. Help us, we ask, to appreciate the full scope of what it means to be a steward of your resources, to know and accept that all we have is only on loan from you. Help us to live comfortably with the knowledge that we are but temporary custodians of the things of this world. In that light help us to hold our belongings loosely, so loosely, in fact, that we may part with them easily when opportunities arise for us to press them into the service of your realm. We know, O God, " 'tis only one life and it will soon be past. Only what's done for Christ will last." Amen.

Sermon Summary

So many Christians worry themselves sick over things. It isn't necessary. In fact, worry is a reflection of a breakdown of trust. What's more, it's not good for us. God wants to provide for all our needs, including our material needs. We need to trust God to make that provision.

Hymn of the Day

"For the Fruit(s) of All (This) Creation"

English hymnist Fred Pratt Green wrote this fresh Thanksgiving hymn in 1970. While celebrating the wondrous gifts of creation, the hymn goes further and gives thanks for those times when we reach out to others, and God's will is done. And it gives thanks, too, for "the wonders that astound us, the truths that still confound us" and "most of all, that love has found us."

While Green originally intended the hymn to be sung to "East Acklan," it has gained popularity sung to the Welsh tune "Ar Hyd Y Nos."

Children's Time

Worry Not

Have you ever thought about how wonderful it would be to be a cat? All day long, you get to lie around in the sun, stretching when you feel like it, going for a prowl or climbing up on a lap. Food appears magically; you don't have to work to earn the money to buy food.

What about being a bird? Do you ever watch the birds and wish that you could be a bird, free to go wherever you please, whenever you please?

Cats and birds live fairly worry-free lives. God has provided all they need: humans and worms, houses and trees, fur and feathers.

What about us? Has God given us all we need? Or should we be worried about that? Sometimes we can't help worrying. But Jesus tells us to trust that God will provide for us. This Thanksgiving weekend, we're thankful for all that God has given us. We count our blessings as we look around the table at all our loved ones. We count our blessings as we eat our Thanksgivings feasts. We know that God has provided for us. So next time we start to worry, let's remember that we can trust God to take care of us.

The Sermon

Crackers and Cheese Christianity

Hymns

Beginning of Worship: "How Great Thou Art"
Sermon Hymn: "God of Grace and God of Glory"
Closing Hymn: "Search Me O God"

Scripture

Matthew 6:25-33 (For additional sermon materials on this passage, see the 2003 May/June planning issue and the August 2003 issue of *The Clergy Journal.*)

One of modern history's greatest exemplars of trust was George Müller of Bristol, England. As a young man Müller was a wild sort. In fact, at the age of 14, while his mother lay dying, he was out with friends partying and getting drunk. But God claimed Müller. By the age of 25, Müller had turned his back on his profligate lifestyle and devoted his life to God. And what a devotion it was!

Müller became distressed over the plight of the poor in Bristol and determined that he should found a house to care for orphans. Within a few years his orphanages were caring for more than two thousand children. What makes this story so remarkable is that Müller never solicited a penny for the work. He took Jesus at his word when he declared in the Sermon on the Mount that God would make material provision for God's children.

"Therefore I tell you, do not worry about your life, what you will eat or what you will drink; or about your body, what you will wear. . . . But strive first for the kingdom of God and his righteousness, and all these things will be given to you as well" (Mt 6:25, 33).

In the Sermon on the Mount, after Jesus counseled his disciples to invest wholly in the lasting treasures of the soul, he directed them to the only logical conclusion of this teaching through the use of the word, *therefore.* "Therefore I tell you, do not worry . . ."

It's interesting to note that the word for "worry" in the Greek has reference to strangling or being choked. And that's precisely what worrying does to us. It strangles the life out of us, choking out the joy of trusting in a God who loves us and promises to take care of us in very specific and practical ways, according to the measure of our need.

How sad and ironic that we Christians worry so much! Pastors' offices are filled with parishioners who are depressed, whose relationships are a mess, and whose lives are lacking purpose. And why? Often, in large measure, because we're treasuring the wrong things and worrying ourselves physically, emotionally, spiritually, and relationally sick as a result.

The apostle Paul clearly got the point of Jesus' message when he wrote to the Philippian church, "Do not worry about anything but in everything, by prayer and supplication with thanksgiving let your requests be made known to God. And the peace of God, which surpasses all understanding, will guard your hearts and your minds in Christ Jesus" (Phil 4:6-7).

How hard it is for us to rest in this assurance and not to fret needlessly, especially in a rugged individualist culture like ours where what we get is generally from the sweat of our own brow. For the sake of our health and well-being, how can we change our ways? How can we worry less and trust more?

Certainly, first and foremost, we need to own – not just believe – that God is completely trustworthy. And that's not easy for anyone whose life experience, perhaps even from childhood, has ingrained the conviction that others can be relied on only conditionally. It's a challenge, a lifelong challenge in fact, to come to know that God is different. Whereas others let us down, God won't. Whereas others love us conditionally, God doesn't. And God's love is manifested not just in principle, but in practical provision. Elsewhere in the gospels Jesus taught his disciples to pray with confidence, "Give us this day our daily bread." We pray that prayer weekly. In the Sermon on the Mount we're summoned to live in the fulfillment of our petition.

Next, if we are to grow in our ability to trust God more and worry less, we need to grasp the full extent of how much God values each one of us. "Look at the birds of the air; they neither sow nor reap nor gather into barns, and yet your heavenly Father feeds them. Are you not of more value than they?" (Mt 6:26).

In addition, if we're to grow in our ability to worry less we must recognize that God's trustworthy promise of provision is not synonymous with an invitation to passivity. It's not so much that birds don't work. Actually, they're among the busiest of all this world's creatures. We, too, should work and work hard, but not from a place of worry. Not from a place of anxiety. Not from a place of running scared. Not from a place of defensive hoarding. We work because it is good and right and natural for us to work. The point is that God will meet us where we need to be met and will ensure that our efforts will more than prove adequate to our need.

Being freed from worry also requires us to sort out the difference between our needs and our wants. Many of us don't and won't trust God because we want more than what we fear God will provide. And that's probably true. Trust in God calls us to recognize that God knows what is best for us. If we're honest, we must admit that most often it's not our needs that make us sick with worry, but our wants. Why then would God give us what in the long run is not for our good?

Yet one more thing to consider as we seek to worry less and trust more: the real beauty we often long for in life, the outward beauty of Solomon, so to speak, is not the kind of beauty we should be worrying about. The natural beauty of the human soul is what we should go after and it's that beauty which God promises to provide in liberal measure if we trust God, just as God adorns the grass and lilies of the field. We have this on the word of Jesus himself.

Years ago a Scotsman was making a journey by ship from Great Britain to America. Worried about spending any extra cash, he lived on crackers and cheese for the entire trip, until the last day. No longer able to stand the sight of crackers and cheese he thought to himself, "Well, maybe on this last day I'll splurge and treat myself to a full meal."

The steward was surprised to see the man seated at the dinner table and when he inquired as to where the Scotsman had been for the entire voyage, the man told how he was anxious about spending too much money. The steward was shocked, "Didn't anyone tell you? The meals are included in the price of the ticket!"

How many of us are sailing through life on a "crackers and cheese" existence, worried sick over earthly treasures? "Give it up," Jesus says. "It isn't necessary. God's provision is included in the price of your trust."

– David Wesley Reid
First Baptist Church
Reading, Massachusetts

November 30, 2003

1st Sunday in Advent

Lessons

RCL	Jer 33:14-16	1 Thess 3:9-13	Lk 21:25-36
Roman Catholic	Jer 33:14-16	1 Thess 3:12–4:2	Lk 21:25-28, 34-36
Episcopal (BCP)	Zech 14:4-9	1 Thess 3:9-13	Lk 21:25-31

Introduction to the Lessons

Lesson 1

(1) *Jeremiah 33:14-16* (RCL/RC)

God promises that restoration will come to the houses of Israel and Judah. A Branch from the lineage of David will establish righteousness in the land and his name will be called the Lord Our Righteousness.

(2) *Zechariah 14:4-9* (Epis)

On a day of the Lord to come, God will fight for Israel against all enemies. There will be dramatic changes, but the living water of God's presence will flow in abundance.

Lesson 2

***1 Thessalonians 3:9-13* (RCL/Epis);**
***1 Thessalonians 3:12–4:2* (RC)**

Timothy reports that the church in Thessalonica is doing well, delighting Paul, who hopes that one day God will open the possibility for him to visit. Until such time, however, his prayer is that God will strengthen and bless the church.

Gospel

***Luke 21:25-26* (RCL); *Luke 21:25-28, 34-36* (RC);**
***Luke 21:25-31* (Epis)**

In the end times there will be cataclysmic changes in the world, warnings of Christ's second coming. Be ready so you can stand confidently before the Son of Man.

Theme

Christ will return for us.

Thought for the Day

All history is incomprehensible without Christ.

– Joseph Ernest Renan

Call to Worship

Leader: Christ will come down from heaven, with a loud command, with the voice of the archangel and with the trumpet call of God.

People: The dead in Christ will rise first.

Leader: We will meet the Lord.

People: And we shall be with the Lord forever. Hallelujah.

– Based on 1 Thessalonians 4:16-17

Pastoral Prayer

Almighty and merciful God we believe, despite all the strange comings and goings of humanity, that our history belongs to you. We give thanks that your eternal purpose is weaving its way through the events of time and space. Sometimes, O Lord, it's a challenge to hold on to this belief, but our confidence is in Christ, your Son and our Savior. We believe his death and resurrection are our confirmation that even though we can't understand the big picture of things, we can know history's final outcome. Gracious God, we watch with eager expectation for the return of Christ. Our souls buzz with anticipation of seeing the One, face to face, who authored and sustains the universe, the One in whom and through whom all things hold together, the One who will one day sit in judgment. We believe that on that last and great day all of history's scoffers will drop to their knees in recognition of your Son. Thank you, Lord. Amen.

Prayer of Confession

O God, we enter your presence now with broken spirits. We have known what is right to say and do, but have failed to say and do it. We know the right and deliberately choose the wrong. Why is that? O wretched people we are! Please forgive us, not on our merit, but on Christ's, who did for us what we cannot do for ourselves – allow us entry into your presence, confident that Christ's perfect goodness is credited to our account. Words escape us, Lord, as we contemplate the magnitude of your grace, mercy, and forgiveness. With hearts of gratitude we praise you. Amen.

Prayer of Dedication of Gifts and Self

Eternal God, how majestic is your name in all the earth. The whole earth is full of your glory. Please accept our humble offerings of our selves and our resources. Please use them to herald your hope to all persons everywhere who are living in physical, moral, and spiritual poverty. We want to love and care for them in the name of Jesus. What a privilege it is for us to be invited to share in such an eternal venture. In Christ's name we pray. Amen.

Sermon Summary

Christ is coming back and his coming will be preceded by many cataclysmic changes in the world. Our challenge, as Christians, is not just to wait, but to watch for his return by living lives of moral and spiritual readiness.

Hymn of the Day

"Let All Mortal Flesh Keep Silence"

Originally sung at the point of bringing in the elements for communion in the ancient liturgy of St. James dating from the fourth century, this hymn also has stong Advent overtones. The haunting French melody "Picardy" seems especially appropriate to this first Sunday of Advent, wherein we begin the mysterious cycle of the Christian year once again. We are caught up in the betwixt and between of preparing for the birth of Christ while acknowledging his presence among us, as well as pondering the mystery of his divinity and humanity.

Children's Time

Christmas Is Coming!

Today is the first day of the season of Advent. Advent is that special season when we prepare to celebrate Jesus' birthday on Christmas. It's the time of waiting. We remember Mary, Jesus' mother, who was waiting for Jesus to be born. For all of us, it's a time of preparation for Christmas. It's an exciting kind of waiting. Jesus' birthday is coming!

What do you do to get ready for a birthday party? *(Allow a moment for responses.)* I usually buy a present and wrap it. Then I make sure my party clothes are clean. What do people do to get ready for a birthday as special as Jesus' birthday?

Some people bake cookies and buy gifts. Some write Christmas cards and wrap presents. Some plan big parties for their families. But we need to be careful. We can get so excited about Jesus' birthday party that we forget to think about Jesus – God's special gift to us!

Remind your families to think about Jesus this month while you're planning for his birthday party. Read some stories about Jesus from the Bible. Thank God for Jesus in your prayers. How else can you remember Jesus as you get ready for his birthday party on Christmas? *(Invite responses.)*

The Sermon

Ready or Not, Here I Come

Hymns

Beginning of Worship: "Joyful, Joyful, We Adore Thee"
Sermon Hymn: "All Glory, Laud and Honor"
Closing Hymn: "Jesus Shall Reign"

Scripture

Luke 21:25-36 (For additional sermon materials on this passage, see the 2003 May/June planning issue and the September 2003 issue of *The Clergy Journal.*)

If we were to survey Christians about the doctrines of faith that are most important in our daily lives, we probably would get a broad spectrum of answers. Some would say that what we believe about God is most important. Others, what we believe about humankind. Still others, it's what we believe about Jesus' life, death, and resurrection that matters most. Some might focus on the Holy Spirit. Others might talk about the church. And so on.

Very few are likely to zero in on their belief in Christ's return, his Second Advent. Most of us probably would say that our belief in Christ's Second Coming doesn't factor into our daily lives much, if at all.

Yet, there are many of Jesus' words recorded in the gospels on this very topic. Jesus admonishes us to live lives of watchfulness in anticipation of that event. "Be alert at all times," Jesus says in Luke 21:36.

So, are you alert? Are you waiting, or are you watching? There's a difference between "watching" for Christ's return and "waiting" for Christ's return.

When a loved one has been away on a lengthy trip and is about to return home, we arrive at the airport early! We make repeated trips to the television consoles that post the flight status, checking again and again to see whether the screen still says *On Time.* And when, after what feels like an interminable season of anticipation, the screen changes to *At the Gate,* our hearts begin to flutter. We race for baggage claim to make sure that ours is the first face our loved one sees coming through the security doors. We stretch and strain to get that first glimpse. We're not just waiting, we're watching.

Contrast that with a person who is merely waiting. He or she sits passively at home and waits for the call from the airport that announces, "I'm in, would you come and pick me up?"

Isn't it true that most of us are waiting – not watching – for Christ's return? Why is this the case? What does it mean to be "on the watch" for Christ anyway?

One reason, and probably the most grievous, may be that we're not really in love with the Lord. We believe in Jesus. We attend church regularly. We're deeply committed to the church's ministries. But, in truth, deep in our hearts, our spirit is not bonded with Jesus' spirit. We're not really "in Christ" as the apostle Paul described himself. Hence, whether Jesus returns or not . . . well, it makes no real practical difference to us. Perhaps we are among those about whom Jesus spoke when he said, "This people honors me with their lips, but their hearts are far from me" (Mk 7:6).

Another reason may be that we haven't thought through the implications of Jesus' non-return. Fact is, were Jesus not to return, he would have lied to us. History could then be construed as a neverending saga. Sin would have perpetual sway over collective humanity. And the Christian community would be stripped of its consummate vision of God's eternal justice coming to fruition.

One more reason we merely wait for the Lord might have to do with spiritual immaturity. We're too caught up in the concerns of the here-and-now. We barely have the time and energy to get through today, let alone think about tomorrow, or some tomorrow after that. Sure, it makes sense that Jesus is coming back. After all, he came once, why wouldn't he come again? But frankly, we have all we can do to live a good life in the present. We can't dwell on or think much about what the future might bring. Such spiritual immaturity preoccupies us with the things of this world and causes us to run against the grain of Jesus' teaching. It's too tempting to lay up treasures here on earth.

Whatever the reason, something's wrong when most of us seldom think about, let alone watch for, the Second Advent of the Christ.

So, what does watching look like? What does it involve? At the very least it involves a clear understanding and acceptance of the fact that for believers, as the song goes, "this world is not our home, we're just a passin' through." First Peter describes Christians as "aliens and exiles" (1 Pet 2:11). Think about that, "aliens and exiles." Our convictions, our morals, our choices – they're different from those of the secular community. It can be a lonely way to live. In that light isn't it logical that we'd long to re-unite with Christ, for whom we've relinquished everything? Of course it is.

Watching also involves spiritual sensitivity to the signs of the times. This is tricky because it's so easy for believers to go off the deep end trying to "read" the events of the day, concluding that this or that cataclysm points to Christ's imminent coming. Many a Christian has looked foolish in this way. Yet, at the same time – in Luke's gospel and in other places – Jesus tells us to keep a close eye on *things* because these *things* will provide a hint, a suggestion, of his approaching Second Advent. So, how do we do that in a level-headed way?

November 30, 2003
1st Sunday in Advent

Truth is, reading the so-called signs of the times should be done more with the heart than with the mind. Our minds are limited, but our hearts can be illuminated with Truth beyond measure, sensitizing us to Christ's arrival in the same way we are suddenly sensitized to a person in the room whom we never saw or heard enter. We just know it. So, in our watching we study the calamities and upheavals of our day. We ponder them. We listen until the Spirit's voice in our souls whispers, "It won't be long."

Certainly, it seems that watching involves some level of chronic heartache, the heartache of longing for the final union with Christ to take place. Is it any wonder that a biblical metaphor for describing Christ's relationship with the church is the metaphor of marriage? We watch for the return of Christ, because in our deep love for him we can't help not watching.

Finally, watching involves obedience. Jesus cautions us in Luke's gospel not to allow our hearts to be "weighed down with dissipation and drunkenness and the worries of this life" (Lk 21:34). The implication is clear. Anticipating Christ's return should cause us, as suggested elsewhere in the New Testament, to prepare ourselves as a bride adorned for her husband, pure and without blemish.

During one of his expeditions to the Antarctic, Sir Ernest Shackleton left a few of his men on Elephant Island, planning to return for them. Time passed, however, the sea froze, and he could not return for his men. Finally, on the fourth attempt, he made it. To his delight and surprise he found them watching for him, all packed and ready to go. Shackleton asked how they knew to be ready. They acknowledged that they didn't know when, but that his coming would be certain. So, every morning the leader of the men arose and said, "Get your things ready, boys. The boss may come today."

We Christians ought to do likewise. We ought to live lives of readiness. Make no mistake, the Boss is coming.

– David Wesley Reid
First Baptist Church
Reading, Massachusetts

December 7, 2003

2nd Sunday in Advent

Lessons

RCL	Bar 5:1-9 or Mal 3:1-4	Phil 1:3-11	Lk 3:1-6
Roman Catholic	Bar 5:1-9	Phil 1:4-6, 8-11	Lk 3:1-6
Episcopal (BCP)	Bar 5:1-9	Phil 1:1-11	Lk 3:1-6

Introduction to the Lessons

Lesson 1

Baruch 5:1-9 **(RCL/RC/Epis)**

This passage is a hopeful call to Jerusalem to step into the future with God, clothed with splendor and awaiting the arrival of all who are returning to Jerusalem. God has made the way safe for Israel and will lead Israel with joy.

Lesson 2

Philippians 1:3-11 **(RCL);** ***Philippians 1:4-6, 8-11*** **(RC);** ***Philippians 1:1-11*** **(Epis)**

Beginning with a detailed salutation, the writer prayerfully remembers the Philippian church with deep love for the church and confidence in the One who will complete the work begun in them.

Gospel

Luke 3:1-6 **(RCL/RC/Epis/Luth)**

Luke introduces the political and religious context for John the Baptist's ministry. The word comes to John in the wilderness, but not to other leaders in various positions of importance. John takes the message to "prepare the way of the Lord" to the public.

Theme

We prepare for Christmas, but it is God who prepares us.

Thought for the Day

Have we become so caught up in our preparations that we actually begin to think we control Christmas? Have we begun to think its success depends on what we manage to cross off our "to do" lists?

Call to Worship

Leader: Prepare the way of the Lord.
People: Make the paths straight.
Leader: Let all be well with your soul,
People: For God's promise is coming.

Pastoral Prayer

O Faithful God, you await our prayers, always to ready to bless them with your Spirit's power. So we bring our thanksgiving and intercession to you. Give us grace to carry the troubles of this world in balance with the joy of this season. We lift up to you the places in the world where people live in fear, where terrorism works unhindered, where wars never really cease. We pray for the rulers of this world, that you will work through them. We give thanks for every victory that honors the sanctity of human life. Help us to see everyone through your eyes of love. We remember that the social excesses of the holiday season are difficult for those who daily battle addictions. Bless their longing for freedom with your strength and encouragement. We remember also those who mourn and the people in our hospitals. Be present where people are anxious or afraid, and answer their fears with your constant love. We thank you for the home we have here among your people, and ask you to bless our congregation with your spirit of welcome. Now add our silent prayers to the one great prayer of Jesus' life, death, and resurrection, in whose name we pray. Amen.

Prayer of Confession

O Patient God, we pause in our many other preparations to prepare ourselves for the coming of your Son. When you ask, "Is it well with your soul?" we hardly know where to begin. The path is not straight within us, and we are not ready for celebration. Let your mercy come to us now with a forgiving touch and a healing hand. Make us a people for whom the apostle Paul would give thanks in his prayers; a people in whom God is completing the work begun in us through Jesus Christ. In his name we pray. Amen.

Prayer of Dedication of Gifts and Self

Receive us, O God, and these our gifts as graciously as you give yourself and your gifts to us. Let us go deeper with you into the promise of Christmas, as we open ourselves to new paths of serving in the ministry of your Son. Complete the work you have begun. Amen.

Sermon Summary

In the midst of preparations for this holy season, Paul reminds us that God is at work in us completing the work already begun. Paul's confidence is in God's ability to complete the work. God will prepare us for Christmas regardless of what we leave undone on our holiday lists.

Hymn of the Day

"There's a Voice in the Wilderness"

This hymn was written by James Lewis Milligan to celebrate the formation of the United Church in Canada. This 1925 merger brought together the Congregational, Methodist, and Presbyterian churches and was later enhanced with the addition of the Evangelical United Brethren in Christ in 1968.

Taking as its basis Isaiah 40, which in turn is quoted in the story of John the Baptist, the hymn fits well in Advent. The tune by H. Hugh Bancroft carries a strong sense of anticipation and celebration.

Children's Time

Write a Letter

(Preparation: Bring a large sheet of paper and markers. Bring an envelope that is addressed to a child or other person who has moved away recently or a member of the congregation who is homebound.)

Today I'd like you to help me write a letter to (*name of recipient of letter)* to tell about what we're doing here at the church to get ready for Christmas. *(Ask the children to suggest sentences and write them down. Finish it up later if need be.)* After worship, I'm going to put our letter and some markers on a table by the door so you all can sign it.

The apostle Paul used to write letters to churches that he had visited in his travels. They loved to get his letters! We have copies of these letters in our Bible. Today in worship we are reading from one of Paul's letters, written to the church in Philippi (what is now Greece). It's pretty special to be able to read this letter almost two thousand years after it was written. It's almost like Paul was sending words of comfort and reassurance to us, too.

I think that *(name of recipient of your letter)* will be excited to hear from us, too.

The Sermon

Christmas Confidence

Hymns

Beginning of Worship: "There's a Voice in the Wilderness Crying"
Sermon Hymn: "What Is the Crying at Jordan"
Closing Hymn: "Long Ago, Prophets Knew"

Scripture

Philippians 1:3-11 (For sermon materials on Luke 3:1-6, see the 2003 May/June planning issue of *The Clergy Journal* and on Baruch 5:1-9, see the September 2003 issue of *The Clergy Journal*.)

It's the second Sunday in Advent. That means there are only 17 shopping days left to find the gifts you still have on your list. And there are only so many free hours left to bake and prepare your special holiday treats. And there are only so many free evenings to squeeze in all your seasonal social obligations. How are you ever going to complete all the work of Christmas before Christmas has come and gone?

I'm beginning to think that retailers may have the right idea. We need a lot more than the four weeks in Advent to get fully prepared for Christmas. Maybe the church should follow their lead and move right out of Halloween into the Christmas season. Residents of the United States could see Thanksgiving as a Christmas dinner rehearsal. We all need more time to complete the things we take upon ourselves, and all the things that others lay upon us as Christmas obligations. I am no longer confident that these things will be completed in time for Christmas.

Now, there's the apostle Paul. It's the second week in Advent and he's in jail. What seasonal faith question could possibly be in this passage besides, "Will he get out in time to carve the turkey?"

But this passage isn't a plea from Paul for help in his situation. It isn't Paul defending himself or worrying about what is going to happen to him at all. Instead, Paul is reaching out to a young community of faith with words of encouragement and affection. He shares his prayer for them, not his prayer for himself. As a young church they get into some heavy discussions about their faith. They have disagreements and they have common passions. They are themselves a "work in progress." They are not yet who they are becoming in Christ. They are not yet ready. They are not yet complete. Will they have enough time to get their act together before that something that Paul calls "the day of Jesus Christ" (Phil 1:6)?

With that phrase, "the day of Jesus Christ," we step into another realm of waiting and preparation. Paul and these believers were in a kind of "advent" period themselves. They were waiting for the fulfillment of God's plan in the return of Jesus Christ and the end of the present age. In this way, we may find common threads between our advent and theirs.

Among all the affirmations that Paul gives his readers, perhaps the most compelling is found in verse 6, "I am confident of this, that the one who began a good work among you will bring it to completion by the day of Jesus Christ." At last someone is confident about something being finished on time! How can we gain the confidence that Paul has and shares with this young church?

Perhaps the first thing to see is that the confidence Paul has is not in the Philippians' ability to get things finished. Rather, it is in God's ability to complete the work begun in them. If we are no longer confident that we will be able to "pull off" the style of Christmas season we feel is necessary, maybe our confidence is better placed in someone else – God.

I think we know that very little of what we feel we must do for seasonal preparations is what God is asking of us. We invest so many hopes and expectations of this season in preparations that are disconnected from the central powerful story of Christmas – the Word made flesh, God among us. Could it be that we, like the Philippians, need to refocus our energies not on what we are doing, but on what God is doing in us?

As we move more deeply into the meaning of the Christmas story, we make it possible for God to prepare us for the coming celebration. As we focus less on the things that are disconnected from the story and turn toward the message of the Bethlehem baby, we open ourselves to the possibility of God working in us.

The number of gifts we have crossed off our lists, the number of cookies stored in the freezer, and the number of parties we attend do not prepare us for the wonder of Christmas. It is God who gets us ready. It is always God who brings to completion the work begun in us, so that when Christmas comes, the Christ child will find a safe, welcoming place in our hearts.

Over the years, there has always been something that we find has been out of our control in Christmas preparations. We can't predict world or local events and how they will affect our holy season. We can't predict illness or job loss that comes into our lives. We can't even predict when relationships will fall apart or turn sour. There is always something at Christmas for which we remain unprepared, no matter how much we manage to get done in the weeks ahead. It is God alone who prepares us for the things of the season that we can never control.

After all, a man writes us from prison a few thousand years ago, and doesn't even know that we will one day read his words a few weeks before Christmas. He doesn't know that his words will be read by harried and stressed people who are making preparations that he would have little hope of understanding. And we who read them are used to an advent cast of ancient prophets, wild and woolly forerunners, and shepherds. But a guy in prison? Have we even noticed this reading before? Yet here he tells us what we need to remember most in this season of waiting and preparation.

Let us allow God to complete the good work that God has started in us. As deadlines crunch, let us be confident that the most important preparations are those that are in God's hands. After all, nothing that we do or don't do can bring Christmas faster or keep it from coming at all. It is God who really gets us ready. It is God who gives us Christmas.

– Diane J. Strickland,
Interim Minister
Springbank United Church
Calgary, Alberta

December 14, 2003

3rd Sunday in Advent

Lessons

RCL	Zeph 3:14-20	Phil 4:4-7	Lk 3:7-18
Roman Catholic	Zeph 3:14-18a	Phil 4:4-7	Lk 3:10-18
Episcopal (BCP)	Zeph 3:14-20	Phil 4:4-7 (8-9)	Lk 3:7-18

Introduction to the Lessons

Lesson 1

Zephaniah 3:14-20 **(RCL/Epis);** ***Zephaniah 3:14-18a*** **(RC)**

These verses are from the last section of the book. In this respect they are its climax, and point to the hope and promise that is driving the prophet's entire ministry. He celebrates a time when Israel will be released from judgment, safe from her enemies, renewed in God's love, and renowned among nations.

Lesson 2

Philippians 4:4-7 **(RCL/RC);** ***Philippians 4:4-7 (8-9)*** **(Epis)**

In this last chapter of Paul's letter, he calls his readers to a lifestyle of rejoicing, gentleness, prayer, and peace. We can embrace these things because the Lord is near, and God hears our prayers.

Gospel

Luke 3:7-18 **(RCL/Epis);** ***Luke 3:10-18*** **(RC)**

John the Baptist outlines the uniqueness of his prophecy, so that his listeners will understand that the one who is coming is unlike anyone who has come before. John calls them to lives of sharing and honesty.

Theme

Live this season with sharing, gentleness, and prayer.

Thought for the Day

Step back from the seasonal activities that are only about gathering things, experiences, and privileges for yourself or your immediate family and friends. Step into seasonal activities that provide opportunities to share, opportunities to offer gentleness, and opportunities to pray for those outside your circle.

Call to Worship

Leader: Rejoice in the Lord always:
People: Again I will say, rejoice!
Leader: God is building a future.
People: And nothing can stop the work of God's grace!
Leader: Rejoice in the Lord always:
People: Again I will say, rejoice!

– Based on Philippians 4:4-6

Pastoral Prayer

O may you hear us in these days before the celebration of Christmas. For as we move into the hope of this season, we see more clearly how the world holds pain for so many people.

The Lord is near. God hears our prayers. We pray for nations where strife is a part of everyday life, and children grow up with fear and conflict all around them. Bind the powers that stir up trouble so that your people may feel safe.

The Lord is near. God hears our prayers. We pray for people living will illness and disease, and for those who are dependent on others for basic needs. May every system, every care facility, and every care worker be called more deeply in the holy work of caring for others in need.

The Lord is near. God hears our prayers. We pray for people with power that the public has entrusted to them. Keep them honest and keep us vigilant in every place of accountability to which we are called. In the complexities of life, give us wisdom to live faithfully.

The Lord is near. God hears our prayers. Amen.

Prayer of Confession

We pray to you, O God, seeking to be ready for your future. Let your Spirit move over our own, to turn us more fully toward faithfulness. A new time is coming! What then shall we do?

Where we have not been generous with our resources, forgive us. Where we have not always been honest in our living, forgive us.

A new time is coming! What then shall we do?

Keepus in your love, O God, and make us walk in the way Jesus showed us. For a new time is coming and by your grace, we'll be ready! Amen.

Prayer of Dedication of Gifts and Self

Generous God, we are glad to share our resources with you. It is not always easy to share our lives, but we know you can be trusted with our greatest treasure. Receive us, and these gifts, that we might live freely as your servants in the world. Amen.

Sermon Summary

Reflecting on Paul's words, we challenge the way we are living through this holy season. Considering the full context of Paul's letter, we find things in common with it. We are invited to choose to focus on the one "big idea" of Christmas and let it be enough to guide our choices for the season, and to bring a more effective witness through rejoicing, sharing, gentleness, and prayer.

Hymn of the Day

"People, Look East"

Eleanor Farjeon wrote this hymn for the *Oxford Book of Carols* in 1928. In lines fairly busting at the seams with joy, enhanced by the vivid French folk tune "Besançon," the hymn conveys the sense of excitement at the arrival of a special guest. We are enhorted to prepare our homes for this important guest, birds are admonished to prepare a nest, the earth to prepare to hold a sacred see, the stars to watch, and the angels to proclaim the new life that is about to unfold upon the earth.

Children's Time

Don't Worry, Be Happy

Rejoice! Christmas is near! In today's reading from Paul's letter to the church in Philippi, Paul gives us some good advice.

First, Paul says to let others know about our gentle sides. Some people think it's better to look tough. But Paul tells us to show others that we are gentle and caring. How can we be gentle and caring while we're waiting for Christmas? *(Invite children to offer ideas.)*

Paul then reminds us that God is always near. That's easy to remember when sitting in church, but how about when we're in a busy shopping mall along with hundreds of other people? Well, we could look at all the people passing by and remember that God loves each and every one of them.

Paul's next piece of advice is to not worry. He tells us to pray. When we do, God's peace will fill us and keep our hearts and minds safe in Jesus' care. What shall we pray for this week? *(Invite children to share ideas.)*

This week, be gentle, remember that God is near, and pray – make it a good week!

The Sermon

What's the Big Idea?

Hymns

Beginning of Worship: "Come Thou Long Expected Jesus"
Sermon Hymn: "Sing 'til Sundown"
Closing Hymn: "Tomorrow Christ Is Coming"

Scripture

Philippians 4:4-7 (For sermon materials on Luke 3:7-18, see the 2003 May/June planning issue of *The Clergy Journal* and on Zephaniah 3:14-20, see the September 2003 issue of *The Clergy Journal*.)

Hunched over the scroll, the writer shifted his weight yet again. It was hard to get comfortable in his current surroundings. A waft of pungent humanity hit his senses as his fellow prisoners paced in their cells. He paused for a moment, remembering where he was and why he was there. But it was only a split second of personal anxiety that ran through him. Paul went back to work. The letter needed to get to the church at Philippi. He was nearly finished – just a few more thoughts. There was too much invested in Philippi to leave them floundering in their new faith.

But even more than that, there was something about Philippi that was familiar to Paul. There was something in them he understood. Philippi was a Roman colony on the main road from Asia Minor to Greece. It had a strategic location, as well as gold and silver mines. It was a bit of a Rome "wannabe." It was a place with ambition. It kept track of its successes, its increasing profile, and its growth. It was a town with big ideas about itself.

Paul had been a bit of a Roman "wannabe" himself. He had had major political ambitions. He, too, had kept track of his successes, his increasing profile, and the growth of his power. He had once been someone with big ideas about himself, too.

Those days were gone now. Paul knew who he had been without Christ, and who he was with Christ. Even in prison, his spirit was not brought low. His message was all about good news – news good enough to inspire him to scratch down these lines, "Rejoice in the Lord always; again I say, rejoice" (Phil 4:4). What kind of soul carries that joy even in jail, carries it well enough to call others to live in it?

Just for a moment, stop thinking about all the things you need to do, all the commitments you have made, all the other places you should be right now. Yes, there's too many and too much of everything. Think instead that in this place at this time you have an opportunity to stop time and think about what you really want, deep within, for Christmas. In this place called sanctuary, as you discover what that might be, let God know.

Now that we've been really honest about what we want most for Christmas, let's move on to another question. What is the quality you would most like to communicate to others over the Christmas season? If you aren't sure how to describe it, Paul gives us some to consider. His list includes the qualities of rejoicing, gentleness, not worrying, praying, giving thanks, and peace. Choose one of these qualities for yourself. Is it presently a quality that others would use to describe your countenance in this season? Are any of these qualities likely to describe you? If not, how do you think you would be described?

Earlier I suggested that Philippi was a Rome "wannabe." And I said that Paul had been a bit of a "wannabe" as well. This season can make "wannabes" out of many people. We may "wannabe" richer, more popular, more attractive, and more successful because this is a time when people make a show of their successes. They buy more and better gifts. They travel. They are invited to big parties with other important people. They create an atmosphere around them that suggests they know more about celebrating Christmas than the rest of us. And we may "wannabe" like that. We may have big ideas about ourselves, and big ideas about Christmas.

There's nothing wrong at all with having a wonderful celebration. But can there really be any "bigger idea" about Christmas than the idea that God has become one of us and is born to a poor young woman in a lowly stable? If we just stay with that idea as the biggest idea of the whole season, is it possible for us to set aside some of our other ambitions and goals and follow where that idea leads us?

Paul's words in this wonderful passage may suddenly find room in us and make a home, just as Mary found room in a stable to deliver Jesus. It becomes possible to rejoice without expensive equipment. It becomes easier to be gentle, because you are steward of this incredible idea that includes a baby who is born. Maybe you don't worry so much, because you're talking to God a little more in prayer and supplication with thanksgiving. And then there comes a peace, sort of like the peace that comes over a big city on Christmas Eve when it snows. It's like all the noise is wrapped in a muffler, and if you listen closely, it might be possible to even hear the angels singing. Oh, I know that doesn't make sense, but Paul says it is a peace that passes all understanding – a peace that will keep our hearts and minds in Christ Jesus.

There was something about the Philippians that was familiar to Paul. There was something in them he understood. I think there is something in us that Paul also understands. And he invites us to accept that the one big idea of this holy season is enough. We don't need any more big ideas or a substitute for the one we have. Paul could have used his letter to ask the Philippians to help him get out of jail. He could have complained about his situation or defended himself. But he did none of these things. Instead he stuck to the one big idea that had moved him to walk away from everything he had gathered to himself. So, when a man in prison – who never knew that his words would be in the Bible or in this sermon – asks us to rejoice during this season, maybe he knows what he's talking about.

As we engage the full and expectant spirit of Paul's writing, we are invited to look around us. With whom do we share our resources? For whom do we pray? Where is gentleness needed? In our own church, in our local community, and in national and global communities we have opportunities to express our joy in knowing the same Christ that Paul knew. We can express it through sharing our resources, offering gentleness, and praying. Here is the most effective way to witness to our faith in this holy season.

– Diane J. Strickland
Interim Minister
Springbank United Church
Calgary, Alberta

December 21, 2003

4th Sunday in Advent

Lessons

RCL	Mic 5:2-5a	Heb 10:5-10	Lk 1:39-45 (46-55)
Roman Catholic	Mic 5:1-4a	Heb 10:5-10	Lk 1:39-45
Episcopal (BCP)	Mic 5:2-4	Heb 10:5-10	Lk 1:39-49 (50-56)

Introduction to the Lessons

Lesson 1

***Micah 5:2-5a* (RCL); *Michal 5:1-4a* (RC); *Micah 5:2-4* (Epis)**

The prophet declares that from one of the least significant clans of Judah will come the one to rule all Israel. This ruler will gather those who have been far off and bring security and peace. He will be God's shepherd.

Lesson 2

***Hebrews 10:5-10* (RCL/RC/Epis)**

This section contains material from Psalm 40 concerning what God really wants from us – faithfulness in doing God's will. The law requiring offerings and sacrifices is abolished by the faithfulness of Christ in doing God's will.

Gospel

***Luke 1:39-45 (46-55)* (RCL); *Luke 1:39-45* (RC); *Luke 1:39-49 (50-56)* (Epis)**

Mary visits Elizabeth, whose own child leaps in her womb at Mary's greeting. Elizabeth offers an inspired greeting and shares her experience with Mary. The optional verses include the Magnificat and a verse indicating how long Mary stayed.

Theme

What does it mean to be open to Christmas?

Thought for the Day

Western Christians often travel an uneven road of low self-esteem and high arrogance. We bump from one place to another, knowing we don't really belong in either place. This story of two humble women, thrilling together at the realization that God has included them in the great story of salvation, includes that uneven road. But it also gives us another path to travel – the way of openness to things of faith.

Call to Worship

Leader: This is a season for humble souls to do the will of God.
People: Let us celebrate the Christmas story of humble beginnings, and begin again ourselves, humbled by God's grace.
Leader: For this is a season for humble souls to do the will of God.

Pastoral Prayer

Great is your name, generous God. We sing and speak many words of praise and thanksgiving to widen our faith in you, and broaden the scope of our response to you. Yet we never fully capture the expanse of your love that embraces the world, or the depth of your commitment to us. We pray this week for those who serve you in places without honor or recognition from others. Bless their lives with joy and wisdom, strength and good health. Draw us more deeply into the unlikely places where you are working without us knowing. Give us your spirit to discern where grace births new spiritual life in others and gives creativity to support and strengthen it. We remember also those women who even now carry new life within them. Keep them safe. We remember women who grieve children they will never have. Encourage them. We remember children born without privilege, those born with special needs, those who are abandoned by fathers and mothers. Advocate for them. And in every way draw us into these questions of life in joy and trouble. Keep us open to what is going on around us, and guide our searching for how your grace calls us to become partners with you in doing your will. These things we pray in Jesus' name. Amen.

Prayer of Confession

Holy God, we gather in this sanctuary with you. Gathered up by your Spirit's nudge in our lives, we pray now about the sin that threatens to scatter us from you, from each other, and from our neighbors in this world. If not for your promise to hear us in our need, we could not bear to bring you the failure in our lives to do your will. Thank you for accepting us as we come to you now. Let your mercy pass over our lives. Humble us with the grace that defeats our pride and restores our self-esteem. Let our song be joined with Mary's song, magnifying you and rejoicing in you, our Savior. Look with favor upon us and choose us again to be your servants. Through Jesus Christ, we pray. Amen.

Prayer of Dedication of Gifts and Self

Let us be open to your call upon our lives, O God. As a sign of our commitment we open our hands to share our resources with you. We open our hearts to share our hearts with you. We open our spirits to share our spirits with you. We open our minds to share our minds with you. We open our strength to share our strength with you. Receive these offerings, and by the power of your Holy Spirit, use them to bring the good news of your grace to the lives of others. Amen.

Sermon Summary

An intimate exchange between two pregnant women is not the heart of this passage. The heart of this passage is how the two women – unlikely choices by many standards – are open to God's will and the things of faith. All the reasons that it would be unlikely for us to be included in this work of God are transcended by our own openness to God's will and the things of faith.

Hymn of the Day

"Mary, Woman of the Promise"

Protestants tend to shy away from hymns and prayers that pay homage to Mary, the mother of Jesus. Yet her role in the life of Jesus, emphasized in the Christmas story, and her involvement in the early church as evidenced by her being mentioned in Acts 1:14, suggest that we ought to acknowledge her importance. This new hymn by Mary Frances Fleischacker provides an excellent opportunity to do just that. The words remind us of the role this courageous woman played, and the German carol tune "Quem Pastores" is a simple one to learn, yet carries a profound and lasting charm.

Children's Time

Unto Us a Child Is Born

(Preparation: Ask a pregnant woman in the congregation to talk with the children. Or, invite a mother to talk about her experience of being pregnant – what it feels like, any worries she might have, her hopes for the baby, and how excited she is.)

Wonder together how Mary might have felt, being pregnant with Jesus. This close to his birth, she would have been very large indeed. She could feel Jesus moving and kicking inside her.

Mary went to visit a relative of hers named Elizabeth who was also going to have a baby. When Mary walked in the door, Elizabeth's baby leapt for joy inside her, and Elizabeth was filled with the Holy Spirit. She told Mary how blessed she was because the baby she was carrying was to be the Savior sent by God. How do you think this made Mary feel? Mary sang a song of joy, thanking God for this baby.

This week, as you and your families finish up your preparations for Christmas, think about Mary and how excited she was about her baby, Jesus. Who can you tell about Jesus' birth? What will you say? *(Invite responses.)*

The Sermon

The Pregnant Pause for Grace

Hymns

Beginning of Worship: "All Earth Is Waiting"
Sermon Hymn: "My Soul Gives Glory to My God"
Closing Hymn: "Long Ago, Prophets Knew"

Scripture

Luke 1:39-45 (46-55) (For sermon materials on Hebrews 10:5-10, see the 2003 May/June planning issue of *The Clergy Journal* and on Micah 5:2-5a, see the September 2003 issue of *The Clergy Journal.*)

Mary is in a hurry to visit Elizabeth. She is the only person that Mary can imagine telling about the angel's visit. She arrives at Elizabeth's house. Together they are free to express what their bodies already communicate – God is birthing a holy promise from Mary's womb.

In the past, some scholars within the church may have treated this text with the sterile surgical gloves of men who knew they didn't know what they were reading but wanted to respect it. It was unfamiliar territory: women talking together, womb business, a secret made known, the soul friendship of pregnancy, and finally, a woman's song of faith like nothing sung before.

I know that the first telephone call I made after telling my husband and my parents that I was pregnant was to my closest girlfriend. I remember buying maternity clothes with her and trading ideas about dealing with nausea. One of the most vivid memories I have is her visiting me with my brand new baby, her own belly swollen with eight months of pregnancy. It was an intense period of women talking, womb business, the soul friendship of pregnancy, and a knowing that we had entered a work of great mystery and sanctity. We were partners with God in a brand new way. We sang a song of faith we had never sung before.

So it does not surprise me that Mary goes to Elizabeth, or that Elizabeth discerns and declares God's special blessing on Mary as her own child leaps in her womb. She needs no angel to tell her anything! I feel a connection to the story of the two women coming together and what passed between them. This visit is set within a long and great tradition of women sharing the joys and the struggles of their pregnancies with each other. And perhaps at some level we understand that the possibility of some extraordinary act of God in our pregnancies is not so far-fetched.

But do we have to be women, or even pregnant women, before we can discern that God is fulfilling the ancient and eternal promise of salvation? What about the rest of humankind who never carry a child within them? Are they excluded from this experience of spiritual discernment and celebration?

The heart of this incredible meeting is not that its main characters just happened to meet specific criteria that excluded everyone but them, or that we have to be people in the same situation before we can enter the story! The heart of this story is exactly the opposite. Unlikely people in every respect receive the capacity to both birth and discern God's fulfilment of the ancient and eternal promise. Unlikely people. If that, then, is the heart of this story, then it is also the gift of it. You do not need to be a pregnant woman, or a woman at all, to share in the miracle of what God is doing!

God chooses the language and images of birth to speak of the way in which grace enters our own lives through Jesus Christ. We are reborn in Christ. And faith is birthed within us. Its seed is planted within, fertilized, and grows to maturity. We then deliver this faith to the world in acts of compassion, justice, mercy, and love. We do not need a womb to do any of this, or to recognize it coming to pass in the life of another person. We are all unlikely places for God to visit with the grace of the gospel.

As we read this story, we may read it as an event far away, long ago, and unlikely to happen here. This is true in some sense. But the sense of "unlikeliness" should always be a clue to this season. It's always a sign that you might have suddenly entered the Christmas story, joining the great cast of those unlikely individuals who first lived it. The only real criteria we can see operating in this story is that these two women were open to God's call and open to God's plan. They had no power, no status, no wealth. But they were open to the things of faith.

When Mary sings her song of faith, called the Magnificat, she sings of how God has chosen the unlikely person and lifted up the lowly person. Her joy is that the humble soul is God's choice as a partner, and that the proud are scattered and the rich leave empty-handed. Think for a moment. What song would you have sung? What song would you sing now if you knew that God had entrusted you with God's greatest treasure?

Maybe it's difficult for you to imagine that song. But can you see what makes you the unlikely partner for God in this enterprise of grace entering our lives and our world? Maybe we have power, status, and wealth. Maybe we have only a loosely formed idea of faith. Maybe we can not imagine God's promise anymore. These make us "unlikely" by the standards of Mary's song. But perhaps we should focus again on the necessary criteria. Being open to things of faith has more power to include us in the story than all the details that exclude us from it.

December 21, 2003
4th Sunday in Advent

We cannot keep God at arm's length and expect to be at God's side in the story. We cannot put conditions on God's communication with us and expect to hear everything God says. We cannot prejudge other people and expect to understand how God is moving in their lives. Being open to things of faith means placing ourselves in God's presence and among God's people. Being open to things of faith means cultivating an attitude of listening through God's Word, through God's people, through dreams, through nature, through art – and on and on it goes. Where are we not open at all? Where are we not open enough? Mary and Elizabeth were simply open. They didn't even bother to dwell on what was likely or unlikely. Instead, they lived openly with God and it brought them to this place.

When we celebrate this story year after year, we do so in the hope that we will find our place in it. We want to find that this story is not about "remember when" but "still today." Still today God finds unlikely people who are open. Still today God plants a seed of promise. Still today God fulfills that promise through our lives. Still today. This very day. Pause in these days of expectancy. We may be pregnant with grace.

– Diane J. Strickland
Interim Minister
Springbank United Church
Calgary, Alberta

December 24, 2003

Christmas Eve

Lessons

RCL	Isa 9:2-7	Titus 2:11-14	Lk 2:1-14 (15-20)
Roman Catholic	Isa 9:1-6	Titus 2:11-14	Lk 2:1-14
Episcopal (BCP)	Isa 9:2-4, 6-7	Titus 2:11-14	Lk 2:1-14 (15-20)

Introduction to the Lessons

Lesson 1

Isaiah 9:2-7 **(RCL);** ***Isaiah 9:1-6*** **(RC);** ***Isaiah 9:2-4, 6-7*** **(Epis)**

This poetic celebration of the messianic king uses powerful images of light and dark, yokes of oppression broken, a child's birth, glorious names for the child, and the way the child will exercise authority. The promises of joy, justice, peace, and growth come with his authority.

Lesson 2

Titus 2:11-14 **(RCL/RC/Epis)**

The writer announces the coming of salvation in Jesus Christ. Moral imperatives for living are given in the context of waiting for our "blessed hope" and the "manifestation of glory." The work of Christ is described as an offering and a redemption from iniquity.

Gospel

Luke 2:1-14 (15-20) **(RCL/Epis);** ***Luke 2:1-14*** **(RC)**

The writer tells the story of Mary and Joseph's journey to Bethlehem and Jesus' birth. The angels appear to shepherds with good tidings. In the optional verses, the shepherds go to find the child and share the message of the angels.

Theme

The Christ child is our new beginning.

Thought for the Day

People often long for new beginnings. But sometimes we do not engage the opportunities we are given for new beginnings because we cannot let go of things we need to leave behind. What do you need to put down in order to hold the baby, the promise, the hope, and the new beginning of this night?

Call to Worship

Leader: Do not be afraid; I have great tidings of joy for all people.
People: Tell us great tidings. We are not afraid.
Leader: A Savior is born for you this day.
People: Where can we find him?
Leader: You can find the child wrapped up with cloth, and lying in a manger.
People: Glory to God in the highest heaven, and peace on earth among God's own.

– Based on Luke 2:10-14

Pastoral Prayer

O God of mercy and truth, tonight your eternal mystery is caught by time, and humanity wraps its arms around the one who holds the universe. We pray for the special needs of people in this season. For those struggling with addictions in an atmosphere that leads them into temptation, grant them strength and wisdom to call on you. For parents who depend on the generosity of others for their childrens' Christmas gifts and food, grant them the freedom to receive these things as from your hands, and to enjoy them. For children who share the secrets of an unhappy home, grant them protection and peace. For those in hospitals and care facilities, for their families and staff who will care for them, grant them your presence and your joy. For people of all ages whose grief is made fresh by the season's memories, grant them comfort and hope. For countries where trouble is often the people's portion, especially remembering Israel, Palestine, Ireland, and Afghanistan, grant that your body in those places will be sources of justice and love. Let us wake tomorrow knowing that we – like the baby – have been born for a holy purpose. Amen.

Prayer of Confession

O Holy God, this night you wait with us for the child to be born. Thank you for your Spirit's presence and for the promise of this night. Lead us into that promise now, and into the hope of the child who has been born for us. Thank you for all that is familiar in the Christmas story, and all that you will make new again in our lives. Take our personal stories and mix them up with the story of the Christ child, that we will find ourselves inside your Christmas miracle, letting its power and its healing transform our lives. May we rise forgiven, renewed, and freed by the glory that shines all around us tonight. Through Christ we pray. Amen.

Prayer of Dedication of Gifts and Self

We respond to you this night, O God, remembering that you came into our world and were born for us. We respond with welcome, celebration, and our offerings. Receive these gifts as a trust between us. Through them may the whole world know you are the Wonderful Counselor, Mighty God, Everlasting Father, and Prince of Peace. Amen.

Sermon Summary

What does a baby mean in your family, your congregation, and your sacred texts? We explore what the baby of this night means to the world through the beautiful words of the prophet Isaiah. We are invited to embrace that meaning in our own lives as new beginnings. But first we may need to put down other things that we are carrying around. If our arms are to be full this night, let them be full of the child who is born for us.

Hymn of the Day

"Star-Child"

Prolific New Zealand hymn writer Shirley Erena Murray has wrapped a number of powerful and complex images and symbols in the simple language of this text. Set to a tune by American composer and hymnal editor Carlton R. Young, the hymn captures Advent hope and longing in the wonder and mystery of Christmas Eve.

The entire hymn can be sung in unison or soloists (including children) can sing the stanzas with the congregation joining in the refrain.

Children's Time

The Light of the World

(Preparation: Bring a flashlight and a string of Christmas lights ready to plug in, with an extension cord if necessary).

Have you ever noticed how beautiful the darkness of night can be? What are things you like about nighttime? *(Invite responses.)*

While darkness can be beautiful and peaceful, we can stumble if we need to move around when it's dark. *(Hold up the flashlight.)* What can I use this for?

Light shows us the way when we need to go somewhere or do something. Light makes it possible to work or play. That's why light has always been so important to people. Light makes people feel safe and hopeful.

At Christmas time, we talk about light and use lights. Our Advent candles give off light. We use lights on our Christmas trees. *(Plug in the string of Christmas lights and leave them glowing.)* Sometimes Jesus is called the "light of the world." Jesus is not a light like these lights, but Jesus helps us feel safe and hopeful. Jesus helps us see God's love.

Think about it – a tiny little baby born in a stable is God's light to the world. What a wonderful God we have, to come to us in Jesus to light up the way to see God's love.

The Sermon

An Armful of Promise

Hymns

Beginning of Worship: "O Little Town of Bethlehem"
Sermon Hymn: "Infant Holy, Infant Lowly"
Closing Hymn: "Silent Night"

Scripture

Isaiah 9:2-7 (For sermon materials on Titus 2:11-14, see the 2003 May/June planning issue of *The Clergy Journal* and on Luke 2:1-14 (15-20), see the September 2003 issue of *The Clergy Journal.*)

Every baby that comes into our lives comes as a chance to begin again. Even a story about the coming of a baby can be that compelling. Perhaps that is why the Christmas story remains so compelling, whether its hearers possess a Christian faith that is certain or uncertain. A baby gives us back the word "miracle" in an age that loves too much the limits of reasons. It gives us back a belief in the future in an age when people don't often think much past today. It gives us back our vocation to nurture others in an age that worries most about self.

The baby that comes into our lives doesn't have to be our baby, a baby in our family, or a close friend's baby. If a baby comes into our congregation, that's enough. If a baby comes into our sacred texts, that's enough. With babies come new beginnings.

We realize that there is something very sad about a congregation with no babies in it. In the drama of the Old Testament stories it is often the case that the Hebrews were one generation away from extinction. They were always on the edge of losing their future. A church without babies is beginning to feel the edge of that abyss under their feet. When a baby is brought into Christian community, we receive a holy commission – to begin anew the process of nurturing disciples, affirming emerging gifts and talents, and sowing seeds of ministry into those who will be the Church long after we are gone. Every baby that comes into our lives as the church is an opportunity to begin again to live into the very purpose for which we exist.

Tonight the prophet Isaiah heralds the coming of the baby who will be Messiah for Israel. The prophet's words are seared into the Christmas memories of the faithful, rising up from the depths of our being and, despite their familiarity, never losing their power to command attention. The hope, longing, trust, and the vision of God's reign that they describe endure. Here prophecy and poetry blend together. And every word of this passage leads into and out of this one line, "For a child has been born for us" (Isa 9:6a). A child has been born for us.

Our lives will go on for 364 days before we next hear the story of the Bethlehem baby. In that time we will face all kinds of things we did not know were coming. Just think for a moment about what you faced this past year. What joys and sorrows came your way? What disappointments and successes did you experience? What did you lose this year, and what did you gain? No matter how you respond to these questions, this story is here tonight for you. Because every baby that comes into our lives also comes as a chance to begin again – especially the baby in our sacred text.

You may never hold a baby in your arms that you call your own, but tonight you can hold this baby. For a child has been born for us. The Christ child. It is your chance and my chance to believe again in the future. It is our chance to believe in our future together as a church. It is our chance to believe in our future together as the people of this planet earth. Tonight the story says that the future comes into our world in our flesh and blood. The future comes as a child born. We can hold the future in our own flesh and blood and know for sure that the future is God's.

This is our chance. But in order to take advantage of this wonderful story, we will have to do something. We will have to put down whatever else we are carrying in our arms in order to receive the Christ child. Isaiah says that the Messiah breaks the yoke of our burden (v. 4) and the rod of our oppressor, but sometimes we hang on to the burden anyway. Too often, we carry things that need to be laid down – old grudges and wounds, regret and guilt, anger and fear. The yoke of our burden may be broken, but we choose to carry its broken pieces. It is as if we don't know enough to put it down. But we cannot carry those things and the Christ child, too.

What have you brought with you tonight? What burden taxes your spirit and uses your energy? What baggage have you hauled around with you for way too long? Where are you dragging anchor? Whatever you have brought here this night, lay it down and let it go. Lay it down and let it go. Because when you've put it down you will find your arms will be free, free to pick up the Son of God, free to let him come close to you, free to let him surprise you with hope and strength, forgiveness and healing, trust and joy.

People come to Christmas Eve service for many different reasons. But each of us needs to hear again this year, "For a child has been born for us." A child has been born for us. And so the Christmas story endures. At its center is a baby, a baby in whom all the potential for new beginnings has been fully realized for our sake. And for that baby people set aside old quarrels, people let their hearts be strangely warmed, and people will explore the possibility of faith. They know as we know that a baby is a chance to begin again.

It's getting late. The candles burn down. Our children need to sleep. The service is almost over. Are your arms free yet? Don't wait too much longer. For even now God is saying, "Here is the one born for you. It's nearly your turn to hold him. Are you ready? Are you ready? Here he is!" Go ahead. Take him in your arms. You can do it. God gives you the strength to do it!

If our arms are to be full this night, let them be full of the child who is born for us.

– Diane J. Strickland
Interim Minister
Springbank United Church
Calgary, Alberta

December 25, 2003

Christmas Day

Lessons

RCL	Isa 52:7-10	Heb 1:1-4 (5-12)	Jn 1:1-14
Roman Catholic	Isa 52:7-10	Heb 1:1-6	Jn 1:1-18 or 1:1-5, 9-14
Episcopal (BCP)	Isa 52:7-10	Heb 1:1-12	Jn 1:1-14

Introduction to the Lessons

Lesson 1

***Isaiah 52:7-10* (RCL/RC/Epis)**

The prophet exalts the beauty of the messenger who brings good news and invites us to sing out the messenger's arrival. We are called to rejoice, for soon the whole world will see God's salvation.

Lesson 2

***Hebrews 1:1-4 (5-12)* (RCL); *Hebrews 1:1-6* (RC); *Hebrews 1:1-12* (Epis)**

God speaks in many ways – through prophets before and now through a son of God's own appointing. The Son of God is imprinted with God, purifying and sustaining all things, finally sitting at the right hand of God.

Gospel

***John 1:1-14* (RCL/Epis); *John 1:1-18* (RC)**

John tells us the story of God's relationship with creation using the "Word" as pretext, prophecy, and incarnation – Jesus Christ.

Theme

The good news still comes, whether or not you've been waiting for it.

Thought for the Day

Often we drift through the activities and events of the Christmas season with less discernment and discrimination than we employ during the rest of the year. We let other people set the meaning for the season. But each year, in the Christmas story, we have an opportunity to hear for ourselves the good news that is very old news. Perhaps we haven't been waiting for the good news, but it comes for us just as well as for those who have been waiting with expectation. Is it time to decide what this day means to you?

Call to Worship

Leader: In the beginning was the Word
People: And the Word was with God, and the Word was God.
Leader: And the Word became flesh and lived among us
People: And we have seen his glory, full of grace and truth.
Leader: Thanks be to God, Jesus has come! Merry Christmas!
People: Thanks be to God! Merry Christmas!

– Based on John 1:1, 14

Pastoral Prayer

O Great Comforter, draw near to us this blessed Christmas day. Let our voices sing with joy and gladness. Let our smiles be given freely and our embraces be certain. Let our prayers also go forth as good news in this world you so treasure. We pray for people caught in memories this day, with grief both tender and raw. We pray for those who on this day of great promise feel even more keenly the edge of injustice and oppression around the world. Sustain those who stand for the promises of this day and those who have yet to receive them. We pray also for people in hospitals and care facilities and those who tend to their needs. We remember people from whom we are separated this day, by distances both physical and emotional. We pray for countries facing war and strife, and remember the people of Israel and Palestine this day, praying for peace and reconciliation. May we live our lives this Christmas season with spiritual depth, witnessing to a true meaning of this day for all people. These things we pray in Jesus' name. Amen.

Prayer of Confession

O God of Christmas, you confound the complexity of human trouble with a simple story of simple people who trusted you completely. Into their hands and their world you placed your own Son. On this Christmas day we pray that Jesus' grace will confound the complexity of our own troubles. Be born, O Christ, in the rude stables of our hearts. Banish fear and soften anger. Temper our ambition and overcome the bonds of sin. Come again by the power of the Holy Spirit, and let us receive you with the joy of our new freedom, forgiveness, and healing. Through Christ we pray. Amen.

Prayer of Dedication of Gifts and Self

Ever-giving God, from the fullness of the Word made flesh we have all received grace upon grace. With open hands and hearts we dedicate these gifts to the ministry of Jesus Christ, and offer ourselves for your service. May your Spirit rest upon us, that the world may know the good news has come. Amen.

Sermon Summary

The prophet's words celebrate the theme of waiting for the arrival of the messenger who brings good news, and foretell how that news will spread to the ends of the earth. Many of us have not really been waiting for much more than "the usual" Christmas celebration. We are challenged to explore ways to engage the good news of this day so that we decide for ourselves what the day will mean, instead of accepting the secondhand meanings that others give this day.

Hymn of the Day

"Joy to the World"

English Congregationalist pastor Isaac Watts frequently used the psalms as a basis for Christian hymns, and this, perhaps his most famous, is no exception. Taking as his primary text Psalm 98, the traditional psalm for Christmas Day, Watts reinterprets its words of praise in light of the nativity.

The tune "Antioch" by Lowell Mason begins with a simple descending D major scale reflecting a peal of bells as might be heard on Christmas Day.

Children's Time

Feet

I'm thinking about feet today. What are you thinking about? *(Invite responses.)* I'm thinking about feet. Not because I got socks for Christmas, but because today's reading from the Bible mentions feet.

Let's take a look at our feet. *(Have everyone hold their feet out and gaze at them.)* Did you know that your feet are important to God? Your feet are important to God, especially on this Christmas Day. The Bible passage we're reading in worship today says, "How beautiful are the feet of the messenger, the messenger who carries the good news of God to all the people."

Now we don't have wings. We can't fly around telling shepherds the good news about Jesus' birth and how Jesus brings God's love to us. But we do have feet, and we can use them to walk up to our friends and people in our family to say, "Merry Christmas! God loves you!" Let's practice that right now, then see how many times you can use your feet and be a messenger of that good news today.

The Sermon

A Day for Meaning

Hymns

Beginning of Worship: "O Come All Ye Faithful"
Sermon Hymn: "What Child Is This?"
Closing Hymn: "Joy to the World"

Scripture

Isaiah 52:7-10 (For sermon materials on John 1:1-14, see the 2003 May/June planning issue of *The Clergy Journal* and on Hebrews 1:1-4 (5-12), see the September 2003 issue of *The Clergy Journal*.)

When we await the imminent birth of a grandchild, or niece or nephew, we live differently. We tell people where we are going to be and how we can be reached. We check our messages more often than usual. If we can't be near a phone we might have someone wait by our phone in case the long-awaited call should come. We may make arrangements to travel to where the baby is to be born. Sometimes parents will make a list of who to call first, second, third – and then those people have a list of people that they call. And if we get the news in person, we hug and kiss the messenger as if he or she was the good news itself. Good news is something we look forward to receiving, and when we finally get it, we want the whole world to know.

Today is that day for Christians all over the world. The child who was promised was born today, two thousand years ago. And we celebrate. Boy, do we celebrate! Our churches are dressed for the season. We sing special songs. We read the most important Bible passages for the season. We give even more back to our communities with special service and mission initiatives. We make special food and share it with each other and with those less fortunate. We have parties and get-togethers. We visit family and neighbors. We phone friends and family who don't live near enough to visit. We dress our homes for the season and give each other gifts to show our love, and to symbolize the great gift that God gave us in the Christ child. In fact, we have made this season into such a big celebration that even people who don't celebrate Christ's birth celebrate our season of giving and sing our songs of faith. And today is the day that started the celebration.

At first we did not know that Jesus was our child, too. We were Gentiles. He was Messiah for Israel. But then, through Jesus' life and love, he made it clear that he came for everyone – everyone who had been waiting for him and everyone who hadn't. So it actually makes a lot of sense for people today to celebrate this season with us, even if they aren't preparing for the celebration of Jesus' birth. Jesus Christ always has and always will come for those who aren't waiting for his birth, as well as for those who are.

Isaiah gives us a great picture of how good news arrives and then spreads. The messenger brings the message the people have waited to hear. Just the way we live differently when we are expecting good news about a baby born, these people lived differently, too. They were so anxious to get the news that they posted sentinels to keep watch for the messenger. And when they saw the messenger – well – was there ever a more beautiful messenger than the one the sentinels spotted that day? Even the messenger's feet are beautiful!

Then the "ruins of Jerusalem" (Isa 52:9) are invited to break out singing as well. Israel has comfort! Jerusalem is redeemed! So, sing! Then stand back, because "all the ends of the earth shall see the salvation of our God" (v. 10). Just imagine the rejoicing as the ripples of good news go out over the whole earth.

One of the things that I notice in today's passage is that by the time the first messenger arrives with the good news, it's already old news. God has already acted in fulfillment of the promises. And with every ripple of sharing the good news, we get farther and farther away from the actual moment. It's old news, but somehow it is still good news, and news worth telling. Here we are, two thousand years later on Christmas morning, on a different continent than Bethlehem, and this is still news that has to be told.

We know this story – its characters, its rhythm, its mystery, and its enduring power. But there is always the possibility that we don't know yet that the news is really for us. We hear it, but perhaps it goes right by us and settles deep into Grandma, or maybe our neighbor, or even our spouse. It goes right by us, year after year after year.

Maybe it's been going right by you – a kind of "same old, same old." The story seems quaint. It's familiar. It's religious. But maybe it has never been good news that makes you want to sing the way these people in this passage sing. We all live with such a commercial build-up to Christmas that it is difficult for the good news to break through the layers of stuff around this day. There is a lot of "giving and getting" in the air, it seems. Most of us know we are going to get something, especially if we asked for it nicely. We might even be anticipating it, and waiting for it, even planning for receiving it.

In between all that you have planned for this Christmas Day, make room for a moment with God and the story of this day. No, do more than make room. Anticipate the moment. Wait for it. Even plan for it. And in that moment, tell yourself the story of this day from memory. You may surprise yourself. I'll bet you can remember whole chunks of scripture, names, phrases, and images. Give yourself the gift of the good news. Spend some time thinking about the details you remember. Imagine how the people are feeling in the story. What if you were Joseph? Or Mary? One of the angels? Or a shepherd? Then just let yourself *be* yourself. What are you feeling? Could this baby make a difference in your life? Do you want him to? Could it be that he is the One who brings God's love to people like us?

December 25, 2003
Christmas Day

The good news of this day belongs to the people who waited a long time for it, as well as the people who never saw it coming their way at all. The ripples of this story are still going out to touch the lives of people everywhere. They will continue to go out until there are no more December 25ths to mark the birth of Christ.

At some point we have to decide what we want this day to mean. Some mean it for profit. Some mean it for holiday. Some mean it for family. But God means it for love, a love that wears our flesh and breathes our air, a love strong enough to save us from death – whether or not we've been waiting for it. At some point we have to decide what we want this day to mean. What, then, will this day mean to you?

– Diane J. Strickland
Interim Minister
Springbank United Church
Calgary, Alberta

December 28, 2003

1st Sunday after Christmas
RC: The Holy Family, Not Listed

Lessons

RCL	1 Sam 2:18-20, 26	Col 3:12-17	Lk 2:41-52
Episcopal (BCP)	Isa 61:10–62:3	Gal 3:23-25; 4:4-7	Jn 1:1-18

Introduction to the Lessons

Lesson 1

(1) *1 Samuel 2:18-20, 26* (RCL)

After committing her son to God's service in the temple, Hannah and her husband, Elkanah, returned annually and brought him a robe. Eli, the high priest, whose own sons were scoundrels, blessed Hannah and Elkanah for offering Samuel to God.

(2) *Isaiah 61:10–62:3* (Epis)

Rejoicing in God's faithfulness, the prophet Isaiah sees himself chosen and welcomed by God. He sings of the hope of God's righteousness made manifest, for the sake of his people who languish under domination. He promises that his nation, worn and discouraged, will soon be a crown of beauty in God's hand.

Lesson 2

(1) *Colossians 3:12-17* (RCL)

How are we to live as God's chosen ones? The writer of Colossians calls us to live in community, bearing one another in love. It is the peace of Christ that grounds us, and it is in Christ's name that we live.

(2) *Galatians 3:23-25; 4:4-7* (Epis)

The faithful at Galatia needed to work out their relationship to the Jewish roots of Christian faith. They had to come to terms with the law, which embodied God's covenant with the people of Israel. In Christ, the demands of the law are fulfilled. Christ makes us children of God.

December 28, 2003
1st Sunday after Christmas
RC: The Holy Family, Not Listed

Gospel

(1) *Luke 2:41-52* (RCL)

Jesus' parents traveled to Jerusalem annually, much as Samuel's parents had. When he was 12, Jesus stayed to learn from and question the teachers there. He was doing his Father's business, beginning the ministry that was foretold at his birth.

(2) *John 1:1-18* (Epis)

In the poetry and rich imagery of this prologue to John's gospel, we hear an introduction and a preview of the depth and profound meaning of Jesus' life and ministry. He was in the beginning. He became flesh. From him, we receive grace.

Theme

Clothed in Grace

Thought for the Day

Our busy lives often rob us of spiritual time – time to reflect and watch for God at work in our world. God invites us to take the time to put on the clothing of grace, to ask and learn and ponder the wonder of God's love for us.

Call to Worship

God-with-us, we gather to worship you, our Prince of Peace. We are hungry for your word and eager to grow in grace. Be with us, guide us, nourish us.

Pastoral Prayer

Christ, our Lord, we have celebrated your nativity. Gather us into your people, children of your promise. Bless this congregation, that in the coming year, all we do is in your name. O Gracious One,

Hear our prayer.

Jesus, you wore compassion and love every moment of your life. Dress us as your disciples, that others may see you in us. We remember before you those in our community in special need of your love and hope. O Gracious One,

Hear our prayer.

We bring before you a world in need of healing. Teach us to ask before we answer, to listen before we decide, to love before we act. Give all leaders an extra measure of humility and patience, and all followers, wisdom. O Gracious One,

Hear our prayer.

O Gracious One, fill us with your grace. Give us courage to see and use the gifts you have given us for ministry in our world. Let the word of Christ dwell in us richly. We look to you for life and hope. In Jesus' name we pray. Amen.

Prayer of Confession

Prince of Peace, word of God incarnate, we doubt your power, your wisdom, and your mercy. We do not consistently respect each other as wonders of your creation, and too often, we approach our relationships with suspicion and envy. We do not cherish the earth as our source, a womb of your making. We confess to you these failings. We ask you to clothe us in your grace, that we might engage our lives sure of your unfailing love, so that, freed from trying always to please you, we might love others and our world with abundant joy.

The God of grace is faithful beyond our imagining. God created us as limited human beings. In the name of Jesus, we are free of needing to compete for God's favor. We are chosen, loved, cherished, and given to be a gift. Amen.

Prayer of Dedication of Gifts and Self

We offer our gifts to you, our newborn King. As you have so generously given yourself, so we give ourselves to you and your service. We commit our lives to the purpose you have created in us, and seek to live together with justice and mercy for the whole creation. Amen.

Sermon Summary

Where we would seek to be clothed in righteousness, God clothes us in grace. We are invited to see the miracle of life beyond our fears and anxieties.

Hymn of the Day

"What Child Is This?"

William Chatterton Dix was a businessman in Bristol, England, who also wrote a number of poems and hymns, this being among his most famous. Some versions repeat the same refrain throughout, although in its original form (preserved in some modern hymnals), the text of the refrain changes each time and carries a sense of foreboding as it speaks of the realities of the cross. While some find this detracts from the Christmas mood, others find it offers a more complete answer to the question that forms the hymn's title.

The tune "Greensleeves" is an English folk tune dating to at least the 15th century.

Children's Time

Jesus Grows Up

The Bible tells us about the many special things that happened around the time Jesus was born. Today the Bible reading tells us about something that happened when Jesus was a boy. Each year, Mary and Joseph took Jesus to Jerusalem for the big Passover festival. Worshiping God was important for this family. They traveled to Jerusalem with a large group of friends and relatives.

When Jesus was 12, they made the trip as usual. On the way back home, Mary and Joseph thought that Jesus was with them. Have you ever been with a large group of friends or classmates and suddenly noticed that a person was missing? That's what happened. After they'd been on the road for a day, Mary and Joseph realized that Jesus wasn't with the group. They raced back to Jerusalem and searched everywhere. They found Jesus in the temple. There he was, sitting with the teachers, discussing the scriptures with them.

When Jesus was a boy, he spent time learning about God's word in the scriptures. What questions would you like to ask about the scriptures, the book we call the Bible? *(Invite responses.)* I hope you will talk about your questions with your families and your teachers, just like Jesus did.

The Sermon

Clothed in Grace

Hymns

Beginning of Worship: "There's a Star in the East"
Sermon Hymn: "Once Again My Heart Rejoices"
Closing Hymn: "Your Little Ones, Dear Lord"

Scripture

Luke 2:41-52 (For additional sermon materials on this passage, see the 2003 May/June planning issue and the September 2003 issue of *The Clergy Journal.*)

"Now, every year his parents went to Jerusalem for the festival of the Passover" (Lk 2:41). Every year. Regular. Predictable. Probably without fail.

Kind of like you – here in church again the first Sunday after Christmas. Such regular faithfulness on the part of parents could drive an adolescent wild. "What, church again?" But those of us who show up on the Sunday after Christmas may very well value the habit of churchgoing and the gifts this discipline affords us.

The Gospel of Luke reveals Mary and Joseph to be the rule-following types. Save their tumultuous beginnings as a couple – surprise pregnancy, post-conception marriage, birth in a stable away from home – they clearly followed the laws of their faith. Jesus was circumcised on the eighth day as was the custom, and when it came time for Mary to be purified after her childbirth (because Jesus was a boy, on the thirty-third day), she and Joseph went to the temple again with the requisite offering. There they met the faithful Simeon and Anna (who never left the temple in her old age) and heard these holy elders offer predictions and praise for their young son.

So it is not a surprise that Mary and Joseph would make an annual trek to Jerusalem for the holy festival of Passover. They were, in many ways, clothing themselves with righteousness, since following the rules was a critical element of faith in their Jewish world. This trip was an act of faithfulness in lives of faith whose motto might have been "keep on keeping on."

We know the wisdom of this kind of steadiness. If you are a regular churchgoer, perhaps you know that funny, incomplete feeling of skipping worship one week – like something is missing from the week and from your soul. Though every week may not be a spiritual high, each week adds to the bank of memory and experience of worshiping, communing, and bonding. And sometimes, isn't it true, the whole thing hits home and you leave worship a changed person – renewed perhaps, or resolved or reconciled. Your life, your outlook, and your understanding is fundamentally changed, generally for the better.

Perhaps this is what happened to Jesus that Passover when he was 12. Perhaps something he heard or experienced in the familiar rituals struck him in a way that was new and inspiring. We can only imagine, because the story does not tell us.

What we do know is that his parents left Jerusalem without him, though they thought he was somewhere with the gang of relatives and friends with whom they traveled. It was not until the next day that they realized he was not along. I do not know what fears possessed Mary's heart, and Joseph's too. Would they have worried about child abduction as we might? Did they think they had a runaway on their hands? What guilt overwhelmed them? He was, after all, only 12. He was alone in a big city. Who knows where he was and with whom?

Three days they searched for him. Perhaps they checked the temple last, thinking that their adolescent son would be anywhere but there. Parents among us can understand Mary's burst of impatience when they finally found him. Perhaps if they had paused a moment before running to Jesus, they would have seen their curious son sitting at the feet of the teachers that they, themselves, admired. Perhaps they would have noticed his engagement, his curiosity, and the mutual respect that must have already been apparent between Jesus and his teachers.

From the sounds of it, Mary and Joseph were overwhelmed. "Child, why have you treated us like this?" (v. 48). They were singularly focused. They could see and feel nothing but their own anxiety. Jesus had broken their rules, and they took it personally.

Those among us who are parents would have, too, is my guess. Three days of panic would be hard to set aside. If and when life doesn't go as planned, don't *you* take it personally? If the circumstances had been different, they would have been proud of him, but they could not see the big picture. They would have seen the wonder of their son emerging, a person of faith, curious to know more about that which grounded them so firmly. They would have been proud, and perhaps they were later, once they had settled down.

Sometimes, our insistence on doing things the right way gets in our way. Sometimes being clothed in righteousness is a burden rather than a blessing. Moments of grace are rarely predictable.

Imagine, for example, the utter surprise that Jesus, this curious 12-year-old, would turn out to be the Messiah – the Prince of Peace long promised. I suspect there had been precocious boys before. Perhaps some of those temple teachers had been just such boys when they were young. But the Messiah?

We know the disruption Jesus would cause in their lives. In 20 short years or so, they would reach the end of their rope with him. Perceived as a profound threat to their carefully tended truce with the Roman occupiers, they will kill him, hoping that the disruptions would end. These teachers in the temple took Jesus' dangerous love quite personally, and tried to snuff it out. They chose murder in order to protect their right-ness.

What if God were to react in such a way? What if our disruptions of God's life were taken so personally, caused such anxiety, conjured such a threat? We do, of course, disrupt God's life quite regularly. What must it do to God to watch us pillage the earth God so carefully fashioned and then gave to us as gift? What grief must we cause when we do not trust God's ability to provide for us, or perhaps even worse, do not trust God's steadfast love for us? Would we blame God for exasperation with our inability to get along with each other, whether it is across the dinner table or across the globe? Wouldn't it be reasonable for God to demand to know why we are treating God this way?

It would be reasonable, but it is not God's way. God does not demand that we make it up, even the score, or grovel in shame. God chooses to love us first, before we do anything. God chooses to bring life into a manger, a baby to the temple, a curious teenager to the feet of teachers, a just, young man to his death, and a dead man to life so that we might know how much we are loved.

God treasures us, cheers for us, and grows us. Like Hannah of old, who brought her son holy clothing that he might continually become the priest he was, God brings us grace as a gift and a promise. Clothed in grace, we are free to see God at work in our world, to love each other, and to give witness to the wonder of God's love.

– Catherine Malotky
Evangelical Lutheran Church in America
Minnetonka, Minnesota

January 4, 2004

2nd Sunday after Christmas

Lessons

RCL	Jer 31:7-14 or Sir 24:1-12	Eph 1:3-14	Jn 1:(1-9) 10-18
Roman Catholic	Sir 24:1-4, 12-16	Eph 1:3-6, 15-18	Jn 1:1-18 or 1:1-5, 9-14
Episcopal (BCP)	Jer 31:7-14	Eph 1:3-6, 15-19a	Mt 2:13-15, 19-23 or Lk 2:41-52 or Mt 2:1-12

Introduction to the Lessons

Lesson 1

(1) *Jeremiah 31:7-14* (RCL/Epis)

Exiled, the people of Israel wondered why God seemed to have abandoned them. They came to believe that it was because of their own disobedience. What words of grace Jeremiah offers them – words of forgiveness and welcome back into God's embrace.

(2) *Sirach 24:1-4, 12-16* (RC)

Wisdom, who came forth from the mouth of the Most High, sings of the time when God directed her to place her tent. She dwells with Israel, is established in Zion, and is rooted in an honored people. Jerusalem is her home, affirming God's presence with God's chosen people.

Lesson 2

***Ephesians 1:3-14* (RCL); *Ephesians 1:3-6, 15-18* (RC); *Ephesians 1:3-6, 15-19a* (Epis)**

These verses celebrate the God who chose and adopted us all in Christ. In Jesus Christ we see God's goodwill – that all things will be gathered to God in the fullness of time.

Gospel

(1) *John 1:(1-9) 10-18* (RCL); *John 1:1-18*

With beauty and care, the Gospel of John unfolds the petals of God's richest treasure, that Jesus is God's own word made flesh, the fulfillment of God's promises, fully scented with grace and truth.

(2) ***Matthew 2:13-15, 19-23*** **(Epis)**
Matthew's gospel gives us a glimpse of the precariousness of Jesus' life. Already perceived as a threat by the local rulers, God warns Joseph to escape with Jesus and his mother to Egypt. In the night, they escape back to the land of their forebears' bondage, now a place of anonymity and safety.

Theme

In Christ, every day is New Year's Day.

Thought for the Day

A new year is an opportunity to re-imagine our lives. How might we live more in the light of faith? So many causes, both personal and global, clamor for our attention. Though it may seem like we cannot make any difference, we can follow Christ's example and "show up," being present and loving to those around us, especially those that many would consider to be less than lovable.

Call to Worship

We begin our worship in the name of our loving God, our newborn King, and the Spirit who has sealed us for all eternity as God's own.

Pastoral Prayer

Blessed are you, O God, who, in wisdom and insight, sent Jesus to be God-with-us. Like the people of Israel, we often need the consolation of your presence, assuring us that we are indeed your precious people. Keep before us the mark of our baptisms, your covenant with us. We pray in the name of Jesus Christ. Amen.

Prayer of Confession

We come before you, gracious God, full of resolutions we have let die. We would like so much to save the rest of the world and ourselves, but we do not have the wisdom or the commitment. We have tried and failed. We come before you, unable to bring permanent peace to our world, full health to the earth, and true contentment to our souls. We so easily lose sight of you, then assume we have been abandoned. We confess that we do not trust you to be God. We do not let you be the savior. Remind us of our human limitations, and remind us of your love for us, limited as we are. Open us to receive the grace you so freely give. Amen.

Prayer of Dedication of Gifts and Self

It is a new year, blessed and blessing God. We bring before you our hopes and dreams for the months ahead and commit them to you. Empower us to be your servants in the world, filled with hope and grace for those around us and ourselves. We are your chosen. We give our resources and ourselves back to you, the source of all blessing in our lives. May we live in the light of Christ. Amen.

Sermon Summary

A new year brings hope because we are chosen and adopted by God into an inheritance of God's presence and power.

Hymn of the Day

"Good Christian Friends, Rejoice"

Dating from around the year 1400, this carol was first written in a mixture of German and Latin, part of a popular trend at that time to mix the "church" language with the vernacular. Translated into English by John Mason Neale, the hymn has remained popular for its joyful exuberance celebrating the birth of Christ, and some of the implications of that birth for humankind.

A variety of rhythm instruments can capture the tune's original joy and add to the festive mood.

Children's Time

Count Our Blessings

Preparation: Print "Blessing" down the left side of a piece of chart paper, leaving room for words to be written after each letter. Bring markers.

Sometimes on New Year's Day, people make resolutions about things they want to do differently or things they want to start doing. Some promise that they'll be kinder to their sister or brother. Some promise to practice piano regularly, others that they'll exercise more or quit eating junk food. Did anyone in your family make a new year's resolution? *(Invite responses.)*

But I want to start a new tradition. To start the new year, I want to count my blessings. Today's Bible reading talks about how richly God has blessed us all, in all sorts of ways. Wouldn't it be great to start the new year by focussing on God's blessings? *(Invite the children – and congregation if need be – to list blessings on the chart paper, writing one that begins with B, one with L, and so on. Other blessings can be written around the edge of the page.)*

I'll hang this chart by the door to remind all of us to count our blessings. Thanks for helping me get this year off to a good start.

The Sermon

In Christ, Every Day Is New Year's Day

Hymns

Beginning of Worship: "A Stable Lamp Is Lighted"
Sermon Hymn: "Lo, How a Rose Is Growing"
Closing Hymn: "Once in Royal David's City"

Scripture

Ephesians 1:3-14 (For additional sermon materials on this passage, see the 2003 May/June planning issue and the October 2003 issue of *The Clergy Journal.*)

Blessed be the God and Father of our Lord Jesus Christ, who has blessed us in Christ with every spiritual blessing in the heavenly places. Amen.

There is something so promising about this season. It's a new year, an opportunity to try again, to set some goals and work at meeting them. Twelve whole months are before us. In the Northern Hemisphere, we have crossed through the winter solstice – the days are getting longer. Nature promises that winter will not last forever. In two days Epiphany will mark the coming of the star of Bethlehem and the light of Christ will spread beyond the manger.

Does this new year feel so good to us because we got bogged down in the old one? The holiday season is a panic for most of us – gift buying, decorating, entertaining, and being entertained. We can easily lose ourselves in the hype and find ourselves exiled in a consumer-driven world moving too fast to appreciate a baby in a manger.

But we may have felt lost and exiled for other reasons, reasons that go beyond the preparation for the holidays just past. Perhaps last year at this time you vowed to work on taking better care of yourself. You were going to eat better, exercise more, drink less, or quit smoking. As the months went by, how did you do? Did you start off with a bang and then find your resolve slipping? Did find yourself making excuses? Re-resolving? Feeling angry and guilty?

Perhaps you resolved to be a better friend or parent. At first, I'll bet it went pretty well. You made that list of people to have lunch with, and even started calling. But then life got busier and busier, and before you knew it, the list had been set aside and life became about schedule survival again.

Perhaps last year at this time, you resolved to live your faith more clearly. You wanted to become more active in the social justice issue that you care about most. You were going to write your elected representatives, support a local serving agency, and give more time and money. And then your own needs kept getting in the way, and every time you needed your money for something else, every time you decided to skip a meeting because you were too tired, it got harder to stay focused on the good you had hoped to do.

You never did resolve to help bring about world peace, to make sure that no child in our world goes hungry, or to make fundamental inroads into the crisis of environmental degradation. Because you knew then as you know now that these problems are of epic proportion – overwhelmingly discouraging and frightening.

Now, what was that about this being a hopeful time of year? It is not hard to find ourselves quite lost, resolutions slowly abandoned, and we're back at zero. The world really is a mess, and each of us is just one part of it all. So where is God, after all?

Our forebears in faith, the people of Israel, surely knew these feelings. Their issues were different, no doubt, but they searched for God as they languished in exile. Their personal problems were thorny, and their national problems certainly seemed insurmountable. They were stuck in a world that was so foreign to them – different food, different language, different values. They had thought they were God's chosen people. They had believed that God loved them, but stuck year after year in exile, they wondered.

Like us. When we are exiled from the promised land of our own health – and the health and vitality of our families, our communities, our country, and our globe – we can begin to think that God has moved on and left us behind to manage this new year on our own.

What are we to God? In spite of appearances to the contrary, we are everything to God. God has not packed up and left us here. In fact, God just moved in. Remember the manger? Remember that newborn, Emmanuel, God-with-us? Are you getting the slightest glimmer of a new star in the heavens? Do you hear the distant sound of camels winding their way to Jerusalem so their riders might worship the newborn king?

Listen to the words of Ephesians: "[God] destined us for adoption as his children through Jesus Christ, according to the good pleasure of his will, to the praise of his glorious grace that he freely bestowed on us in the Beloved" (Eph 1:5-6). This is not a god who abandons us to the fates. This God took on flesh and blood, time and space, to walk with us in life. Jesus has been born!

Now make a scan of Jesus' life. Did he pick and choose his compatriots? Not, if we mean that he was above the people around him. Did he pick and choose? Yes, he did. Jesus chose guys who made their living fishing, women who sold their bodies in prostitution, turncoats who fleeced their neighbors when they collected taxes, and members of the religious elite who came at night to ask him questions. Yes, he did. Jesus picked and chose everyone to love. He challenged the social pecking order that oppressed so many of his day, and stirred up quite a firestorm as he did so.

This was God at work, not hiding from the mess, but walking right into the middle of it. That was true then, and it's true now. At your baptism, God picked and chose you, the unique and wondrous you. You were sealed with the Holy Spirit, a pledge of your inheritance as one of God's own. When you eat at the Lord's table, God comes to you in bread and wine, nourishing you for the challenge of this year's resolutions. When we come together, we are the body of Christ, called to be God's hands in the world, gathering all on earth and in heaven into God's embrace.

It's a new year. When its luster starts to fade, God will still be here. We will still be sealed by the Spirit, forgiven and chosen. When the luster of the new year starts to fade, we can still look for the light of Christ. We can trust God's steadfast presence. In Christ, every day is New Year's Day.

– Catherine Malotky
Evangelical Lutheran Church in America
Minnetonka, Minnesota

January 6, 2004

Epiphany

Lessons

RCL	Isa 60:1-6	Eph 3:1-12	Mt 2:1-12
Roman Catholic	Isa 60:1-6	Eph 3:2-3a, 5-6	Mt 2:1-12
Episcopal (BCP)	Isa 60:1-6, 9	Eph 3:1-12	Mt 2:1-12

Introduction to the Lessons

Lesson 1

Isaiah 60:1-6 **(RCL/RC);** ***Isaiah 60:1-6, 9*** **(Epis)**

Jerusalem lay in ruins. Isaiah prophesies that Jerusalem's light will come again, and God's glory, instead of being hidden and absent, will be what illumines the great city. Long-lost relatives will stream home and everyone will proclaim the praise of God.

Lesson 2

Ephesians 3:1-12 **(RCL/Epis);** ***Ephesians 3:2-3a, 5-6*** **(RC)**

Paul lays out clearly the result of the first great theological debate of the early church – are Gentiles included in the Messiah's good news, or not? Paul said yes, and the church came to agree with him.

Gospel

Matthew 2:1-12 **(RCL/RC/Epis)**

Isaiah prophesied that kings would be drawn to the brightness of Jerusalem's light (60:3). Matthew tells how this prophecy is fulfilled. Gentile astrologers came from the East to inquire about the child born King of the Jews. The glory of God shines in a star they followed to where Jesus lay.

Theme

The Epiphany star is the light in the darkness.

Thought for the Day

Epiphany celebrates the coming of the star. It shines the light of Christ throughout the world. In Jesus, we see God as clearly as we ever could, an infant king who will love us without fail. We live in this light. When it is hardest to believe in God's love, this light can draw us to life again.

Call to Worship

We stand in the presence of the ruler of the universe, our Creator, who knows all and sees all. We remember today that God also gave all, coming in the form of a child to bring the light of this love to the whole creation. We gather at his cradle to adore him.

Pastoral Prayer

Infant Christ, the Magi came to honor you and bring you gifts. They did not know the religious rules that governed your world, yet they came to worship. Let us see the light of your star in our lives, that we might be inspired by your presence to the love, justice, and mercy that marked your life among us. Amen.

Prayer of Confession

We gather in your light and confess the ways we have not trusted your goodness and love. We have failed too often to acknowledge our limited vision and wisdom. We have failed to lean on each other for help, failed to bring our gifts to bear where they are needed, and failed to trust that your love is the sturdy ground of our worth and value. Let us see ourselves as you do – precious first, and then called to be and bring your light to the world. Fill us with your vision of life and give us the courage to live it. Amen.

Prayer of Dedication of Gifts and Self

Christ, our light and our life, we bring our gifts and ourselves to you this day. We set them at your cradle, as the Magi did so long ago, in honor of their origins with you. We commit ourselves to trusting your love for us, and turning our sights on the world to bring healing and peace. Bless our efforts for the sake of the whole creation. Amen.

Sermon Summary

Our hope in Christ is renewed. Jesus is God's most profound gift of love to us. We live in the midst of the light God gives to us. There is no earning it. The Magi's worship is ours as well.

Hymn of the Day

"I Am the Light of the World"

Jim Strathdee based his lyrics on a poem by Howard Thurman. This is one of the few hymns written specifically for after the season of Christmas, answering the rhetorical question, "So what do we do now?" Both text and tune can be easily learned, and the hymn works well accompanied by guitars and/or piano. The hymn can be sung year round, either with or without the first verse. Either way, the piece reminds us of the words of Ebenezer Scrooge (after his dreams) who promised to "keep Christmas all through the year."

Children's Time

Epiphany

Today is Epiphany, the day when we hear the story of some Wise Men. These men lived far from where Jesus was born. They saw the bright star that God placed in the sky when Jesus was born. This star told them that a special king had just been born and so they left on a long journey to find him. Can you imagine how it felt to travel for weeks on their camels, crossing the desert as they followed the brightly shining star?

Well, they found the baby Jesus, but he wasn't living in a palace like they might have thought a king would be. He didn't have lots of servants. Did this stop the Wise Men? Did they turn around and go back home disappointed?

No. They knew that fancy palaces weren't necessary for a true king, for God's Son. They brought their gifts of gold, frankincense, and myrrh to Jesus. They knelt down and worshiped him.

Epiphany is a word that means uncovering a surprise or revealing a mystery. And that's what those wise men did. They uncovered the mystery of the star that was shining brightly. They followed the star and found Jesus, God's love brought to earth for us.

The Sermon

The Gift of This Day

Hymns

Beginning of Worship: "Bright and Glorious Is the Sky"
Sermon Hymn: "Oh, Love, How Deep"
Closing Hymn: "We Are Marching in the Light of God"

Scripture

Ephesians 3:1-12 (For sermon materials on Matthew 2:1-12, see the 2003 May/June planning issue of *The Clergy Journal* and on Isaiah 60:1-6, see the October 2003 issue of *The Clergy Journal.*)

At one time, January 6 was the day the sun began to come back. For some of our pagan ancestors, this was the solstice – the shortest day of the year, the turning point of winter in the Northern Hemisphere. This day began the last cycle of dormancy before the time of plenty began again – the time of gathering, planting, harvesting, storing. In spite of the darkness and cold, it was a promise of the summer to come.

Well before the time of Christ, the civilizations that had discovered a way to measure the sun and the stars claimed an earlier date for the winter solstice, December 25. Both were wrong according to the ways we now measure such things, but the movement through the shortest day of the year was sacred to our forebears and a deeply spiritual time, regardless of which date was claimed.

Both dates have remained holy to our contemporary spiritual sensitivities. In Puerto Rico, presents are exchanged on Epiphany, not Christmas, in memory of the gifts brought by the Magi to the newborn King. In the Eastern Church, today is the day to mark Jesus' baptism, to remember how God publicly claimed him in the waters of the Jordan.

The gift of this day is both simple and impossible to grasp. The prophecy of Isaiah points to it. "Arise, shine, for your light has come . . . the Lord's glory will appear over you" (Isa 60:2, 4). This was spoken to a people whose sacred places were in ruins, who lived under occupation, who longed to return to home. Isaiah sang of homecomings. He gave voice to the people's yearnings to have their history and their story brought together, to reunify the children of Abraham, no matter what bad blood had passed between them over the years. Isaiah's word was an offering of hope to a people who dearly needed it.

In Ephesians, Paul spoke confidently to Gentile Christians of the mystery with which he had been entrusted, a truth for which he had paid dearly and was still paying. Is the good news of Jesus Christ for Jews alone, those who waited for the Messiah? Or are the Gentiles considered God's children as well? Jesus was a Jew, after all, but his news of love for all was a challenge to the apparent exclusivity of the origins of the faith. This was the first great challenge to the church, this profound theological question. Paul's ministry was to preach to the Gentiles and to convince the church that they were to be included in the body of Christ. Paul's ministry and the letter to the Ephesians were words of hope to the Gentile Christians who had heard the good news of Jesus. They were affirmed in their hope of salvation.

What of us? Who are *we* this day? For what do we need hope? We live at a time when dreams and ideals are as dashed as those of any generation. Though we are financially wealthy by the world's standards, we suffer from other poverties. When our homes are constantly invaded by the precise psychology of advertising, we may yearn for a home that is our own. When we watch our children ever more burdened by the poisons that surround us – the poisons we eat and breathe every day because we cannot seem to harness our appetite for progress at almost any cost – we must begin to see that we are exiling ourselves by degrading our planet. When we look around at all the ways we worship gods other than the One who comes to us – when we know ourselves to be addicted to success, security, material wealth, or other things that numb us – we know that we have missed the whole point of Christmas. We have come to Epiphany needing a revelation of God's goodness to ground us in something solid and worthy.

Just as our forebears relied on the regularity of the earth's seasons, we can rely on Epiphany to come on January 6 to offer us a revelation of God. Here is the mystery of which Paul spoke. Here is the vision Isaiah painted for his people. In spite of all that wearies or frightens us, in spite of our shortsightedness and destructive ways, God loves us.

The gift of this day is both simple and nearly impossible to grasp. In Bethlehem, God came in human flesh. The God of the whole universe, who created the stars and the seas with a word, took on flesh and blood, so that God could tell us of divine love in a way we could understand. The

Magi followed the star to find the newborn king, but he was a baby, suckling at Mary's breast, cooing at Joseph's smile. This was God's surprise and promise, that God holds our created form as precious from the beginning. God does not keep score; in Jesus there is no score to keep. We do not have to earn God's favor; we have it.

Simple, yes, but nearly impossible to believe. How do we make sense of who we are without keeping score, comparing, and measuring? Yet, these are not God's way. God's way is to bring light, not demand it. We are heirs of God's grace. As Ephesians says, we are members of Christ's body and we share in the promise in Christ Jesus through the gospel (see Eph 3:6).

The heavens have been opened – the light of Christ is all around us. In him, all God's children are gathered together, all wounds healed, and wisdom born. Even now, the star is shining on you.

– Catherine Malotky
Evangelical Lutheran Church in America
Minnetonka, Minnesota

January 11, 2004

1st Sunday after Epiphany/ The Baptism of Our Lord

Lessons

RCL	Isa 43:1-7	Acts 8:14-17	Lk 3:15-17, 21-22
Roman Catholic	Isa 42:1-4, 6-7	Acts 10:34-38	Lk 3:15-16, 21-22
Episcopal (BCP)	Isa 42:1-9	Acts 10:34-38	Lk 3:15-16, 21-22

Introduction to the Lessons

Lesson 1

(1) *Isaiah 43:1-7* (RCL)

The powerful imagery of Isaiah 43 speaks to the desolation of its first hearers. These words reassert the promise of God's steadfast commitment to the people God created. God will gather sons and daughters from every direction and all will call on God's name.

(2) *Isaiah 42:1-4, 6-7* (RC); *Isaiah 42:1-9* (Epis)

Isaiah's first Servant Song came to be understood as a pointer to the long-promised Messiah. Now we see in these words and foretaste of the Christ, whose light cannot be extinguished, and who brings God's justice to the earth.

Lesson 2

(1) *Acts 8:14-17* (RCL)

Soon after Stephen was martyred, the apostles heard that the word of God had been accepted in the far territories of Samaria. Samaritans and Jews had a long and fractious rivalry, but the apostles came to understand that their bond as believers could heal their history.

(2) *Acts 10:34-38* (RC/Epis)

Who could be counted among the faithful? Could Gentiles? This profound theological question challenged the early church. God came to Peter in a dream and revealed the universal nature of the good news, and Peter responded by going to the house of the Gentile Cornelius, to preach the truth he had come to believe.

Gospel

***Luke 3:15-17, 21-22* (RCL); *Luke 3:15-16, 21-22* (RC/Epis)**

John the baptizer points to the one who comes after him. He paints a picture of one who commands the elements of life – earth, fire, and water. Then Jesus joined him in the water and was claimed by God. The dove and the voice from heaven confirmed that God had come to earth.

Theme

God claims and calls us in baptism.

Thought for the Day

Most ancient religions believed the gods were fearful and threatening. This understanding weaves its way through the Old Testament as well. Certainly, the Ruler of the whole universe could be regarded in this way. In Jesus, however, we see another side of God – one of compassion and deep love. This is the God who breaks into our world in the life of Jesus, whose baptism we celebrate today.

Call to Worship

We gather in the Spirit of God, who comes to us in the person of Jesus, who calls us to live and love, and who welcomes us through the waters of baptism into God's holy will and way. Blessed are you, O God.

Pastoral Prayer

Oh, God, shall we see your face and live? Break open the barriers between your wonder and our humanity. Bless us in our baptisms as you blessed your son, Jesus, in his. In your steadfast love, we can release our fear to you. Amen.

Prayer of Confession

God of courage, you took the risk to send your Son among us. You were not content to let the world spin as it would, but came to be one of us so that we might know your love. We confess that we have not been courageous. When you have called us to justice and mercy, too often we have hidden ourselves, lest we risk our safety and security by giving to others. We are afraid, and we do not need to be. Remind us of the baptismal welcome you offer us daily, so that we might be and do all that you desire for us. Amen.

Prayer of Dedication of Gifts and Self

We were baptized to lives of service and love. We commit our resources and ourselves to do your work in the world. Bless these gifts with your goodness and hope, that we might do your will for the sake of the world. Amen.

Sermon Summary

Jesus is more than a decoration for the holidays. He is God at work in our world, calling us to the sacred work of justice and mercy. In him, the Spirit is let loose in the world, and in baptism so are we.

Hymn of the Day

"Wash, O God, Our Sons and Daughters"

On this day that the church celebrates the baptism of Jesus and many congregations have baptisms or renewal of baptismal vows, this hymn of Ruth Duck's is particularly appropriate. Each stanza carries its own powerful message and poignancy. The tune "Beach Spring" has been used for a number of hymns and is easily learned, if not familir. The hymn can be sung in unison, or in two parts with the second voice joining in at the word "sons."

Children's Time

My Beloved Son

(Preparation: Bring a bowl and a pitcher of water.)

Ask the children if they remember their own baptisms or the baptism of a sibling. Talk about the rituals that your church follows for baptism; then tell the story.

John the Baptist was a prophet who came before Jesus to tell people to get ready for Jesus. John lived a simple life and preached to people to remember all that they had done wrong and to ask for God's forgiveness. As a sign of this forgiveness, he called them to come and be baptized in the river Jordan, where the water could wash away their sins. *(Pour water from the pitcher into the bowl as you tell this.)* Water represented new life.

One day, Jesus came to John to be baptized by him. John baptized Jesus with the water in the river. After Jesus was baptized, the heavens opened, and the Holy Spirit came down like a dove. And a voice from heaven spoke and said: "You are my Son, the Beloved; with you I am well pleased."

In our church, we still baptize people. *(Say a little about what your church teaches about the meaning of baptism.)*

The Sermon

Not Just a Decoration

Hymns

Beginning of Worship: "The Only Son from Heaven"
Sermon Hymn: "I Bind unto Myself Today"
Closing Hymn: "We Know That Christ Is Raised"

Scripture

Luke 3:15-17, 21-22 (For additional sermon material on this passage, see the 2003 May/June planning issue and the October 2003 issue of *The Clergy Journal.*)

Have you come down yet after Christmas? Feeling bad that you still have holiday decorations hanging around? Most of the rest of our society moved on long ago. Even the Christmas clearances at the mall have ended.

We Christians know about Epiphany, and for some of our brothers and sisters in the faith, it's a bigger celebration than Christmas. But even Epiphany is past. Now it is just January.

That is, unless you are a Christian.

It's funny how out-of-step we Christians are. We try to observe Advent when the world wants to do Christmas. We want to celebrate the days of Christmas when the rest of the world is cleaning up and moving on. And we celebrate Epiphany, the coming of God's light into the world, right through these dark days of winter.

We are out of step in other ways, too. The cultural celebration of the holidays is all about getting ready, staging the celebration, and then, once the day is past, it's over. Not for us. For us, "the day" launches a whole new life. Think about it. Jesus has been born. He's been called the

Wonderful Counselor, Mighty God, Everlasting Father, and Prince of Peace (see Isa 9:6). His mother predicted that Jesus would scatter the proud, bring down the powerful, and send the rich away empty. She sang that he would lift up the lowly and fill the hungry with good things (see Lk 2:51-53). John the Baptist said Jesus would clear his threshing floor and gather the grain into his granary, but burn the chaff with an unquenchable fire (see Lk 3:17). Isaiah promised that the messiah would not break a bruised reed, but would bring forth justice (see Isa 42:3-4).

Clearly, Jesus is not intended to be a decoration put out for display on his birthday and then stored away until Christmas time next year. Jesus came to change the world. He is not a noun. He's a verb.

How did he begin? In our gospel text, we see Jesus, standing in the waters of the Jordan River with others who had been baptized. Then the heavens were opened and the Holy Spirit hung over him as a dove and a voice came from heaven: "This is my Son, the Beloved; with you I am well pleased" (Lk 3:22). Jesus is not a noun. Jesus is a verb, but not just any verb. He is God at work in our world. He was claimed at baptism, empowered at baptism, revealed at baptism, and sent out at baptism.

Now, it was no small thing that the heavens opened. It is no small thing that the Holy Spirit descended in a dove. And the voice – no small thing either. Our forebears in faith understood that a little space between us and God was a really good thing, a life-saving thing. Jacob, after wrestling with God in the night, named the place where he had struggled, for he had seen God face to face, and lived (see Gen 33:30). When Moses realized that the burning bush he was staring at was God, Moses hid his face, for he was afraid to look at God (see Ex 3:6).

Yet, over the river Jordan that day, the heavens opened. Suddenly we are face to face with God – in Jesus. Jesus opened the heavens for us, and we do not have to be afraid anymore.

It would be safer, of course, if Jesus *were* just a decoration. It's more challenging to have him as a force for justice in the world, even more dangerous. Certainly our security-hungry souls would be happier to be dealing with a noun, a mere decoration. Then we could name Jesus clearly, once and for all. We could hold on to him, and in holding him, hold God. We could get a sure handle on God's will and follow through to Jesus' glory and our gratification.

But Jesus is not a noun.

Instead, Jesus works his way into our very beings. Instead, he becomes a part of the way we live and breathe. Instead, he feeds us for the work ahead. In baptism, we are joined to his works of justice and mercy for the whole world. In communion, we "eat this bread" and "drink this cup," and Jesus is alive and at work in us.

We will try to make Jesus into a holiday decoration. It's so much easier when we aren't asked to question every single thing we hold dear, when we are not asked to join him in the work of bringing life to the world. It's so much easier just to look at a picture and get nostalgic. But that's not the way God intends. The deal is that we don't have to be afraid, even though God is right here, because God is just and merciful. When we shrink into our need for safety, predictability, and security, God is there to remind us of our calling. God will surround us with love and God will invite us to take the risk of faith. God's affection for us is unwavering, God's encouragement is endless.

In baptism, you are sealed by the Holy Spirit and marked with the cross of Christ forever. In baptism, you are claimed and called by God. You are claimed and called for holy work. You can stand face to face with God, and live.

– Catherine Malotky
Evangelical Lutheran Church in America
Minnetonka, Minnesota

January 18, 2004

2nd Sunday after Epiphany

RC/Pres: 2nd Sunday in Ordinary Time

Lessons

RCL	Isa 62:1-5	1 Cor 12:1-11	Jn 2:1-11
Roman Catholic	Isa 62:1-5	1 Cor 12:4-11	Jn 2:1-11
Episcopal (BCP)	Isa 62:1-5	1 Cor 12:1-11	Jn 2:1-11

Introduction to the Lessons

Lesson 1

***Isaiah 62:1-5* (RCL/RC/Epis)**

This may be the urgent prayer of a post-exilic prophet or the promise of God to break silence and restore Zion. Either way, Jerusalem will be given a new name, mission, direction, and purpose. Various images of vindication are included: glory, crown of beauty, delight, and rejoicing.

Lesson 2

***1 Corinthians 12:1-11* (RCL/Epis);**
***1 Corinthians 12:4-11* (RC)**

Probably in response to a question about manifestations of the Spirit, Paul instructed the Corinthians about the multiplicity and diversity of spiritual gifts. God distributes gifts, not for our personal possession or as a reward for achievement, but so we can do God's work. This is the first of three chapters Paul devotes to a discussion of gifts of the Spirit.

Gospel

***John 2:1-11* (RCL/RC/Epis)**

In a passage filled with symbolism, Jesus miraculously changes water into wine. This first of his signs indicated who he is. His presence at the wedding and his power to recycle and re-create were clear signs that his ministry would bring about a time of great joy, since wine represented abundant life for the Jews.

Theme

God gives us gifts that are to be used in service to others.

Thought for the Day

"Like good stewards of the manifold grace of God, serve one another with whatever gift each of you has received . . . so that God may be glorified in all things through Jesus Christ" (1 Pet 4:10-11).

Call to Worship

Leader: This day is a gift from God.
People: Let us rejoice and be glad in it.
Leader: This time of worship is our gift to God.
Leader: Let us give our best to God, offering our gratitude with gladness.

Pastoral Prayer

Gracious, giving God, we come before you aware of how often we have been on the receiving end of your generosity. You give us light for our lives, truth that we can trust, strength for our struggles. From your storehouse you pour out upon us mercy and grace. You give to each of us special gifts: our time, our talent, and even our treasure. We thank you for those who share with us the gifts they receive from you. The words that are spoken, the songs that are sung, the smiles that are offered, all ultimately come from you. It is your Word that we hear. It is your presence that we celebrate. It is your joy that fills us. We are aware this day of those who may feel they have been passed over or left out and those who find it hard to believe that you have been generous to them. When we wish we were more talented, or had more time, or could accumulate more wealth, help us to do an honest appraisal of who we are and what we already have. May we, in the self-giving spirit of your Son, Jesus, be more willing to give away the blessings we have received. Amen.

Prayer of Confession

Loving God, we confess before you and one another the things that have kept us from being both more grateful and more useful. While there are those who are hypocritical in thinking they are better than they really are, we confess that sometimes we are no better when we think we are less than we really are. We forget you have given to each of us unique talents and abilities. Forgive us if we have failed to discover and develop them, buried them, or hidden them. Ease our fears, that our gifts will be rejected or not needed. Remind us that we are not to just enjoy your gifts, but are also to employ them in your service. Let us hear again the words of Jesus, "From everyone to whom much has been given, much will be required; and from the one to whom much has been entrusted, even more will be demanded" (Lk 12:48b). Amen.

Prayer of Dedication of Gifts and Self

Leader: Were the whole realm of nature mine,
People: That were an offering far too small;
Leader: Love so amazing, so divine,
People: Demands my soul, my life, my all.
– "When I Survey the Wondrous Cross" Isaac Watts, 1707

Sermon Summary

Christians are gifted with gifts that are to keep on giving. God gives a variety of gifts to us, as different as we are as individuals. God also expects us to use these gifts for "the common good."

Hymn of the Day

"Come, O Fount of Every Blessing"

Attributed to the early Methodist preacher Robert Robinson, this hymn complements Psalm 36 well. The tune "Nettleton" provides a strong backdrop for the rich images of the text.

Some newer hymnals have reworked the second stanza after generations of singers have stumbled – and corresponding generations of children have giggled – over the phrase "Here I raise my Ebenezer." Meaning "stone of help" in Hebrew, the word *Ebenezer* is used in the King James Version of 1 Samuel 7:12 wherein Samuel set up a stone as a memorial of God's help.

Children's Time

Different Gifts

(Preparation: Write many types of gifts on index cards: musician, listener, parent, teacher, friend, scientist, person who cares for the earth, nurse, preacher, farmer, and so on. Put cards in a basket.)

Can you imagine what our world would be like if God had made all people the same? What if everyone had black hair and brown eyes? What would happen if everyone was a teacher? Would that be good? What if someone got hungry? Who would grow the food?

Fortunately, God is wise and created many different kinds of gifts to give to people. Here is a sample of some of the different ones. *(Invite the children to pull cards from the basket and read them aloud.)* What other ones can you think of?

Did you know that God has given each and every one of us special gifts – talents and interests that make us different from everyone else? Sometimes it seems obvious what our gifts are. Sometimes, it takes us awhile to figure out what our gifts are. But have patience – trust in God. Your gifts are inside of you, just waiting to be found. Your gifts are waiting to be used for the good of everyone.

The Sermon

Unwrapping Your Gifts

Hymns

Beginning of Worship: "Many Gifts, One Spirit"
Sermon Hymn: "Christ, from Whom All Blessings Flow"
Closing Hymn: "Of All the Spirit's Gifts to Me"

Scripture

1 Corinthians 12:1-11 (For sermon materials on Isaiah 62:1-5, see the 2003 May/June planning issue of *The Clergy Journal* and on John 2:1-11, see the October 2003 issue of *The Clergy Journal*.)

There are many ways to think of the church. It's obviously more than a group or institution. Some have thought of it as an army. Others have suggested it should resemble a flock of geese. We often think of it as one big, happy family. Sometimes it may seem like a giant jigsaw puzzle, with myriad parts that we try to fit together. Paul, of course, thought of it as a body. How about thinking of it as a beehive? In his book, *The Vital Congregation,* Herb Miller uses what he calls the "beehive principle" to describe what Paul wrote to the church at Corinth:

> Honeybees have a highly developed social structure. A beehive may house as many as 80,000 bees, each of which performs a specialized duty. Some are forager bees, which fly great distances to collect food. The guard bees protect the hive entrance from intruders. The scout bees keep the hive alert to opportunities and dangers in the outside world. A few bees serve as undertakers, responsible for removing dead bodies from the hive. Others are water collectors . . . some are plasterers. . . . The scent fanners station themselves at the hive entrance and blow the scent outward so that disoriented bees can locate their home base. (Herb Miller, *The Vital Congregation* [Nashville, TN: Abingdon Press, 1990], p. 55.)

Our churches can be veritable beehives of activity. Increasingly, congregations are becoming community centers offering something for everyone. Church calendars fill up and compete with personal calendars. So much needs to be done. So many depend upon us. We can buzz around as busy as bees. Unfortunately, that's where the analogy breaks down. We may not be as well organized as bees are, but that's why one of our greatest needs is to shift our thinking from having "jobs to do" in the church to having "gifts to give."

Paul said the Corinthians were uninformed when it came to spiritual gifts. We, too, may be uniformed about the whole idea of God's gifts. We have neglected the concept of spiritual gifts as we have gone about the business of filling vacancies on the leadership team. We have discounted the potential of discovering our spiritual gifts as we have bemoaned the fact that "we can't get anybody to teach . . . to work with the youth . . . to sing in the choir . . . to go on our mission trips . . . to reach out to the unchurched . . ."

Here's the good news. As Brian Bauknight reminds us in his book, *Body Building,*

> God provides the gifts necessary to do what God needs us to do through the church in any given situation." (Brian Bauknight, *Body Building,* [Nashville, TN: Abingdon Press, 1996], p. 59.)

One of the tasks of the church is to help each person discover, develop, and deploy her or his God-given gifts. Too few of us have any idea that there are so many ways that the church can use our gifts. These gifts are more than our talents and abilities. Talents tend to serve the person who possesses them, as in hobbies and careers. Spiritual gifts, on the other hand, are other-directed. When a congregation helps persons understand they are gifted, it ends up with a teaching, healing, giving, helping, administering, evangelizing force that ministers powerfully to the community and world.

There is not a single person here who has not been given a gift for ministry! The gifts are widely different. Rather than institute a professional clergy who must do it all, God gifted a church, in which all serve together. A preacher isn't the only one who teaches, evangelizes, and witnesses. It takes all of us to do that. No one person can have it all or do it all. In Paul's day, the titles "apostles," "prophets," "teachers," and "pastors" did not refer to ordained ministers as we know them today. They were individuals who were called and gifted for ministry.

Paul's list of spiritual gifts includes utterance of wisdom, utterance of knowledge, faith, healing, the working of miracles, prophecy, discernment of spirits, and interpretation of tongues. Additionally, the New Testament lists serving, teaching, giving, leading, and showing mercy. That diversity of gifts sounds a bit like the jobs of those bees in a beehive! Each of us has something to contribute. We can't all be greeters and ushers. We dishonor God when we fail to do our part and render the church less effective in its ministry to the world.

God's gifts are given for the common good, Paul says. They are to be passed on, used in serving others. As diverse as they are, these gifts contribute to the unity of the community. George Bernard Shaw put it this way: "I am of the opinion that my life belongs to the whole community and as long as I live it is my privilege to do for it whatever I can."

What do you do when you receive a gift? Toss it aside? Ignore it? Use it once and discard it? Sometimes we are nothing more than packages containing gifts that need to be unwrapped. Remember that Michelangelo is quoted as saying he saw an angel "that wanted to come out" of an old piece of stone. Too often, pastors have neglected to discover and call forth those gifts that are in abundance in a congregation. A discovery and recovery of the whole idea of gifts can move us from always asking, "What can I get?" to asking, "What can I give?" Too many of us in the church ask "What's in it for me?" rather than "What's in me for it?"

January 18, 2004
2nd Sunday after Epiphany
RC/Pres: 2nd Sunday in Ordinary Time

The question becomes, then, what is your gift? In an interview for ordination, a young minister told of having the gift of healing. He explained how he went to visit a woman in his church who had one leg shorter than the other. He prayed for her healing, and said he could watch the other leg grow. One of the older pastors interviewing him scoffed at such an idea. So the young candidate looked at him and said, "I believe we all have gifts. Mine is healing. What is yours?" The pastor had no answer. Perhaps he had never thought of it before.

There are no greater or lesser gifts. Each is important. As the old gospel hymn *There Is a Balm in Gilead* reminds us, "If you can't preach like Peter, if you can't pray like Paul, just tell the love of Jesus, and say he died for all." There was an associate pastor in a large congregation who was often on the receiving end of good-natured fun because he could not sing a note. The other pastors didn't want to stand by him when they were leading worship and hymns were being sung. But he was an outstanding pastor, and his caring and compassion were obvious. One day, when the other pastors were laughing about his monotone, a lay person interrupted: "You might not want to stand by him when he sings, but I sure want him to stand by me when I'm hurting."

We do not need to think of our gifts only in terms of those that draw attention to ourselves. The youth group in a small church spent a summer afternoon picking up trash in a nearby housing project. They told the residents who gathered to watch that they were "picking up trash for the Lord." Before long, some of the children came up, asking what they were doing. They joined in, and soon the youth were playing with the younger children. Friendships were made. The minister decided to invite the children to vacation Bible school. The van driver knocked on doors. Three vanloads of children came. The children were encouraged to come to Sunday school. A ministry started from picking up trash.

You may have wrapped up your gift and put it aside, or buried it like the one-talent servant in Jesus' parable. You might need to hear what Paul wrote to the young Timothy, "Do not neglect the gift that is in you . . . " (1 Tim 4:14) and "I remind you to rekindle the gift of God that is within you" (2 Tim 1:6). Is it time for you to unwrap your gift?

– William M. Schwein
Sunrise at Geist United Methodist Church
Indianapolis, Indiana

January 25, 2004

3rd Sunday after Epiphany

RC/Pres: 3rd Sunday in Ordinary Time

Lessons

RCL	Neh 8:1-3, 5-6, 8-10	1 Cor 12:12-31a	Lk 4:14-21
Roman Catholic	Neh 8:2-4a, 5-6, 8-10	1 Cor 12:12-30 or 12:12-14, 27	Lk 1:1-4; 4:14-21
Episcopal (BCP)	Neh 8:2-10	1 Cor 12:12-27	Lk 4:14-21

Introduction to the Lessons

Lesson 1

***Nehemiah 8:1-3, 5-6, 8-10* (RCL);**
***Nehemiah 8:2-4a, 5-6, 8-10* (RC); *Nehemiah 8:2-10* (Epis)**

Standing before the people, Ezra read from the scroll containing the Mosaic law. The Levites helped the people understand what they were hearing. They responded with sorrow, because of their failure to obey the law. Ezra reassured them that there were reasons for them to rejoice.

Lesson 2

***1 Corinthians 12:12-31a* (RCL);**
***1 Corinthians 12:12-30* (RC); *1 Corinthians 12:12-27* (Epis)**

Paul continues to teach about the meaning of unity and diversity in community. He describes the Church in a well-known metaphor, "the body of Christ." The various parts of a body are complementary and interdependent; each is indispensable; none are more important than the others.

Gospel

***Luke 4:14-21* (RCL/Epis); *Luke 1:1-4; 4:14-21* (RC)**

The ministry of Jesus began in Nazareth, his hometown. Jesus reads from Isaiah and interprets it. In doing so, he indicates who he is and what his role as Messiah will be. Jesus was faithful to Judaism – observing the Sabbath, reading from the scriptures, and spending time in the synagogue.

January 25, 2004
3rd Sunday after Epiphany
RC/Pres: 3rd Sunday in Ordinary Time

Theme

The apostle Paul gives us one of the most helpful analogies for the church: the Body of Christ.

Thought for the Day

The simple movement of a finger requires 60 muscle-impulses. The movement of the leg when we walk requires 300. One scientist has said that the body is "a masterpiece of precise planning, a delicate and complex apparatus whose various components work as a unit."

Call to Worship

Leader: May God lift our dropping hands and straighten our weak knees.
People: May God open our eyes, that we may behold wondrous things out of God's law.
Leader: May God open our ears to God's teaching, and may our lips praise God.
People: May God prosper the work of our hands, and guide our feet into the way of peace.

Pastoral Prayer

Eternal God, we have gathered out of our need for you and for one another. You have called us to be your people, your children, the body of your Son, Jesus Christ. We thank you for all the ways you remind us of your dreams for us to be one. There is a grand design and eternal purpose for all that you have made. You call us to restore relationships and the interconnectedness of all things. Nothing exists on its own. We cannot survive on our own. We confess that we have not always lived up to your intention for us. We have separated into special interest groups. We are guilty of forming cliques. We naturally gravitate to those who like us and who are like us. And yet we know that in this great tapestry of human life, we need to be woven together into one beautiful pattern. Weave us, knit us, and hold us together in your love and purpose for us. Amen.

Prayer of Confession

Merciful God, when our ears do not hear and our eyes do not see and our minds do not understand, we limit what you are able to do in our lives. So often we listen, but do not understand; look, but do not perceive. Our hearts have grown dull, our ears are hard of hearing, and we have shut our eyes. It is the same with the body of Christ, to which we belong. We confess that not all the members of the body of Christ are working properly. When we fail to fulfill the roles you have assigned to us, the ability of Christ to continue his ministry is limited. Forgive our envy. Forgive us for disconnecting ourselves from the rest of those with whom we are to share ministry. Give us a renewed sense of being in this together and a renewed commitment to do our part. Amen.

Prayer of Dedication of Gifts and Self

God, we know the world is waiting for us to open our hands, to open our hearts, and to open our purses and pocketbooks. You have given to us enormous resources for healing human hurt, bringing hope to the hopeless and help to those who cannot help themselves. Enable us to be good stewards of who we are and what we have, and to be held accountable for what we do with what you have given us. Amen.

Sermon Summary

Each part of the body has an important role. One part is not more important than another. When each of these parts is fully involved and working properly, the body is alive and well.

Hymn of the Day

"Many Gifts, One Spirit"

This text by Al Carmines works well with any scripture about the gifts of the Spirit, including today's epistle from 1 Corinthians 12.

Upon first hearing, the timing in the tune can seem difficult to grasp. However, like many songs in folk tradition, once it has been heard a few times, it plants itself in one's memory never to fade. A soloist or choir could introduce the stanzas, with the congregation joining on the refrain. The tune works best on guitar or piano.

Children's Time

All Are Equal

My eyes and my hands are having an argument. My eyes think they're more important to my body than my hands. But my hands think they're more important. Which do you think is more important? Let's take a vote. *(Invite a show of hands for eyes and then hands.)*

The apostle Paul talked about this question one day. He pointed out that all the parts of our bodies are important. The heart and the brain work together, and so do the lungs and the blood. You can't single one part out as being more important than all the others are.

Paul teaches us that the church is like the body of Christ. Have you heard that phrase before? Paul says that each person is important in the body of Christ, just like the eyes and the hands are both important to a human body. Each person is important and we all need to cooperate to make the body of Christ work.

This means that children are as important in our church as the pastor, and that the people in the back pew are as important as the people in the front pew. We worship a wonderful, amazing God, who loves us all equally.

The Sermon

Incorporated

Hymns

Beginning of Worship: "Jesus, United by Thy Grace"
Sermon Hymn: "Blest Be the Dear Uniting Love"
Closing Hymn: "Where Charity and Love Prevail"

Scripture

1 Corinthians 12:12-31a (For sermon materials on Nehemiah 8:1-3, 5-6, 8-10, see the 2003 May/June planning issue of *The Clergy Journal* and on Luke 4:14-21, see the October 2003 issue of *The Clergy Journal*.)

At a church staff retreat, the leader drew an outline of the human body and posted it on the wall. She explained that each staff member was to take a marker and put her or his name on the part of the body that represented how they perceived themselves.

Each person went to the drawing and wrote her or his name in a particular part of the body. Some were hands. Others were feet. One was a heart. Another the head. Still another a mouth. One an ear. Then they talked about their choices. It certainly dramatized for them what Paul meant when he wrote to the Corinthians about being a part of the Body of Christ.

At the concluding session of that staff retreat, the leader had the participants write letters of recommendation about themselves. They were to list what they appreciated about themselves, both as individuals and as members of the staff. It proved to be a unique time of self-affirmation.

Increasingly, congregations are becoming incorporated, formed into legal corporations. What is needed more is for churches to become incorporated in terms of being united, blended, and combined thoroughly to form a consistent whole. When a group of individuals act as a single person, it is a corporation.

Paul made many references to the Body of Christ in his epistles. That image implies unity, but also diversity. God always creates diversity. We go against God's design by trying to make everything the same. Like "birds of a feather," we tend to associate with those who are similar to us. But the church encourages – sometimes even forces – us to be in fellowship with all sorts of people. We have often used the phrase, "Well, it takes all kinds." It does! There is no more profound description of the church. It does take all kinds of people. A homogeneous world would be boring. That's why Paul lists eight body parts: foot, hand, ear, eye, nose, head, and what he calls our unpresentable parts. All are necessary. All are part of the whole. We don't all have curly hair. God didn't make every day Monday, or every rose pink, or every animal an eagle. God loves our differences!

These days there seems to be little cooperation among churches, and not much more cooperation within them. The continuing task of the church is to bring us together, to enable us to get along, work together, and fit our differences into some sort of unity. In the church, we intentionally provide a place for human interaction and connectedness. Rather than the image of a "melting pot," the better image is that of a "stir-fry." The church is called to bring individuals together in ways that allow flavoring to take place while the elements retain their unique identities.

Paul had to instruct the Corinthians in how to maintain unity within the church. Nearly everything had become a source of division – even their awareness of God's gifts. Paul had to tell them that even though these spiritual gifts were different, they were all inspired by the same Spirit. One was not more important than the others. What they had in common was their source. What they were to do was enhance the body.

We tend to discount our own gifts and the part that we play in the body. We tend to envy the gifts and roles of others. We may end up resenting what another can do. When we say, "I wish I could do that," are we denying whatever it is we might have for the good of the body? We expend far too much energy watching others. The time comes when we have to say, as Noah did in the play, *Green Pastures*, "I ain't much, but I'se all I got!" As an old poem has the squirrel say to the mountain, "If I cannot carry forests on my back, neither can you crack a nut." Thomas Merton said that "For each one of us, there is only one thing necessary: to fulfill our own destiny, according to God's will, to be what God wants us to be." God would never ask why we aren't like someone else. God's only question to us would be why we aren't more fully who we are.

The result of comparison is competition. Envy is the one deadly sin that is not about satisfaction, but dissatisfaction. Paul warned that when persons "measure themselves by one another, and compare themselves with one another, they do not show good sense" (2 Cor 10:12).

Henry Van Dyke once said, "Use what talents you possess: the woods would be very silent if no birds sang there except those that sang best." General Dwight D. Eisenhower would not tolerate having one of his generals refer to a foot soldier as "just a private." He firmly believed that the war would be won by the soldiers, not the generals. Likewise, congregations grow and thrive by the efforts of each member.

In one church, a picture of Christ as the good shepherd was being painted on the wall behind the altar. Only the outline of his head and shoulders were visible. A stranger stepped into the church and noticed the sketchy outline. He asked one of the painters when the picture would be finished. The workman replied that is was finished. The visitor pressed him, saying that most of it was missing: the eyes, mouth, arms, hands, legs, and feet. In fact, he said, the whole body of the Lord is missing. The workman replied, "You won't see it on a wall. The body of Christ is this congregation."

Just as the Word became flesh in the person of Jesus Christ, we are to embody the work of God as the Body of Christ. The spirit of Jesus Christ lives on today in the gathered community of his disciples. St. Teresa once said that "Christ has no body now on earth but yours, no hands but yours, no feet but yours; yours are the eyes through which to look with Christ's compassion on the world, yours are the feet with which to go about doing good, and yours are the hands with which he is to bless others now." Following the resurrection, the disciples found the body of Jesus missing from the tomb. We pray the body of Christ won't be missing today.

– William M. Schwein
Sunrise at Geist United Methodist Church
Indianapolis, Indiana

February 1, 2004

4th Sunday after Epiphany

RC/Pres: 4th Sunday in Ordinary Time

Lessons

RCL	Jer 1:4-10	1 Cor 13:1-13	Lk 4:21-30
Roman Catholic	Jer 1:4-5, 17-19	1 Cor 12:31–13:13 or 13:4-13	Lk 4:21-30
Episcopal (BCP)	Jer 1:4-10	1 Cor 14:12b-20	Lk 4:21-32

Introduction to the Lessons

Lesson 1

***Jeremiah 1:4-10* (RCL/Epis); *Jeremiah 1:4-5, 17-19* (RC)**

When the youthful Jeremiah is called to speak forth God's word, he joins the other prophets in being reluctant, even resistant to God's commission. As always, along with God's command, there is a reassuring promise for divine authority and empowerment.

Lesson 2

(1) *1 Corinthians 13:1-13* (RCL); *1 Corinthians 12:31–13:13* (RC)

Though this passage is often read at weddings, Paul intended it to be read to the church. Love was to control the other gifts of the Spirit.

(2) *1 Corinthians 14:12b-20* (Epis)

Paul continues his teaching about spiritual gifts. He is concerned about those who would place "speaking in tongues" at the top of the list of those gifts. The Christian's speech is to be understandable and helpful to those outside the community of faith as well as to those within it.

Gospel

***Luke 4:21-30* (RCL/RC); *Luke 4:21-32* (Epis)**

Jesus received a mixed reaction to the sermon he preached in his hometown. It becomes obvious Jesus was not a crowd-pleaser. He did not seem concerned with merely meeting the expectations of his listeners. The angry response he received from some would escalate, until the time he was crucified.

Theme

Learning to love as Christ loved us ought to be the life-long goal of the Christian.

Thought for the Day

The love we experience from God is an "in spite of" kind of love that we are to express in our relationships with others.

Call to Worship

Leader: Beloved, let us love one another, because love is from God;
People: Everyone who loves is born of God and knows God.
Leader: Whoever does not love does not know God,
People: For God is love.
Leader: Beloved, since God loved us so much,
People: We also ought to love one another.

– Based on 1 John 4:7-11

Pastoral Prayer

Lord, show us once again what it means to love others as you love us. You love us when we are not lovable or loving; you care for us when we are uncaring. You do not wait for us to measure up to your expectations, or even return your love. You just love us. Unconditionally. Just as we are. You are patient, you never give up on us, you do not keep account of our sins but forgive us again and again. You are always seeking to do good to us. We thank you for those within our circle of friends and church fellowship who love us as you love us. We thank you for the ways they make your love real: with an encouraging word, with a pat on the back, with a shoulder to cry on, with a willingness to overlook our mistakes. Help us to learn from you and from them what it can mean for us to make love the greatest gift we can give to others. Amen.

Prayer of Confession

Gracious and forgiving God, we confess to you that we have done little to take seriously Jesus' words that others will know we are his disciples if we have love for one another. Our relationships at home, at work, and in the church do not always identify us as followers of Christ. Teach us how to accept one another. Teach us how to overcome evil with good. Encourage us to make love a priority in life. Too often we waste opportunities we are given to do the loving thing. Too often we make love dependent upon our feelings rather than upon being faithful to what your Son has commanded us to do. God, love us into being more loving. Amen.

Prayer of Dedication of Gifts and Self

Loving God, you loved us so much you gave us your Son, Jesus Christ. May these gifts be the evidence of how much we love you. May they be the indication that we want to be more loving. Encourage us to give and not to count the cost, but only to see the value of the difference we can make. Amen.

Sermon Summary

Following Paul's instructions to the Corinthians about spiritual gifts and the varied roles we are to play in Christ's body, Paul brings it all together with a beautiful hymn to love – the greatest gift.

Hymn of the Day

"Though I May Speak"

This hymn, a lyrical paraphrase of 1 Corinthians 13:1-3 by Hal Hopson, is often sung at weddings. Yet its invocation of God's Spirit of love to guide and govern our daily living makes it suitable for all times.

Hal Hopson adapted the English folk melody "O Waly Waly" in a very singable fashion. The hymn works well with a soloist singing the first stanza, joined by choir on the second, and full congregation on the third.

Children's Time

Love Above All Else

(Preparation: Bring in a picture of someone who loves you and another picture of someone you love.)

Ask the children: Who loves you? Who do you love? *(Invite responses.)* Tell them about the people in your pictures.

Love is the most powerful force in the world. Today's reading from the Bible is all about love. It's a beautiful passage that is often read at weddings. Listen while I read part of it.

If I talk, but don't have love, then all I make is a dreadful noise.

If I am smart and trust in God, but don't have love, then I am nothing.

If I give away all I own, but don't have love, I get nothing.

For love is the most important thing of all.

True love is patient and kind.

Love is not grumpy.

Love is not happy when someone does something wrong.

Love rejoices when the truth is told.

Love trusts and believes.

Love hopes and lasts forever.

Faith, hope, and love are all great, but love is the greatest.

The Sermon

The Best Gift Ever!

Hymns

Beginning of Worship: "Love Divine, All Loves Excelling"
Sermon Hymn: "How Can We Name a Love"
Closing Hymn: "The Gift of Love"

Scripture

1 Corinthians 13:1-13 (For sermon materials on Jeremiah 1:4-10, see the 2003 May/June planning issue of *The Clergy Journal* and on Luke 4:21-30, see the October 2003 issue of *The Clergy Journal*.)

I suspect that at every birthday or anniversary or Christmas, there is one gift we receive that we value above all the others. It is probably the gift that was selected with our deepest needs in mind. It perfectly matches who we are. We exclaim, "Oh, thank you! That's the best gift ever!" We may even forget about all the other gifts we receive.

Paul had been writing about the gifts that God gives us. The list was extensive. He wrote about the need to make good use of those gifts. Even if we get everything we want and have everything we need, unless we receive this one, great gift, the rest of what we have amounts to little more than the wrapping it came in.

In order to fully understand this all-too-familiar passage from 1 Corinthians, it helps to go back to the conclusion of chapter 12. Paul says, "But strive for the greater gifts" (1 Cor 12:31). He then went on to call love the "greatest gift." Love, Paul said, was of more significance than any other gift from God. The truth is, we can do a lot of very good things without doing the very best thing, which is to love.

In some ways, it is unfortunate that the reading of this passage has pretty much become just another wedding tradition. Paul did not write it for weddings, but for the whole church. Specifically, he wrote it to the church with which he had been struggling in an effort to confront the division, strife, and disunity that threatened to tear them apart.

In a *Peanuts* cartoon, Lucy tells Charlie Brown, "You know what I don't understand? I don't understand love!" Charlie replies, "Who does?" So Lucy asks him to explain love to her. But he protests, "You can't explain love." Does Paul try to do the impossible? To explain love? In this text, Paul does not really explain love or define it. He describes what it was and wasn't. Love, for Paul, takes care of a lot of deficiencies. It is the best way to accomplish what he had been talking about in 1 Corinthians up to this point. It relates to his concerns about conflict over spiritual gifts and about feelings of superiority (and inferiority) among the members of the body of Christ.

There is a scene from the play about Helen Keller's life in which Anne Sullivan spells out the word "L-O-V-E" in Helen's hand. Perplexed, she spells back the question, "W-H-A-T I-S L-O-V-E?" I know few people who do not want to love, who set out to be intentionally hateful or hurtful, or to withhold love. It's just that we do not know exactly what love is. I once saw a bumper sticker that said, "Love means nothing in tennis. What does it mean to you?" Good question, isn't it?

It is difficult, if not impossible, for us to express love until we experience it. It is hard to love until we feel loved. That is why some believe that Paul is just outlining what it means to understand how God loves us unconditionally. For the Christian, it is not just enough to love. We are commanded to love as Christ loved us. It is out of the great reservoir of God's love for us that we draw the strength and motivation and means to love others.

Victor Hugo wrote, "The supreme happiness of life is the conviction that we are loved." It is not enough for us to be liked; we want to be loved. I knew of a psychiatrist who maintained that most all the problems in our lives stem from the absence of unconditional love and that most of the problems in our lives could be resolved by the experience of unconditional love. Is that too bold a statement? Can love really undo the hurts and pains we have known? Can love indeed cover a multitude of sins – both those we have committed and those committed against us? Can love really bring peace to the world? Can love really restore what has been broken? How will we know until we have tried it?

James Thurber once said, "Love is what you've been through with someone." It has an "as is," "no matter what," "in spite of," quality to it. When we have tried everything else, we might try love.

Columnist Ann Landers once responded to an inquiry by writing, "If you have love in your life, it can make up for a great many things you lack. If you don't have it, no matter what else there is, it's not enough."

Paul seemed to suggest that if we have and can do everything, but have no love, it is as useless as multiplying by a minus. You end up with a minus. Less than nothing. If we can preach with the eloquence of Billy Graham, or keep a clean house, or name the 66 books of the Bible, or quote all the *Chicken Soup for the Soul* books, or teach Sunday School, or work with Habitat for Humanity, or help out in the food pantry – but have no love – we are nothing much to brag about.

There is a danger that just as we talk about love so glibly, Paul's hymn to love may be too familiar to us. It sometimes helps to hear the words in a different translation. J. B. Phillips paraphrases this passage beautifully:

> This love of which I speak is slow to lose patience – it looks for a way of being constructive. It is not possessive: it is neither anxious to impress nor does it cherish inflated ideas of its own importance. Love has good manners and does not pursue selfish advantage. It is not touchy. It does not keep account of evil or gloat over the wickedness of other people. . . . Love knows no limit to its endurance, no end to its trust, no fading of its hope. . . . It is, in fact, the one thing that still stands when all else has fallen." (J. B. Phillips, *The New Testament in Modern English,* [New York, The Macmillan Company, 1964], p. 371.)

It might help to personalize this passage further. The suggestion was once made that we substitute our names for the word "love." You might try it. It would help you discover if you are patient, kind, envious, boastful, arrogant, or rude; if you insist on your own way, or are irritable or resentful. Love is expressed in how we relate to one another. Is has less to do with an emotion than with devotion. Sometimes doing the loving thing means being a bit more patient with a friend or family member who irritates us. Sometimes it means doing a random act of kindness. Sometimes it means we can rejoice in someone else's good fortune. Sometimes it means we need to quit drawing attention to ourselves. Sometimes it means being humble. The impact of these kinds of loving actions would be enormous.

The pastor of a large church was telling a friend how he had changed the priorities of his ministry as he came closer to retirement. He said, "I used to think that the ultimate was to build this building. You know, the old edifice complex. Now that it's built, I think a lot about love. What good is a building if the people aren't changed? I'd like to spend the rest of my ministry teaching people how to love."

What a great gift he gave his people!

– William M. Schwein
Sunrise at Geist United Methodist Church
Indianapolis, Indiana

February 8, 2004

5th Sunday after Epiphany

RC/Pres: 5th Sunday in Ordinary Time

Lessons

RCL	Isa 6:1-8 (9-13)	1 Cor 15:1-11	Lk 5:1-11
Roman Catholic	Isa 6:1-2a, 3-8	1 Cor 15:1-11 or 15:3-8, 11	Lk 5:1-11
Episcopal (BCP)	Jud 6:11-24a	1 Cor 15:1-11	Lk 5:1-11

Introduction to the Lessons

Lesson 1

(1) *Isaiah 6:1-8 (9-13)* (RCL); *Isaiah 6:1-2a, 3-8* (RC)

This passage, "the call of Isaiah," tells us what can (and should) happen in worship. Isaiah has a vision of God's heavenly throne and senses God's presence in an act of adoration. He responds with confession. God calls and Isaiah responds.

(2) *Judges 6:11-24a* (Epis)

This is another story about how God calls persons to do specific tasks in their time and place. Through an angel, God commissions Gideon to deliver Israel. Gideon is hesitant, making excuses about his inadequacy. God is persistent, and promises to be present with him.

Lesson 2

***1 Corinthians 15:1-11* (RCL/RC/Epis)**

Paul proclaims the resurrection of Jesus as the central tenet of the Christian gospel and the foundation of the Christian faith. Some in the Corinthian church had doubts about the resurrection. Paul is confident because the risen Christ appeared to Paul.

Gospel

***Luke 5:1-11* (RCL/RC/Epis)**

The "miraculous catch of fish" is Luke's account of the call of the first followers of Jesus. As in the passage from Isaiah, Peter is overcome with fear in the presence of such power. He acknowledges his sinfulness, and receives and responds to the call to be sent out in ministry.

Theme

The resurrection of Jesus Christ has significance for us not just when we die but also as we live.

Thought for the Day

Easter, by which I mean the assurance of the presence of Christ, has a way of coming at unexpected times in unexpected places. The fact is, you never know when, suddenly, it will be Easter.

– W. Merlin Schwein Sr.

Call to Worship

Jesus, stand among us, in thy risen power. Let this time of worship be an holy hour.

– William Pennefather, 1816–1873

Pastoral Prayer

Loving God, regardless of our circumstances, you help us to think in terms of resurrection and rejoicing, in terms of new beginnings. May the great truth of Christ's return from the grave bring a word of life to those for whom there has been death; a word of courage to those for whom there has been discouragement; a word of promise to those for whom there have been problems; a word of hope to those for whom there has been disappointment. Let our hearts be open to the presence of a risen and reigning Christ. We know that Christ is present whenever and wherever we need confirmation of the trust that we have placed in you. May he come into our lives in new and real ways, as Savior, Redeemer, Lord, and Friend. Amen.

Prayer of Confession

We confess, O God, that we do not always live as people who believe in the resurrection of Jesus. We are so quick to give up and to give in. We do not allow you to use the power that raised Jesus from the dead to lift our spirits in life. We try to do too many things on our own. We forget that you are able to overcome the most tragic of circumstances with a power to make all things new. We pray for an experience of Christ this day, so that his spirit of forgiveness, the touch of his healing hand, and his willingness to offer grace may be as real to us as is the awareness of our sins and shortcomings. Amen.

Prayer of Dedication of Gifts and Self

Lord, we would like to think that if we were to see you hungry, we would give you food; if we were to see you thirsty, we would gladly give you something to drink; if we were to see you naked, we would give you clothing. Is that what we are doing by bringing these gifts to you this day? Amen.

Sermon Summary

Easter is an open-ended story. It can only reach its conclusion when we have experienced the presence of the risen Christ. The resurrection of Jesus Christ is an event that did not end with his ascension. The risen Christ continued, and continues, to appear to those who are in need of an encounter with him.

Hymn of the Day

"I, the Lord of Sea and Sky"

While borrowing words from the call of the prophet Isaiah, this hymn readily fits any situation in which we explore biblical stories of call or our own. Hymnwriter Dan Schutte has captured the mission of the church in each stanza, and likewise our own ambivalence in the refrain: "Here I am, Lord. Is it I, Lord?"

The tune builds momentum as the piece is sung. It is difficult to sing this hymn without feeling a sense of growing commitment as the tune and words progress. Some congregations sing the last refrain with everyone facing the doors of the church, ready to go out and serve.

Children's Time

Who Is Paul?

We've talked about the apostle Paul, and we've read some of his letters. If someone came in and sat down with us right now and told us he was the apostle Paul, would you believe him?

It's always hard to know how to trust what a stranger tells you, and Paul ran into this problem when he traveled around telling people about Jesus. He often told them about how he came to know Jesus.

Paul lived at about the same time that Jesus did, but never actually met him while Jesus was alive. At first, Paul was against the early church and the people who followed Jesus. In fact, Paul was determined to stop them from telling other people about Jesus.

One day, Paul was traveling when a bright light flashed out all around him and he heard a voice asking, "Paul, Paul, why are struggling against me?" Paul asked the light who it was, and the voice answered, "I am Jesus."

Paul was blind for three days, until God sent a man to heal him. After that, Paul was baptized and began to preach about how Jesus was the Son of God. Paul started many churches and wrote many letters, which we still read today in the Bible.

The Sermon

Personal Appearance

Hymns

Beginning of Worship: "Ask Ye What Great Thing I Know"
Sermon Hymn: "Easter People, Raise Your Voices"
Closing Hymn: "Cristo Vive" ("Christ Is Risen")

Scripture

1 Corinthians 15:1-11 (For additional sermon materials on this passage, see the 2003 May/June planning issue of *The Clergy Journal* and on Luke 5:1-11, see the October 2003 issue of *The Clergy Journal.*)

Read the ending to Mark's gospel. Scholars do not know how Mark originally ended the story. Some believe it ended with verse 8, "So they went out and fled from the tomb, for terror and amazement had seized them; and they said nothing to anyone, for they were afraid" (Mk 16:8). Other scholars believe Mark went on to write a "longer ending." "Now after he rose early on the first day of the week, he appeared first to Mary Magdalene, from whom he had cast out seven demons" (Mk 16:9). From there, Jesus appeared to two disciples "as they were walking into the country" (vs. 12), and to the eleven as "they were sitting at the table" (v. 14).

The shorter ending is not very satisfying. We are left hanging. There is no "closure," as we like to use that word. The disciples are left to wonder about what had happened to Jesus and what would happen to them. Would they not need some personal confirmation that Jesus was alive, like a personal appearance of the risen Christ? Didn't the disciples need to know that Jesus intended to meet them in the midst of their lives somewhere, sometime? Don't we?

After the television production of *Jesus of Nazareth* had been filmed and was being previewed, someone noticed that they had omitted the resurrection. So they reassembled the cast and went back into production on location in North Africa in order to film a new ending – in which Jesus was resurrected.

One of Dwight L. Moody's students was preaching at a tent meeting in Chicago one night when his professor slipped in unannounced. The young man talked at length about the crucifixion, and then invited folks to return the next night when he would preach on the resurrection. Moody took him aside and scolded him for preaching only "half the gospel," and taking the chance that those who couldn't return would never have the opportunity to hear the "rest of the story."

One Easter season a store had placed a picture of the crucifixion in their window as part of a seasonal display. A little boy was studying that picture when a man, walking down the street, stopped to talk with him. The little fellow tried to explain what he was looking at: "That man on the cross is Jesus. And the Roman soldiers put him to death. And that woman crying there is his mother." The man barely acknowledged the story the boy told him, and moved on down the street. In a few moments, he heard feet hurrying behind him. It was the young boy, who said, "And, mister, I forgot to tell you. He rose again."

How important it is that we hear the "rest of the story." But it's not really the conclusion. In a sense, the resurrection did not end the story, just as the crucifixion was not the end. In fact, Easter is open-ended. Jesus didn't disappear. He reappeared. He came back to make a number of "personal appearances." That means God is always able at any time to re-write our life stories so that they come out right.

Robert Raines, in *To Kiss the Joy,* wrote that Paul's words "he appeared also to me" "underline the nature and the meaning of the resurrection event. The earliest New Testament tradition speaks not of an empty tomb (those stories in the Gospels come later) but of appearances of the risen Jesus." He further points out that the verb "appeared" is used to both describe his encounter with the risen Christ and to describe the encounters the first disciples had with Jesus. (Robert Raines, *To Kiss the Joy* [Word Books, Waco, Texas, 1973,] p. 131.)

What is of first importance? That Christ died for our sins? That he was buried? That he was raised on the third day? That he appeared to Peter and to the other apostles and disciples? That he appeared to Paul? That he can appear to you?

Further, what is the proof of the resurrection of Jesus? That the original disciples were eyewitnesses? That the risen Jesus appeared to them on 11 occasions during the 40 days following Easter? That the emphasis of their preaching was the resurrection? That they were literally transformed from cowering followers to courageous proclaimers of the resurrection, and that they were willing to go to the death for their beliefs? That the tomb was empty? That the church came into being? That Paul was converted from public enemy number one to primary missionary through an encounter with the risen Lord? For the most part, the disciples didn't really believe in the resurrection until they encountered the Risen Lord and knew him to be alive.

Charles Jordan wrote

The proof that God raised Jesus from the dead is not the empty tomb, but the full hearts of his transformed disciples. The crowning evidence that he lives is not a vacant grave, but a spirit-filled fellowship. Not a rolled-away stone, but a carried-away church."(Clarence Jordan, *The Substance of Faith and Other Cotton Patch Sermons* [New York: Association Press, 1972,] p. 29.)

The resurrection is incomplete until it affects us personally, one way or another. A manufacturer said his company didn't sell drills, but holes. The results are what are important. Maybe the best proof is to experience what happened when Jesus went to the tomb of Lazarus. Martha went to tell her sister Mary, "The Teacher is here" (Jn 11:28).

Certainly the reason many of us believe in the resurrection of Jesus Christ is the difference that he continues to make in human lives. Have you thought about how many of the negative words in our vocabulary and personal experience begin with the letter "D"? Despair, disbelief, disappointment, divorce, depression, defeat, death. Think about how many of the really good words begin with the letter "R," which is, obviously, how the word resurrection begins: renewal, rest, rebirth, reclaim, repair, revive, return, resuscitate, refreshment, restoration, reconciliation, redemption, re-creation, rejoice, and even recycle. The prefix "re" means "again, or anew." What I believe the power of the risen Christ can do is change the "D" words into "R" words. Like despair to repair.

You may be writing the story of your life with too many "D" words and not enough "R" words. Jesus came back so that you can make a comeback. The church should witness to the fact that Jesus is among us in his risen power. The gospels record the post-resurrection appearances of Jesus in unusual places and unexpected times: in the Upper Room; on the road to Emmaus; in a home; on the lakeside. Regardless of where you are, the risen Christ can show himself and his power to you: in a hospital room; in a doctor's office; in the funeral home; even in church.

The resurrection enables us to face our own death with confidence. Winston Churchill planned his own funeral. He instructed a bugler to play "Taps" after the benediction. But as soon as he finished, another bugler, on the other side of the dome of Saint Paul's Cathedral, was to play "Reveille."

Someone has said that we put down a period where God only puts down a comma. The truth is, we give up too soon. It's like getting up from the theater before the last act. Or leaving the game when your team is behind and learning later the game went into overtime and your team won. We may feel we can never win. That's why we have to wait until God has "last bats." When we do that, we will discover that triumph comes out of tragedy. The presence of the risen Christ can give you that assurance.

– William M. Schwein
Sunrise at Geist United Methodist Church
Indianapolis, Indiana

February 15, 2004

6th Sunday after Epiphany

RC/Pres: 6th Sunday in Ordinary Time

Lessons

RCL	Jer 17:5-10	1 Cor 15:12-20	Lk 6:17-26
Roman Catholic	Jer 17:5-8	1 Cor 15:12, 16-20	Lk 6:17, 20-26
Episcopal (BCP)	Jer 17:5-10	1 Cor 15:12-20	Lk 6:17-26

Introduction to the Lessons

Lesson 1

***Jeremiah 17:5-10* (RCL/Epis); *Jeremiah 17:5-8* (RC)**

The prophet Jeremiah bears the unhappy task of bringing a word of doom to Jerusalem and Judah. Unlike most of the prophecies in the beginning of the book, in this passage Jeremiah offers a word of hope following judgment.

Lesson 2

***1 Corinthians 15:12-20* (RCL/Epis);**
***1 Corinthians 15:12, 16-20* (RC)**

Chapter 15 in 1 Corinthians focuses on the topic of resurrection, beginning with the resurrection of Christ. Paul, in this lesson, postulates the impossible, from the Christian point of view, by using "if" clauses seven times. However, the "in fact" in verse 20 cancels out the futility of "if."

Gospel

***Luke 6:17-26* (RCL/Epis); *Luke 6:17, 20-26* (RC)**

Luke's "Sermon on the Plain" begins with blessings and woes. These blessings and woes are not prescriptive, but rather descriptive of the condition of those to whom Jesus speaks. Some of them have left everything to follow Jesus and are blessed with the necessity of the mission. Others are content with this world's charms.

Theme

We drink deeply by trusting in the Lord.

Thought for the Day

Food, clothing, shelter – these are the three necessities of life, as we have been taught from childhood. Consider some other necessities: oxygen, without which we would die in minutes; water, without which we would die in days; the Lord, without whom we die like a shrub in the desert.

Call to Worship

Leader: Happy are those who do not follow the advice of the wicked, or take the path that sinners tread;

People: Happy are those whose delight is in the law of the Lord, and on this law they meditate day and night.

Leader: They are like trees planted by streams of water, which yield their fruit in its season. In all that they do, they prosper.

People: God watches over the way of the righteous, but the way of the wicked will perish.

– From Psalm 1

Pastoral Prayer

O God, we long to come to the plain and hear Jesus say, "Blessed are you." We know that we are blessed in ways too numerous to count, yet we still seek your reassuring and affirming word.

There are so many people in so many places who long for your blessing, who are suffering from hunger, from evil perpetrated by governments, from natural disasters, from catastrophes brought on by hatred and greed. Give us the power of your Spirit to extend a hand of blessing and healing to all in need. Help us conduct ourselves in ways that honor all peoples and all lands.

We wonder, Lord, about the "woes" of which your Son speaks. Fill us with humility so that we do not view the blessings you have freely given to us as a right, but receive them only as undeserved gifts from your bounty. And strengthen us to be good stewards of these gifts to be a blessing to others.

Bless us in these remaining days of Epiphany, that we may manifest your love to the world. We pray in the name of Christ, the first fruits of the dead. Amen.

February 15, 2004
6th Sunday after Epiphany
RC/Pres: 6th Sunday in Ordinary Time

Prayer of Confession

O Lord of water and life, left to ourselves we would lead ourselves into the desert of death. Our sins threaten to cut us off from you, from each other, and from your creation. Our bones are dry. Our sins have caused us to waste away. Can there be any life in us? We are dead and need the life that only you can give. Our sin dries us up, Lord; it dries us up as plants that are parched in the heat of summer. We drink, O Lord, of your forgiveness. We thirst for your reassuring word. Send your sin-quenching love and forgiveness to all and nourish us with your loving kindness. Amen.

Prayer of Dedication of Gifts and Self

Creator God, even in the dead of winter you prepare your earth to spring forth with new life. Winter rains come to the desert to reawaken plants that have waited for sustenance. Snow piles high in the mountains to provide water. The frozen plains will soon become the fertile, moist soil of planting, growth, and harvest. Even so, O God, you prepare your people to spring forth with life. You nourish us in many ways, including the blessings we receive in this time of worship. We ask your Spirit to move in us and strengthen our will to take the nourishment you have given us. Make us, in turn, blessings to others. Help us share the life-giving water and word that you give and make disciples of all nations. We pray, in Jesus' name. Amen.

Sermon Summary

God, through Jeremiah, challenges the people to trust the Lord and be like trees drinking deeply from the river. Those who do not are like shrubs that die in the desert. God desires that we be filled with life and bear good fruit.

Hymn of the Day

"We Have This Ministry"

It has been said that, unlike Matthew's beatitudes, Luke's version would never end up on a needlepoint sampler. Today's gospel includes both blessings and woes, and reminds us of the joys and challenges, pleasures and pitfalls of Christian ministry. This hymn by Californian Jim Strathdee captures much of that sense. An unbridled celebration of many aspects of ministry, the text of this hymn contains a blend of beauty and realism. The tune supports the text with a strength and majesty befitting the sense of commitment.

Children's Time

Trust in the Lord

(Preparation: Bring a potted plant.)

What would happen if I didn't water this plant for a month? *(Invite responses.)* Plants need regular watering to grow deep roots to withstand occasional dry periods.

The prophet Jeremiah said that people who trust in God are like trees that are planted by water. Because the trees can send their roots out deep under the stream, storing up water, they are all right when a long dry spell comes. Their roots have stored up enough water to see them through and they can still bloom and bear fruit.

God gives us faith that is like deep roots on a plant. When bad things happen to us, we've got these deep faith roots to lean on – our faith in God can see us through the trouble. We can keep on growing and loving. We can trust God to give us this faith. God never forgets to water us with faith.

Blessed are they who trust in the Lord, says the prophet Jeremiah. I think he's right.

The Sermon

Drinking from the River

Hymns

Beginning of Worship: "Baptized in Water"
Sermon Hymn: "Shall We Gather at the River"
Closing Hymn: "I've Just Come from the Fountain"

Scripture

Jeremiah 17:5-10 (For sermon materials on Luke 6:17-26, see the 2003 May/June planning issue and on 1 Corinthians 15:12-30, see the November/December 2003 issue of *The Clergy Journal.*)

God has graced our planet with an amazing array of trees, shrubs, and plants. Have you ever noticed how the same variety of plant can look very different depending on its environment? A sunflower seed sown in a well-tended field or garden grows differently than a sunflower planted by a seed dropped accidentally at the side of a busy road or a sunflower trying to grow in the shade of a tree. Plants adapt themselves to their environment, obviously, or they die.

Consider how adaptable trees are. At the southernmost tip of the United States, the very southern outpost of the big island of Hawaii, there is a most unique tree. One would think that the uniqueness of the location would warrant the creation of a tourist trap; far from it. To get there one has to turn off the highway and follow a dirt road many miles to a place where there are no buildings. It is an unforgiving outcrop of land with prevailing winds constantly blowing in from the ocean. The waves seem to be coming from two directions at once and provide the illusion of threatening to destroy the tip of the island.

On this point of land, one tree has adapted and survived. It grew upward like most trees for a number of years, but then it took a 90-degree turn and began growing parallel with the ground. Why did this one large tree turn and not the others? This tree found a way to drink deeply and to survive the unforgiving wind.

Other trees have found ways to survive arid conditions. For example, the Sonoran Desert of Arizona gets two periods of rain each year. There are lighter rains in the winter and heavy downpours in the summer. The water from the summer downpours collects in basins that don't dry up immediately. Trees like mesquite grow next to these basins and drink deeply in the weeks in which water is available. They store up enough water so that they are able to go without for the long periods when there is no rain. It is truly amazing to see these marvels of nature growing next to what appear to be dry stream beds and basins. (http://helios.bto.ed.ac.uk/bto/desbiome/sonoran.htm)

Most of us live in areas where rainfall and snowmelt are more abundant, so that trees get watered more regularly. For instance, a mature silver maple tree can draw up to 58 gallons of water per day through its roots. (http://www.remodelonline.com/directories/garden/tips/trees/01801006.html)

Without question, trees need water for survival. Through the prophet Jeremiah, God tells us that some sources of life-giving water are better than others for trees. There are some trees that will not survive. They are like shrubs in the desert that grow for a while, but eventually perish in the parched land. On the other hand, there are those who are like trees planted by rivers – trees that send out roots to drink deeply and often from the flowing water of life.

Without question, we need water for survival. Through the prophet Jeremiah, God tells us that some sources of life-giving water are better than others for us. Those who put their trust in mortals are those who die in the desert. Those who put their trust in the Lord are the thriving trees by the river.

We all know people who have put their trust in mortals and have figuratively died. Most Americans are attached to the stock market in some way, and the fluctuations in recent years have caused many to despair of their financial health. Some have even killed themselves over having lost their entire savings or pensions. Other people have trusted human medicine and become despondent when doctors inform them that there is no more that medicine can do to heal. Some have placed all their hope in their families, only to be disappointed by some family member.

So, where do you place your trust? Are you going to trust your 401K, your nice house, or your business? Or are you going to heed the word of the prophet Jeremiah and drink deeply from the river of God from the river of life?

Here again, there are many ways that the people of God respond to the gift of living water. Some plant themselves by the river of life that flows endlessly. Some see to live in more arid land, but drink deeply when the water of life is available to flow to their roots. Some spring up quickly, then die like shrubs in the desert.

How are you drinking from God's life-giving river – 58 gallons a day, a few gallons a year, or are you parched? Thanks for gathering at the river this day. "Blessed are those who trust in the Lord." You will not cease to bear fruit. Amen.

– Norman W. Wahl
Bethel Lutheran Church
Rochester, Minnesota

February 22, 2004

Transfiguration

Lessons

RCL	Ex 34:29-35	2 Cor 3:12–4:2	Lk 9:28-36 (37-43)
Roman Catholic	Dan 7:9-10, 13-14	2 Pet 1:16-19	Lk 9:28-36
Episcopal (BCP)	Ex 34:29-35	1 Cor 12:17–13:13	Lk 9:28-36

Introduction to the Lessons

Lesson 1

(1) *Exodus 34:29-35* (RCL/Epis)

In the presence of the Lord, Moses' appearance takes on a brilliance of which he is unaware. Is the veil to protect the people from the reflected brilliance of God or perhaps to disguise the fading brilliance of Moses?

(2) *Daniel 7:9-10, 13-14* (RC)

In this reading we hear of one who is a "Son of human beings" coming with the clouds of heaven. Some Bible translations name this one as a "Son of Man." Is this a reference to the one who is transfigured in the gospel for today? "Son of Man" is a title that Jesus reserves for himself in the gospels.

Lesson 2

(1) *2 Corinthians 3:12–4:2* (RCL)

Paul declares that only in Christ is the veil removed from hardened hearts. Those who turn to the Lord will have the veil removed and be transformed through the Spirit.

(2) *2 Peter 1:16-19* (RC)

Peter offers an eyewitness account to the transfiguration of Jesus on the mount. We are not eyewitnesses, however, and regard Peter's account as a matter of faith. It is faith that is our lamp in the dark places of our lives.

(3) ***1 Corinthians 12:17–13:13*** **(Epis)**
Like the disciples at the transfiguration, we only see dimly, we only know in part. It is as if the clouds obscure the fullness of the glory of God. In the absence of complete knowledge, however, we are shown the excellent way – the way of love.

Gospel

Luke 9:28-36 (37-43) **(RCL);** ***Luke 9:28-36*** **(RC/Epis)**

Dozens of sermons suggest themselves in this reading: moving to the mountain after Peter's confession; transfiguration with Moses and Elijah; Jesus' "exodus"; the voice from the cloud echoing the voice at Jesus' baptism; silence after the transfiguration; returning to the real world of demons. Our God is great.

Theme

Witnesses to the Son, the chosen.

Thought for the Day

On this last Sunday of the season after the Epiphany, we are witnesses to the glory of Jesus' manifestation – a pinnacle just short of the cross and resurrection. Who will bear witness to this epiphany of light, power, and healing?

Call to Worship

Leader: God is king; let the peoples tremble!
People: God sits enthroned upon the cherubim; let the earth quake!
Leader: The Lord is great in Zion;
People: The Lord is exalted over all the peoples.
Leader: Let us praise your great and awesome name.
People: God is holy!
Leader: Mighty king, lover of justice, you have established equity;
People: You have commanded justice and righteousness.
Leader: Extol the Lord our God in worship.
People: God is holy!
Leader: Extol the Lord our God, and worship at God's holy mountain.
People: God is holy!

– Based on Psalm 99:1-5, 9

Pastoral Prayer

O Lord, we pray for the mountaintop, we prepare for the plain. We watch, Lord, as your servant Moses climbs the mountain into your glory. We wait. We wait. We become impatient, even worried with the waiting. We take matters into our own hands and make our own gods – false gods. Your servant, his face glowing with the radiance of your glory, comes to face us, and our sin against you breaks the stone tablets. We watch, Lord, as your Son, the chosen one, climbs the mountain to pray. With the disciples we are awestruck at the glory and appearance of Jesus – dazzling white. We are speechless in your presence. We climb down the mountain and meet demons. O God of the mountaintop, inspire us and strengthen us to your service. O God of the plain, help us to endure the travails of this life and to put away the sin that is ours. May we all respond in love to the greatness that is your Son, Jesus, in whose name we pray. Amen.

Prayer of Confession

O God of forbearance, you suffer the faithless and perverse generations that come and go. So often we lack even a mustard seed of faith that would help us to move mountains, a seed that would help us to see the truth of the Mount of Transfiguration. Like Moses' face, our hearts are veiled. Our veils prevent us from seeing you clearly. Our veils are of our own making. Our minds and hearts are hardened. Forgive our foolishness. Unveil our faces, particularly as we journey into the lenten season of repentance and preparation. Help us to see our own faults clearly so that we can see just as clearly the grace and favor that you offer to us in Jesus Christ, whose life and words speak forgiveness and peace. Amen.

Prayer of Dedication of Gifts and Self

Today we offer gifts to build up the work of your church. For some of us, these gifts represent a true sacrifice. Some of us have responded sincerely to your gifts of grace and love. Others have offered only what is convenient to us at this time. Others of us are wondering how we can offer anything of ourselves to you.

Unlock our hearts so that we might give freely of the gifts we have received – our time, our possessions, and ourselves. Make us disciples who do not keep silent, but who are bold to shout from the mountaintop the news of your beloved Son, the chosen one. Amen.

Sermon Summary

The transfiguration of Jesus is an unlikely story that gives us unlikely witnesses to the good news of Christ. We don't often expect nonhuman elements to give testimony to God, but the Bible is full of examples. Where are the unlikely witnesses to the gospel today?

Hymn of the Day

"Shine, Jesus, Shine"

Arguably British hymnwriter Graham Kendrick's most popular hymn outside of the UK, this hymn combines text and tune in a powerful invocation of Christ as light of the world. Kendrick is fond of exploring the image of Jesus as king, and crafts his lyric so that we find ourselves not merely praising Jesus with words, but inviting him to fill us that we may be living testaments to Christ's glory.

This hymn is best at the conclusion of worship, as its inherent energy invites a smooth transition into daily living.

Children's Time

A Special Trip

We're going to go on a special trip today, in our imaginations. So settle down and close your eyes to listen.

Imagine that you're standing with Jesus and three of his disciples, Peter, John, and James. Jesus invites you to climb a mountain with them. You start to climb together, winding round and round, passing some trees and some sheep. You stop to catch your breath. Finally, you climb up and there you are on top of the mountain, looking out over the countryside.

Jesus starts to pray. All of a sudden, his face and clothes become shining white, so bright you can hardly look at him. And wait! Two more men have appeared! Peter whispers to you that it's Moses and Elijah, two prophets who died many years ago. Suddenly a cloud comes and covers you all. You hear a loud voice saying, "This is my Son, listen to him!" The cloud disappears, and so do Moses and Elijah, and you're there again with Jesus and his disciples. Silently you all walk back down the mountain.

Open your eyes now. What you just imagined was called the "Transfiguration," which is a big word meaning that Jesus was changed by the light. I think the disciples were also changed by what they saw. What about you?

The Sermon

Unlikely Witnesses to the Son

Hymns

Beginning of Worship: "Oh, Wondrous Type! Oh, Vision Fair"
Sermon Hymn: "Let All Mortal Flesh Keep Silence"
Closing Hymn: "How Good, Lord, to Be Here!"

Scripture

Luke 9:28-36 (37-43) (For additional sermon materials on this passage, see the 2003 May/June planning issue and the November/December 2003 issue of *The Clergy Journal.*)

On this Transfiguration Sunday, we are treated to some remarkable witnesses to the divinity of Jesus – the Son, God's chosen one. No less than the purveyor of the law, Moses, and the archetype of the prophets, Elijjah, appear on the mountain for a three-way conversation with Jesus. There is no mistaking the importance of this group of three.

At the same time, there is a trio of remarkable disciples – Peter, James, and John – who accompany Jesus on this mountain journey. Consistently in the gospel writings, these three form an inside cabal of Jesus' closest followers. Of course, in this particular story, these three do not distinguish themselves as particularly apt in interpreting the significance of the event. They prove through time, however, their magnitude in the Christian mission.

There is another set of three witnesses that appear or are implied in our story from Luke's gospel today – a cloud, some stones, and a demon.

The Cloud

This story of Jesus on the Mount of Transfiguration is not the first instance of a cloud being an instrument of God's work in the world. In the first lesson, Moses comes down from Mount Sinai with the two tablets of the law. He has been on the mountain for 40 days and 40 nights – in a cloud. Previous to this time on the mountain, God had led the people out of Egypt with a pillar of cloud by day and pillar of fire at night (see Ex 13:21-22). Throughout the wanderings of the Israelites in the wilderness, God appears in a cloud. Nineteen times in the book of Numbers, God's presence is described as a cloud around the tabernacle. Much later, 2 Kings reports how Elijah is not taken off the earth in a cloud, but in a whirlwind (see 2 Kings 2:11). Elijah and Moses come back to this earth at the moment of Jesus' transfiguration and they are accompanied by a cloud.

In the Gospel of Luke, when Jesus foretells the second coming of the Son of Man, Jesus says that he will come in a cloud with power and great glory (see Lk 21:27). In Acts, Jesus ascends into heaven in a cloud in the presence of his disciples (see Acts 1:9).

In our gospel lesson for today, the cloud speaks. There can be no mistaking that this is the voice of God the Father: "This is my Son, my chosen; listen to him!" (Lk 9:35). Even clouds can be witnesses to Jesus' glory.

Stones

And maybe even stones. The transfiguration event has ended, and the disciples see Jesus on the mountain, alone. When this story is told in the gospels of Matthew and Mark, Jesus orders the disciples to tell no one about what they have seen. Luke's gospel, however, doesn't indicate that Jesus orders the disciples to tell no one of the experience. Luke simply says that the disciples were silent.

They were silent? They had just seen two of the greatest figures in history along with Jesus, the one Peter had declared to be "the Christ of God" (Lk 9:20)!

They were silent? It calls to mind another event in Jesus' life, an event toward which we are headed. Jesus is riding on a donkey to the praises of the disciples and the crowd, "Blessed is the king who comes in the name of the Lord!" (Lk 19:38). Some Pharisees in the crowd object and ask Jesus to make the people stop their praising. Jesus replies, "I tell you, if these were silent, the stones would shout out" (vs. 40). Even stones would testify to Jesus if we did not raise our voices.

In the gospels, Jesus' presence does, at times, call forth a reaction of silence in those who witness his power. He orders demons to remain silent (see Lk 4:31-35). He notices lawyers and Pharisees watching him on the Sabbath and asks if it is lawful to heal on that holy day. They are silent; they don't know what to say (see Lk 6:6-10). In the last week of Jesus' life, Pharisees try to trap him into saying something incriminating. But instead they are amazed by his answers and remain silent (see Lk 20:20-26).

Even the disciples remain silent at times – after the transfiguration and during the trial and crucifixion of Jesus. But I tell you, if we do not raise our witness to Jesus Christ today, even the stones will cry out.

The Demon

We have seen already that Jesus can command the silence of demons. On the day after his amazing transfiguration, Jesus confronts a demon (see Lk 9:37-43). From the glory of the mountain, Jesus is brought to the reality of evil as a man implores Jesus to cast out an evil spirit from his son. The demon dashes the boy to the ground as the boy is brought to Jesus. Luke writes simply that Jesus rebukes the unclean spirit and gives the boy back to his father. All were astounded and amazed.

This is as they should be. A demon is no match for Jesus, God's own Son, the chosen one. Maybe the people that day would never hear about how Moses and Elijah were with Jesus when he was transfigured on the mountaintop because of the disciples' silence, but a demon would testify to the power of Jesus.

You would expect Moses and Elijah to bear witness to God's Son. You would expect Peter, James, and John to come to be witnesses to the Christ. But would you expect much out of clouds, stones, and demons?

Who and what are the unlikely witnesses to Jesus today? How does the transfigured Son reveal himself in your life each day? We are no longer called to remain silent. We are commissioned to be witnesses unto the ends of the earth. Amen.

– Norman W. Wahl
Bethel Lutheran Church
Rochester, Minnesota

February 25, 2004

Ash Wednesday

Lessons

RCL	Joel 2:1-2, 12-17 or Isa 58:1-12	2 Cor 5:20b–6:10	Mt 6:1-6, 16-21
Roman Catholic	Joel 2:12-18	2 Cor 5:20–6:2	Mt 6:1-6, 16-18
Episcopal (BCP)	Joel 2:1-2, 12-17 or Isa 58:1-12	2 Cor 5:20b–6:10	Mt 6:1-6, 16-21

Introduction to the Lessons

Lesson 1

Joel 2:1-2, 12-17 **(RCL/Epis);** ***Joel 2:12-18*** **(RC)**

The prophet Joel has witnessed a massive locust plague and sees the day of the Lord's judgment approaching. Joel calls for true repentance. The day of the Lord will bring punishment to all the unfaithful, including those in Israel. Restoration and blessing can take place only with sincere repentance.

Lesson 2

2 Corinthians 5:20b–6:10 **(RCL/Epis);**
2 Corinthians 5:20–6:2 **(RC)**

On this day in which repentance is a major theme, Paul implores us to be reconciled to God – something made possible because of Christ's sacrifice for our sin. Our righteousness leads us to certain behaviors befitting those who are upright in God's sight, but this righteousness comes through grace, not our behavior.

Gospel

Matthew 6:1-6, 16-21 **(RCL/Epis);**
Matthew 6:1-6, 16-18 **(RC)**

Millions of Christians around the world bear an ashen mark of the cross on their foreheads this day. Jesus warns us that our motivation for this or any other mark of piety determines its value. If we wear the mark (or pray or fast or give alms) in order to receive earthly recognition or rewards, our ultimate treasure will be only earthly rewards.

Theme

Can God use calamity to bring about change in the world?

Thought for the Day

There are many for whom this very day is one that brings dread and pain. Woes such as the deaths of family members or friends, unemployment, irreversible illness, psychological diseases, hunger, and a host of other plagues surround them. May God offer a blessing to those who live in distress.

Call to Worship

Leader: Create in me a clean heart, O God,
People: And put a new and right spirit within me.
Leader: Do not cast me away from your presence,
People: And do not take your holy spirit from me.
Leader: Restore to me the joy of your salvation,
People: And sustain in me a willing spirit.
Leader: The sacrifice acceptable to God is a broken spirit;
People: A broken and contrite heart, O God, you will not despise.

– Based on Psalm 51:10-12, 17

Pastoral Prayer

O Lord, your prophet Joel calls us to return to you with all our heart, even with fasting, weeping, and mourning. At the beginning of this season of Lent, we are called to mark our foreheads with ashes and return to you, hearing that we once were ashes and to ashes we will return. We come to you with different spirits, even somber spirits, recognizing that our Christian journey involves more than love and joy – it includes suffering. Your Son invites us into that way of suffering. We are called to return to you and to walk that journey to Jerusalem with Jesus over these next weeks. There are times, Lord, when we would avert our eyes from that journey. We want to look away from times of betrayal, especially those times that we betray. We want to bury the stories of misunderstanding and ignorance, knowing that these stories mirror our own lack of understanding and knowledge. We want to hurry over death so that we can celebrate life. Yet, our journey with you would be incomplete without Jesus' suffering and death. Compassionate

God, attend to us on our journey in this lenten season and always. Make us faithful to the one who journeyed to the cross for us, Jesus Christ our Lord. Amen.

Prayer of Confession

O God, it is your will that your people repent and live. We offer our prayers of repentance on this day in which ashes bring fresh meaning to our mortality. Our confessions, O God, are often too quick and too shallow to disturb the core of our unfaithfulness and captivity to sin. Help us to use this time of worship to acknowledge how far we fall from your will for our lives. With the apostle Paul, we do not do the good that we strive to do. Instead, we do evil deeds that shock and surprise us. Our sins are sometimes apparent to us and to others. Our sins are sometimes cloaked in our attempts at righteousness. May the ashes that we carry on our foreheads this day not lead to earthly reward or acclaim. May the prayers that we pray not be offered in pomposity. May the alms that we give be offered so as to glorify you and not ourselves. Forgiving God, have pity on your people assembled here. Create new hearts within us and grant us fresh spirits. Amen.

Prayer of Dedication of Gifts and Self

God, on this day, we begin a season of preparation. You offer this time to ready ourselves for great and unparalleled joy. You offer us 40 days to focus on our commitment to the good news of Jesus Christ. With these gifts we offer back a small portion of what you have given to us. Inspire us to use what we have kept for ourselves in such a way that our belongings give honor to you. May our houses or apartments be dwellings of your Spirit. May the food that we eat be fuel for our service in Jesus' name. May our times of recreation and quiet make us more ready to act on your behalf. Jesus dedicated himself entirely to us. May we dedicate ourselves to you in return. Amen.

Sermon Summary

Calamitous events are common in our lives. Such events may be natural disasters (locusts or hurricane), national disasters (9/11/01), or individual tragedies (death or disease). Do disasters drive us closer to the God who offers us blessings instead of woe?

Hymn of the Day

"Sunday's Palms Are Wednesday's Ashes"

Another hymn set to the tune "Beach Spring" (see January 11), this hymn by Rae E. Whitney refers to the custom on Ash Wednesday of burning palms from the previous year's Palm Sunday. The text moves from this ritual to a confessional mood appropriate to the beginning of Lent, and the first and third stanzas end with a plea for pardon and renewal. The middle stanza suggests that aduring the lenten season we let go of our failings as an appropriate offering to God.

Children's Time

Return to God

Today is Ash Wednesday, the beginning of Lent. Lent is the 40 days (not counting Sundays) before Easter when we learn more about God's love and about Jesus' life.

Forty days was an important number in the Bible. Forty days is how long it rained when Noah and his family (and all those animals!) were on the ark. Forty days is how long Jesus spent in the wilderness at the beginning of his ministry.

And now we have 40 days to spend praying that God will draw us close and hold us in God's loving arms. We have 40 days to learn about Jesus' ministry when he lived on the earth. We have 40 days to get ready for Easter.

God wants us to come closer. If we've done or said things that are against God's way, God wants to forgive us and draw us closer. God wants us to trust and love God. God want us to return again and again for God's love and care.

The Bible tells us to gather together all the generations, the old folks and the children, even the little babies to worship God. We all gather today, thinking about what we've done wrong and how sorry we are, and returning again to God's loving care. It's good to be here today.

The Sermon

The Day of the Lord

Hymns

Beginning of Worship: "O Lord, Throughout These Forty Days"
Sermon Hymn: "A Mighty Fortress Is Our God"
Closing Hymn: "I Want Jesus to Walk with Me"

Scripture

Joel 2:1-2, 12-17 (For sermon materials on Matthew 6:1-6, 16-21, see the 2003 May/June planning issue of *The Clergy Journal* and on 2 Corinthians 5:20b–6:10, see the November/December 2003 issue of *The Clergy Journal*.)

The prophet Joel announces, "The day of the Lord is coming, it is near" (Joel 2:1).

So, just what does a day of the Lord look like? In Joel's time it looked like a swarm of locusts so massive that the sky grew dark, even black, with the insects that would render the region nearly uninhabitable. In the verses omitted from the reading for this Ash Wednesday, Joel describes this army of locusts vividly. They leave nothing but a desert wasteland behind them. All who see this army of destruction are in anguish, and their faces turn pale.

The day is coming and the day is near when the Lord will judge God's people.

In our own recent history, we in the United States experienced a cataclysmic event that has captured our minds, attention, and spirits. Does September 11, 2001, or 9/11 as it is usually called, seem like very old news to us? Or do repercussions of that day still reverberate in our daily lives?

For one group of Christians in New York City on that fateful day, 9/11 will always be a day that changed their world. St. Paul's Chapel used to be a thriving Episcopal parish just kitty-corner from the World Trade Center. Having fallen into disuse, St. Paul's was incorporated into the ministry of Trinity Episcopal Church a few blocks away. St. Paul's Chapel was in the process of being transformed into a successful alternative ministry for the Trinity Parish. Then, 9/11.

February 25, 2004
Ash Wednesday

Trinity is a parish with many blessings, including a television production studio. On 9/11 a group of people were at the church, filming a piece on Christian spirituality. Notables from across the country and world were gathered there, including Rowan Williams, Archbishop of Wales (who, 10 months later, was named Archbishop of Canterbury, head of the worldwide Anglican communion).

When disaster struck on 9/11, the people gathered at Trinity were forced to seek shelter from the collapsing buildings nearby. They crowded into a stairway. The air became so filled with fumes and smoke that breathing became difficult. It didn't take much imagination or despair to believe that the end was near. One of the people in that stairway went up to Rowan Williams and said, "If we are going to die, I am glad I am dying with you." Prayers, faith, and hugs were offered.

Is that what a day of the Lord looks like? Instead of hordes of locusts darkening the sky, is it the aftermath of terrorism? Is it fire, smoke, and ash that blot out the sun and sky and threaten to undo us? Will it be, as the prophet Joel suggests, a day of darkness and gloom, a day of clouds and thick darkness? Blackness, Joel writes, will be spread upon the mountains, perhaps not unlike the black and gray ashes of 9/11 that covered everything in the area of the twin towers.

It would be too bold to suggest that 9/11 was a day of the Lord. To the contrary, most people have attributed the day to great evil, not to some recompense from the Lord. Maybe two centuries from now theologians will look back on this day as having particularly apocalyptic significance, but we are far too close to the event for any defining perspective. At the same time, is it possible that the Lord can use hordes of locusts, or even the evil destruction of terrorists, to wake up God's people? The prophet Joel declares that God is gracious and merciful and calls the people to return to God and receive blessing.

In New York City, Trinity Church and St. Paul's Chapel became instruments of God's mercy and blessing. For almost nine months following the tragedy, the chapel served as a healing place. It started out simply as a place where the weary and the grieving could find food and rest. It quickly evolved into a place where rescue workers could find almost every necessity they needed, from over-the-counter medications, replacement boots, and gloves to a healing word of grief counseling. And always, a place to rest. The chapel became a display of good wishes and God's blessings from around the city, nation, and world.

Trinity Parish will never be the same again, nor will the many families who live with the horrific aftermath of that day each and every day. What about you? Did 9/11 change your life in some unalterable way?

What would a "day of the Lord" look like in your life? Maybe you know, because you have experienced a personal "day of the Lord." Maybe it was the day you heard the diagnosis of cancer or the day when that dreaded telephone call came. Maybe it was the day you were shipped overseas for military service or the day you thought your marriage was unraveling. Maybe it was today. Maybe it will be tomorrow.

On all days, return to the Lord your God, for God is gracious and merciful – even in the worst of darkness and gloom. In the ashes of New York City, in the ashes of your own worst days, and in the ashes of this worship service, there is a blessing. God's mercy abounds.

– Norman W. Wahl
Bethel Lutheran Church
Rochester, Minnesota

February 29, 2004

1st Sunday in Lent

Lessons

RCL	Deut 26:1-11	Rom 10:8b-13	Lk 4:1-13
Roman Catholic	Deut 26:4-10	Rom 10:8-13	Lk 4:1-13
Episcopal (BCP)	Deut 26:(1-4) 5-11	Rom 10:(5-8a) 8b-13	Lk 4:1-13

Introduction to the Lessons

Lesson 1

***Deuteronomy 26:1-11* (RCL); *Deuteronomy 26:4-10* (RC); *Deuteronomy 26:(1-4) 5-11* (Epis)**

The book of Deuteronomy is unwavering in setting the expectation that all of life will be lived before the Lord. This action on our part is a response to being God's chosen people and not an attempt to earn a relationship with God. Twenty-five times, the book of Deuteronomy declares that worship is carried out "before the Lord." God's people are called to worship only the "Lord your God."

Lesson 2

***Romans 10:8b-13* (RCL); *Romans 10:8-13* (RC); *Romans 10:(5-8a) 8b-13* (Epis)**

Paul recalls the Law of Moses in this passage, establishing with the book of Deuteronomy the truth of the way of righteousness. This way is possible for us because the word is near to us, as near as our own hearts and mouths. Such righteousness may best be exemplified by one of the earliest confessions of faith, "Jesus is Lord."

Gospel

***Luke 4:1-13* (RCL/RC/Epis)**

This is a story about obedience. Three times Jesus quotes scripture in response to the devil's temptations. The people of Israel were unfaithful in the wilderness. The Son of God proves his faithfulness in the wilderness as he completes the preparation for his public ministry.

Theme

Let us bow down before the Lord our God.

Thought for the Day

What would happen if everyone in the world obeyed the First Commandment perfectly? Would there be war? Likely not, for there would be a distribution of goods to satisfy everyone and no need for war. In our own little part of the world, let us live each day as those who have but one God, the maker of heaven and earth.

Call to Worship

Leader: We who live in the shelter of the most high, who abide in the shadow of the almighty, say to the Lord,

People: "You are our refuge and our fortress; our God in whom we trust."

Leader: Because we have made the Lord our refuge and the Most High as our dwelling place,

People: No evil shall befall us, no scourge come near our tents.

Leader: God will command angels concerning us to guard us in all our ways.

People: The hands of angels will bear us up, so that we will not dash our feet against a stone.

Leader: We call on the Lord, who will answer us.

People: God, be with us in times of trouble. Rescue us, honor us, and show us your salvation.

– Based on Psalm 91:1-2, 9-12, 15-16

Pastoral Prayer

It is with wonder, God, that we journey with Jesus in the wilderness this day. We wonder about the vexing of the devil and the strength of your Son in his time of great need. We even wonder about the Holy Spirit who led Jesus while he was in the wilderness. It is a tempting world in which we find ourselves. Everywhere we look there are temptations to buy what we don't need and to find happiness in the trappings of this world. Children and youth face temptations of which their elders never dreamed. Vast sums of money give rise to unethical behavior. Lead us not into temptation, Lord. Deliver us from evil. Fill us, too, with your Holy Spirit, that we might be led and strengthened as we march through the wildernesses of our lives. Prove us worthy to bear the name of Jesus into the world. Lead us to worship only you, and guide us to bring you the first fruits of our lives and our labor. O God, we do not live by bread alone. We live by the word, in whose name we pray. Amen.

Prayer of Confession

O Lord our God, if the devil led us to a high place and showed us all the glories of the world – all the money, all the glory, all the land – and offered them to us for worshiping him instead of you, how strong would our faith prove to be? By our actions in this past week we have given evidence that we would offer even our souls to the devil if the price were right. When the clerk gave us too much change, we worshiped money rather than your commandment to deal honestly with people. When we had a chance to tell a gossipy story at work or school, we worshiped personal satisfaction rather than your commandment to not bear false witness. When we had a chance to help our neighbor, we put our own needs and desires first, thereby putting ourselves above you. Forgive us our wandering ways. Incline us toward the path of righteousness. We pray in the name of the Son who worshiped only you, Jesus Christ our Lord. Amen.

Prayer of Dedication of Gifts and Self

Thousands of years ago, gracious Lord, you gave your people a land and an inheritance. It was a place flowing with milk and honey, with an abundance of fruit. In these days you have blessed us even more bountifully. Bring us to give thanks for the richness in which we live. Strengthen and guide us to share our riches with those in need – for those living in areas that suffer from drought or flood, for those whose homes are ravaged by war and strife. Help us also to share of the eternal riches that we have been given in Jesus Christ. May we dedicate our lives each day to being gospel bearers to those around us, even as Jesus who is the good news leads us to the cross. Amen.

Sermon Summary

From the beginning of time, people have been tempted to bow before gods other than the one true God. The writer of the book of Deuteronomy leaves no room for error in exhorting the people to serve only the one God, the God who saved the chosen people from slavery in Egypt and who has given them wondrous blessings.

Hymn of the Day

"Jesus Walked This Lonesome Valley"

This traditional, anonymous American folk hymn fits well with the beginning of Lent, often referred to as a journey or a voyage. As we reflect on the story of Jesus' temptation, we think of all he endured during the final weeks and days of his life, and contemplate what that means for us. In this same context, the stanzas of this hymn invite us to recognize our individual need to experience, in all its fullness, the annual season of Lent, that we might experience in even greater fullness the never ending season of Easter.

Children's Time

Be Grateful

(Preparation: Bring an offering plate and your offering envelope.)

How many of you get an allowance? What do you do with the money? *(Invite responses.)* When I get some money, I do three things with it. I give some to the church or another good cause that helps people; I save some; and I spend some for things I need like food and gas for the car.

The Bible story today tells us about a way of showing God how grateful we are for all that we are given. In this story, farmers are told to take some of the first part of the grain or fruit that they harvest and place it in a basket and take it to the temple as an offering to God. The farmers were told to remember their families and the important times in their lives while they made their offering, and to give thanks to God for all they have.

Imagine if we did this! As I give my offering to God, I might say, *(fill in here with your own history as you put your offering envelope in the collection plate)*. What might you say as you give your offering? *(Invite responses.)*

The Sermon

Kneeling Before the One God

Hymns

Beginning of Worship: "Holy Majesty, before You"
Sermon Hymn: "Let Us Break Bread Together on Our Knees"
Closing Hymn: "Savior, Again to Your Dear Name"

Scripture

Deuteronomy 26:1-11 (For sermon materials on Romans 10:8b-13, see the 2003 May/June planning issue and on Luke 4:1-13, see the November/December 2003 issue of *The Clergy Journal.*)

If you are a student of American history, you remember the name of Robert E. Lee, the general who was instrumental in leading the Confederate Army during the American Civil War in the 1860s. General Lee was a superb military strategist and was able to win many battles over the Union Army even though he generally had fewer soldiers, fewer munitions, and fewer supplies.

However, the sheer numbers and resources of the North wore down the military efforts of the South. By April of 1865, the southern capital of Richmond, Virginia, was threatened and the Confederate forces made plans to retreat and entrench themselves deeper in the South.

"April 2, 1865, began in Richmond with the steady tolling of bells that awoke a slumbering city. It was Communion Sunday." (Jay Winik, *April 1865: The Month that Saved America* [New York: HarperCollins Publishers, 2001], p. 102.) In spite of recurring losses, southern pride was evident everywhere, even in the church. It would probably be fair to say that most every warring people has believed God to be on their side, and they have invoked God's name for victory. It was no different during the Civil War – both sides were sure that they would win the war with God's help.

St. Paul's Episcopal Church in Richmond was the house of worship of choice for the city's elite (ibid, p. 104) including General Robert E. Lee and Confederate President Jefferson Davis. On April 2, however, Lee was engaged with his men while Davis was worshiping. After the invocation, a military messenger hurried to pew number 63 and handed Davis an urgent message from Lee. The message indicated that fall of Richmond was imminent.

During numerous battles during the next week, tens of thousands of lives were lost on both sides. General Grant of the Union Army proposed surrender to General Lee. And about one week after the fall of Richmond, Robert E. Lee surrendered the Confederate Army of Northern Virginia at Appomattox.

It was only a matter of a few more weeks in April of 1865 before the rest of the Confederate Army laid down their arms in surrender. In spite of great southern pride and resistance to admit defeat on the part of some people, Robert E. Lee was chief among leaders in the South to encourage citizens to become loyal to the Union.

Late in the spring of 1865, there was another Communion Sunday at St. Paul's Episcopal Church. As the communion began, a black man approached the communion rail along with the white members. Customarily in this church, blacks had waited until whites had finished communing before coming to the altar. Listen to the account of what happened:

> The black man slowly lowered his body, kneeling, while the rest of the congregation tensed in their pews. For his part, the minister stood, clearly uncomfortable and still dumbfounded. After what seemed to be an interminable amount of time – although it was probably only seconds – another white man arose, his gait erect, head up and eyes proud, and walked quietly up the aisle to the chancel rail. His face was a portrait of exhaustion . . . with quiet dignity and self-possession, Robert E. Lee knelt down to partake of the communion, along the same rail with the black man. (Ibid, pp. 362–363)

In the text from Deuteronomy that is our lesson today, the writer implores us four times to respond, to kneel, to worship "before the Lord your God." It is no accident that the first commandment is "You shall have no other gods." Were we to fully comply with this commandment, there would be no need for the other nine. We need to be continually reminded that there is but one God, and that One is the God before whom we kneel; that One is the God we worship.

We are prone to allowing other gods to capture our hearts. It would have been easy in a time of Civil War to allow one's allegiance to one's culture to eclipse one's faithfulness to God. It would have been easy for

Robert E. Lee to be embittered over the end of the war and to encourage southern partisanship for the rest of his life.

Lee recognized, however, that there is but one God. And that God is the God before whom he bowed. In a time in which it might have been scandalous or even dangerous to kneel beside a black man at the communion rail, Lee led the way, at least for that moment, for the children of God to come together in worship in the way that God intended.

Bow down before the Lord your God. There is no other. Amen.

– Norman W. Wahl
Bethel Lutheran Church
Rochester, Minnesota

March 7, 2004

2nd Sunday in Lent

Lessons

RCL	Gen 15:1-12, 17-18	Phil 3:17–4:1	Lk 13:31-35 or Lk 9:28-36
Roman Catholic	Gen 15:5-12, 17-18	Phil 3:17–4:1 or 3:20–4:1	Lk 9:28b-36
Episcopal (BCP)	Gen 15:1-12, 17-18	Phil 3:17–4:1	Lk 13:(22-30) 31-35

Introduction to the Lessons

Lesson 1

***Genesis 15:1-12, 17-18* (RCL/RC/Epis)**

The passage reflects God's covenant renewal with Abram. Graphically portrayed in this passage is the Hebrew concept of cutting a covenant. The covenant is sealed when the torch passes between the cut animals as a sign of God's faithfulness.

Lesson 2

***Philippians 3:17–4:1*(RCL/RC/Epis)**

Citizenship in heaven gives us new life in Christ. It saves us from destruction and through Christ we become transformed so that we are not only imitators of Paul, but are also conformed to the body of Christ's glory.

Gospel

(1) *Luke 13:31-35* (RCL); *Luke 13:(22-30) 31-35* (Epis)

Jesus responds to the Pharisees who say that Herod is about to kill him. After predicting that he will finish his work on the third day, Jesus laments that Jerusalem has killed the prophets and stoned those who have been sent to it.

(2) *Luke 9:28b-36* (RC)

The transfiguration scene is punctuated by the theophany of God in a cloud that envelops the disciples. Rather than a sign of judgment, this cloud from God becomes a sign of hope, inviting the disciples to listen to Jesus, God's chosen.

Theme

God gives life. False gods destroy.

Thought for the Day

Our heavenly citizenship helps us keep our eyes focused on Jesus Christ, and his life, death, and resurrection for our sake. God gives us life eternal through Jesus Christ. In contrast, the gods that the world reveres lead us into our own destruction.

Call to Worship

Gracious God, you are the giver of every good and perfect gift. We thank you for the gift of your son, and the life that you have given us through his suffering and death. Help us as we worship to keep our lives centered on God, and the life that you give to us daily.

Pastoral Prayer

Lord God we recognize that our world continually tempts us with the voices of those who would claim to be gods and deceive us by claiming to offer to us what only you can give. Help us, O God, when we hear those voices and are tempted by their claims. Help us, O God, to resist the temptation to follow those gods. Let us look to you for strength and fortitude in the face of such temptation. Help us resist the invitations that those gods present, instead strengthening us to celebrate always with joy and thanksgiving the many ways in which you surround us with the gifts of your grace and the power of your Holy Spirit. In the end, O God, remind us of our heavenly citizenship. Empower us to lead others to enjoy the life that you bring us each day, and lead them to know the life-giving power of your holy name. Amen.

Prayer of Confession

Loving God, we humbly confess that all too often we are more interested in the voices of this world than we are in listening to your voice. We seek to control that which is beyond our power, and we want to own that which only you can claim. We acknowledge that as we hunger and thirst for more material possessions, we ignore our hunger and thirst for you. We need you, God, and the forgiveness you bring to save us from our wayward paths and lead us away from the sources of our destruction. Help us look toward you as our source of power and life. Give us the strength to make decisions that reflect our faith and our trust in you, so that when confronted by the gods of this world, we might live in hope and certainty, trusting that you never leave us nor forsake us. We ask this, O God, in the name of your son Jesus Christ, our Lord. Amen.

Prayer of Dedication of Gifts and Self

Merciful God, you have blessed us richly with every good and perfect gift. Help us not only to appreciate and give thanks for those gifts, but lead us to be faithful stewards of these gifts. Remind us of the privilege that you give to serve you and to worship you each day. Help us see in the ordinary events of our lives, the extraordinary power of your grace and mercy. Renew us, O God, with the gift of your Holy Spirit, so that drawn to you and the life that you give, we might in turn renew others with the promise of your presence and the gift of your love. Send us out into the world that you have created, to faithfully serve you and, through our service, point others to your never ending gifts. Help us as to invite others into your kingdom to enjoy the love of your heavenly rule. Amen.

Sermon Summary

Our world is filled with competing forces that invite our commitment and command our response. Our heavenly citizenship helps us commit our lives to God, and through that choice, celebrate the life that only God can give.

Hymn of the Day

"When Twilight Comes"

This beautiful hymn from the Philippines picks up on the image presented in today's gospel where Jesus compares himself to a mother hen. The text rejoices in the loving nurturing and healing presence of Christ. The closing line, "by a mother's love embraced in the blessed Trinity" provides a bold way of naming the godhead. The text was written by Moises Andrade and translated by Australian Anglican priest James Minchin.

The tune by Francisco Feliciano is in a minor key, and yet it conveys the gentle joy of the words.

Children's Time

Copy This!

(Perform several simple motions and ask the children to imitate *you.)* If I threw some orange paint on the floor in here and asked you to imitate me, would you do it? Why or why not?

Our Bible reading this morning is from our old friend, the apostle Paul. Paul has some advice for us as we live as God's children. Paul says to be careful of imitating other people. Have you ever thought about this? We see lots of people at school, on television, or at the mall. Some people behave in caring and responsible ways. They love God and they love their neighbors. Other people do things that hurt themselves or others or the Earth.

So, how do we know when it's OK to imitate someone? *(Invite responses.)* Sometimes it's easy to tell. Sometimes it's not.

It's good to ask ourselves some simple questions. Does this person take care of other people? Does this person do things that are healthy for her or his own body? Does this person take care of the earth? The apostle Paul warns us to make careful decisions about imitating other people. Maybe when we're looking for another person to imitate, we should choose Jesus. He's the best one to imitate!

The Sermon

The Life-Giving Choice

Hymns

Beginning of Worship: "Let Us Ever Walk with Jesus"
Sermon Hymn: "O Savior Precious Savior"
End of Worship: "Lift High the Cross"

Scripture

Philippians 3:17–4:1 (For additional sermon materials on this passage, see the November/December 2003 issue of *The Clergy Journal* and on Genesis 15:1-12, 17-18, see the 2003 May/June planning issue of *The Clergy Journal.*)

"False gods destroy! Only God gives life!" The confirmation teacher made the statement after she summarized her guest's presentation for the evening. The class was studying the first commandment, and the guest was a recovering alcoholic. He described his downward spiral into the world of chemical dependency and drug addiction. What had seemed so attractive to him as a high-school senior had turned his life into a quagmire of chaos. What had been a way for him to escape the horrors of the Vietnam War ultimately prevented him from seeing the potential beauty of God's world and all that this world offered him. What had appeared to be an exciting adventure had robbed him and made him confront the possibility of his own death. He ended his presentation by saying that alcoholism is a progressive and fatal disease.

The teacher knew what she was doing. She knew that the world the guest speaker described was no different than the world her students experienced. It was far different than the world she wanted them to experience. She thought about his presentation, as well as the lives of these young people that she had the privilege of teaching every week. She knew that false gods destroy. Would they learn that same message? Would the message from the visitor and from God's word prevent them from wandering off to try to discover the truth of that message on their own – in their own time?

That's why it was so important for her to invite her friend to share his experience with her students. She knew that chemical dependency is not only a physical crisis of epic proportions. It is a spiritual crisis as well. She wanted her students to hear what would happen when they moved away from their center. She wanted to let them know that such a move would not give them freedom; it in fact would make them slaves. It ultimately would lead to their destruction. In going away from their center, they would give up their ability to choose to serve God and their Lord and Savior, Jesus Christ.

No matter what age we are, it can be tempting to mistake the glamour of the demons of our society for that which is enlightening and truly life giving. Such demons and temptations can be extremely devious and difficult for us to discern. Whether the issue is chemical dependency or gambling, whether it is our own inability to control our anger or our need for more material goods, we are tempted to wander. We are tempted to wander away from our roots – from the God who has rooted us in the body of God's son, Jesus Christ.

Now, as Paul wrote this letter to the Philippians, he acknowledged that they were a strong congregation. They were a congregation that had given him much joy. They had responded emotionally as well as financially to the appeals Paul had made on behalf of the Jerusalem church. They had supported him and continued to support him, even though as he wrote this letter, Paul was in prison.

Yet, Paul still makes every effort to warn the Philippians of the temptation to wander off. Paul is concerned about all the gods that would try to seduce the Philippians into believing that they could go it on their own. Paul was concerned about the false gods who would try to lure them away from their center, their heavenly citizenship. Paul's warning is stark and to the point. He says that the Philippians and us have a choice of whether we will be imitators of him or will live as enemies of the cross. If we choose to live as enemies of the cross, we will be faced with our own destruction.

That is why it is so vital for Paul to help the Philippians remember who they are, and in whom they are centered. Paul speaks about this center by telling the Philippians that they are citizens of heaven. He boldly proclaims that God has the power to move them – transform them into the body of Christ. Once transformed into that body, Paul is confident that the Philippians will help others be transformed as well.

A father once told his son before he went away to college, "Son, remember who you are and you will always be in good hands." Perhaps the father's advice is meant for us as well. Only we might take some liberties and transform his message in this way. It is important for us – who claim to be members of the body of Christ – to remember not only who we are, but also whose we are. We belong to God. We have been given the sweatshirts that say, "Property of Yahweh." And since we belong to God, God has given us an eternal citizenship in heaven.

It is that citizenship – that gift – which should make all the difference in the world to us. For it is our heavenly citizenship that helps us trust that we are grounded in the very grace of God. From that grace it is God, through the power of the Spirit, who helps us to remember our center – to remember whose we are. It is God's grace that allows us to make choices that will glorify God, and in turn, empowers us to continue to be faithful in our service to God and to one another. We have become transformed into Christ's body, and citizens of heaven. Amen.

– John R. Bucka
House of Hope Lutheran Church
New Hope, Minnesota

March 14, 2004

3rd Sunday in Lent

Lessons

RCL	Isa 55:1-9	1 Cor 10:1-13	Lk 13:1-9
Roman Catholic	Ex 3:1-8a, 13-15	1 Cor 10:1-6, 10-12	Lk 13:1-9
Episcopal (BCP)	Ex 3:1-15	1 Cor 10:1-13	Lk 13:1-9

Introduction to the Lessons

Lesson 1

(1) *Isaiah 55:1-9* (RCL)

This reading looks with anticipation to the day when Israel will be restored. On that day, God will renew the covenant that was made with Israel. Israel will once again be a witness to the nations, and all the wicked will repent.

(2) *Exodus 3:1-8a, 13-15* (RC); *Exodus 3:1-15* (Epis)

This account highlights the call of Moses through the theophany of the burning bush. The identification of the sovereign who calls Moses is simply, "I am." The phrase probably is derived from the Hebrew word for God, *Yahweh* or *the one who causes to be.*

Lesson 2

1 Corinthians 10:1-13 (RCL/Epis);
1 Corinthians 10:1-6, 10-12 (RC)

Paul uses an incident from Israel's time in the wilderness to warn the Corinthians against behavior that would lead them away from God. At the same time, Paul says that even in the midst of temptation, God will provide them with strength to withstand that temptation.

Gospel

Luke 13:1-9 (RCL/RC/Epis)

The theme of repentance is the focal point of this passage. Jesus' audience questions him about Pilate and the Galileans, then Jesus expands on the theme of repentance as he discusses the parable of the fig tree.

Theme

Repentance leads us to live without fear and bear fruit.

Thought for the Day

It is not always easy for us to admit that we have sinned. It is even more difficult for us, once we have confessed our sins, to change our ways. God, however, gives us the strength to confess and to change, through the gift of the Holy Spirit.

Call to Worship

O God, help us to see how far we have fallen from your ways and your will. As we worship you, come to us as you do each day of our lives. We offer thanks for the power of your forgiveness and the strength of your love.

Pastoral Prayer

Loving God, you have given us many blessings and supplied us with everything that we need. We are your servants, the people that you have created. When we are tempted to move away from you, O God, bring us back by your benevolent mercy. When we fail to use the gifts and the talents that you have given us, renew us with the strength of your will and the wisdom of your direction. When we would rather stand idly by than to become involved in the passion and the suffering of this world, move us to act with the gift of your compassion. When we surround ourselves with images that would lead to our destruction, renew us with the Spirit of your life-giving love. When we walk away from you and the lives to which you have called us, lead us to repentance so that our broken and sinful hearts might be healed by your Word. All this we ask not only for our sake, but also for the sake of your Son, Jesus Christ our Lord. Amen.

Prayer of Confession

Merciful God, what is it about answering your call to faithfulness that makes us afraid? What causes us to shrink away from all that you would have us do? Why is it, O God, that we are attracted by the easy life, the life that invites us to stand by and watch the innocent suffer and the victims of injustice continue to cry out? We confess to you, merciful God, that we have not grown in your word and your love as you want us to grow. Not only have we not done what you have desired, we often have done that which the world has desired. We seek your forgiveness for what we have done and what we have failed to do. Help us change, so that we might be transformed by the power of your almighty grace. Give us the joy of that transformation so that as we faithfully respond to your call to be your son's disciples, we might bear the fruit of repentance and reflect the power of your love. Amen.

Prayer of Dedication of Gifts and Self

We come to you this day, O God, grateful for the gifts that you have given us. You have blessed us with what we need; you provide for us each day, even those days when we forget to ask for your blessings. Help us appreciate your gifts, O God, and give us the strength and dedication to use those gifts to your glory. May our lives reflect what you have given us, so that we bring honor to your name and bring others to your love. Help us, gracious God, to continue to grow as if our lives were wonderful plants rooted in your word. Give us power to grow in faith toward you and in love toward all people, that all people might come to know the joy of your blessings. Amen.

Sermon Summary

The idea of bearing fruit – or of seeing our lives from the perspective of God as the gardener and we as fig trees – seems frightening until we realize that God helps us bear the fruit of repentance.

Hymn of the Day

"There's a Wideness in God's Mercy"

Originally part of a much longer poem, the verses of this hymn use simple words such as kindness, justice, welcome, and healing to depict the mercy of God, which author Frederick William Faber depicts as being as vast as the sea.

The hymn's simple majesty is supported by the anonymous Dutch tune "In Babilone."

Children's Time

Whose Fault Is It?

Long ago, people used to believe that if it didn't rain for many months, it was because they had been bad and some god was angry at them. Or if there had been a huge storm and houses had been blown down, they thought that it must be some kind of punishment for something they had done wrong. To be honest, there are still people who believe this today. But I don't. And Jesus, in today's Bible passage, says that he doesn't either.

Jesus tells about a tragedy that happened in Jerusalem: a tower fell on eighteen people and killed them. Some people said that this happened because they were bad people, but Jesus said that was not true.

If something bad happens to us, it does not mean that God thinks we are very bad. Bad things happen to ordinary people. It's very sad, and God is sad, too. Bad things just happen – that's the way of our sinful world.

It is true that each one of us does things that do not make God very happy, but God does not punish us for them by doing things like sending storms to blow down our houses. Our sins do make God unhappy, and Jesus teaches us to say "sorry" to God and ask God for forgiveness.

The Sermon

The Trouble with Gardening

Hymns

Beginning of Worship: "Lord of Glory You Have Bought Us"
Sermon Hymn: "We Plow the Field and Scatter"
End of Worship: "Lord I Lift Your Name on High"

Scripture

Luke 13:1-9 (For additional sermon materials on this passage, see the November/December 2003 issue of *The Clergy Journal* and on 1 Corinthians 10:1-13, see the 2003 May/June planning issue of *The Clergy Journal.*)

I remember the year that I finally decided to give up gardening for good. I always wanted to garden because my parents had gardened. My in-laws had been successful gardeners as well. So I tried. I planted, I hoed, I weeded, and I fertilized. I cultivated. In spite of it all, the yields that I received were paltry in contrast to what friends and neighbors would produce. I do believe that the straw that finally broke my proverbial back came when potato bugs attacked, and threatened to destroy completely all the work that I had done.

As I look back on that experience, I realize that somehow I was taking the whole enterprise much too personally. It wasn't just that my crops had failed or had failed to produce. I felt that I was the one who had failed. My lack of agricultural-horticultural skill had caused the production failure to occur. It was my own propensity to blame myself that caused me to quit gardening for good. The weeds weren't to blame. The lack of water or the potato bugs weren't the culprits. I was all of the above. I had failed to make the crops produce to their own maximum potential.

That was my experience with gardening, but I wonder if there is a universal lesson to be learned by that experience. It isn't only gardening that pressures us to produce fruit from our labors, so to speak. We experience this pressure at every level of life. It starts as early as toilet training and continues through elementary and grade school. We need to make the grade, toe the line, or win the reward. We need to succeed, earn an income, provide for our families, and gain recognition. And yet in this growing season that we call life, more often than not we emphasize the moments of our lives when we do not achieve. We remember our failures. More often than not, we are our own worst critics and our own worst enemies.

Perhaps that recognition alone contributes to our difficulty when we first approach this text. If the gospel is indeed good news, just where does the good news reside as we hear the words of this text? If parables are earthly stories with heavenly meanings, then even our heavenly fate appears to be called into question. If Jesus seems to be so harsh on this poor unsuspecting fig tree, will he not be just as harsh with us? We at least do have some semblance of control over what we do or say. We are able to recognize when we fail and when we fail to succeed.

So our first reaction to this text is truly one of avoidance. In fact, some would cite this text as one of the reasons why people leave organized religion. It's pretty much gloom and doom. It's seen as another attempt to scare people into being good and manipulate people into doing what they are not good at doing in the first place. After all, if we experience such a difficult time in meeting our own goals and fulfilling our own expectations, how much more impossible can it be for us when it comes to doing what God desires? In the face of questions such as these, who could blame people for shutting down and walking away, believing that the Bible gives them no hope, but only failure and judgment?

We need to pause for a moment and take into account the context of this story, as well as the one who tells it. When we recognize what is occurring in this text, we can turn our sadness to joy and our fear into faith. In this text Jesus offers us a small view of the greater portrait we call our salvation story. In this story we are the ones for whom Jesus comes and dies. In the salvation story, God sends forth the son precisely because of our inability to produce. Jesus suffers and dies because we have not been the faithful producers that God initially desired us to be. Thus, the destruction that we deserved, Jesus endured.

Viewed in that light, the gospel becomes even more important for us. For it is Jesus Christ himself that removes the burden of that law from our shoulders. The gloom of judgment does not belong to us. God has taken that from us and places it squarely on the shoulders of Jesus. That exchange then should lead us to a great sense of freedom and joy. No longer do we need to look on what God wants with suspicion and fear. No longer do we have to see our response to God in terms of obligation, burden, or drudgery. No longer do we have to view our lives as God's children from the perspective of what we need to do or should do.

It is God who created our lives from the very dust of the earth. It is God who breathed life into us with the breath of God's Spirit. It is this same Spirit that lives now grows us in grace and in faith. What God first planted in us, God continues to tend, nurture, and grow. What God first began within us, God will bring to completion.

It is God, then, who never quits gardening and never walks away from the seeds that have been planted. It is that same God who sends Jesus, the shepherd, to look for us, the lost sheep. Jesus the shepherd finds a way to bring us back to the fold. When we are returned to the family of God, we are surrounded once more by the love of the Master Gardener. From the strength of the Gardener's love, the seed of faith that has been planted in our hearts will continue to grow and produce the fruit that God knows can be produced. Thanks be to God! Amen.

– John R. Bucka
House of Hope Lutheran Church
New Hope, Minnesota

March 21, 2004

4th Sunday in Lent

Lessons

RCL	Josh 5:9-12	2 Cor 5:16-21	Lk 15:1-3, 11b-32
Roman Catholic	Josh 5:9a, 10-12	2 Cor 5:17-21	Lk 15:1-3, 11-32
Episcopal (BCP)	Josh (4:19-24); 5:9-12	2 Cor 5:17-21	Lk 15:11-32

Introduction to the Lessons

Lesson 1

Joshua 5:9-12 **(RCL/Epis);** ***Joshua 5:9a, 10-12*** **(RC)**

The Israelites finally reach their destination of Canaan and began to enjoy the fruit of the land, instead of the manna that they had been receiving. At Gilgal the commander of the Lord's army visits Joshua and pledges his assistance.

Lesson 2

2 Corinthians 5:16-21 **(RCL);**
2 Corinthians 5:17-21 **(RC/Epis)**

The coming of Christ changes humans from those who were once a part of the old creation to people who are members of the new creation in Christ. The old has passed away and the new has come.

Gospel

Luke 15:1-3, 11b-32 **(RCL);** ***Luke 15:1-3, 11-32*** **(RC);**
Luke 15:11-32 **(Epis)**

The texts tell the familiar parable of the prodigal son. Some interpreters retitle this story, the waiting father. Whatever the title, the story emphasizes God's patience and God's way of dealing with those who are lost.

Theme

God's grace often brings results that we do not expect.

Thought for the Day

God's grace rarely operates in ways that humans predict. We often believe that only those who behave in prescribed ways will earn God's favor, then are amazed when God is gracious to those whom we believe least deserve it.

Call to Worship

O God, your love for your people is boundless and your patience without end. As we begin our worship, help us trust that you give us that same patience and that endless love. May that patience and love give us hope through Jesus Christ

Pastoral Prayer

God of grace and God of glory, pour out your power. From your great store of wisdom and strength, give us willing minds and welcoming hearts so we might continue to be bearers of your grace. Through our witness, help us reflect the glory that you have given to us through your son, Jesus Christ our Lord. As we go out into the world help us to see in each person not that which divides us but that which unites us. As we recognize our differences, help us search for our similarities as well. Remind us, O God, that you are a patient and loving God. You extend the welcome of your grace to all people. Nourished by your grace, may we welcome and love others as you have welcomed and continue to love us. Amen.

Prayer of Confession

God, we have failed to realize the all-encompassing circle of your grace. It is so difficult to imagine how you can love and welcome all people, no matter what they have done or have failed to do. When we look at the magnitude of your grace, we realize how the circles we have drawn have not included all people. We have used the circles of our communities, our families, and even our churches to exclude those with whom we differ and those who make us uncomfortable. Forgive us, God, for our failure to welcome the stranger, and to show love and kindness even to the people we love. Continue to love us and draw us into the circle of your family, reassuring us that when we are tempted to exclude others, you continue to include us as your precious children. From the circle of your grace, give us that same spirit of hospitality so that all people might come to know the power of your everlasting love. Amen.

Prayer of Dedication of Gifts and Self

God, as we respond with joy and thanksgiving to the grace that you have given us through Jesus Christ, help us share your love with all people. Give us a measure of your grace so that we might dedicate ourselves and all that you have given us to serving all people. Help us to see that your Son gave his life not to exclude, but to include all people as members of your realm. Strengthen us in the hope of your promise and gift, the gift of eternal life with you. Amen.

Sermon Summary

Do we draw the circles of our lives to include all, or do we exclude those who are different? In spite of our attempts to exclude people, God continues to include us as members of the body of Christ through the gift of God's never ending grace.

Hymn of the Day

"Softly and Tenderly"

The words and music to this hymn were written by Will L. Thompson, and the hymn grew in popularity through its use as a hymn of invitation and commitment at Dwight L. Moody's evangelistic gatherings. The image is of Jesus, like the father in the story of the prodigal son, waiting patiently and lovingly for the return of us, the wayward children. In earlier times it was frequently sung at funerals.

Children's Time

Celebrate!

Jesus told this story:

There was a farmer who had two sons. The younger son wanted to enjoy life in the city. So he went to his father and asked if he could have his share of the inheritance. The father gave him his money and the younger son went to the city. He wasted his money on all sorts of things that seemed fun at the time.

After a while, he had no money left. He was hungry, so he got a job taking care of pigs. He realized that the pigs had better food than he did!

This young man decided to go home and ask for his father's forgiveness, hoping that maybe his father would hire him as a servant.

When his father saw him coming, he raced out to meet him. He was so happy to have him back that he hugged him and kissed him. The son told his father how sorry he was for all the things he'd done wrong.

Why did Jesus tell this story? Jesus wants us to know that God is always happy when we go to God. God is waiting with open arms for us and will forgive us when we do or say something that is wrong. This is good news to celebrate!

The Sermon

Expanding the Circle

Hymns

Beginning of Worship: "The King of Love My Shepherd Is"
Sermon Hymn: "There's a Wideness in God's Mercy"
End of Worship: "Son of God, Eternal Savior"

Scripture

Luke 15:1-3, 11b-32 (For sermon materials on Joshua 5:9-12, see the 2003 May/June planning issue of *The Clergy Journal* and on 2 Corinthians 5:16-21, see the November/December 2003 issue of *The Clergy Journal.*)

The pastor was leading a retreat for the church council and administrative leaders when she asked, "Can I have eight volunteers come to the front and form a circle?"

After the circle had been formed, she commented, "Why is it that when we are asked to form a circle we always look inward, at one another? What would happen if the circles we formed looked outward, toward the people who are not a part of our circle?"

"Our circles would grow!" one leader replied. "Our church would not remain the same!" another person answered. "Why would we want to change?" another person queried. Needless to say, this retreat started with an intense discussion about the role and the mission of the church.

Which way do we choose to draw our circles? Do the circles we draw with our families, our work places, and our communities reflect our desire to be open? Do we draw them in ways that preserve what we hold dear and exclude that which threatens? In so many respects it seems natural for us to do the latter. After all, isn't that what families are for? Aren't we first and foremost called to look out for ourselves and the members of the groups to which we belong? After all, that's why we join groups, isn't it? We are looking for safety. We are looking for people who share things in common with us. We look to those who are like us for support and encouragement.

Yet, all too often we use our circles of familiarity to exclude – to keep us from venturing into areas where we might expand, learn, and contribute. It happens in churches, and it happens in communities as well. I saw it when I lived in a rural area. We would look at the town six miles down the road and say, "Thank God we live here, and not there." I've seen it when rural folks compare their way of life to life in cities. "Thank God we live here. This is a place where our kids will be safe, and we don't have to worry about gangs and drugs." City people do the same thing with people in rural areas.

In this familiar story about the parable of the prodigal son, the story begins with the Pharisees who complain, "This fellow welcomes sinners and eats with them." The circle of the scribes and Pharisees was an exclusive circle. Only those who obeyed the law perfectly were included. Within this circle, members would constantly thank God that their circle was different and unique. Throughout scripture, Jesus' encounters with these two groups reinforce that point. The Pharisees used not only the law, but also their interpretation of the law, to make sure that people who were dissimilar – people they named as sinners – would never be included within the reinforced boundary of their circle.

In response to their stubborn resistance to welcoming those who were different or who failed to measure up to their standards, Jesus tells this story of the prodigal son or the waiting father. The importance of the story is not only that the wandering son comes to his senses and returns to the good graces of his father; rather the story itself is told in contrast to the older son who believes that his brother should be excluded from the circle of his father's family. In the end, the father reassures this recalcitrant older son that his property has always belonged to this older son. The return of his younger brother does nothing to change the love that this father has for both sons.

March 21, 2004
4th Sunday in Lent

How do we draw the circles of our communities, our families, and our churches? Even as we ask that question, we need to acknowledge that were it not for Jesus' suffering, death, and resurrection, we too would be outside the circle of God's grace. We would be nothing more than prodigals; and even if we would come to our senses and try to return to the circle of God's family, we could never do so. Jesus Christ, however, has changed that for us. Jesus Christ brings us to God who is patient and loving, and ever willing to expand the circle of the family to include all people. Such is the power of God's grace.

Rather than make rules and regulations to exclude, grace brings us the love of the eternal God, who sent Jesus Christ on our behalf and throws a party for our return. For in every respect the words that the father says about this prodigal are the words that God says about us, "But we had to celebrate and rejoice, because this brother of yours was dead and has come to life; he was lost and has been found" (v. 32).

As we realize the magnanimous power of God's grace and the impact that it has upon our lives, this news should help us celebrate our lives with joy and thanksgiving. It should allow us to look at each day and each opportunity to serve as a gift of God's grace. Most importantly, it should challenge us to draw circles that include. It should help us expand our own circles of hospitality so that all the people we touch might know the touch of God's wonderful, welcoming, inclusive grace. For Jesus' sake! Amen.

– John R. Bucka
House of Hope Lutheran Church
New Hope, Minnesota

March 28, 2004

5th Sunday in Lent

Lessons

RCL	Isa 43:16-21	Phil 3:4b-14	Jn 12:1-8
Roman Catholic	Isa 43:16-21	Phil 3:8-14	Jn 8:1-11
Episcopal (BCP)	Isa 43:16-21	Phil 3:8-14	Lk 20:9-19

Introduction to the Lessons

Lesson 1

***Isaiah 43:16-21* (RCL/RC/Epis)**

This passage looks forward to the restoration of Israel. It anticipates Israel's return from exile by portraying a way home for the exiles through the wilderness. The return is accentuated by God's promise to do a new thing, and not to remember the things of old.

Lesson 2

***Philippians 3:4b-14* (RCL); *Philippians 3:8-14* (RC/Epis)**

Paul encourages the Philippians to run the race to which God has called them – to attain the goal of their heavenly call of God in Christ Jesus. It is a goal that is only reachable because Jesus Christ has claimed them and made them his own.

Gospel

(1) *John 12:1-8* (RCL)

Jesus returns to the house of Lazarus, where Mary anoints Jesus' feet and wipes them with her hair. The passage serves as a dramatic foreshadowing of that which is to come. In effect, Jesus is anointed for his burial in the presence of Judas who will betray him.

(2) *John 8:1-11* (RC)

The Pharisees and the scribes bring to Jesus an adulterous woman, wanting Jesus to comment on her guilt. Rather than reinforcing their verdict, Jesus says, "Let anyone . . . without sin be the first to . . . stone her."

(3) ***Luke 20:9-19***
There was a man who planted a vineyard and leased it to his tenants. The tenants killed the servants that the owner sent, including the owner's son. Jesus completes the story by discussing how the stone that the builders rejected will become the cornerstone.

Theme
Although we do not know what the future holds, we know who holds us in the future.

Thought for the Day
Since Jesus Christ has already made us his own, the race that we run is not a marathon to be endured, but an event to be celebrated. The race in which we participate is invigorated by the presence of Jesus, as well as the Holy Spirit who renews us daily.

Call to Worship
O God, you have called us to follow you and from the riches of your love you have given us the power to remain faithful to that call. Be with us, O God, as we worship you and as we continue to run the race that you have set before us.

Pastoral Prayer
Loving God, you have set us on the path and by your grace we travel the road of life with the power of your presence and the gift of your Holy Spirit. Set before us the gift of faith. Give us confidence that as we run the races of our lives, you have already given us the assurance and the promise of the heavenly prize that has been awarded through Jesus' suffering, death, and resurrection. Empower us to forget what is behind and strain for that which is ahead, trusting that you will never leave us nor forsake us. Allow us to complete the journey knowing that you will greet us at the last day. Amen.

Prayer of Confession

God, we often look at our lives as competitive struggles in which we vie not only for recognition from one another, but recognition and validation from you. So many times, we mistakenly think that it is completely up to us to finish this race – especially when the struggles of life overwhelm us. Forgive us for those times, O Lord, when we look only to our own power. Remind us that when the struggles of life occur, and the journeys of our lives become difficult, you are there to restore us and give us strength. You are with us through the Holy Spirit to empower us and keep us faithful to you. Continue, O God, to instill within us that faith and trust. Amen.

Prayer of Dedication of Gifts and Self

Loving God, we want to dedicate our gifts and ourselves totally and completely to you and your service. We bring to you our hearts, our love, our talents, and our abilities. We offer the gifts of our time and our possessions. We pray that what we bring will glorify you and help others to see the gift of your love. We dedicate these gifts to you – gifts that you have given us through your Son Jesus Christ and the power of the Holy Spirit. Amen.

Sermon Summary

As we travel the road of life and face life's struggles, we can be immobilized by our fears. Faith, however, empowers us to look toward the future, trusting that although we do not know what the future holds, we know who holds us as we move into the future.

Hymn of the Day

"Said Judas to Mary"

English schoolteacher Sydney Carter (perhaps best known for "I Danced in the Morning") wrote this hymn as an imagined conversation between Judas and Mary of Bethany. A paraphrase of today's gospel reading, the text and tune both carry a sense of the confrontation between these two biblical characters.

The hymn can readily be sung by a congregation as the folk-like tune is quite easy to learn. However, it can also be effective sung by three soloists, each one taking the part of Judas, Mary, or Jesus.

Children's Time

Winning the Big One

Preparation: Bring in an award ribbon or trophy.

This is a prize for *(explain the award).* What prizes have you or someone else in your family won? *(Invite responses.)* How did you celebrate winning the prize? *(Invite responses.)*

It's great to win a prize, isn't it? When we've worked and practiced hard, it feels good to win a prize, whether it's in sports or music or schoolwork. It's fun to celebrate when we win a prize, or when someone we know wins one.

The apostle Paul talked about winning prizes, but Paul didn't talk about prizes for running races or piano competitions. Instead, Paul said that being loved by Jesus is the biggest prize of all. All other prizes are nothing compared to the prize of belonging to Jesus.

The best part is, this is a prize we already have. That's right. Even if we never win any other prize in our whole lives, this prize is ours. Because of Jesus' life, death, and resurrection, we belong to Jesus. We win the prize of life with Jesus and God forever. Let's give a cheer for this great prize: "Thanks be to God!"

The Sermon

The Race Is Won

Hymns

Beginning of Worship: "Guide Me Ever, Great Redeemer"
Sermon Hymn: "Jesus, Lead Thou On"
End of Worship: "Praise to the Lord, the Almighty"

Scripture

Philippians 3:4b-14 (For additional sermon materials on this passage, see the 2003 May/June planning issue of *The Clergy Journal* and on Isaiah 43:16-21, see the November/December 2003 issue of *The Clergy Journal.*)

Nervously, anxiously she waits with a group of a thousand runners who are about to run the 26.2 mile race known as the marathon. The starter pistol sounds, and the herd of humanity begins to move forward, slowly at first. She feels like she is in a vacuum, being pushed, sucked, and shoved forward. Her heart begins to pound, and her breath starts its rapid repetitions as she feels her diaphragm moving up and down. In the middle of the race, she hits her stride. Everything is in harmony; her body, her limbs, the ground beneath her feet all meld into one symphonic verse. She glides as if she were carried by the wind, wondering if she can last forever in this euphoric state. Then suddenly without warning it hits. Some call it a wall. For her, it is more like a collision, a realization that every cell within her wants to shut down. Her body is crying out for her to stop. She truly begins to feel each pebble in the pavement below her tired aching feet. Will the finish line ever come?

Such is the life of a long-distance runner. Perhaps it is a life with which very few of us will ever identify. Most of us will never experience running a marathon; yet, the experiences of a marathon runner may be closer to us than we imagine. Some people refer to life as a race. We begin slowly, then come to a crawl. Then, incredibly, our lives begin to speed up until we limp, emotionally and physically, to the finish line. As we run this race, there are the proverbial peaks and valleys. Walls come up to hit us in the face and knock us flat. We run with elation, and we run with pain. And no matter where we run or how we run, we wonder about the purpose and meaning of it all. We investigate the deep questions of our lives and ask if God has anything to do with our running. We wonder about the purpose of running at all. What does all this running accomplish?

As Paul wrote his letter to the Philippians, he asked questions like these. He wondered about the purpose of everything that he had done. He questioned his life as a Pharisee. When Paul examined it all, he saw the futility of his former life. He recognized that his life as a student of the law did nothing to assure him that God was with him. He had been circumcised on the eighth day, a member of the people of Israel, the tribe of Benjamin. He had been a persecutor of the church, and viewed from the standards of the law, he was blameless. All of this, however, was to no avail. For Paul still did not believe and trust that God was with him, nor did Paul experience any vision of God's grace.

Paul's meaning came finally from Jesus Christ. In verse 8 he states, "I regard everything as loss because of the surpassing value of knowing Christ

Jesus my Lord." It was this knowledge that empowered Paul to run. And as he ran, Paul knew that his ability to finish the race was not up to him. His only responsibility was to keep on. Keep on running. Keep on moving. Keep on serving. In his words, "Christ Jesus has made me his own" (vs. 12). Paul's new identity in Christ made him realize that when the race finally ended, there would be nothing more and nothing less than that very same Jesus. That same Jesus motivated Paul to say earlier in the letter, "For to me, living is Christ and dying is gain" (1:21).

Jesus became the object of Paul's faith as he traveled life's road. Paul knew that the outcome at the end of his travel was not in doubt, for it would not be up to him to obtain that heavenly prize. That prize would be a gift to him as a result of how Jesus had made him his own on the cross.

As we run this race of life, questions are certain to arise. In the midst of the speed bumps that surprise us as well as the storms that surround us, we have more than our share of questions and doubts. We experience times when we wonder whether we are running alone, without support from anyone – including God. Yet the same Christ that made Paul his own has claimed us and named us. Certainly we do not know what our futures hold, but we know that Jesus holds us as we move into the future. Strengthened by faith in a present and risen Jesus, we need not look back in our past and stay stuck there. We can proceed down the road of life. Even as we continue to press on toward the goal of eternal life, we know that this prize already has been won and given to us through the gift of God's grace.

So in the end, we realize that our lives are not marathons to be endured; they are events to be celebrated. With a sense of celebration then, we continue. We continue to press on, to serve, to praise, to worship, and to proclaim that we are Christ's own. We will continue to be faithful to the heavenly call of God in Christ Jesus our Lord. Amen.

– John R. Bucka
House of Hope Lutheran Church
New Hope, Minnesota

April 4, 2004

Passion/Palm Sunday

Lessons

RCL	Isa 50:4-9a	Phil 2:5-11	Lk 22:14–23:56 or Lk 23:1-49
Roman Catholic	Isa 50:4-7	Phil 2:6-11	Lk 22:14–23:56 or Lk 23:1-49
Episcopal (BCP)	Isa 45:21-25 or Isa 52:13–53:12	Phil 2:5-11	Lk (22:39-71) 23:1-49 (50-56)

Introduction to the Lessons

Lesson 1

(1) *Isaiah 50:4-9a* (RCL); *Isaiah 50:4-7*

Taught by God, the Servant brings God's comfort to the weary. Though they abuse him, the Servant remains sure that God will vindicate him.

(2) *Isaiah 45:21-25* (Epis)

All nations are called to bow before the one God and sing God's praises.

Lesson 2

***Philippians 2:5-11* (RCL/Luth); *Philippians 2:6-11* (RC)**

God-in-Christ came to us as fully human; he died for us. For Jesus' humility, God has exalted and glorified Christ, so that all creation will some day worship Christ's holy name.

Gospel

***Luke 22:14-23:56* (RCL/RC);**
***(Luke 22:39-71) 23:1-49 (50-56)* (Epis)**

The Lord's Supper is instituted. Jesus and the disciples go out to the Mount of Olives, where he is betrayed.

Theme

The humility of the Suffering Servant will be vindicated. God will raise the Servant in glory, so that all creation will confess that Jesus is Lord.

Thought for the Day

God-in-Christ came to us, not in earthly pomp or with blasts of heavenly trumpets, but humbly, as one of us. We, too, are called to humility, and join with all creation in the joyous affirmation, "Christ Jesus is Lord!"

Call to Worship

Come, worship at the end of our lenten time of preparation. Let us look to the example of Jesus, coming before God in humility and obedience. Let us follow in Jesus' footsteps. Let us join with the church throughout the ages in the acclamation, "Christ Jesus is Lord!" Amen.

Pastoral Prayer

O God, your tender mercy and favor are poured out upon the humble and lowly. Help us, in this most holy time, to reflect on the awesome works you have done for us through the sacrifice of your Son. Make us worthy to join with all creation in praise of our Lord, Christ Jesus, the glorious ruler of all. Amen.

Prayer of Confession

God of Compassion, we confess before you that we have not loved you with heart, mind, and soul. Too often we fail to give to those in need. In our arrogance and self-importance, we seek to seize that which only you can give. Forgive us our trespasses and strengthen us to follow the example of your Son in humility and obedience. Amen.

Prayer of Dedication of Gifts and Self

We bring to you, O Generous One, our gifts and tithes. Guide our hands and hearts to use these gifts to extend the hand and heart of Christ to those in need. Create in us a fresh resolve to love you above all and our neighbors as ourselves. In Jesus' name we pray. Amen.

Sermon Summary

As Holy Week begins, we are called to remember what Christ has done for us, and to imitate his humility and obedience as we await his coming in glory.

Hymn of the Day

"Ride On! Ride On in Majesty"

Anglican priest Henry Hart Milman wrote this text for Palm Sunday in the early 1800s. It captures well the dual nature of this day – a sense of triumph, and yet also of impending gloom. Palm/Passion Sunday is a day filled with varied emotions, as the day of Jesus' entry into Jerusalem must have been for the disciples then. Certainly they all knew something was going to happen, but what?

The tune "St. Drostane" was written by John Bacchus Dykes specifically for this text, although the hymn regularly appears with other tunes, most notably "Winchester New" and "The King's Majesty."

Children's Time

One of Us

Have you thought about how wonderful it is that Jesus came to earth and became a human being like us? Jesus chose to come and live with us. This is really quite amazing.

Jesus knew that when he was born on earth, he wouldn't be the kind of king who is born into a rich palace with lots of servants to look after him. He knew he would be born into a poor family.

Jesus knew that some people would be angry with him for teaching the things that he did. Jesus knew that he would suffer and be killed before he was raised from the dead to live with God forever.

But Jesus came to earth anyway. Jesus did this for us, because God loves each one of us so much. Jesus wanted to teach everyone about God's love and lead us all to God.

Today is the beginning of what the church calls Holy Week. This week we'll tell the stories from the Bible about the sad things that happened to Jesus, but we'll also give thanks for how much Jesus loves us. We listen to these stories knowing that because of Jesus, God gives us the best Easter gift ever.

The Sermon

What Did Jesus Do?

Hymns

Beginning of Worship: "Ride On, Ride On in Majesty"
Sermon Hymn: "At the Name of Jesus"
Closing Hymn: "I Wonder as I Wander"

Scripture

Philippians 2:5-11 (For additional sermon materials on this passage, see the January 2004 issue of *The Clergy Journal* and on Luke 22:14–23:56, see the 2003 May/June planning issue of *The Clergy Journal.*)

We have all seen the great variety of goods – mugs, bracelets, T-shirts – emblazoned with the letters WWJD: What Would Jesus Do? Today's lesson from Philippians calls us to reflect on a different question: What *did* Jesus do?

We have come now to Holy Week, the most solemn period in the Christian year. The church calls this day both "Palm" and "Passion" Sunday. Knowing what is ahead, we can appreciate all too fully the irony of Jesus' triumphal entry in Jerusalem. "Hosanna!" the crowds cried. "Blessed is the one who comes in the name of the Lord!" becomes, in a few short days, "Crucify him!" The king they were hoping for was not the king they got.

That is the theme of the great hymn of the early church, which Paul records in this passage from Philippians. God-in-Christ came to us, not in earthly pomp or with blasts of heavenly trumpets, but humbly, as one of us. He came to die, and by that death has been glorified.

Those who wrote this hymn and those who sang it were steeped in the Hebrew Scriptures. Throughout the Christian scriptures we hear echoes of Isaiah, a prophet of the exile. The early church saw in Christ the fulfillment of the prophecies of the Suffering Servant.

And so it is in this hymn. In the verses which describe Christ's self-emptying, we hear again Isaiah's song of the Suffering Servant: "he poured out himself to death and was numbered with the transgressors" (Isa 53:12). Paul adds that this death was on a cross, a cruel way to die, a death reserved primarily for rebellious slaves.

Isaiah puts forward, "He was oppressed, and he was afflicted, yet he did not open his mouth" (Isa 53:7). But humiliation and death are not the end, for Isaiah earlier prophesies, "See, my servant shall prosper; he shall be exalted and lifted up, and shall be very high" (Isa 52:13).

Not only did this early church recall the prophecies of Isaiah, in this hymn we see that Paul and the other Christians also saw in Christ Jesus the Second Adam:

> the First Adam, who was created in God's likeness, sought to seize parity with God, and through his disobedience lost the glorious image of his Maker. But the Second Adam, Christ, who is the Heavenly Man, although he pre-existed in the true likeness of God, humbled himself obediently and accepted the status of a servant . . . he chose the way of meek submission to God's will, which ended in a cross. This obedience . . . reverses Adam's primal disobedience and leads to Christ's exaltation by the Father. (A. M. Hunter, *The Layman's Bible Commentary*, vol. 22, [Richmond: John Knox, 1959], p. 94.)

For his obedience, Jesus was given the "name that is above every name" (Phil 2:9). Names, we know, are extraordinarily important and meaningful in the Bible. A change in status often was accompanied by a new name: Abram became Abraham and Sarai changed to Sarah when they received the promise of God (Gen 17:5). Jacob became Israel when God entered a new relationship with him (Gen 32:28). Saul, when the Holy Spirit filled him, became Paul (Acts 13:9). Now, in his exaltation, Jesus, the humble, obedient, crucified slave becomes Lord.

Perhaps the earliest creed is the acclamation, "Jesus is Lord!" All creation rings out with it; it is heard on the lips of angels, powers, and principalities.

Well, that is what Jesus did. And what are we called to do? How are we to respond to this amazing love? Paul tells us quite specifically; indeed, this hymn is included in his letter to the church at Philippi as part of an exhortation to persistence in faith in the face of opposition, including opposition from within the church itself, and even when faced with the threat of death. Forget yourselves, Paul says, think about your neighbors: "Do nothing from selfish ambition or conceit, but in humility regard others as better than yourselves. Let each of you look not to your own interests, but to the interests of others. Let the same mind be in you that was in Christ Jesus . . ." (Phil 2:3-5).

The Greek culture, which formed the cultural backdrop for Paul's churches, took a dim view of humility. They would have agreed with Lancelot in the play *Camelot,* "I find humility means to be hurt; it's not the earth the meek inherit, it's the dirt." We, too, have trouble with humility. We tend to see humility as an indicator of that psychological vice, low self-esteem. Yet, Christ made humility a virtue. Will we follow Christ's example or that of our culture?

We, with the community at Philippi, are called to practice in our lives as a Christian community what the Spirit produces in our hearts through our relationship with God and Christ. This week, we follow the footsteps of Jesus as he goes to die on the cross. In our sorrow, it is tempting to turn inward. Self-examination is appropriate during this holiest of weeks. Yet it must not overwhelm our concerns for others or our outreach to our brothers and sisters.

As we understand more fully what Jesus did, perhaps we can better answer the question, "What would Jesus do?" in the situations of our daily lives. Let's spend this week reflecting on what it means to "let the same mind be in us that was in Christ Jesus." In doing so, may we move through the Passion and crucifixion and, at the remembrance of the resurrection, affirm with all our hearts, "Jesus is Lord!"

– Katherine Ellison
Montclair State University
Upper Montclair, New Jersey

April 8, 2004

Maundy Thursday

Lessons

RCL	Ex 12:1-4 (5-10), 11-14	1 Cor 11:23-26	Jn 13:1-17, 31b-35
Roman Catholic	Ex 12:1-8, 11-14	1 Cor 11:23-26	Jn 13:1-15
Episcopal (BCP)	Ex 12:1-14a	1 Cor 11:23-26 (27-32)	Jn 13:1-15 or Lk 22:14-30

Introduction to the Lessons

Lesson 1

Exodus 12:1-4 (5-10) **(RCL);** ***Exodus 12:1-8, 11-14*** **(RC);**
Exodus 12:1-14a **(Epis)**

God commands the Passover and tells Moses and Aaron how to observe it.

Lesson 2

1 Corinthians 11:23-26 **(RCL/RC);**
1 Corinthians 11:23-26 (27-32) **(Epis)**

Paul writes to the Corinthians the words that are familiar to many Christian communities as the words of institution for Holy Communion.

Gospel

John 13:1-17, 31b-35 **(RCL);** ***John 13:1-15*** **(RC/Epis)**

At the Last Supper, Jesus washes the feet of the disciples and exhorts them to serve each other in the same spirit of humility.

Theme

Jesus and the disciples celebrate Passover; Christ is revealed as the Lamb that is slain for us.

Thought for the Day

Christ, the Passover Lamb goes forth in deepest humility to be sacrificed to save and redeem us. We are exhorted to remember the sacrifice and keep the feast.

Call to Worship

Come, behold the Lamb of God that takes away the sin of the world. God has laid on this Lamb the iniquity of us all. Come, behold the Lamb of God before his time of trial. Prepare to love and serve one another, as imitators of the Lamb.

Pastoral Prayer

God of the humble, you exhort us to humility. In the example of our Lord, you have shown us that total obedience to your will is the path to glory. The death of your Son reveals the essence of your holy love. Help us now to be instruments of your love. We ask this in the name of the Lamb that was slain, our Lord and Savior, Jesus Christ. Amen.

Prayer of Confession

God of love, we confess that we have not loved you with our whole hearts nor cared for our brothers and sisters as you have commanded. As we search our hearts this day, help us to see the ways and times we have been tempted to act like Judas: betraying you as we betray others. As Jesus washed the disciples' feet, wash our hearts in the blood of the Lamb, and make us whole. Amen.

Prayer of Dedication of Gifts and Self

Giving God, as Jesus offered thanks over the bread and the wine, we offer thanks to you over these gifts that we bring. Be with all who are stewards of these resources and strengthen them to serve the needs of others in your name. Open our eyes each day to new opportunities to be your humble servants. In Jesus' name we pray. Amen.

Sermon Summary

On this day, we are called to remember that Christ, God's Passover Lamb, was sacrificed for us. We, too, are called to the service of others in humble love.

Hymn of the Day

"Go to Dark Gethsemane"

This hymn has a history of revision. First published by James Montgomery in 1820, it was reworked substantially by the author five years after and republished. More recently, the first line (and title) were changed to move away from perpetuating the equation of darkness with negativity.

Set to a tune known by a number of names (most commonly "Redhead" or "Gethsemane") the hymn invites us to observe the last night of Jesus' life. It works well in Maundy Thursday worship, especially as congregations transition from the last supper "scene" to the arrest in the garden.

Children's Time

Follow My Example

Preparation: Bring a pair of slippers, a bowl of warm water, and a towel.

How do you welcome people who come to your house to visit? Do you take their coats or jackets? Do you offer them slippers to wear? *(Show the slippers.)* Do you offer them a snack?

In Jesus' time, people wore sandals or sometimes, if they were really poor, just walked in their bare feet. This meant that people's feet were usually covered with dust. When they arrived at a friend's house for dinner, a servant would be sent to the door with water to wash their feet. *(Show the bowl and towel.)*

One day when Jesus was having dinner with his disciples, he did something very unusual. Jesus tied a towel around his waist and began to wash his disciples' feet. *(Ask for a volunteer and wash her or his feet as you tell the next part.)*

The disciple named Peter was very upset about this. Jesus wasn't a servant – he was their leader! Jesus shouldn't be washing people's feet! But Jesus insisted – and he told the disciples to follow his example and serve others. Jesus tells us to follow his example, too. Find a special way to care for others this Easter weekend.

The Sermon

Awash in Blood, Awash in Love

Hymns

Beginning of Worship: "Bread of the World in Mercy Broken"
Sermon Hymn: "Jesu, Jesu, Fill Us with Your Love"
Closing Hymn: "Ah, Holy Jesus"

Scripture

John 13:1-17, 31b-35 (For sermon materials on Exodus 12:1-4 (5-10), 11-14, see the 2003 May/June planning issue of *The Clergy Journal* and on 1 Corinthians 11:23-16, see the January 2004 issue of *The Clergy Journal.*)

The time had come to celebrate the Passover. The lamb was ready, a young male, without blemish. Its blood, the Lord's portion of the sacrifice, would be smeared on the holy places of the house, and the Destroyer would pass over the house during the plague of the firstborn (Ex 12:1-14). The blood of the lamb was the sign of deliverance.

Jesus and the disciples were gathered for the Festival of Passover. For the disciples, an exciting and somewhat troubling week was drawing to a close. Jesus had entered Jerusalem in triumph. But again, Jesus had spoken in riddles. He had told them that his soul was troubled. He spoke of walking in darkness and in light. He spoke of judgment. Did they understand? Probably not.

The meal was under way. The disciples must have thought it just another feast, or perhaps the beginning of Jesus' triumphal march toward an earthly kingdom. How wrong they were – and, in the end, how right.

But the gospel lets us know that Jesus knew there was much more to come. How shocked the disciples were when Jesus got up from the table, took off his outer robe, wrapped a towel around his waist, and began to wash their feet!

Now a good host knew that, after a day on the dusty roads, sandal-clad feet were grimy. Guests were provided with water to wash their feet. Not even a Jewish slave was expected to wash the feet of another person. Yet here was Jesus, the Master, performing this act of utmost humility and service.

Earlier in the week, Mary had anointed Jesus' feet with costly ointment and dried them with her hair. When Judas protested, Jesus said, "She bought it so that she might keep it for the day of my burial" (Jn 12:7). Death foretold.

Death also is foretold in the footwashing. It is not the physical washing that is so important, of course, but what it symbolizes – Jesus' death brings salvation. The water is important here. Scripture is full of water symbols. God leads us beside still waters and restores our souls. Moses strikes the rock and water gushes forth. The psalmist cries, "Wash me and I shall be whiter than snow" (Ps 51:7).

Water is life, yes, but water also is death. The Great Flood covered the earth, the Sea of Reeds closed over the Egyptians. The Gospel of John is replete with symbolism. Perhaps he means for us to see this water, with which Jesus washes the feet of his disciples, as the waters of baptism. In baptism, as we go under the water, we die to the old self. We emerge clean and new. In the early church, baptism was performed during the Easter Vigil. The candidates had gone through a long period of initiation. They were stripped of their old clothes, went under the water, and when they emerged they were given new clothes as a symbol of their new life in Christ.

The footwashing, then, tells us that submission to a cleaning at Jesus' hands means being taken into the events as the cross, the resurrection, and the glorification. But Jesus reminds us that not all who are washed are clean (see Jn 13:11). The act of washing does not ensure a future of living without sin.

Further, the disciples are exhorted to follow the example of their Master. Soon he would no longer share the earth with them. They are to serve each other – wash each other's feet – as he has served them. We hear echoes of Matthew's Great Commission: "Go, therefore, and make disciples of all nations, baptizing them in the name of the Father and of the Son and of the Holy Spirit, and teaching them to obey everything that I have commanded you" (Mt 28:19-20).

The supper ended. Judas received the piece of bread; Satan entered into him. He went out to "do quickly what you are going to do" (Jn 13:27).

Jesus gathered the disciples around him for a farewell speech, a speech like one that a dying parent might give to a child. Jesus spoke to them tenderly: "little children," he called them. Jesus prepared them for his departure – and his coming again in glory. That glory would be a visible manifestation of God's majesty in acts of power. Jesus would lay down his life and take it up again.

Jesus gave them a new commandment, a new covenant. New? Hebrew Scriptures commanded that we love one another as ourselves (Lev 19:18), even to love the foreigner (Lev 19:34). The newness of Jesus' commandment did not lie only in love for one another, but is related to the theme of covenant at the Last Supper. Jesus fulfilled prophecy of Jeremiah: "The days are surely coming, says the LORD, when I will make a new covenant with the house of Israel and the house of Judah" (Jer 31:31). The new covenant was to be marked by the people's intimate relationship with God. Jesus' words that night speak to this knowledge.

On this day, the waters of death are about to roll over our thoughts as we come to remember again the Passion and death of our Savior. The Passover celebrated God's saving of the firstborn children of the Israelites in the time of Pharaoh. But Jesus, God's first and only Son, was not passed over. God's Passover Lamb went meekly to the slaughter. The blood of the Lamb was shed for us and for our salvation. Because of his blood, his sacrifice, death passes us over. At the last day "mourning and crying and pain will be no more" (Rev 21:4). Even now, God's home is among mortals. We, too, are called to humble service and love, so that Christ may be glorified through us.

Those first disciples could not possibly have comprehended all that Jesus was telling them. We, who know the continuation of the story, hear only in part as we grow in faith in the risen Lord.

Christ's saving blood was shed for us. We are washed in the blood of the sacrificial Lamb. His love washes over us, conquering death.

Join in this holy meal, Christian sisters and brothers, to "proclaim the Lord's death until he comes" (1 Cor 11:26). Go forth, remembering Jesus' sacrifice on the cross. Go forth, remembering that this sacrifice was not in vain. Go forth to serve the Lord in love.

– Katherine Ellison
Montclair State University
Upper Montclair, New Jersey

April 9, 2004

Good Friday

Lessons

RCL	Isa 52:13–53:12	Heb 10:16-25 or Heb 4:14-16; 5:7-9	Jn 18:1–19:42
Roman Catholic	Isa 52:13–53:12	Heb 4:14-16; 5:7-9	Jn 18:1–19:42
Episcopal (BCP)	Isa 52:13–53:12 or Gen 22:1-18 or Wis 2:1, 12-24	Heb 10:1-25	Jn (18:1-40) 19:1-37

Introduction to the Lessons

Lesson 1

***Isaiah 52:13–53:12* (RCL/RC/Epis)**

The suffering of the Servant is described. The Servant is vindicated.

Lesson 2

(1) *Hebrews 10:16-25* (RCL); *Hebrews 10:1-25* (Epis)

Christ offered himself for all time as a sacrifice for sin. Through Christ's death on the cross, our salvation is assured. Therefore, let us encourage and support one another.

(2) *Hebrews 4:14-16; 5:7-9* (RC)

Jesus, our sinless great high priest, was tested as we are. Therefore we can receive mercy and find grace in time of need.

Gospel

John 18:1–19:42* (RCL/RC); *John (18:1-40) 19:1-37

The betrayal, trial, crucifixion, and burial of Jesus are described.

Theme

Christ, the Servant of God, suffers and dies for us.

Thought for the Day

On this somber dreadful day, we are called to remember all that God has done for us through the sacrifice of God's Son. May we also be willing to sacrifice ourselves for Christ's purpose.

Call to Worship

Day of sorrow, dark night of the soul! Come weeping as we remember the sacrifice that has been made for us and for our salvation. Go again with Jesus to the cross; kneel in horror and awe at its base. See what our Lord has done for us.

Pastoral Prayer

God of the Sacrifice, you gave your Son, your only begotten. You did not stay the hand of Annas or Caiaphas, the hand of Pilate, or the hand of the soldier who hammered in the nails and lifted high the cross. Teach us to proclaim your love, that all the world will know your sacred name, your sacrificial love. Through Christ, the Lamb, we pray. Amen.

Prayer of Confession

For the times that we have taken your sacrificial love for granted, forgive us. For the times that we have failed to witness faithfully to the good news of the gospel, forgive us. For the times that we have sought to earn our own salvation, forgive us. Forgive us, O God, and bring us to amendment of life for the sake of your Son, Jesus Christ. Amen.

Prayer of Dedication of Gifts and Self

What gifts can we offer, O God, in thanks for the great love and sacrifice of Jesus on the cross? Accept the gifts we offer now – ourselves, our time, and our possessions, signs of your gracious and saving love among us. Bless these offerings to the glory of Christ's love and the work of your realm. Amen.

Sermon Summary

We follow Jesus to the cross. As we go, we hear again the words of the ancient prophet, Isaiah, describing the obedient Suffering Servant.

Hymn of the Day

"O Sacred Head, Now Wounded"

This anonymous latin hymn captures the mood of Good Friday in tragic and personal tones. The original text contained seven stanzas, each addressed to a different part of Christ's body. The version sung today focuses on Christ's head, inviting us to look upon his face and see there the pain borne on our behalf.

The haunting tune "Passion Chorale" was originally a secular piece, and was incorporated by J. S. Bach in a number of works, most notably *St. Matthew's Passion.*

Children's Time

Out Of Death

Preparation: Bring a flower bulb, raisins, sunflower seeds, and instant milk powder.

This flower bulb looks dead. If you found it lying on the ground, you might be tempted to throw it in the garbage. And yet, if you plant it in the ground in the fall, what happens? *(Invite responses.)*

These things also look dried up and dead, but still they contain life. *(Show the raisins, seeds, and milk powder you brought.)* The raisins can be eaten right now *(offer them to the children)*, the seeds can be planted to bloom in the summer, and this powder can be mixed with water to produce milk, which gives life to hungry people.

Death isn't final. It's just a step along the way to something else. Death is like this flower bulb. It looks like nothing is alive, yet a flower will grow from it. From death comes new life.

Today we hear about Jesus' death on the cross and we feel very sad that he died. But we also remember that out of his death came new life – for him and for us. So when you feel sad today, remember that it's not the end of the story. Wait for what's coming on Easter Sunday.

The Sermon

The Servant Goes to the Cross

Hymns

Beginning of Worship: "Were You There?"
Sermon Hymn: "Go to Dark Gethsemane"
Closing Hymn: "O Sacred Head, Now Wounded"

Scripture

Isaiah 52:13–53:12 (For additional sermon materials on this passage, see the 2003 May/June planning issue of *The Clergy Jourmal* and on John 18:1–19:42, see the January 2004 issue of *The Clergy Journal.*)

It is finished. Supper is over. Come. Walk with the disciples through this night of trial. Go to dark Gethsemane, go into the horror of the day of suffering and death. See so many fall away and, in terror for their own lives, abandon the one in whom they had put so much hope, the one they had called Lord, Master, Teacher.

Come. Hide in the dark recesses of the courtyard of the high priest as Jesus is taken to Annas, then to Caiaphas. The cold that creeps into our bones goes beyond the chill of early morning; these are the chill fingers of despair. Hear Peter deny the Lord; hear the cock crow.

Slink after the soldiers, the priests, and Jesus. Enter the headquarters of the prefect, Pontius Pilate. Hear the questioning. Hear Pilate ask, "What is truth?"

See the wounds from Jesus' flogging, the mocking crown of thorns and purple cloak. Hear the crowds shout, "Crucify him!"

Come. Walk along the Way of Sorrows, as Jesus carries his own cross to the Place of the Skull. Come with his mother, with Mary Magdalene and the other women, and with John to the foot of the cross. Stand a bit away from them, with the rest of the crowd that gathers at a crucifixion to watch – some in horror, others with a terrible glee. "See what happens to malcontents and blasphemers!" they say.

Jesus is nailed to the crossbeam. The crossbeam, and those of the two others, are raised up and attached to the posts that have been standing ready.

But look! Jesus' cross is different from the others. There is an inscription above his head. Anyone who can read can tell what it says, for it is in all the languages common in the region. "Jesus of Nazareth," it reads, "the King of the Jews." When Pilate had ordered this, the chief priests had been angry. "Don't write, 'The King of the Jews,' " they cried. Don't legitimate this blasphemer! Make his blasphemy plain. "Write 'this man said, I am King of the Jews' " (Jn 19:21). But Pilate refused to relent: "What I have written, I have written" (v. 22).

Stand there and watch as the soldiers divide his clothes, cast lots for his seamless tunic. As we watch, the words of the ancient psalm come into our heads: "They divide my clothes among themselves, and for my clothing they cast lots" (Ps 22:18).

Then other ancient scriptures come to mind: the words of Isaiah. Jesus had been so like that Servant the prophet had described. He had grown up unobtrusively, come out of nowhere, a nobody of whom it had been said, "Can anything good come out of Nazareth?" (Jn 1:46). "He had no form or majesty" (Isa 53:2b).

Jesus had done so much for so many, and yet, like the Servant of the prophecy, here he was, "despised and rejected by others, a man of suffering and acquainted with infirmity; and as one from whom others hide their faces he was despised and we held him of no account" (vs. 3).

Jesus had preached against oppression, and yet like Isaiah's Servant, "He was oppressed and he was afflicted, yet he did not open his mouth; like a lamb that is led to the slaughter and like a sheep that before its shearers is silent, so he did not open his mouth. By a perversion of justice he was taken away. Who could have imagined his future?" (vv. 7-8).

Oh, who could have imagined this as Jesus' future? Certainly not those of the faithful gathered at the foot of that awful cross. Certainly not those who had run away. He had done no violence, and there was no deceit in his mouth. This was to be the king who would defeat the legions of Caesar and restore the land to them. This was to be the king who would reign in majesty, greater than the Maccabees, greater than David, greater than Caesar. Less than a week ago that had seemed to be the future.

Why had it come to this? He seemed to have known what was waiting. Why hadn't he run and hidden? Run away, perhaps to gather an army? Why? And so our thoughts run, as we wait.

Listen! Jesus is speaking now. Low, a voice dulled with pain. He gives his mother into the keeping of the disciple whom he has loved. He asks for drink. Then: "It is finished" (Jn 19:30). Jesus bows his head and gives up his spirit.

April 9, 2004
Good Friday

Minds, hearts, and spirits dulled with pain would have heard only part of the prophecy of Isaiah: the pain and suffering of the innocent Lamb. How, in those hours, could they have understood the nature of Jesus' sacrifice – what it was for them and for all of humanity?

Jesus was not like the sacrificial animal that had no power over the circumstances of its fate. Rather, as John tells it, he went knowingly, willingly, obediently.

Jesus did not go to his death to appease a vengeful God, for our God does not delight in the blood of sacrifices (Isa 1:11). Rather, Jesus died to break the power of sin, the power of Satan, the arch-deceiver. "Jesus lets the violence of the world system defeat itself on his dying body – instead of this being a sacrifice to a vengeful God, it is a paradoxical defeat of the torturer. . . . The only sacrifice by Jesus is his offering of his innocent body to the fury of the sacrificial system that is being canceled." (Garry Wills, *Papal Sin* [New York: Doubleday, 2000], p. 307.)

Through Jesus' suffering, nations and their leaders – the whole world – will come to see the power of God that brings peace and harmony to all. As they see, they will be astonished at him: "kings shall shut their mouths because of him" (Isa 52:15).

Ah, but at the moment of death, and in the hours that follow, as Jesus lies in the grave, how could the followers of the sinless Suffering Servant, now slain, have believed that the other words of the prophecy might come to pass? Jesus himself said those anguished words: "It is finished" (Jn 19:30). How could the disciples have imagined that God's "servant shall prosper; he shall be exalted and lifted up, and shall be very high" (Isa 52:13)? How could they have known that Jesus had borne their iniquities and carried their sorrows? How could they have seen any light?

No, on this night of sorrows, the disciples do not understand yet. We do not understand yet. That must wait until the third day. For now, we will keep the vigil. Come, let us wait for the dawning of the New Day.

– Katherine Ellison
Montclair State University
Upper Montclair, New Jersey

April 11, 2004

Easter Day

Lessons

RCL	Acts 10:34-43 or Isa 65:17-25	1 Cor 15:19-26 or Acts 10:34-43	Jn 20:1-18 or Lk 24:1-12
Roman Catholic	Acts 10:34a, 37-43	Col 3:1-4 or 1 Cor 5:6b-8	Jn 20:1-9
Episcopal (BCP)	Acts 10:34-43 or Isa 51:9-11	Col 3:1-4 or Acts 10:34-43	Lk 24:1-10

Introduction to the Lessons

Lesson 1

***Acts 10:34-43* (RCL/Epis); *Acts 10:34a, 37-43* (RC)**

Peter's sermon sums up the gospel – beginning with the baptism of John and ending with the message that Christ is the judge from whom all who believe receive forgiveness.

Lesson 2

(1) *1 Corinthians 15:19-26* (RCL)

Paul describes the significance of the resurrection.

(2) *Colossians 3:1-4 (*RC/Epis)

The Christian life is described. Christians are to set their minds on things above, so that, when Christ is revealed, they, too, may be revealed with Christ in glory.

Gospel

(1) *John 20:1-18* (RCL); *John 20:1-9* (RC)

John describes the events of Easter morning at the tomb, with Mary Magdalene, Simon Peter, and the disciple whom Jesus loved.

(2) *Luke 24:1-10* (Epis)

The women come to the tomb and find the stone rolled away. They are greeted by two men in dazzling clothes, who tell them that Jesus is risen, as he had said. The women tell the apostles.

Theme

Christ is risen, bringing forgiveness and salvation to all who believe.

Thought for the Day

Even as we rejoice in the Resurrection, we are called to spread the good news of forgiveness to all.

Call to Worship

Leader: Christ is risen!
People: Risen, indeed!
Leader: Christ is risen from the dead, the first fruits of them that sleep!
People: The grave could not hold Jesus!
Leader: We fear death no more! Our salvation is assured!
All: Christ is risen! Risen, indeed! Hallelujah!

Pastoral Prayer

O God, you have blessed us with the gift of your Son, now risen victorious over sin and death. We come this day to celebrate all that you have done for us. As you show no partiality, help us truly to do likewise. Give us the power of your Spirit to go from this place to spread the gospel to all. Amen.

Prayer of Confession

God of forgiveness, we confess that we have shown partiality, in opposition of your own loving way. We have favored those who are like us and despised those who are different in nationality, race, social status, behavior, and belief. Through the gospel you call us to repent, and we do. Forgive us and help us to turn again to you and to the world. Amen.

Prayer of Dedication of Gifts and Self

Loving God, we offer our gifts and tithes with thanks for your great love this Easter day. Bless these first fruits of your abundance in our lives, that your will may be done on earth. Receive our thanks and make us ever mindful of the needs of others. In the name of the risen Christ, amen.

Sermon Summary

After the resurrection, the church grew. Peter was led to understand that "God shows no partiality." We, too, are to hear that message and respond by spreading the good news and welcoming all into the body of Christ, the risen Savior.

Hymn of the Day

"Because You Live, O Christ"

Assuming that most English-speaking churches will use "Christ the Lord/ Jesus Christ Is Risen Today" as an opening hymn on this day, this hymn is an excellent hymn with which to conclude Easter Sunday worship.

The words by Shirley Erena Murray of New Zealand were written precisely to inject new life into the delightful tune "Vruechten" – most familiar as the setting for "This Joyful Eastertide" which Murray found outdated. She has succeeded admirably in restoring this energetic tune to comfortable use with those Easter congregations that are bursting with unbridled joy this day.

Children's Time

Raised from the Dead!

Preapration: Bring a blooming Easter lily or other flowering plant used in your church for Easter decoration.

Look at the flowers around you this morning. *(Pass around one plant for children to smell.)* We like to have these plants in our church on Easter to celebrate that God raised Jesus from the dead and that God gives us new life, too.

When Jesus was first born, do you remember what the Wise Men from the East said about him? And what the angels told the shepherds? They said that a great king had been born!

All through his life, people were excited to see Jesus. They were waiting for a king who would help them overthrow their harsh government. They wanted a king who would free them and look after them. They thought Jesus was that king.

So when Jesus was put to death on the cross, just like a criminal, Jesus' disciples were really upset. But on that first Easter morning, so long ago, the disciples found out that Jesus was alive again and they were really happy. They knew that because Jesus died, they would have God's forgiveness and love forever. They went out to tell the good news to everyone.

We're still celebrating today, almost two thousand years later. That's how important Jesus is to us. Let's shout out "Hallelujah" together!

The Sermon

Christ Is Alive! Now What?

Hymns

Beginning of Worship: "Christ the Lord Is Risen Today"
Sermon Hymn: "Christ Is Alive"
Closing Hymn: "The Church of Christ in Every Age"

Scripture

Acts 10:34-43 (For additional sermon materials on this passage see the 2003 May/June planning issue and the January 2004 issue of *The Clergy Journal.*)

Christ is risen! Christ is risen, indeed! We shout out the joyous Easter acclamation. The dark season of Lent and the week of Jesus' Passion are past. We cry "Hallelujah" once again, as we acknowledge the glorious Risen Lord.

Now what? The lectionary text from the Acts of the Apostles puts us on fast forward. But first let us rewind a bit, to the beginning of the Acts passage, to get the full impact of Peter's message to Cornelius and his household.

Christ has been taken up into heaven. The Spirit has come at Pentecost; the church is born. Peter has been preaching to the Jews, and many have been converted.

The church is growing. Oh, there have been setbacks. Peter and John were arrested, then freed. Saul and others persecuted the first believers. Stephen was killed for his preaching. But none of this stopped the spread of the gospel.

God is working God's purpose out. The church is growing. Saul, the great ravager of the church, has become Paul, God's chosen instrument.

The disciples are heeding the call of Christ to "be my witnesses in Jerusalem, in all Judea and Samaria, and to the ends of the earth" (Acts 1:8). They are preaching and healing. To this point, however, the good news was preached mainly to those who considered themselves God's chosen people. Indeed, there are those in the Jerusalem church who argue fervently that to be a Christian one must first become a Jew.

But all this is about to change. For the Lord has spoken to Cornelius, a member of a group triply despised: Gentile, Roman, soldier of the oppressors. Peter, too, has had a vision, one that will force him to move beyond the confines of Jewish believers to open the world to Christ's message of salvation. God has redefined the meaning of what is clean and what is unclean. As Peter, greatly puzzled, is pondering his vision, messengers come to him from Cornelius, asking him to hear the message an angel has brought and to come to speak to Cornelius and his household.

What a radical thing for Peter to do! We can hardly comprehend it! When Jesus had associated with sinners, even eaten with them, his conduct had scandalized the pious. To associate with Gentiles was unlawful (Acts 10:28); it made Jews unclean, unable to enter the synagogue or temple, subject to all the rites of ritual purification. And yet Peter heeded the vision from God and went into the house of Cornelius.

Cornelius tells Peter and those who have come with him of his vision. "All of us are here in the presence of God," he says, "to listen to all that the Lord has commanded you to say" (Acts 10:33).

And so Peter begins to speak, slowly perhaps, fumbling with the Greek, his sentences disjointed. But the message is clear. It is the good news of the gospel – of Christ's baptism, good works, and healing. Of his death and resurrection and appearance to his chosen witnesses. Ah, but this is not to remain a secret, a mystery revealed only to the few. For Peter's vision has taught him that "God shows no partiality" (Acts 10:34).

No partiality! Yes, the message came to the Jews first, but then to the Greeks and to the Romans. As Paul says, "There is no longer Jew nor Greek, there is no longer slave or free, there is no longer male and female; for all of you are one in Christ Jesus" (Gal 3:28). All are to hear the good news and repent. All will receive forgiveness of sins through Christ's name.

What a word Peter spoke that day to the Gentiles in the house of Cornelius! The Holy Spirit was poured out on them, just as it had been on the disciples on the day of Pentecost. They, too, received the gift of tongues, shocking the Jews who had come with Peter. "Can anyone withhold the water for baptizing these people who have received the Holy Spirit just as we have?" Peter asks (Acts 10:47). Water was brought, and they were baptized in the name of Jesus Christ.

What a word Peter spoke that day to the people in the house of Cornelius! What a word for us today! Too often we have shown partiality. We have clung to those who are like us; some have even turned the church of Christ into their own exclusive little club. We have not welcomed the stranger, the outcast, those who are different. Instead, we have shunned them, railed against them, even tried to call God's curse down upon them. At the extreme, people who call themselves believers have declared themselves as the arm of the Lord to exact vengeance on those whom they fear and abhor.

Peter reminds us that God's forgiving grace is open to all. On this Day of Resurrection, we, too, are called to examine our hearts and to repent of any partiality. We are called to spread the good news so that all may believe, repent, and receive the gifts that God offers to us through Christ. Peter must have trembled as he entered the house of the Gentile Cornelius, breaking with his life-long customs and beliefs. We, too, may have to rethink old customs, old beliefs, old judgments. We, too, may tremble, but must push on for the sake of the one who died, was raised, and has gone to sit at the right hand of the Father, from where he will come to give judgment.

Rejoice, Christians. Shout the glad news: Christ is risen! Christ is alive! "Hallelujah! Salvation and glory and power to our God, for his judgments are true and just!" (Rev 19:1-2). "Hallelujah! For the Lord our God the Almighty reigns, let us rejoice and exult and give him the glory" (Rev 19:7-8).

Hallelujah! Christ will come again. The Risen Lamb will wipe every tear from our eyes. Death will be no more; mourning and crying and pain will be no more. This is the good news of Easter. Tell it abroad, so that all may come to know the good news of forgiveness and salvation.

Amen! Come, Lord Jesus.

– Katherine Ellison
Montclair State University
Upper Montclair, New Jersey

April 18, 2004

2nd Sunday of Easter

Lessons

RCL	Acts 5:27-32	Rev 1:4-8	Jn 20:19-31
Roman Catholic	Acts 5:12-16	Rev 1:9-11, 12-13, 17-19	Jn 20:19-31
Episcopal (BCP)	Acts 5:12a, 17-22 25-29 or Job 42:1-6	Rev 1:(1-8) 9-19 or Acts 5:12a, 17-22, 25-29	Jn 20:19-31

Introduction to the Lessons

Lesson 1

***Acts 5:27-32* (RCL); *Acts 5:12-16* (RC); *Acts 5:12a, 17-22, 25-29* (Epis)**

Acts provides an account of the beginnings of the church. In these scriptures we witness Peter and the apostles boldly teaching, healing, and defending the faith in the midst of opposition, persecution, and imprisonment. They are a model of committed discipleship.

Lesson 2

***Revelation 1:4-8* (RCL); *Revelation 1:9-11, 12-13, 17-19* (RC); *Revelation 1:(1-8) 9-19* (Epis)**

Revelations encourages Christians to be strong of faith in a time of increasing persecution. It affirms God's coming victory against Satan, and the vindication of the faithful. Here, John reviews his own belief and testifies to the presence of Jesus himself as the herald of this message.

Gospel

***John 20:19-31* (RCL/RC/Epis)**

After the resurrection, Jesus appears first to Mary Magdalene and then to the disciples. Through closed and locked doors he enters, dispels fear, pronounces peace, transfers power, proves himself to the doubting Thomas, and instructs the disciples. Jesus does the same for us.

Theme

Jesus gives us power to face life with peace.

Thought for the Day

Through faith in Jesus, we have peace and power for life. Jesus faced the worst that life can offer and triumphed. Jesus gives us, through faith in Christ, the strength to rise, go out, and meet all of life's challenges.

Call to Worship

As we gather in this holy place, let us claim the peace of Christ. Let us worship, unafraid to praise the Lord. Let us praise God with our songs, our words, and our hearts, and receive the blessing of God's love!

Pastoral Prayer

We come before you as humbly as we know how, thanking you for the gift of our lives and the grace of your love. As the womb of night has given birth to the wonder of this new day, keep us in the womb of your love that we might birth more of you in the world. Help us to walk boldly in faith as we seek to serve you. Let our faith be seen in our actions and words, and help us not to be afraid of witnessing to your presence in our lives. We pray for those in pain here in our church, in our community, and in the world. We pray for leaders to make decisions for peace instead of conflict. We pray for more awareness of the sacredness of our earth, that we may treat it with more reverence and respect. Comfort those who are ill. Send your peace to those who are worried. Give strength to those who are afraid, that they may meet the circumstances of their challenges with hope and faith. We ask these things in the name of the One who saves. Amen.

Prayer of Confession

We confess, O God, that even though we have seen you work wonders in our lives, we still have times of doubt. We have worried when we should have claimed your peace. We have waited for proof when we should have had more faith. We have desired signs instead of trusting your promises. We have wondered where you were when we should have claimed your presence in the midst of our troubles. We have complained loudly instead of quieting our souls to hear your still, silent voice. We have acted alone when we should have waited for your guidance. We have lost sight when we should have walked in the light of your wisdom. And when we have passed through our times of trouble we have not thanked you for your grace. Forgive us, O God. Create in us clean hearts and renew a right spirit within us. Amen.

Prayer of Dedication of Gifts and Self

We thank you for the blessings you have allowed us to experience, and return to you a portion of that which you have given to us. We dedicate these tithes and offerings to your service in furthering the great work to which are called. Lead us in giving more of ourselves, that more of this earth may be blessed through the grace and peace you have bestowed on us. Amen.

Sermon Summary

Jesus enters the closed and locked areas of our lives, offering the peace and power, which can overcome fear. We must respond with acceptance and trust, relying on his promise to be with us. We can then move forward in faith and live into our call as people of God.

Hymn of the Day

"O Sons and Daughters"

This rather lengthy ballad tells the story of Easter Sunday and the events a week later. Accordingly, it works well to sing either the first five stanzas on Easter Day, or stanzas 1 and 6–9 on this Sunday when the lectionary provides the gospel account of Jesus' appearance to Thomas.

Both text and tune date to 15th-century France, with the original Latin words having been written by Jean Tisserand, a Franciscan friar. The medieval melody invites the use of tambourines or hand drums, as would have been common in those times.

Children's Time

Believe!

In our Bible story today, the disciples are hiding in a locked room, feeling scared. Remember that Jesus, their leader, had been put to death. While the disciples know that God has raised Jesus from the dead, none of them have actually seen him. They're not sure what's going on.

Suddenly, even though the door is locked, there's someone standing there with them. It's Jesus! Jesus says, "Peace be with you," then he breathes on them and gives them the Holy Spirit.

One disciple, Thomas, wasn't there that day. When he got back, the other disciples crowded around, telling him what had happened. Poor Thomas! Can you imagine how he felt? He refused to believe the others.

One week later, when the disciples were all gathered together again, Jesus came again and Thomas got to see him. At last, Thomas believed that Jesus was raised from the dead.

Jesus told Thomas it was easy for him to believe because Jesus was standing right there. Jesus said that people who believe without seeing are even more blessed. That would be us, since we can't see Jesus with our eyes, but only with our hearts. Jesus says we are blessed. Spread this blessing to others using Jesus' words, "Peace be with you."

The Sermon

The Power of Christ's Peace

Hymns

Beginning of Worship: "Let There Be Peace on Earth"
Sermon Hymn: "I've Got Peace Like a River"
Closing Hymn: "Lord, Make Us Servants of Your Peace"

Scripture

John 20:19-31 (For additional sermon materials, see the 2003 May/June planning issue and the January 2004 issue of *The Clergy Journal.*)

Fear is a powerful force. It can drive us to exhibit behaviors or commit actions from which we might refrain if we had a sense of peace. We may strike out at a person or assert ourselves in a given situation before thinking things through. Or, we may tighten up, close ourselves off, or shut ourselves in. Most of us know that aggressively striking out may cause unwanted backlash, exacerbating the situation. We know that hiding keeps us from moving forward, and that denial only puts off the inevitable. Yet, we are prone to such responses because of the power and influence of fear, or, more precisely, because of a lack of peace.

Fear is a normal reaction to the vicissitudes of life, and admittedly, there is much to be afraid of in this world filled with wars, crime, and the confrontations that will surely come from dealing with other humans. But to succumb to fear is, in essence, to display a distrust of the faith that gives us power for life; power to face, deal with, and triumph over every circumstance that life may present.

Facing one's fears takes courage. It means risking something, venturing into unknown territory. We cannot with surety know what is on the other side. Jesus reminds us in John 16:33, "I have said this to you, so that in me you may have peace. In the world you face persecution. But take courage; I have conquered the world!" Jesus spoke these words to the disciples, but they did not seem to sink in. Peter denied Christ because of his fear. And now, we see in today's gospel lesson, fear that prompted the disciples to lock themselves in a room.

In this setting of fear, doubt, and locked doors, Jesus enters. He comes into the room where the disciples are hiding, afraid of being recognized as followers of Jesus amidst the backlash and opposition to the cause of Christ. We have here, in Jesus' actions, a demonstration of his unconditional love, and his power and willingness to seek us out – to step into our situations and our fears. Jesus greets the cloistered disciples with a powerful message – peace.

Jesus' first words to the disciples (and to us present day believers), is, "Peace be with you" (Jn 20:19). He is offering a gift; one that is able to give a person a sense of total well-being and inner rest of spirit. No one can give what they do not possess. Jesus can extend his peace because his very nature is one of peace. Now, within this offering of peace is compassion – for what the disciples have gone through, for what we go through in troubling times and tough situations. In addition, there is forgiveness in Christ's peace. Jesus knows we are human, and that our faith needs propping up. Jesus forgives our lack of faith and takes away our guilt, so that we might again be able to move forward. Jesus sends us forward, confident in our ability through God's power, to go into the world giving praise and glory to God and Christ Jesus in all that we do.

Jesus had already told them, "Peace I leave with you; my peace I give to you. I do not give to you as the world gives" (Jn 14:27). The world gives peace and takes it back all too easily. From the year 1500 B.C.E. to 1860 C.E., more than 8,000 treaties of peace were signed between countries and peoples, each meant to remain in force forever. The average time they remained in force, however, was two years. Jesus' peace offering is a lasting one; a divine promise devoid of the equivocations of human commitment. It overcomes all fear concerning Jesus' continued love for us in our weaknesses. It addresses and assuages any doubts concerning Jesus' willingness to be with us – to be our shepherd, providing renewal, guidance, wisdom, salvation, and power to live lives of engaged discipleship.

Jesus acts first; but we must also act. We must respond "yea" or "nay" to him. We must break through to *claim* the peace Jesus offers. The word *breakthrough*, coined by Meister Eckhart, a 13th-century Dominican priest, emphasizes the radical change needed in us to complete the peace that Jesus seeks to bring into our lives. The breakthrough needed is *trust*; trust that the power and love of Christ can indeed be relied upon. When this happens, we are able to claim and bring into our souls Christ's peace. Christ's promise of peace is a living word, one that passes human understanding. We must be willing to receive it. Trust allows that to happen.

Now, after Jesus extends his peace and shows his wounds to the disciples, he again offers peace. In doing this, Jesus demonstrates his willingness to reassure, knowing the fragile nature of human belief. Afterwards, Jesus offers a special blessing. Jesus breathes on the disciples, and in a very visual and physical way, transfers power to them. He encourages them to receive what he is giving them; not only his peace, but the ability and authority to forgive and bless others. In essence, he performs an action that affirms his offering of peace. We are called to do the same. When we confer our peace, let it not be just in words, but in action and deed. We may not breathe on someone as Jesus did, but the "airs" of our own attitudes are passed to others just the same. The Spirit of God is with us through our relationship with Christ. It surrounds us and blows in and through our words and actions.

The disciples were fortunate to have Jesus appear in person. Thomas, however, was not present, and merely hearing that Jesus was alive again was not enough for him. Many Christians are like Thomas. They need conclusive proof that Christ is with them. The testimony of Christ's presence with other believers in their tough, maybe even similar situations, does not inspire their faith. The consequence of this lack of faith, besides a lack of peace, is the inability to move forward; to act with trust that God is working things out. In addition, there can be no celebration, no joy. For Thomas, as well as many Christians, the hidden God needs to be seen, and nothing short of this will do. But "seeing is believing" is not faith. Faith resides in the area between the good news of Christ's hope and proof. Faith is the evidence of things unseen.

Jesus, in his great love and mercy, proves himself to Thomas. Thomas believes, whereupon Jesus lovingly chastises him for his lack of faith. But what about us? How are those persons who doubt Jesus' presence in their lives and immediate circumstances to be convinced if Jesus is not here to prove himself?

Ah, but, Jesus is here! We, the Church, are the body of Christ today. We can present the living Christ, prove his aliveness, and show his wounds in the way we, as a community, offer peace and sacrifice for Christ's sake. Jesus' peace, transferred to us through trust and acceptance, allows us to endure opposition while offering forgiveness. Jesus' wounds are seen in our loving sacrifices of time, effort, and talents to help others. His triumph is seen in our ability to continually offer peace in the midst of challenges and challengers.

Faith allows us to "see" Christ without seeing. It is the key that opens the door to Christ's blessings for us. As we trust, Jesus gives us his peace, dispels our fear, transfers his power, and guides us as we live our lives. Praise be to God, and his risen son, Jesus Christ!

– David Preston Sharp
Presbyterian Church (USA)
San Jose, California

April 25, 2004

3rd Sunday of Easter

Lessons

RCL	Acts 9:1-6 (7-20)	Rev 5:11-14	Jn 21:1-19
Roman Catholic	Acts 5:28-32, 40b-41	Rev 5:11-14	Jn 21:1-19 or 21:1-14
Episcopal (BCP)	Acts 9:1-19a or Jer 32:36-41	Rev 5:6-14 or Acts 9:1-19a	Jn 21:1-14

Introduction to the Lessons

Lesson 1

(1) *Acts 9:1-6 (7-20)* (RCL); *Acts 9:1-19a* (Epis)

Saul, a persecutor of Christians, is confronted by Jesus on the road to Damascus. This divine encounter blinds Saul for three days, until Ananias heals him. Transformed, he begins to preach that Jesus is the Son of God. Here, we are reminded of our own encounters with Christ.

(2) *Acts 5:28-32, 40b-41* (RC)

The apostles are brought before the Sanhedrin where they boldly witness to their faith and defend their teaching and preaching of Christ. After being flogged, they rejoice, happy to be found worthy of suffering disgrace for the name of Jesus. Are we so joyous in serving God?

Lesson 2

***Revelation 5:11-14* (RCL/RC); *Revelation 5:6-14* (Epis)**

John tells of seeing the elders, the throne guards, tens of thousands of angels, and all creatures in heaven and on earth worship and sing to Christ and affirm his worthiness to be praised. John's vision should fill all believers with renewed inspiration to worship and praise Christ.

Gospel

***John 21:1-19* (RCL/RC); *John 21:1-14* (Epis)**

This scripture challenges our commitment to follow Jesus, who will provide for our needs. The disciples, who have gone back to fishing after the Resurrection, have empty nets. Jesus guides them, demonstrating that success comes from obedience to God's will. Christ calls us to follow.

Theme

Jesus calls us, guides us, nourishes us, and challenges us.

Thought for the Day

As we live each day, expect Jesus to come to us. When we slip into old patterns and ways, Jesus will show up to give us new direction. When we follow Jesus' leading, we will accomplish things beyond our own abilities. Jesus knows our best destiny.

Call to Worship

Come let us worship Christ, who meets us on the road of our lives, and gives us wisdom and guidance. Let us cast our dreams on the side of righteousness that we may catch the hope of Christ's promise. Let us celebrate Christ's presence on the shores of our days.

Pastoral Prayer

We praise you, O God, for the majesty of this wondrous universe. You have filled it with awe-inspiring mystery and breathtaking beauty. You have blessed it with all manner of living beings. Your strength is like a mountain; your grace like the rising of the sun. Your Spirit is sensed in the comforting breeze of a warm day; your peace in the calm of a still night. You announce your presence through the glory of creation and the beauty of nature. We acknowledge you and revere you as worthy to be praised. You are ancient and always new; unchanging and renewing; merciful and just. We thank you that you have loved us enough to send us Jesus of Nazareth to be our Sure Hope and model of how to live and love. We pray for those who need his love right now – for those who are in need of forgiveness, renewal, and salvation. May we go out into our community and the world as the disciples did, unafraid to witness to new life found in Christ Jesus. As the heavens praise you, may we shout praises to you on earth, through our actions, words, and deeds. Amen.

Prayer of Confession

We confess, God, that we have sometimes heard you call and failed to respond. There are times we have seen you, but were too distracted or too busy to recognize you. There are times you have tried to guide us, but we did not listen. You have offered nourishment, but we did not partake. There are times we have known what was right to do, and have left things undone. We confess that there are times we have done what is right and suffered for it, complaining instead of rejoicing that we were suffering for your sake, as you suffered for ours. Forgive us and strengthen our resolve to be your people in good times or bad, whether we are ridiculed or honored, knowing that all we are and all we endure is for the glory of your name. Amen.

Prayer of Dedication of Gifts and Self

We bring these tithes and offerings and dedicate them to your service, O God. As you have nourished us in your love and grace, may these be used to nourish others. As you meet our needs and bless us with the material necessities to live life, we pray for guidance as we seek to serve and meet the needs of others in our church, our community, and the world. Amen.

Sermon Summary

As Christians, we are called to live and work with a new focus. Left to our own devices, it is tempting to go back to old ways of thinking, being, and living. Christ challenges us to stay committed to the new life he has called us to.

Hymn of the Day

"Jesus Calls Us"

Cecil Frances Alexander first wrote this text in conjunction with St. Andrew's Day (November 30) and in its original form the second stanza reads "As of old St. Andrew heard it . . ." while more recent hymnals have broadened application of the hymn with a change to "As of old the apostles heard it . . ." Further, the line "Christian love me more than these" has echoes of today's gospel and the risen Christ's admonition to Peter.

The hymn is sung to a variety of tunes in various traditions, the two most common being "Galilee" and "St. Andrew."

Children's Time

Feed My Sheep

Preparation: Bring a children's Bible.

After Easter, Jesus appeared to the disciples one time when they really weren't expecting it. They'd been out fishing all night and hadn't caught a single fish. As the sun came up, they could see someone standing on the shore. This person told them to try casting their nets over the right-hand side of the boat and so they did.

Suddenly they realized it was Jesus and, with a net full of squirming fish, they rowed the boat to shore. There they found that Jesus had prepared a breakfast of bread and fish for them.

After breakfast, Jesus asked Peter three times if Peter loved him. Each time, Peter said, "Yes!" Each time, Jesus said, "then feed my sheep."

Jesus said that we are his sheep. Jesus is the good shepherd. Jesus was telling Peter to feed other people – with food if they were hungry but also with food for their hearts. We feed each other's hearts when we talk about Bible stories *(hold up the children's Bible),* when we pray, and when we are for each other. When Jesus says, "Will you feed my sheep?" we can say, "Yes."

The Sermon

A Call to Commitment

Hymns

Beginning of Worship: "Today We All Are Called to Be Disciples"
Sermon Hymn: "Just as I Am, without One Plea"
Closing Hymn: "Lord, You Have Come to the Lakeshore"

Scripture

John 21:1-19 (For additional sermon materials on this passage, see the January 2004 issue of *The Clergy Journal* and on Revelation 5:11-14, see the 2003 May/June planning issue of *The Clergy Journal.*)

Backsliding. This is a term used to define the process of gradually turning away from one's religion, or relapsing into sinful ways. Christian living is not easy and there are countless reasons for backsliding; but at the core is temptation. We do not get a free ride through life because we have become followers of Christ. Many Christians find that the more they try to live godly lives, the more difficult their lives become. It can be tempting to go back to old ways and patterns of living.

Jesus does not usurp our free will. He does not make anyone live a godly life. It is a decision we make; one which takes constant commitment and resolve. Paul reminds us in 2 Corinthians 5:17, "So if anyone is in Christ, there is a new creation: everything old has passed away; see, everything has become new!" But without proper encouragement, guidance, and even challenge, it is surprisingly easy to revert back to old ways. That is why new Christians must be cared for by the members and leaders of the church. We must guard our faith, as there is much that seeks to take us away from our new life with Christ. Think what would have happened if the disciples had permanently gone back to their old lives. Perhaps the faith we share would have declined to the point of nonexistence.

This is not idle conjecture. Lest we lose perspective, it should be noted that during the first 500 years after Christ, the gospel was hardly a blip on the radar screen. Christianity spread, declined, and almost died out. And during these centuries most of the planet had not yet heard even the name of Christ. With the benefit of looking back on history, what takes place on the shores of Tiberias is no small event in the formation of our faith as a movement and religion.

Simon Peter, probably the most outspoken, and certainly the most boastful and self-righteous of the disciples, decided to go fishing. The others decided to join him. They had not gone fishing for three years; not since the day Jesus called for them to join him and become fishers of people. We don't know whether they went back to fishing for reasons of pleasure, to recapture old memories, or if they were truly going back to their old lives. But after three years with Jesus, it is at least curious that they would do this after Jesus' resurrection. He had shown them another work they were to do now, and had demonstrated how their needs would be provided for in this cause.

In any case, after fishing all night and catching nothing, daylight breaks. Jesus shows up on the shore. He calls to them, addressing them as "children." The Greek word here, *paidion,* means *infant* and is a term of endearment. It also implies that the disciples are still growing spiritually.

As we know, children must be watched and constantly guided. They must be reminded over and over of correct ways of being and acting.

Jesus begins a dialogue that, ironically, reenacts his calling of these disciples three years before. He guides them to cast their nets on the right side of the boat, whereupon they haul in a large catch. Just as the disciples go back to their old ways, Jesus shows up and corrects their behavior. He demonstrates that to be successful they must adhere to his guidance, his direction.

Though it is barely daylight, this action sparks a recognition that it is Jesus who stands on the shore. Peter, naked, puts on clothes, jumps into the water, and hurries to Jesus, who is waiting with lit charcoal, fish, and bread. How did Jesus get fish? Are we to presume that he had gone fishing earlier? Did he buy fish? The Greek word *phaneroo* describes Jesus as manifesting his glory, power, and ability to provide all that is needed. Jesus was showing the disciples, again, that they did not have to go back to the fishing business to make a living – in doing the work Jesus called them to, their needs would be met.

When Jesus invites the disciples to eat, none dare ask if it is Jesus. This scriptural inclusion is interesting in that it invites speculation on Jesus' appearance. He may have looked different to them or appeared in a form they didn't recognize; but Jesus was recognized in his actions and manner of being. For us Christians today it is a reminder that Jesus may come to us in ways that are unrecognizable at first glimpse. Jesus' manner, though, remains the same.

Jesus may appear through seeming coincidences, or in the synchronicity of moments and events, or through timely conversations with friend or acquaintance. In other words, the Holy Spirit may break through the unfolding events of our lives, in the midst of the circumstances and situations, which challenge our lives. When confronted with temptation, Jesus is there to guide us, or correct us if we succumb to the temptations we face. The question he asks is, "Do you recognize me?"

Now, after breakfast, Jesus begins to question Simon Peter, asking three times if Peter loves Jesus. This questioning, which hurts Peter, is poetic justice. Peter had denied Jesus three times before the cock crowed. Jesus absolved Peter's three denials with his three questions. As Peter responds we hear a new tone, one of humility. This was good news.

April 25, 2004
3rd Sunday of Easter

Humility is a must if we are to serve God effectively. In addition, those of us who are preachers, teachers, and leaders in the church cannot serve effectively if we are seeking personal ambition, respect, honor, or other self-interests. All Christians are called to serve for the glory of God.

Jesus told Peter that he would die for Christ's mission. If we are truly believers and have complete faith in Christ, we too must be willing to give our very lives for God's sake. Most of us will not have to go this far or think much about this kind of resolve; but there have been a host of Christians from the time of the church's formation to the present day who have died for the cause of Christ. The point is, our faith is only as powerful as our commitment. Jesus proved that we can live every moment for God. We have seen many people, including church leaders, take great falls when temptation overtakes their commitment. We must guard our faith, lest we become backsliders.

But Jesus is there when we stray, calling us back, testing our hearts, reminding us whom we serve. Just as Jesus called the disciples into new livelihoods, Jesus may guide our paths in surprising new directions. We are called to follow where Jesus leads, even if it means changing jobs, going back to school, or doing something we had never thought of doing. We are called to change our ways and, when tempted to go back to old ways of thinking and being and living, Jesus will call to us just as he did the disciples, telling us to cast our nets on the right side.

Yes, Jesus watches us, and will guide us in the direction that will best serve us and allow us to reach our best destiny in the service of the kingdom of God. Amen.

– David Preston Sharp
Presbyterian Church (USA)
San Jose, California

May 2, 2004

4th Sunday of Easter

Lessons

RCL	Acts 9:36-43	Rev 7:9-17	Jn 10:22-30
Roman Catholic	Acts 13:14, 43-52	Rev 7:9, 14b-17	Jn 10:27-30
Episcopal (BCP)	Acts 13:15-16 26-33 (34-39) or Num 27:12-23	Rev 7:9-17 or Acts 13:15-16, 26-33 (34-39)	Jn 10:22-30

Introduction to the Lessons

Lesson 1

(1) *Acts 9:36-43* (RCL)

Peter is summoned from the town of Lydda after the disciple Tabitha dies. He enters the room where she lays. After praying, he commands her to get up. This demonstration of God's healing power causes many to believe in the Lord, who gives us his healing spirit.

(2) *Acts 13:14, 43-52* (RC)

Paul, with Barnabas, preaches in Pisidian Antioch for two Sabbaths. Stirring up jealousy and opposition, they defend their actions and announce that they will preach to the Gentiles. After being expelled from the region, they continue on, filled with joy and the Holy Spirit.

(3) *Acts 13:15-16, 26-33 (34-39)* (Epis)

Paul here teaches both Jews and Gentiles that Jesus is the fulfillment of the prophecies, using Psalm 2 as evidence. He teaches that Jesus was sinless, that God raised him up, and through him whoever believes is forgiven and freed from their sins. Christ supercedes the law of Moses.

Lesson 2

***Revelation 7:9-17* (RCL/Epis); *Revelation 7:9, 14b-17* (RC)**

John describes his vision of a countless multitude from every tribe and nation wearing white robes and worshiping God and Jesus. This is a model of praise given by those who have come out of the great tribulation, who will never again experience want and pain.

Gospel

***John 10:22-30* (RCL/Epis); *John 10:27-30* (RC)**

This scripture dramatizes Jesus' courage and the decision all must face – to believe in Christ or not. The Jews want to trap Jesus into giving a direct statement about being the messiah, but Jesus offers his works as evidence.

Theme

Have courage and remain faithful in difficult moments.

Thought for the Day

God places us in positions to be blessings to others. We must be willing to speak God's word and act faithfully in all situations and circumstances.

Call to Worship

Let us celebrate the Lord! Let us renew our spirits! Come, all who need healing, and receive hope! Bring your concerns for the earth, for nations, for our community, for loved ones, for your challenges. Let us be of one body, one mind, and one spirit as we pray, sing, and celebrate God.

Pastoral Prayer

We gather our hearts before you in prayer, O God, thanking you for all the blessings you have bestowed upon us. We thank you for allowing us to rise to see another day, and for the gift of communing with you in prayer. We pray that this church will continue to be a bright beacon of hope to a world in need of your touch – growing in faith and trust, seeking your will in all that we do. Send a fresh touch of your healing spirit to those who are hurting. Make the way clear and straight for those who are questioning your direction for their lives. Hear us, O God, as we join the chorus of those around this city, across the nation, and around the world who gather today to honor, praise, and celebrate you and your son, Jesus the Christ. We thank you for the gift of salvation, for the promise that nothing can separate us from your love, and for the joy you give through our relationship with you. Help our unbelief, attend to our brokenness, and strengthen us where we are weak. In the name of Jesus Christ. Amen.

Prayer of Confession

O God of grace and mercy, we humbly submit ourselves to you, asking for your forgiveness. We have allowed opportunities to pass when we could have been instruments of your blessing in the lives of others. We have been silent in our praise when others needed our faith to be spoken. We have been afraid to interfere when we could have been peacemakers. We have been too distant to comfort when others needed words of encouragement and hope. Forgive us, and strengthen our faith that we may not be afraid to boldly share our great heritage as children of God. Amen.

Prayer of Dedication of Gifts and Self

As you have blessed us with the gift of your sacrifice, we return to you these tithes and offerings, as symbols of our willingness to sacrifice that which you have given us for the sake of others. We dedicate this offering to the building of the realm of God, here in this community and through our missions across the world. May it be used in our ministry to bring new hope to those in need, nourishment to the hungry, help to the indigent, and comfort to those in despair. In the name of the One who saves. Amen.

Sermon Summary

In Jesus' confrontation with the Jews, he demonstrates wisdom, courage, commitment, and resolve to be who he is in the midst of immediate danger. He speaks boldly, challenging the intellect and heart of the Jewish leaders.

Hymn of the Day

"God Is My Shepherd"

Without question, Psalm 23 is the most familiar passage of scripture amongst Christians, and even arguably amongst many non-Christians. The text has been adapted to several different tunes, the most famous being "Crimond" and "Brother James' Air," which is the tune used here in this fresh text by Lavon Bayler.

Adapting the version from the Scottish Psalter of 1650 (itself a compilation of earlier versions) Baylor infuses the familar psalm with new life, inviting us to reflect on the images in new ways, within the comforting arms of a familiar tune.

Children's Time

Let Those Who Have Ears to Hear . . .

Has anyone ever said to you, "Pay attention!" What was happening? What were you doing? Did you just not hear this person or did you choose to ignore her or him? *(Invite responses.)*

Sometimes, we only hear what we want to hear. We don't always want to pay attention. It was like that in Jesus' time, too. The Bible story today tells about something that happened before Jesus was put to death. The people were asking Jesus whether he was the savior they had been waiting for. So, Jesus points out that he has told them over and over that he is. Jesus has healed many people, too. Still, these people refuse to believe that Jesus is the savior they've been waiting for. They just have not been paying attention!

Finally, Jesus says, "I've been doing these things so that you will know and understand that God is working in me and I am working with God."

The Bible gives us plenty of chances to learn about Jesus' message of love and to learn about who he is. All we have to do is listen and pay attention.

The Sermon

The Crucible

Hymns

Beginning of Worship: "Be Thou My Vision"
Sermon Hymn: "My Hope Is Built on Nothing Less"
Closing Hymn: "I'm Gonna Live So God Can Use Me"

Scripture

John 10:22-30 (For additional sermon materials on this passage, see the February 2004 issue of *The Clergy Journal* and on Revelation 7:9-17, see the 2003 May/June planning issue of *The Clergy Journal.*)

The scene captured in this scriptural setting evokes the image of a crucible. A crucible is a heat resistant bowl or cup used to melt ores and metal. It is also a severe test. In the same manner, this scene finds Jesus in the midst of a severe test – the crowd's emotions have become very heated because of what he is saying. As we listen to the text, we become witnesses, watching to see how Jesus responds to and handles the anger of the crowd and how the crowd reacts to his responses.

This is high drama that tests both Jesus and those who oppose him. On the one hand, it tests the human part of Jesus to stay on task – to stay committed to that purpose for which he came. It tests Jesus' courage in the midst of immediate danger, and his ability to reason in the heat of the moment. On the other hand, it is a severe test of the intellect and heart of those who assail him. They must withstand Jesus' bold, compelling defense as they look to trap him into saying something for which they might accuse him before Pilate.

We are not used to speaking of Jesus in terms of his courage, but we must remember that Jesus was human. He had been born, was a child, was part of a family, and loved life. Though his destiny was authored and ordained by God; though he knew his mission was to die; though he voluntarily took on this role; still, it took great courage for him to follow through. We see that courage displayed in these verses.

The crowd wants Jesus dead, even as he promises to give eternal life to those who follow him. He speaks boldly of his authority and power even as he is outnumbered by those who seek to overpower him. It is the Lamb of God surrounded by hungry wolves. It is a test of his courage and love.

The word *courage* comes from the French, and means "large heart." That is what Jesus has, a heart large enough to love each one of us completely and unconditionally. A heart large enough to love his enemies and face the coming suffering of the cross, because of his compassion for humankind. Jesus has a heart with courage born of love – a heart large enough to face this dangerous crowd and speak his truth.

This scene comes after Jesus had made bold, if indirect, statements concerning his deity (John 4:26; 8:58). It comes after he has said, "Very truly, I tell you, before Abraham was, I am" (Jn 8:58). It comes as the culmination of a speech where Jesus states that he is the good shepherd. Jesus doesn't say, "I am the Messiah." Instead, he uses symbolic language that speaks to the heart of the listener. While it is true that belief can be achieved through intellectual persuasion, it is, ultimately, the heart of a person that accepts Christ.

May 2, 2004
4th Sunday of Easter

When we pull back and take a long view of what has been said and done immediately before this present scene, we see an inspiring progression. When Jesus says, "My sheep hear my voice. I know them and they follow me" (Jn 10:27), Jesus is saying he wants us to hear. Now, he speaks of belief, which employs the heart. Jesus wants us to believe. Jesus wants us to believe with our hearts what he says and does.

That being said, the Jews (Pharisees, members of the Sanhedrin, and other leaders) want Jesus to end the suspense and state plainly if he is the Messiah. Clear, precise language is what they want; and it is what Jesus provided. His statement, "I have told you, and you do not believe" (vs. 25), is precise. It allows Jesus to avoid the trap of making a statement for which they can then accuse him before Pilate. In addition, it gives their hearts one more chance to receive the truth of who Jesus is. There was no suspense, just an unwillingness to believe.

Jesus does not make anyone believe. Eyes can be open, yet blind. Ears can be open, yet deaf. Hearts can be open, yet unwilling. Jesus states in v. 26 that the Jews do not believe; not that they could not. Jesus, in essence, says, "Look at my works. Actions speak louder than words; seeing is believing; a picture is worth a thousand words."

Jesus boldly deals with their lack of faith, and states quite succinctly the rewards for those who believe. But because of who and what they are, they do not believe. Jesus has not asked for blind faith. He wants us to know, and demonstrated his deity over and over. But the Jews' hearts were hardened.

The reasons for their disbelief were many. For these religious leaders, there was much at stake. If Jesus indeed were the Messiah, the prestige of their positions as religious leaders would certainly suffer. Income would be lost as their flock turned to Christ. Their power and influence would suffer, as Christ gave believers power through faith in him. They could not afford for Jesus to be who he said he was, even though his coming was prophesied, even though everything about him fit the prophecies.

Jesus places the consequence of their disbelief squarely on the shoulders of their refusal to believe his works. Infuriated, the Jews pick up rocks to stone him right there. Jesus responds by using Psalm 82:6 to challenge their reasoning. Angered even more, the Jews try again to arrest him, but Jesus manages to escape. We are not told how Jesus accomplishes his escape, but it demonstrates the power of Christ to avoid capture until he himself is ready, according to God's purpose. It is the same power of protection he promises believers in verses 28 and 29.

What does this story mean for us today? Jesus lays out the very serious situation that every person faces – belief in Christ or not. We should all have courage enough to speak our faith in Christ.

Jesus gives us an opportunity to recognize who he is; not based solely on what he says, but also by what he has done. When Jesus says, "you do not believe, because you do not belong to my sheep. My sheep hear my voice. I know them and they follow me" (vv. 26-27), he challenges the openness of our hearts and our willingness to see and hear the truth for what it is. Jesus' voice is filled with the very vibration of divinity, and must be heard with the heart, for that is where Jesus rules.

"The Father and I are one" (v. 30), Jesus says. The word *one* in Greek means *one thing.* Jesus and God share the same essence or nature. Even though history is replete with efforts to anthropomorphize God, the person of God is seen most clearly through the incarnation of Jesus.

Ultimately, the questions become: Do we see? Do we hear? Do we believe? If we do, then we, too, can have courage through the grace of Christ to speak our faith in any situation or circumstance. We know that we are protected – that no power can snatch us from Christ, or from God's promise of love and eternal life. Amen.

– David Preston Sharp
Presbyterian Church (USA)
San Jose, California

May 9, 2004

5th Sunday of Easter

Lessons

RCL	Acts 11:1-18	Rev 21:1-6	Jn 13:31-35
Roman Catholic	Acts 14:21-27	Rev 21:1-5a	Jn 13:31-33a, 34-35
Episcopal (BCP)	Acts 13:44-52 or Lev 19:1-2, 9-18	Rev 19:1, 4-9 or Acts 13:44-52	Jn 13:31-35

Introduction to the Lessons

Lesson 1

(1) ***Acts 11:1-18*** **(RCL)**

Peter reveals the vision God gave him of Gentile inclusion in salvation and the need for justice and equality in relationship with others. The Jewish Christians hear it and praise God.

(2) ***Acts 14:21-27*** **(RC)**

After Paul had been stoned in Lystra, dragged from the city, and left for dead, we read here of Paul and Barnabas traveling through several cities – preaching, teaching, appointing elders, and encouraging the churches. Upon returning to Antioch they report all that God has done through them.

(3) ***Acts 13:44-52*** **(Epis)**

In Pisidian Antioch most of the city comes to hear Paul preach with Barnabas. They defend their mission against opposing Jews and announce the inclusion of Gentiles. They are expelled, and leave the region filled with the joy of the Lord.

Lesson 2

(1) ***Revelation 21:1-6*** **(RCL);** ***Revelation 21:1-5a*** **(RC)**

John sees a new heaven and earth. He describes an earth without a sea, the Holy City coming down from heaven as a bride, and God living among people. There will be no more death, mourning, crying, or pain as God makes everything new.

(2) ***Revelation 19:1, 4-9*** **(Epis)**
John records a vision of heaven, with a multitude worshiping and praising God. An angel directs him to write of the blessedness of those invited to attend the wedding of the Lamb, the final triumph of God's intimacy with believers.

Gospel
John 13:31-35 **(RCL/Epis);** ***John 13:31-33a, 34-35*** **(RC)**
Jesus states succinctly the fruits of his sacrifice, the coming salvation available to humanity. Jesus states that his earthly mission is about to come to a close. Jesus gives the great command to love – the distinguishing mark of the believer.

Theme
Jesus is the Lamb of God and the hope of our salvation.

Thought for the Day
Faith, hope, and love are powerful forces available to believers – forces which can help, heal, and transform the world for the glory of the Lord.

Call to Worship
This is the day that the Lord has made, let us rejoice and be glad in it. O give thanks to the Lord, for God is good, for God's steadfast love endures forever.

– Based on Psalm 118:24, 29

Pastoral Prayer
O merciful and loving God, we gather our hearts before you, praising you for your majesty and the beauty of creation. We are awed by the mystery of our universe, the vastness of space. We marvel at the beauty of a single flower. The depths of the oceans and the height of mountains humble us. In the vastness of your creation, you have shared your Spirit with us and know each of us by name. Help us to grow in our understanding of this privilege and to seize every chance to share the joy of your presence. With the freedom of will, you have blessed us. We have turned from you and

have filled this world with our sins, causing us to endure trials and tribulations. We thank you for Jesus and his power to heal and restore a right relationship with you, O God. Strengthen our faith that we may encounter challenge with good cheer, counting it as joy, because your word gives us power. Help us to be committed stewards of our earth, and to make this world a home worthy of your presence. Amen.

Prayer of Confession

As you, Jesus, have given your life through sacrificial love, and have commanded us to love our neighbors, we confess our shortcomings. You have asked us to follow you, yet we do so at a great distance; lagging behind and slow to catch up. We lose our way because we do not stay close to your leading. We get distracted by temptation, and do not pause to refocus our hearts. We refuse to give of ourselves sacrificially because we are afraid of losing what little we have, be it time, energy, or material things. We forget that all we have comes from you, and we horde our lives instead of freely giving. In your mercy, forgive us and help us to remember that you can and will supply all that we need. Amen.

Prayer of Dedication of Gifts and Self

As all blessings come from you, O God, we thank you for what you have given us. We thank you for our jobs and for work that is meaningful and beneficial to our families and community. We dedicate these tithes and offerings to your service, and pray that we may grow in faith, giving more of our time, talents, and lives where you direct us. Amen.

Sermon Summary

As Jesus is sharing the Last Supper with the disciples, he gives a final command – a call to love as he loves. This commandment marks the Christian life, a life that calls for sacrifice, including loving enemies and being willing to lay down one's life for another.

Hymn of the Day

"Marching to Zion"

Originally a lengthy poem by Isaac Watts, the text was shortened and adapted by John Wesley, and was first placed with the tune "St. Thomas" by Aaron Williams in the 18th century. In 1867, however, Robert Lowry recast the text to the contagiously joyful "Marching to Zion" tune, named for the brisk refrain he added. The hymn speaks well to the vision of the new Jerusalem presented in today's epistle.

Some hymnals list the hymn only by the title, while others list it only by its first line, variously rendered "Come, We (or Ye) that Love the Lord" or "Come, We Who Love God's Name."

Children's Time

Have Love

Preparation: Bring in a cross necklace, a lapel pin or other item with a Christian fish symbol, and other items that people might use or wear to show they are Christian.

Have you ever seen someone wearing a necklace like this? *(Hold up the cross.)* Or perhaps wearing a pin like this? *(Hold up fish symbol pin.)*

What would you think if someone wearing a necklace or pin like this came along and gave you a hard shove that knocked you to the ground? Or stole your money? What would people think if they saw Christians behaving like that? They'd be pretty shocked, wouldn't they?

Jesus told his disciples that they were to treat each other – and everyone else – with love, because that's how everyone would know they were Jesus' followers. When we treat others with love, then we show that we belong to a loving God. And when we share God's love, we draw others closer to Jesus.

You may wear things or have things at home that tell others you are a Christian. These are nice to have. Jesus wants us to remember, though, that it is most important to let other people know we are Christian by what we say and do.

The Sermon

The Glory of Love

Hymns

Beginning of Worship: "Breathe on Me, Breath of God"
Sermon Hymn: "Lord, I Want to Be a Christian"
Closing Hymn: "They'll Know We Are Christians by Our Love"

Scripture

John 13:31-35 (For additional sermon materials on this passage, see the 2003 May/June planning issue and the February 2004 issue of *The Clergy Journal.*)

When Jesus uttered the words captured in the first part of this passage, there must have been some very confused expressions. He had just told the disciples that he would be betrayed by the one to which he gives bread. He then gives bread to Judas, and tells him to quickly do what he must. The scriptures record that no one understood why Jesus said this to Judas, even though he had just told them he would be betrayed by the one to which he gave bread. Yes, there was confusion present among them; and for good reason – Satan was nearby. Where there is Satan, there is bound to be confusion.

Jesus, in this passage, begins to clear the confusion and set the record straight one last time. Jesus resets the context of his life's mission. He uses the term "Son of Man" here to describe himself. This title is never used by anyone except Jesus. We see it first in Daniel 7:13, referring to a figure who is entrusted by God with authority, sovereign power, and glory. As the Jews believed a person's name summed up their whole person, Jesus employs this moniker to identify himself to those who would believe. He is affirming, once again, that as his time on earth is coming to a close, Jesus knows who he is and what must take place to complete his mission. When he says, "Now the Son of Man has been glorified . . ." (Jn 13:31), Jesus means that all is happening as it should.

The second half of verse 31, "and God has been glorified in him," refers to the oneness Jesus shares with God. He previously says in 10:30, "The Father and I are one," and repeats it eight verses later, saying, "believe the works, so that you may know and understand that the Father is in me and I am in the Father" (v. 38). Whatever Jesus does reflects on God, even as God is reflected in the personhood of Jesus. They are separate beings but are of the same essence. This is why we can say that Jesus is our clearest indication of what God is like.

Now, we can understand more clearly verse 32 of John 13: "If God has been glorified in him, God will also glorify him in himself." Jesus utters these words as a prophecy, foreshadowing God raising Jesus from the dead. When this is done, the glory of both God and Jesus is seen in Jesus' triumph over the grave. God is glorified in Jesus and Jesus is glorified in God.

Jesus refers to the disciples as "little children." This endearing term also points to the truth that they do not yet understand what is really unfolding. As children look for their parents, the disciples will look for Jesus. But where he goes they cannot follow. If, however, his influence has truly become a part of them, it will be seen in their behavior, actions, and works. It is in this context that Jesus gives them a new commandment – to love.

Jesus has reminded the disciples of his authority as the Son of Man to give this command. Jesus has affirmed his role as Savior, also confirming his right to give this command. Jesus has stated his oneness with God, which emphasizes that what he commands is from God. In other words, there is no way out of honoring this command for those who follow Jesus. It is binding. It must be!

This commandment, though new, is based on an old commandment. We find it in Leviticus 19:18: "but you shall love your neighbor as yourself." There is, however, a new twist to what Jesus says. When we look at the Greek rendition of "new commandment," *kainos,* we see that the word means *renewed.* Jesus is not so much issuing a new commandment; he is renewing the commandment by adding a new focus: "Just as I have loved you, you also should love one another" (Jn 13: 34). "Just as I have loved you" is the new focal point, and it has ramifications unseen in any moral system before or since Jesus. To love as Jesus loves is to be able to die for another. No system has ever prescribed anything so pure and unselfish.

Jesus does not give this commandment arbitrarily, lightly, or without example.

Jesus offered his life for the salvation of humankind. Jesus loved his neighbor as himself, as we all must strive to do. Jesus, however, takes this a step farther. Looking two chapters ahead, we hear Jesus repeat this great call to love in John 15:12-13: "This is my commandment, that you love one another as I have loved you. No one has greater love than this, to lay down one's life for one's friends."

Now, we may not have to live this outright, but we must be willing to love this much. The modern precept (and no doubt ancient sentiment as well), that says, "Look out for number one," meaning one's self, is trumped by Jesus' call for us to love sacrificially, as he does. That is the mark of the Christian – the mark of Christian love. It supercedes merely sharing what you have. It is more than bending over backwards. It is *giving,* taken to its highest expression.

The followers of any leader can be seen and identified by their actions or their creeds. Christ's followers are to be known by their love for one another. Furthermore, that love must extend to one's enemies. This is radical love, to be sure. It is a breakthrough in living life, and it stretches our potential as created beings.

It can be said that much of the world loves, or feigns love, for reasons of ambition, envy, or striving for supremacy. But the motivation for Christian love must be in the very virtue of it; for the glory that it brings to God, and for the mark that it leaves on the world and us. You have heard the saying that virtue has its own reward. Well, the virtue within the kind of love Jesus calls us to express has the power to heal, transform, and make whole through the grace of God.

We do not, however, have to bear this call with our own strength. Most of us could not, anyway. It is Christ who gives us the courage and strength to live this commandment. His strength becomes ours. His love fills us. His compassion flows through our sense of caring. Remember Paul's statement: "I can do all things through him who strengthens me" (Phil 4:13).

In the final analysis, as Christ died that we may live, we must die to ourselves and live in Christ. Only then can we truly gain the ability to love as Christ has loved us. Jesus has made it clear. We must be resolved to a greater love than the world knows.

Wherever we go in life, whatever challenges we face, we leave our mark. We leave it in our manner of being, in the words we send forth, and through the deeds we commit. As followers of Christ Jesus, let the mark we leave be the mark of Christ: love.

– David Preston Sharp
Presbyterian Church (USA)
San Jose, California

May 16, 2004

6th Sunday of Easter

Lessons

RCL	Acts 16:9-15	Rev 21:10, 22–22:5	Jn 14:23-29 or Jn 5:1-9
Roman Catholic	Acts 15:1-2, 22-29	Rev 21:10-24, 22-23	Jn 14:23-29
Episcopal (BCP)	Acts 14:8-18 or Joel 2:21-27	Rev 21:22–22:5 or Acts 14:8-18	Jn 14:23-29

Introduction to the Lessons

Lesson 1

(1) *Acts 16:9-15* (RCL)

Paul's first proclamation of the gospel in Europe is to a gathering of women. There he meets Lydia, a Gentile who worships God but is not a Christian. Counterpart to Cornelius, this businesswoman is in contact with the elite of Philippi. Her house becomes the center of the first congregation in Europe.

(2) *Acts 15:1-2, 22-29* (RC)

Is the Christian gospel only for circumcised Jews or also for Gentiles? A historic decision by the council in Jerusalem welcomed uncircumcised Gentile men into the fellowship if they kept certain basic rules of conduct.

(3) *Acts 14:8-18* (Epis)

After healing a lame man in Lystra, Paul and Silas are welcomed as Greek gods, which gives them opportunity to proclaim the good news of the true God, source of all healing and salvation, who blesses the whole world with whatever providence is needed.

Lesson 2

***Revelation 21:10, 22–22:5* (RCL);**
***Revelation 21:10-14; 22, 23* (RC); *Revelation 21:22–22-5* (Epis)**

The gates of the heavenly city, named for Israel's 12 tribes, open the wall with 12 foundations bearing the names of the Lamb's apostles. The triumphant church and the realm where God reigns form a unity that will include all creation; this new Jerusalem becomes a light for all nations.

Gospel

***John 14:23-29* (RCL/RC/Epis)**

God will give Jesus' followers "another Advocate," as well as the gift of God's shalom. God and the risen Christ together give these gifts to sustain the disciples and the future church as Jesus finishes his work by going to the Father.

Theme

The Spirit empowers the church to reach out to the world.

Thought for the Day

God's shalom and the Holy Spirit sustained the disciples when Jesus went to the Father. The same gifts continue to sustain the church as we proclaim the mighty power of God's healing love to all nations.

Call to Worship

Leader: May God be merciful to us and bless us,
People: May the light of God's countenance come to us.
Leader: Let your ways be known upon earth;
People: Your saving health among all nations.
Leader: Let the nations praise you, O God; let all the peoples praise you.
People: May God bless us and may all the ends of the earth stand in awe of the Lord.

– Based on Psalm 67

Pastoral Prayer

We give you thanks, Almighty God, for all the blessings of our lives: for food and family, job and leisure, home and good neighbors, health and rest, and all your gifts to us. We ask the blessing of peace with justice for the world. Take from us all hatred and prejudice and whatever disturbs the unity of your people. We ask your blessing on our community so that its people may resolve their issues and live together in your shalom.

We pray for your healing in body, mind or spirit, for all who are ill in our congregation, our community, our world. Be with those whom death draws near. Console those who mourn. Heal caregivers so they may continue their works of mercy. Above all, hold fast in your loving care those who have departed this life until we can be reunited with them in your holy presence. We pray these things in the name of Jesus Christ, your Son, our Savior and Lord who reigns with you and the Holy Spirit, one God, now and forever. Amen.

Prayer of Confession

Most merciful God, we confess we have done the things we should not have done and have not done the good you desire us to do. We have walked where we desire rather than following your ways. We have not loved our neighbors as you have loved us and have not forgiven our neighbors or ourselves as you have forgiven us. We ask your forgiveness for all that we have done wrong. We long for your loving presence, so that we may amend our lives and walk in your ways in the coming days. In Jesus' name we pray. Amen.

Prayer of Dedication of Gifts and Self

Gracious giver of all good gifts, we offer with joy and thanksgiving what you have first given us: life, time, talents, and possessions. Receive them for the sake of One who offered himself for us, Jesus Christ, our Lord and Savior. Amen.

Sermon Summary

At the Last Supper, Jesus' disciples were overwhelmed by the realization that they would soon lose him. We, too, are often overwhelmed by problems, illness, loss, and hopelessness. God's gifts of shalom and the Holy Spirit are more powerful than any problems we will ever encounter.

Hymn of the Day

"Shall We Gather at the River?"

Robert Lowry, composer of "Marching to Zion" (see last week's Hymn of the Day) provided both text and tune for this hymn in 1864. The inspiration was the soul-searching brought about by tragedy: pastor Lowry was troubled by the deaths of many in his congregation from an epidemic.

The text uses imagery from Revelation 21 (today's epistle), and the tune provides a defiant affirmation in the face of uncertainty. Further, the hymn calls to mind the riverside meeting between Paul and Lydia, recounted in Acts 16.

Children's Time

The Holy Spirit

Preparation: Bring in pictures of a dove and a fire, and also bring in a small fan that you can plug in.

Before Jesus died, he talked to his disciples to prepare them for the fact that he would be leaving them soon. They were sad, of course, and so he reassured them that he wouldn't be leaving them all alone. He promised that he would send the Holy Spirit to be with them.

The Holy Spirit is part of God. The Holy Spirit supports and encourages us.

There are many images associated with the Holy Spirit. It's often pictured as a dove *(show picture),* especially as the dove that descended above Jesus' head just after his baptism. Or it's associated with flames *(show picture)*. The Holy Spirit is also thought of as a wind or the breath of God *(turn the fan on)*, blowing through and into us. Jesus promised that the Holy Spirit would keep on teaching us and would remind us of all that Jesus teaches.

Thanks be to God! We still have the Holy Spirit with us today, teaching and guiding us!

The Sermon

Rejoice in Shalom and the Spirit

Hymns

Beginning of Worship: "Christ Is Alive! Let Christians Sing"
Sermon Hymn: "Son of God, Eternal Savior"
Closing Hymn: "Praise the Savior, Now and Ever"

Scripture

John 14:23-29 (For additional sermon materials on this passage, see the 2003 May/June planning issue of *The Clergy Journal* and on Revelation 21:10, 22–22:5, see the February 2004 issue of *The Clergy Journal*.)

Jesus said to his disciples: "(T)he Advocate, the Holy Spirit whom the Father will send in my name, will teach you everything and remind you of all that I have said to you. Peace I leave with you; my peace I give you" (Jn 14:26, 27a).

Someone once said, "I do not know why so much mainline Protestantism has become a joyless religion. Perhaps we're more impressed by the problems of this world than by the power of God."

Today in the gospel reading we meet Jesus and his disciples at the Last Supper. The disciples are somewhat more impressed by the problem of Jesus' coming departure – his crucifixion will happen on the next day – than by the power of the Holy Spirit and the peace of God, the shalom that Jesus is promising them. How is it with you this morning? Are you more impressed by the difficulties you face this week or by the power of God to walk with you through the coming days? Do you believe the loving God will only lead you where the grace of God will see you through?

All three readings today invite us to be more impressed by the Spirit's power and the healing peace of God than by our fears. Jesus describes these two gifts. In Acts we see Paul living in faith, led by the Spirit into territory he had never visited, and being blessed by the leading of God. (Alternatively, we see the power of the Holy Spirit sending out new preachers of the gospel with a mandate to welcome Gentiles and Jews alike.) In Revelation we see a vision of the coming reign of God, the Father, Son, and Holy Spirit, and the peace of God descending into the world as the New Jerusalem becomes the promised light to all the nations.

Jesus' two gifts, the Holy Spirit and the shalom of God, will sustain the disciples after his resurrection and ascension. They guide Paul throughout his journeys; they lead all who are sent by the Jerusalem congregation where the Spirit calls them. In the New Jerusalem the leaves of the tree of life bring healing to the nations and the water of life sustains all peoples of the world who believe. All stand before the throne, see God's face, and worship God forever in peace and thanksgiving and joy.

Now, how is it with you? Is the Holy Spirit your reassuring and powerful ally in the midst of the troubles or difficulties you are facing this morning? Or is much of life a joyless rut, rat race, or routine?

Jesus calls the Holy Spirit an advocate. That word can also be translated helper. In Psalm 46, the psalmist tells us God is our refuge and strength, a very present help(er) in trouble. The Hebrew word, EZER, used here, is also used for the companion God creates for the first earth creature. Here the word is use by the psalmist for God. An EZER is an equal or a superior who graciously helps you because you are beloved and treasured. An EZER is what God means by a neighbor; it is the kind of neighbor God is to each one of us and the kind of neighbor that we are called to be in the Ten Commandments.

The Holy Spirit that Jesus promised on the night in which he was betrayed will come to be neighbor to the disciples as long as they live in this world. The same Holy Spirit is given to each Christian at baptism. From that day on, we are never alone. The Holy Spirit is God's very presence that never leaves our side. The Spirit is our constant neighbor, our faithful companion, and our friend. Does that make you feel good? Maybe joyful? The Holy Spirit is Jesus' first gift to his friends as he leaves them.

Jesus' second gift is peace, which in Hebrew is the shalom of God. It is peace that nothing or no one else in all creation can give to us. It includes all blessings needed for life. When we fall short of the mark, God's grace – part of this shalom – restores us in love with forgiveness. God's shalom includes the gift of a steadfast faith which trusts God forever, will not let go of us, and keeps us confident.

In God's shalom we are called to live as neighbors who help each other as God comes to us with power to bless, love, serve, and hold fast. In that peace we help each other, never fearing our help will give the other an advantage over us, but believing that loving service to others is, in the end, the best possible gift we can give ourselves. God's peace can never be taken from us by the world, no matter what life brings or what others do to God's faithful followers. Martyrs have died rather than give up that relationship of peace with their God.

Jesus told his followers: "Those who love me will keep my word, and my Father will love them, and we will come to them and make our home with them" (Jn 14:23). A friend tells the following story about a man who knows what those words mean.

Tom had a stroke and went through an operation in which a heart valve was replaced. After he recovered, he described how he had survived. He said, "As my wife got me into the car after my stroke, and then down to the hospital, I was scared. After I got through the initial scare, I asked myself, 'What do I do now?' Well, I could do nothing. I wanted to pray but I couldn't remember even the Lord's Prayer. All I could say was, 'Lord, hold my hand.' I could hardly talk to anyone those first few days, during which at least 20 people came and just held my hand. As I look back, I feel that the Lord was in each person who held my hand, each person who reached out to me. My prayer was, 'Lord, hold my hand,' and the Lord, through those people, held it."

In Acts, God held Paul's hand and led him and empowered him to build a new congregation. God held the hands of the Jerusalem Council and led them to a new insight and vision of mission. Here this morning God comes again to take your hand and walk with you through the coming week. To grant you peace through blessings that nurture and comfort you, through grace that loves and renews you, and through a family of sisters and brothers who cherish and delight in you.

In all these ways God and Jesus come to make their home with us by giving us to each other to know and to love as companions in our pilgrimage on earth. By blessing and caring for us, by forgiving and walking with us, God's gifts of the Spirit and abiding peace and faith bring us joy.

Let us overflow with eagerness to share that joy and love with each other and with others in our world. Let us rejoice in God's blessings and become the people who are much more impressed with God's blessings, grace, and peace than by the problems we encounter in our lives. Amen.

– LaVonne Althouse
Interim Pastor
Lititz, Pennsylvania

May 20, 2004

Ascension Day

Lessons

RCL	Acts 1:1-11	Eph 1:15-23	Lk 24:44-53
Roman Catholic	Acts 1:1-11	Eph 1:17-23	Lk 24:46-53
Episcopal (BCP)	Acts 1:1-11 or 2 Kgs 2:1-15	Eph 1:15-23 or Acts 1:1-11	Lk 24:49-53 or Mk 16:9-15, 19-20

Introduction to the Lessons

Lesson 1

***Acts 1:1-11* (RCL/RC/Epis)**

After 40 days of instructing the disciples, Jesus ascends, promising the gifts of the Holy Spirit. Jesus charges the disciples to be witnesses "in Jerusalem, in all Judea and Samaria, and to the end of the earth." This charge continues to be our challenge.

Lesson 2

***Ephesians 1:15-23* (RCL, Epis); *Ephesians 1:17-23* (RC)**

Christ's resurrection includes his ascension, exaltation, reign with God, and the victory over all hostile powers of this world. The church as the body of Christ lives toward Christ's cosmic reign over all things; its growth will finally embrace the whole creation.

Gospel

***Luke 24:44-53* (RCL);**
***Luke 24:46-53* (RC); *Luke 24:49-53* (Epis)**

After his resurrection, Jesus appears to the disciples and demonstrates to them the continuing identity between the Jesus they have known and the risen Christ. He tells them to wait in Jerusalem, where the apostolic church will be constituted as the new Israel that will fulfill God's plan.

Theme

Christians today continue to be witnesses to Christ's ascension and reign.

Thought for the Day

This festival reminds us that Christ reigns with power for all eternity. We are loved and sent into the world to tell everyone the reign of Christ has come. We are to live this message in the way we share our blessings with all in need, love our neighbor, and care for the earth.

Call to Worship

Leader: Christ is risen and reigns forever.
People: Christ is Ruler of rulers and Lord of lords.
Leader: Hallelujah! We will give thanks to the God with our whole hearts
People: In the assembly of the upright, in the congregation.
Leader: Great are the deeds of God
People: Whose work is full of majesty and splendor; whose righteousness endures forever.
Leader: The works of God's hands are faithfulness and justice;
People: God has sent redemption to all who glorify God's holy name. Hallelujah!

– Based on Psalm 111

Pastoral Prayer

Creator God, risen and ascended Christ, Holy Spirit, we give you heartfelt thanks for all the blessings you shower upon us day by day. Keep us mindful of the needs of others and make us as willing to be blessings to our neighbors. We thank you for the ministry of Christ among us and for your continuing companionship on our daily journeys through this life. We ask your healing blessing on all we name in our hearts, who need healing in body, mind, or spirit. Be the companion of all caregivers and renew them so they may continue their ministries. Bless the work of all in healing professions; strengthen them for their ministries. God, who sets us in families, bless all families everywhere. Enable parents to care lovingly for their children. Renew them and strengthen their love for each other so they may be for each other sources of comfort and support. All these things and whatever else you see we need, grant us, God of the risen and ascended Christ and giver of the Holy Spirit, whom we worship as one God, now and forever. Amen.

Prayer of Confession

Righteous and loving God, forgive all that we have done that is unrighteous and unloving, selfish and thoughtless. We have not shared with others the love, support, and forgiveness that you have given us day by day. We have done things our way instead of following your lead. We have preferred our advantage to showing mercy on our neighbor. We are sorry for the wrongs we have done and ask your gracious forgiveness. For the sake of your risen and ascended Son, renew and lead us so we may delight in your will and walk in your ways. We pray in the name of Jesus Christ, your Son, our Lord. Amen.

Prayer of Dedication of Gifts and Self

Lord God, we ask you to accept these gifts as tokens of the lives we give for the work of your eternal reign. With them we rededicate ourselves to your service. May each gift you have given us be returned for use in proclaiming your provident rule. We pray in the name of Jesus Christ our risen and ascended Lord and of the Holy Spirit. Amen.

Sermon Summary

Today we celebrate Jesus' return to God. Christ is now present everywhere for all eternity – our constant friend. As Christ's friends and followers, we continue to be witnesses of God's eternal reign and the bountiful and unending providence and grace of our triune God.

Hymn of the Day

"Lord, You Give the Great Commission"

Episcopal bishop Jeffrey Rowthorn has provided a number of hymns, in addition to collections of litanies and prayers. The text readily reminds us of the duties of Christian ministry, making the hymn highly suitable for services of commissioning and ordination, or other celebrations of ministry – both lay and ordered – in the life of the church. The story of the election of Matthias as apostle in today's first reading, and Luke's version of Jesus' parting words, suggest the use of this hymn.

Children's Time

Last Moments Together

(Talk about a time when a special visitor was getting ready to leave. How did you feel? What were the last things you talked about? Ask the children for their memories of leave-takings with loved ones.)

It's always hard to say good-bye to someone we love, isn't it? Even when we know we'll see them again, we still don't want to let them go. It's pretty common to feel sad and lonely for a little while after they've gone.

That's how the disciples must have felt, too, during their last few days with Jesus on earth. Jesus spent the time teaching them everything he could and reminding them of all that they had seen and done together. He told them that something special was going to happen and asked them to wait in Jerusalem. Then Jesus lifted his hands above them, and blessed them all. While he was blessing them, Jesus was carried away to be with God.

I bet the disciples felt sad, but also glad. Yes, their beloved Jesus was gone, but Jesus had promised that they would live in heaven with him one day. They went back to Jerusalem to wait for their surprise. They praised God. They knew they could trust Jesus.

The Sermon

Christ, Our Constant and Eternal Friend

Hymns

Beginning of Worship: "Look, the Sight Is Glorious"
Sermon Hymn: "Alleluia! Sing to Jesus"
Closing Hymn: "A Hymn of Glory Let Us Sing"

Scripture

Luke 24:44-53 (For sermon materials on Ephesians 1:15-23, see the 2003 May/June planning issue of *The Clergy Journal* and on Acts 1:1-11, see the February 2004 issue of *The Clergy Journal.*)

May 20, 2004
Ascension Day

Ascension Day recalls the day Christ was crowned Lord of all creation for all eternity. Before Jesus' crucifixion, he was anointed by a nameless woman. At the time, Jesus said the anointing was for his burial – and that was most certainly true. It was the custom to anoint corpses to dedicate them to God's eternal care. But today we see that Jesus' anointing was also for Jesus' coronation as Ruler of rulers for all eternity. We do not, however, see the coronation festival. We only see Jesus taking leave of his followers to return to the God who sent him.

Traditionally this leave-taking is pictured, as someone has said with a smile, as "an on-the-scene report of a take-off as if the disciples had gathered at an ancient Cape Canaveral." The paintings of the event almost always show it in this way. But the Greek in verse 52 speaks of Jesus being "carried away." He parted from them. What looked like an ascending has become, in the age of space travel, a kind of going out to another place. In Jesus' case the "going out" was to return to God.

John Calvin has some beautiful things to say about the meaning of the ascension for us. Let us look at them together. But first let me remind you of what Jesus said was the significance of this leave-taking. Jesus told his followers: "You are witnesses of these things" (v. 48). These things included his teachings, his death, his resurrection, and his ascension.

Those followers – and you and I who follow him today – are to tell the world about all these things because, Calvin said, "As Jesus' body was raised up above all the heavens, so his power and energy were diffused and spread beyond all the bounds of heaven and earth." Like God the Creator and God the Holy Spirit, Jesus now can be everywhere at once. Therefore Jesus, like the Creator God and the Holy Spirit, can be our eternal friend and constant daily companion. The ascension's blessing to each one of us is that in Jesus Christ we have a friend indeed, forever.

Calvin said further that through ascension faith we experience Christ's "transfusing us with power." Calvin envisioned Jesus as high and lifted up, seated at the right hand of God, where he "lavishes spiritual riches" upon "his own people."

Calvin, together with many others, also says Christ ascended as "constant advocate and intercessor" who "prepares a way and access for us to the Father's throne." Calvin says, further, that Christ is a kind of holy distraction for God. He "turns the Father's eyes to his own righteousness to avert (God's) gaze from our sins." Calvin sees Christ persuading the

Father's heart to look with favor on us so that we do not have to dread God's anger, but may enjoy God's continuing forgiveness.

Most important, says one Calvin scholar, ascension faith shows us that Christ's ascension "has opened the way into the Heavenly Kingdom, which had been closed through Adam." In this understanding, the ascension inaugurates God's eternal reign over all creation, God's final victory over sin and death.

Also most important, says Calvin, "Since Christ entered heaven in our flesh as if in our name, it follows, as the apostle says, that in a sense we are already with God in the heavenly places in Jesus Christ." At the ascension, according to this thinking, our "flesh" has been "taken" by God's Beloved One into the very heart of God. One scholar points out that "this is profound good news for us as Christians and for our whole world. It means that we are more deeply valued, loved, and held by God than we may ever have known before."

Wow! Jesus has returned to God and now can be present everywhere for all eternity – our constant and eternal friend. Christ can lavish all divine spiritual riches on us. Christ can intercede for us continually before the throne of grace. Christ has taken our humanity into the Godhead so nothing in all creation can ever separate us from the love of God in Christ Jesus, our Lord. Of all these things we are witnesses!

Luke says that Jesus told his followers to stay in Jerusalem until they were clothed with power from on high. Then they would become his witnesses to the whole world, beginning in Jerusalem, then Judea, then Samaria, and to the ends of the earth.

We live in those ends of the earth nearly 2,000 years later. As the followers of Jesus were clothed with power from on high at Pentecost, you and I were clothed with power from on high in our baptisms. As they received the Holy Spirit in tongues of fire and blowing wind, you and I received the same Holy Spirit when water flooded over us as we were made children of God forever.

Of all these things we continue to be witnesses. The ascended Jesus Christ is our friend and companion. We are continually blessed by the Triune God with every blessing we need for life. Our sins are continually forgiven. Nothing in all creation can separate us from that powerful, caring, blessing, and sustaining love of God that we receive through Christ Jesus our Lord.

May 20, 2004
Ascension Day

Today Jesus Christ is crowned Ruler of rulers for all eternity to assure us we are loved. Christ sends us out into the world to tell everyone this reign of God has come. The reign offers us a peace that enables us to live together in trust and confidence. We are called to share our blessings – all wealth, whether spiritual or material – and to share the land on which we live and all its resources. We are to see that no one lacks anything necessary for life. We are to love each neighbor as we love ourselves and to care for the needs of the other as we care for our own. In short, we are to live shalom, the peace of God, which passes all understanding. It is that peace which God sends us through Jesus' ascension. It truly will sustain and enlighten our hearts and minds forever and ever through Jesus Christ our Lord. Amen.

– *LaVonne Althouse*
Interim Pastor
Lititz, Pennsylvania

May 23, 2004

7th Sunday of Easter

Lessons

RCL	Acts 16:16-34	Rev 22:12-14 16-17, 20-21	Jn 17:20-26
Roman Catholic	Acts 7:55-60	Rev 22:12-14, 16-17, 20	Jn 17:20-26
Episcopal (BCP)	Acts 16:16-34 or 1 Sam 12:19-24	Rev 22:12-14, 16-17, 20 or Acts 16:16-34	Jn 17:20-26

Introduction to the Lessons

Lesson 1

(1) *Acts 16:16-34* (RCL/Epis)

Because healing a woman of her spirit of divination deprived her employers of income, Paul and Silas were falsely charged, beaten, and imprisoned. When God delivered them, their witness convinced the jailer to be baptized and to help heal the wounds the authorities had inflicted.

(2) *Acts 7:55-60* (RC)

Stephen, deacon and evangelist, becomes the first Christian martyr. He reminds hearers of the crucifixion of Jesus when he forgives those who stone him to death. Saul, who consents to this martyrdom, will also suffer greatly for his faith in Jesus Christ.

Lesson 2

***Revelation 22:12-14, 16-17, 20-21* (RCL)**
***Revelation 22:12-14, 16-17, 20* (RC/Epis)**

Christians pray for and expect the return of Jesus Christ, confident that Christ will make all things new and will ban the present order of injustice, oppression, and death. John, in his vision, assures the world that this promise is true and Christ is faithful.

Gospel

***John 17:20-26* (RCL, RC, Epis)**

This prayer pictures an ecumenical church constituted by mission and unity. The unity is basically one of love, reflecting the mutual love of Father and Son and demonstrating God's infinite love for God's people in the world.

Theme

God desires the unity of the church in mission to the world.

Thought for the Day

Current efforts of Christian communions in dialogue and declarations of pulpit and altar fellowship are some of our generation's efforts to be faithful to Jesus' high priestly prayer, that we may be one as Father and Son are one.

Call to Worship

Leader: Clap your hands, all you peoples.
People: Shout to God with a cry of joy,
Leader: For God reigns over the nations,
People: Seated upon the holy throne of grace.
Leader: The nobles of the peoples have gathered together,
People: With the people of the God of Abraham.
Leader: The rulers of the earth belong to God
People: Who is highly exalted among the nations.

– Based on Psalm 47

Pastoral Prayer

Provident God, source of all blessings of our lives, we give you thanks for your church and its mission to tell the world of your nurturing and sustaining love. Lead us to do all we can to preserve and strengthen the unity of the church so that it may witness continually to your loving care for all. God of peace, grace our world with economic justice for all people. Establish among the nations that peace which is the fruit of righteousness. Take from us all hatred and prejudice, and increase mutual understanding among all peoples. Bless and prosper loving relationships of every kind by strengthening our willingness to forgive each other as you forgive us. God of life, we give you thanks for those who have served you on earth and who now rest from their labors. All these things and whatever else you see we need, grant us, Provident God, in the name of Jesus Christ, your Son, our Lord who lives and reigns with you and the Holy Spirit, One God, now and forever. Amen.

Prayer of Confession

Holy and merciful God, we have strayed from your ways like lost sheep. We have done what we should not have done and we have not done what you command. We are heartily sorry for all our offenses and ask that you forgive us for the sake of Jesus Christ, your Son, our Lord. Be with us and strengthen us so that we may walk in your ways in future days. Amen.

Prayer of Dedication of Gifts and Self

God who made all things, through your goodness you have blessed us with these gifts. We offer a token of what you have given, and dedicate our lives to your service in thanksgiving for all your mercies. Receive what we offer for the sake of the One who gave himself for us, Jesus Christ our Lord. Amen.

Sermon Summary

The unity many Christians seek is that of being welcome to the Lord's Table wherever they worship – with family or friends or when traveling. The modern ecumenical movement and dialogues between communions have begun to make such fellowship increasingly possible.

Hymn of the Day

"Leaning on the Everlasting Arms"

This hymn began with its tune and refrain, both from the hand of prolific composer Anthony Showalter as he sought to console two grieving friends. He urged his friend, pastor Elisa A. Hoffman, to write additional words, and Hoffman produced the three stanzas. The hymn works well at a slow, reverent pace, or as a more boisterous song of celebration. Its defiant faith against all odds echoes the types of hymns probably being sung by Paul and Silas in prison.

Children's Time

Jesus in Our Hearts

Preparation: Bring in a mirror and some pictures of Jesus.

What does Jesus looks like? *(Talk about any pictures of Jesus that are in your worship space. Show the ones that you brought and discuss how the artists have expressed their ideas of what Jesus might have looked like.)*

There's another way to see Jesus. All you need to do is look into a mirror. *(Hold mirror so children can look at themselves.)* That's because we are made in God's image, which means that when we look at ourselves, we can see the love of God and Jesus shining through.

When we look into the faces of other people, we also can see Jesus. The Bible tells us that all people are made in God's image, which means that when we look at each other, we can see God shining through. Jesus promised his disciples that he would be in them always. And Jesus is in us, too.

So, stop and look at yourself. You are made in the image of God, and you have Jesus' love right inside you. Remember that when you look into the faces of other people you meet, too, and look for Jesus' love in them.

The Sermon

The Unity of Altar Fellowship

Hymns

Beginning of Worship: "I Know That My Redeemer Lives"
Sermon Hymn: "The Church's One Foundation"
Closing Hymn: "O Spirit of the Living God"

Scripture

John 17:20-26 (For additional sermon materials on this passage, see the February 2004 issue of *The Clergy Journal* and on Revelation 22:12-14, 16-17, 20-21, see the 2003 May/June planning issue of *The Clergy Journal.*)

Jesus said to his disciples, "The glory you have given me I have given them, so they may be one, as we are one, I in them and you in me, that they may become completely one, so that the world may know that you have sent me" (Jn 17:22, 23a).

"In essentials, unity. In nonessentials, diversity. In all things, charity." An early church leader charged the church to behave in this way. Perhaps that leader had in mind the verses of John's gospel we have read this morning.

The history of the church became a series of divisions when we did not follow this wisdom. The divisions were always a scandal. For centuries they caused us to wage war against each other and persecute each other until we Christians were, ourselves, revolted by our own behavior. In horror we began to experience our divisions as scandal, and to regard our differences as decidedly more tolerable than out mutual persecution.

The great American experiment introduced two novel ideas: the separation of church and state and the idea that Christians of differing understandings could live peaceably as neighbors – could tolerate each other, even cordially. The worldwide missionary movement which arose at the end of the 18th century and was revived with vigorous enthusiasm in the 1880s brought to our attention the scandal of our differences as we found ourselves in competition while proclaiming the gospel. The scandal was often most apparent in Asia and Africa, but urban and rural missions in Europe and North America also sometimes seemed competitive. What should we do?

The modern ecumenical movement was a worldwide response to that question. Beginning in about 1890, Christians have worked to create ecumenical structures and dialogues with other communions that have led to closer relationships with each other. Among Protestants a series of developments led to the formation of the World Council of Churches in 1948. During the past four decades Protestants in North America and Europe have entered into inter-communion dialogues that have resulted in a number of declarations of pulpit and altar fellowship. Vatican II resulted, among other developments, in the canon of hospitality which has allowed Roman Catholic priests in some places to welcome Protestants to share the Lord's Table under special circumstances.

All of these developments have been impelled not only by the scandal of our divisions, but positively, as efforts to be obedient to the vision of oneness Jesus set before his disciples in the night in which he was betrayed. The vision of unity in Jesus Christ has long been cherished and celebrated in the church's proclamation of "One Lord, one faith, one baptism."

To many Christians, these words can be catch phrases until life abruptly confronts them with personal issues. A family may move to a community where they come to love attending a church different from the communion in which they have formerly worshiped – and they learn they must be re-baptized because the baptism they had is not recognized or their confirmation is not recognized. There are still Protestant communions that will admit to communion only persons formed within the teachings of that denomination. There remain also barriers to sharing communion with Roman Catholic and Orthodox Christians.

Yet changes are also evolving. Since World War II Protestants in many places and through their denominations have increasingly adopted policies of open communion. Today in many places around the world, all baptized persons are welcome to share the Sacrament of the Altar as visitors in communions other then their own.

Where Christian communions declare full pulpit and altar fellowship, there is often the agreement to disagree about things that interfaith dialogues over several decades have come to consider important but not central to faith. The faithful worshipers in these communions have frequently been sharing the Lord's Table in each other's congregations for some years and are surprised, often, to learn that the agreement of full fellowship is necessary. Asking questions and learning about the reasons for these new steps in one way of learning more about what it means to be obedient to the vision Jesus sets before us in the gospel reading for today.

Jesus calls us to be one so that the world may know that God has sent the only Son so that through Christ all people might be saved. That was Jesus' final prayer for his disciples. Each step of repentance we take to understand our differences, and the unity that overcomes them, allows Jesus to reunite us more and more deeply.

Of course we can move ahead only one step at a time. Finally, only Jesus Christ can make us one. But any decision to live as though we want to be more united feels like a step toward living out Jesus' high priestly prayer in our daily lives. That is the great privilege we gain by learning whatever we can about the dialogues our own communion is having with other Christians – by taking every opportunity to learn about the ecumenical movement and support it. Jesus is waiting and listening, holding all of us together in the body of Christ, the Christian church, while we struggle to shape our obedience to the holy vision of unity. Amen.

– LaVonne Althouse
Interim Pastor
Lititz, Pennsylvania

May 30, 2004

Day of Pentecost

Lessons

RCL	Acts 2:1-21 or Gen 11:1-9	Rom 8:14-17 or Acts 2:1-21	Jn 14:8-17 (25-27)
Roman Catholic	Acts 2:1-11	1 Cor 12:3-7, 12-13	Jn 20:19-23
Episcopal (BCP)	Acts 2:1-11 or Joel 2:28-32	1 Cor 12:4-13 or Acts 2:1-11	Jn 20:19-23 or Jn 14:8-17

Introduction to the Lessons

Lesson 1

***Acts 2:1-21* (RCL); *Acts 2:1-11* (RC/Epis)**

The Jewish Festival of Pentecost marked the giving of the Mt. Sinai covenant. After Jesus' ascension, God's presence that Pentecost day in wind and fire fulfilled the promise to pour out the Spirit on all flesh, welcoming Gentile and Jew, slave and free, male and female into the new covenant.

Lesson 2

(1) *Romans 8:14-17* (RCL)

The gift of the Holy Spirit poured out upon all flesh enables each of us to become children of God and joint heirs with Jesus Christ. We are invited to suffer with Christ in order to share Christ's glory and to live as God's holy new creation.

(2) *1 Corinthians 12:3-7; 12-13* (RC);
***1 Corinthians 12:4-13* (Epis)**

The Holy Spirit enables us to say, "Jesus is Lord." The Spirit gives us gifts with which to serve the mission of the church of Jesus Christ. We live together as the body of Christ.

Gospel

(1) *John 14:8-17 (25-27)* (RCL)

Jesus tells the disciples that the Holy Spirit will empower them to know and do God's holy will. The Spirit will teach what they must know and the peace of God will sustain them to live in faithful trust and without fear.

(2) *John 20:19-23* (RC/Epis)
On the first Easter evening the risen Christ appears to his followers to offer both God's holy peace and a transmission of divine power and authority. They are sent not only to proclaim the gospel but also to forgive sins, a distinctive mark of the church.

Theme

The Holy Spirit comes to set the world on fire, beginning with you.

Thought for the Day

On each Pentecost Day, the Holy Spirit is poured out again on God's holy church to set worshipers on fire, to renew each baptismal covenant, and to empower each Christian again for mission in daily life.

Call to Worship

Leader: O God, how manifold are your works;
People: In your wisdom you have made all living creatures.
Leader: All creatures look to you to give them their food in due season.
People: You open your hand and they are filled with good things.
Leader: You send forth your Spirit and they are created,
People: And so you renew the face of the earth.
Leader: May the glory of the Lord endure forever.
People: I will praise my God while I have my being.

– Based on Psalm 104:24-34

Pastoral Prayer

Spirit of the Living God, blow through our world to expel violence, war, and danger and grant us your peace. Fall fresh on us. Holy Spirit, blow into our family lives and strengthen the love we share for each other. Teach us to work out our differences and bind us together in affection and joy. Fall fresh on us, Holy Spirit. Blow across our world to bring a spirit of community. Blow out of our hearts all prejudices against people who are different from us. Help us to rejoice in differences that bring new experiences into our lives. Fall fresh on us. Holy Spirit, pour out your healing on all whom we love who need healing in body, mind, or spirit. Strengthen caregivers to continue their loving work. Befriend the lonely. Comfort the distressed. Console those who mourn. Fall fresh on us. Into your hands we commend all for whom we pray, trusting in your mercy for the sake of Jesus Christ, our Lord who reigns with the Father, one God, now and forever. Amen.

Prayer of Confession

Gracious God, forgive us. We have been too selfish, too anxious, too busy, or too lazy to follow your commandments. We have not loved others as you have loved us. We have put ourselves first and gained at the expense of others. We have not walked in your ways. We are heartily sorry for all these offenses and ask your pardon for the wrongs we have done. We pray in the name of Jesus Christ, our Lord. Amen.

Prayer of Dedication of Gifts and Self

The gifts we present this morning, Loving God, are only tokens of the blessing you have showered on our lives. All that we have belongs to you. Help us to live to serve you day by day in all that we do. We offer these gifts and pray this prayer in the name of the one who offered himself for us, Jesus Christ our Lord. Amen.

Sermon Summary

Day by day, but especially on each Pentecost Day, the Spirit comes again to set the world on fire with passionate love and gracious service. We are to love God with heart, soul, mind, and strength, and to love and serve our neighbors.

Hymn of the Day

"Spirit, Spirit of Gentleness"

Pastor James K. Manley credits the Holy Spirit with inspiring the first three stanzas of this hymn, which was first sung at Waiokeola Congregational Church in Honolulu. Upon hearing it, someone in the congregation urged Manley to write another verse, which completed the hymn.

The hymn recounts many of the actions of God's Spirit throughout biblical history, and the moving refrain celebrates the spirit as gentle and soothing, while at the same time inspirational and challenging.

Children's Time

As Promised

Do you remember the story when Jesus asked his disciples to wait in Jerusalem because something special was going to happen? Today's the day we celebrate that special event. Today is Pentecost! Some people call today the birthday of the church, because on Pentecost the church really began to grow.

What a wonderful day that first Pentecost Day was. The disciples had gathered to remember Jesus' promise and to wonder what might be coming.

Suddenly, they heard a roaring noise, like a strong wind, and it filled the whole house. Then as they looked at each other, they saw flames appear above each head, but no one got burned! And they were speaking in languages they didn't even know.

A huge crowd gathered to see what was going on. The people couldn't believe it when the disciples started talking in their own languages. "How could this be?" they asked. "What on earth is going on?"

Peter stood up to speak to the crowd. He told them all about Jesus. Peter urged the crowd to love Jesus and have faith in Jesus. From that day on, more and more people flocked to hear about Jesus and the church grew. And that's why we celebrate Pentecost.

The Sermon

Setting the World on Fire

Hymns

Beginning of Worship: "Come, O Come, O Quickening Spirit"
Sermon Hymn: "Come Gracious Spirit, Heavenly Dove"
Closing Hymn: "Spirit of the Living God, Fall Fresh on Me"

Scripture

Acts 2:1-21 (For additional sermon materials on this passage, see the 2003 May/June planning issue and the February 2004 issue of *The Clergy Journal.*)

"I don't want to set the world on fire. I just want to start a flame in your heart." Is there anyone here who remembers that song? Was it a long time ago that we sang it? Well, in fact, God does want to set the world on fire. God also wants to start that fire by kindling a flame of zeal for mission and passion for the gospel in the heart of each person worshiping here this morning.

How about it? Are you ready to be fired up?

When each of you were baptized, the Holy Spirit came to you once with a message from God: "You belong to me." But many in our world who have been baptized may have forgotten this message. Do you continue to hear God telling you of that divine love day by day?

As we affirm our faith by saying the (Nicene) (Apostles') Creed this morning, let that action be a kind of renewing of our own baptismal vows. Let us all recall that God has come to set our hearts on fire with love for God and Jesus Christ. In Baptism we have also been given gifts of loving friendship and support for each other in this congregation. Finally, in baptism we are called to loving outreach to the world. This outreach may mean that we serve the needs of others, but as we do, let us also tell them about the God who created them, blesses them daily, forgives all wrongs, and comes to them to love them.

In short, let us pray together this morning that each one of us will experience a burning flame of passion to know God better and to become more aware of what God is doing in our lives.

Let us also commit ourselves to nurturing and feeding this flame by continuing weekly Bible study or study of issues we face in light of what we learn in our faith. Let us learn always to ask where God is in our struggles. Let us, like those who received the flames on the first Pentecost, share with others what God is doing in our lives. Finally, let us promise to give thanks daily to God for blessings, for guidance, for joys of the day, and for the love with which God surrounds our lives.

So let us commit ourselves to nurturing and feeding the burning flame of passion for knowing God better. Let's be more aware of what God is doing in our lives. Let us share our insights with each other.

To do this we must gather face to face in small groups for regular study, prayer, and fellowship. One hour a week of corporate worship is simply not enough to keep alive the flame of passion for loving God and serving the church's mission.

Those who received the gift of the Holy Spirit on Pentecost knew this. On that birth day God called the church into being by giving voice and spirit and zeal to about 120 frightened followers of Jesus and sending them out on a mission that would turn the world upside down and would last until the end of time. Before the day ended, 3,000 joined their community of faith and witness.

Symbolic of this new mission was the gift of languages: no matter what words any individual needed to tell another about the love of God, those words were given to the disciple in the moment they were needed. Love needs no prepared speech. The right words come from the heart. The Spirit gives language; the words are found as the occasion requires.

At the same time, the Holy Spirit can only give the words to hearts informed by the love of God and aware of its power. After the church was called into being on Pentecost, it had a lot of growing and changing to do. On that day only Jews who had come to Jerusalem to celebrate Pentecost – the feast of first fruits and the giving of the Covenant on Mt. Sinai – heard about God's providence in sending the Messiah and raising Christ from the dead. Both those who told the story and those who were baptized had a lot to learn to prepare them to offer the same gospel to the Gentiles. Or to build the community in which Jew and Greek, slave and free, male and female, were equally regarded by each other as they were equally loved by God and sent to share the gospel mission.

To get them ready for the changes that were to come, and without telling them what changes they would be required to assimilate, the Holy Spirit led them to set up many opportunities for prayer, worship, and mutual admonition. They worshiped weekly in the temple. They shared the Eucharist in a common meal on the First Day (what we call Sunday, our little Easters). They met regularly for times of prayer; they engaged in works of serving as the need arose. Never, never did they stop talking about the wonderful God who raised Jesus from the dead and called them together to tell the whole world this story.

When each of us was baptized (for some of us, when each was confirmed), we took responsibility for building our own lives of faith and faithfulness. Pentecost is one of the occasions when each Christian is called to review her or his commitment; life of faith, proclamation, and service; and willingness to learn more about Christian faith.

May the God who sent the Holy Spirit on the first Pentecost bless all of us here this morning. May that powerful Spirit rekindle in each heart a deeper faith, continuing spiritual growth, more earnest witness, and more generous service in the name of Jesus Christ our Lord. Amen.

– LaVonne Althouse
Interim Pastor
Lititz, Pennsylvania

June 6, 2004

Trinity Sunday

Lessons

RCL	Prov 8:1-4, 22-31	Rom 5:1-5	Jn 16:12-15
Roman Catholic	Prov 8:22-31	Rom 5:1-5	Jn 16:12-15
Episcopal (BCP)	Isa 6:1-8	Rev 4:1-11	Jn 16:(5-11) 12-15

Introduction to the Lessons

Lesson 1

(1) *Proverbs 8:1-4, 22-31* (RCL); *Proverbs 8:22-31* (RC)

Wisdom is personified and speaks, identifying her origin in God and acknowledging her benefits for humankind. Wisdom finds joy in God and delights in all creation, especially in the highest order of God's creation.

(2) *Isaiah 6:1-8* (Epis)

In a crisis moment filled with grief, the prophet Isaiah goes to the House of God in order to worship God. When his recognition of the majesty and glory of God makes him aware of his own finitude and sinfulness, Isaiah experiences God's compassion and forgiveness. The climax of worship for Isaiah comes in his immediate, positive and unconditional response to God's call for service – "Here am I! Send me."

Lesson 2

(1) *Romans 5:1-5* (RCL/RC)

Paul affirms the hope derived from a person's relationship with God through Christ. Not even suffering can obliterate this hope. God's love made known through the gift of God's Spirit provides assurance that this hope will never prove disappointing.

(2) *Romans 4:1-11* (Epis)

Salvation, righteousness, justification, a right relationship with God – call it what you will – comes from grace. If a relationship with God, the blessing of God, were dependent upon a person's works, salvation would exist as a wage or a reward – something that God owed someone. Salvation is a gift from God. That was true of the relationship between Abraham and God a long time ago and it is true in anyone's relationship with God today.

Gospel

John 16:12-15 **(RCL/RC);** ***John 16:(5-11) 12-15*** **(Epis)**

Before his departure from the earth, Jesus tells his disciples that there is much more truth than he has been able to share with them. Stated another way, believers do not yet know everything that is true. However, the discovery of truth is not over. One of the ministries of God's Spirit will be that of guiding people into truth.

Theme

The doctrine of the trinity provides us a way to talk about how we experience God.

Thought for the Day

The greater our knowledge of God, the greater our awareness of how much we do not know.

Call to Worship

Leader: We gather to praise God the Creator.
People: We gather to praise God in Christ the Savior.
Leader: We gather to praise God's Spirit the Comforter.
People: All praise be to God – Creator, Savior, Spirit. Amen.

Pastoral Prayer

O God, is a lack of certainty a sign of growth, a mark of humility, or an indicator of a weakened state of spirituality? Whatever it is, honesty demands that we confess reality; and reality is that what we don't know far outweighs what we know. We celebrate the trinity today. But we don't dare try to explain the trinity. It is another way of speaking of your love for us and of your presence with us, is it not? Your relationship to Jesus fills us with more questions than explanations. To acknowledge you as Spirit is to tiptoe into the realm of a mystery that sometimes seems more like abject confusion. Deliver us, God, from doctrines that attempt to make easy beliefs that retain their significance only if they challenge the depths of our minds and hearts. Save us from stereotypes that provide us with security at the expense of destroying our sense of wonder. Stop us from making you over in our images, that we may experience you as the Creator, Redeemer, and Lover whose nature defies encapsulation in any category that we can imagine. We seek an honest faith, O God. Amen.

Prayer of Confession

"God of wisdom," we acknowledge as one of our greatest needs that which is one of your greatest gifts. Grant us wisdom, God; grant us wisdom. We prize being smart more than being wise. We speak when we need to be quiet, we meditate when we ought to act, we challenge when it is in order to affirm, we support when it would be best to challenge. Forgive our lack of wisdom and help us to know when to conserve and when to expend, how to use our bodies without abusing them, how to offer critique without violating love, and how to love whether or not the loving results in a critique, when to offer comfort and when to make people uncomfortable, when to laugh and when to cry. God of wisdom, be our God and make us your wise children. Amen.

Prayer of Dedication of Gifts and Self

O God, even as Isaiah's experience of your glory and receiver of your forgiveness nurtured him, we too offer you the entirety of our lives. We dedicate the mouths with which we have praised you to sharing the good news of your love. We dedicate ourselves to finding creative ways to share your truth. We dedicate the hands and feet with which we have moved through worship to ministries that touch others with your mercy. Here we are, God; use us for the good of others and for your glory. Amen.

Sermon Summary

The doctrine of the trinity provides us a way to talk about how we experience God.

Hymn of the Day

"God of Many Names"

Of Brian Wren's many hymns exploring the nature of God (see also July 4), this one seems most appropriate to Trinity Sunday. This day provides opportunity to reflect on the many images of God presented to us in scripture, and this hymn gently urges us to stretch our imaginations as we explore how God is revealed to us.

The tune by William P. Rowan is not the easiest to learn, with its unique tempo, but is worth the effort. Soloists can sing the stanzas while the congregation sings the refrain. Percussion instruments can enhance the refrain.

Children's Time

Three in One

Bring in a simple child's puzzle with just a few large pieces. Bring in a stiff piece of board to assemble the puzzle on, so that you can lift it up afterwards to show to people.

Today is Trinity Sunday, so I thought it might be good to talk about the Trinity, which is how we refer to our three-in-one God. Do you ever get confused when you hear people talk about God, Jesus, and the Holy Spirit? Do you ever wonder which one is the big one? The head honcho? The main boss?

It's not very easy for us to understand how God can be in three equal parts and still be one God, and yet, in some ways, it's quite simple. Can any of you tell me what this is? *(Hold up one piece of the puzzle.)* Yes, it's a puzzle piece. Can you tell what the picture is, just from looking at it? Let's put the puzzle together, so that we can see the picture. *(Do the puzzle with the children, then hold it up so all can see the picture when you're done.)*

There, now we can see how that one puzzle piece fit into the picture. I wonder what the picture would be like if we took that piece back out? *(Remove the one piece and ask for the children's reactions.)* The picture no longer works properly.

In some ways, God is like a puzzle. God the parent, Jesus the Son, and the Holy Spirit are all parts of one picture. We refer to them separately, but we also know that they are parts of one whole experience that we call God.

The Sermon

The Trinity – A Non-Sermon

Hymns

Beginning of Worship: "Holy, Holy, Holy"
Sermon Hymn: "O Wisdom, Breathed from God"
End of Worship: "When Minds and Bodies Meet as One"

Scripture

John 16:12-15 (For additional sermon materials on this passage, see the 2003 May/June planning issue and the February 2004 issue of *The Clergy Journal.*)

"What could be more boring than a sermon on the trinity?" several members of the congregation asked me. Here is the conversation that ensued.

"That's theological stuff," assert those questioning the value of a sermon on the trinity, "It's irrelevant to people like us. We are not theologians. We deal with tangible realities – taking inventory, contacting clients, developing marketing strategies, watching Wall Street, going to school, managing households. We're not into theory, trying to figure out how many angels can stand on the point of a pin or speculating about the nature of heaven. Save your trinity sermon for those who enjoy an obtuse discussion of theology."

"Maybe I will," I said, "But I think you protest too much about your disinterest in theology as well as about your involvement in it. You are theologians. You think seriously about whether or not life has any meaning. You argue with your friends about what is luck and what is providence. You question and try to explain terrible tragedies that take the lives of innocent people. All of that is theological talk; you are doing theology whether or not you acknowledge it. So, I cannot let you off the hook of hearing a sermon on the trinity – especially on Trinity Sunday – because you fail to qualify as theologians. I know you too well.

"If you really want to throw up a barrier to keep me from delivering a sermon on the trinity, a far better tack is to charge me with escapism. Say to me something like this: 'Pastor, you are about to preach a sermon on the trinity as a strategy for not preaching on subjects that really matter. Why don't you talk to us about economic justice, the need to eliminate AIDS, a revision of American foreign policy, inclusiveness in the institutional church, or something else that is important?' That gets my attention.

"I am willing to respond positively to your question about a sermon on critical issues. Please know, though, that as soon as I start addressing social and moral issues, I will have to talk about God. I will need to speak of how God is involved in all of these matters. Though the word *trinity* may never surface, our interchange will require attention to the subject of the trinity.

"Let me give you the best argument that I know for *not* doing a sermon on the trinity even though today is designated as Trinity Sunday on the Christian calendar. Nowhere in the Bible is a doctrine of the trinity explicitly discussed. Jesus never mentioned it. You will find implicit suggestions of a doctrine of the trinity only in one or two passages in the New Testament that date some 50 to 60 years after the ascension of Jesus."

"Trinitarian statements began to appear within the Christian community toward the end of the first century. However, those thoughts about the trinity were not incorporated into any kind of doctrinal confession until 150 CE, when the Old Roman Creed took on a Trinitarian form. Not until the adoption of the Nicene Creed nearly 200 years later did the trinity become a doctrine accepted by both the Eastern Church and the Western Church. At no point was an affirmation of the doctrine of the trinity made a requirement for accepting the Christian faith. The doctrine of the trinity developed as Christian people speculated about the object of their faith, seeking to understand the nature of God.

"So, why not let the matter rest? That is my question as well as yours. Before answering that question, though, I need to ask you some other questions.

"Do you believe in God? If your answer is no, then I would like to inquire what kind of God you do not believe in. If your answer is yes, then I would like for you to tell me about this God. Likely your description of God will end up affirming God as the loving creator of all that is who was best revealed through Jesus. Such an assertion leads to my next question.

"Who was Jesus? Was Jesus a revelation from God or *the* revelation of God? You are aware, of course, that the New Testament answers this latter question with a yes followed by an exclamation point.

"So, was all of God in Jesus? Let me state this inquiry another way. When Jesus died, did God die?

"I should tell you that I believe Jesus was as much of God as can become a person. Jesus was all God and all man. If we want to know what God is like, we can look at Jesus and find out. This understanding of Jesus will also let you know why I don't think we can talk about God without talking about social issues. The revelation of God in Christ resulted in God's radical involvement in the world. Why, at one point, Jesus even said that when we feed hungry people and ease the pains of those who hurt, we minister to him – we serve God.

June 6, 2004
Trinity Sunday

"I am guessing that we can agree that the loving God whom we meet in the scriptures and see revealed in the Christ is the Redeemer God as well as the Creator God."

"Right," someone interrupts, "But all of that is in the past. Once Jesus ascended, God, for all practical purposes, was out of the world." "Do you really believe that?" I ask. "I don't want to," the speaker says, "But it makes good sense. How can we say that God is in our midst today?"

I continue, "I am glad you asked. God continues among us today through the presence of God's Spirit. The Spirit of God is every bit as real here and now as the incarnate Jesus was in Galilee centuries ago or as the Creator God was when causing the first rays of light to shoot through the primeval darkness. Personally, that means that we are not alone. The God of beginnings remains with us, living among us as perfect love, absolute grace, and unconditional hope."

Another person in the group speaks up, "I don't want to oversimplify this, but it seems to me that God allows the divine nature, which is one, to be known in different ways."

"Precisely!" I respond. "God is Creator, Redeemer, and Sustainer. God is Father, Son, and Holy Spirit. God is Yahweh, Jesus, and Paraclete. Talking about the trinity provides us with a way of talking about God. The trinity is important not so much as a doctrine about God but as a way of understanding how we experience God. The God who brought the world into being and sent Jesus into the world to do the work of redemption has not left this world – and will not leave us – for one second. God is with us!

"Perhaps we can do without a sermon on the trinity, but we cannot do without an understanding of God that allows us to affirm the sovereignty and singularity of God while experiencing God as creator, redeemer, and comforter. The truth involved in the concept of the trinity is crucial to meaning and purpose in our lives.

"So, I will leave the matter there. Maybe at another time I will offer to share with you a full-blown sermon on the trinity. But for this Trinity Sunday, this conversation will be enough."

I offer these words in the Name of the Father, Son, and Holy Spirit. Amen.

– C. Welton Gaddy
Northminster Church
Monroe, Louisiana

June 13, 2004

2nd Sunday after Pentecost (Proper 6)

RC/Pres: 11th Sunday in Ordinary Time

Lessons

RCL	1 Kgs 21:1-10 (11-14), 15-21a	Gal 2:15-21	Lk 7:36–8:3
Roman Catholic	2 Sam 12:7-10, 13	Gal 2:16, 19-21	Lk 7:36–8:3 or 7:36-50
Episcopal (BCP)	2 Sam 11:26–12:10, 13-15	Gal 2:11-21	Lk 7:36-50
Lutheran	2 Sam 11:26–12:10, 13-15	Gal 2:15-21	Lk 7:36–8:3

Introduction to the Lessons

Lesson 1

(1) ***1 Kings 21:1-10 (11-14), 15-21a*** **(RCL)**

King Ahab and his wife Jezebel conspire to acquire a piece of property that the owner, Naboth, did not want to sell. Their evil plan results in dishonesty, manipulation, and ultimately murder. The prophet Elijah confronts the king with his injustice, condemns his immorality, and informs Ahab of the disasters that will result from his evil deeds.

(2) ***2 Samuel 12:7-10, 13*** **(RC);**
2 Samuel 11:26—12:10, 13-15 **(Epis)**

Fired by the passion of an adulterous relationship, David has the husband of his lover killed. In response, God sends a prophet named Nathan to make David realize the evil that he has done. The prophet tells David a parable that kindles the king's anger toward an evildoer in the story. When David decries the man's action, Nathan tells David that he is the man.

Lesson 2

Galatians 2:15-21 **(RCL/Luth);** ***Galatians 2:16, 19-21*** **(RC)**
Galatians 2:11-21 **(Epis)**

Salvation comes through faith; it is not a reward for personal accomplishments or even the result of an individual's fidelity to the law. The life of faith is a life of grace made possible by Christ living in us and through us.

Gospel

***Luke 7:36–8:3* (RCL/Epis/Luth); *Luke 7:36-50* (Epis)**

A devotee of the law fails to show Jesus the kind of unselfish love and to give to Jesus the kind of generous service demonstrated by a woman of the streets. Jesus uses this occasion as an opportunity to speak of how people who have been forgiven most are the people who will love most and serve most in expressing their faith.

Theme

With God's help, through the practice of forgiveness we can change the future.

Thought for the Day

People who have been forgiven most are the most forgiving people.

Call to Worship

Leader: Come to worship and praise God.
People: "We praise God from whom all blessings flow."
Leader: Come to worship and confess your sins.
People: "We confess our sins and seek forgiveness."
Leader: Come to worship and declare your faith.
People: Forgiveness and salvation come through the grace of God made known in Jesus Christ the Lord.

Pastoral Prayer

O God, what language will we speak in heaven? And, as for the present moment, is there a vocabulary that is immediately understandable to everybody? Do you suggest a word, one word, around which all of us, despite our vast diversity, can come together in unity? In the awkward silence that often follows these difficult-to-answer questions we hear a whispering of the word *love*, a commendation of a vocabulary of acceptance, and a strong commission about speaking the language of compassion. Is it only a hope that we hear, God, a hope as strong as breath, a hope of such substance that its anticipation of love becomes a quiet articulation of love? What language do we speak? How do our vocabularies reflect our faith? Can people who do not know us well listen to us talk and discern instinctively that we embrace the commission to love recklessly? Holy God, given our devotion to you, how can love not be the solid center of our lives from which both our words and our actions emerge? Guiding God, enable us to live out of the center of our beings that what we say and do on earth may resonate totally with what is said and done in heaven. Amen.

Prayer of Confession

O God, we spend most of our time between the revealed truth found in Jesus' teachings as recorded in the scriptures and the recognized realities that make up our daily lives. God, we need you in that gap. All of the great values of our faith, indeed faith itself, are our sparring partners in the space between vision and reality, truth and its application. Love, forgiveness, comfort, grace, and hope evoke our highest praise, loudest affirmation, and firmest embrace until we try to love someone who strikes us as unlovable, forgive a person who has inflicted great pain on us, comfort an individual who seems to need reprimand more than comfort, extend grace to an insensitive person who takes but never gives, and live by hope when emotionally dark clouds have more justification than sunshine. God, forgive us and join us in that gap so that together we may join truth to life and the greatest values in the scriptures may become the basic character traits in our lives. Amen.

Prayer of Dedication of Gifts and Self

Having meditated on the various words in your Word for today, O God, we aspire to the kind of life that brings you pleasure. Like the prophets Elijah and Nathan, we dedicate ourselves to challenging injustice wherever it is found. Like the apostle Paul we commit ourselves to a life based on faith and vibrant with grace. Like the woman whom Jesus praised, we promise to love generously, even lavishly. As a part of our offering in worship, we also dedicate our financial gifts to you in order to support the work of challenging injustice, practicing grace, and loving lavishly as it is done by other people. Amen.

Sermon Summary

With God's help, through the practice of forgiveness we can change the future.

Hymn of the Day

"Amazing Grace"

Arguably the most familiar of all Christian hymns, the story of its composition is almost as familiar. Many people who know of no other hymns have heard the story of slave trader John Newton's conversion, recounted in those immortal words, "amazing grace, how sweet the sound, that saved a wretch like me."

Some have argued for replacing "wretch" with "soul" as less self-deprecating, while others strongly urge retention of Newton's original word because it speaks of his self-image at the time.

Certain musical scholars have suggested that the tune may have originated with slaves aboard ship – the pentatonic scale being common in African music – and that Newton overheard the melody.

Children's Time

Women in the Bible

We've heard a lot of stories about men in the Bible – about the disciples and the apostle Paul and all that they did and said. Today we're going to hear a story about a woman who loved Jesus so much that she gave up an entire bottle of expensive ointment for him. And about some other women who took care of him.

Jesus was having dinner at someone's house. His feet were dusty and tired and he was lying on a couch eating when a woman with long hair burst into the house carrying this pot of ointment. She washed his feet and dried them with her hair and then covered them with the lovely-smelling paste. I'm sure that made them feel much better!

Jesus' host was very upset. The woman had done a lot of bad things in her life. But Jesus told him that she was forgiven just because of her great love. He pointed out that the woman had treated him better than his host had, since his host hadn't even offered him water to wash his feet.

That brings me to another point. Do you think Jesus had a job, like your parents do? Do you think he earned money? No, he was too busy healing people and talking to them. But someone had to take care of him and his followers and the Bible tells us who did it. Women. Mary Magdalene, Joanna, Susanna, and other women, all provided the money and resources that Jesus and his friends needed to be able to travel around the countryside and rent boats when they needed to cross lakes and stay in Jerusalem and other places.

We don't hear about the women in the Bible often enough. But they were there, loving and caring for Jesus, playing important roles in his ministry. And that's important to know.

The Sermon

Can We Change the Future?

Hymns

Beginning of Worship: "Come, O Fount of Every Blessing"
Sermon Hymn: "God of Earth and Heaven"
End of Worship: "There's a Wideness in God's Mercy"

Scripture

Luke 7:36–8:3 (For additional sermon materials on this passage, see the 2003 May/June planning issue of *The Clergy Journal* and on Galatians 2:15-21, see the March 2004 issue of *The Clergy Journal.*)

Easter and Pentecost – the resurrection of Jesus and the first realization of the Spirit of God – prompted unsettling inquisitiveness as well as joyful exuberance among followers of Christ. The very same people who responded to the resurrection of Jesus whispering the declaration "He is risen" or shouting the responsive affirmation "Hallelujah" also raised urgent questions, "What has happened here? Who was this man Jesus, really? What was the cross about? Did Jesus have to die?" and pondering the meaning of what they had experienced. "Could *we* have prevented the death of Jesus?" they must have wondered, "And how do we best *follow* him now?"

Of course, those are some of the very same questions involving various dimensions of religious meaning with which we grapple today. So, for us, how goes this year's journey from Easter to Pentecost and beyond? What now?

We know the past well. Across the years, at crucial turning points, ill-informed actions and politically motivated initiatives adversely shaped both the substance of faith and the nature of Christianity. The negative consequences of those actions persisted for centuries, some even into the present. Could things have gone differently? Yes, of course. Can we alter that history? No.

What about the future; are we destined to repeat the errors of the past? The answer is no again. Does that mean *we* can change the future? Precisely! We *can* change the future. Be aware, though, that such change requires, with God's help, honesty, resolve, courage, discipline and, perhaps most important of all, forgiveness.

The narrative about the post-Pentecost Christian community is a story about God's help. All of the dramatic symbolism related to the gift of God's Spirit points to the provisions of God that enable us to alter the course of history – our future personally and the future of the world in which we live. God provides *forgiveness that frees* and *power that enables.*

Changing the future requires an honest evaluation of the past, a bold review of history coupled with straightforward self-evaluation, including self-criticism. A person who cannot honestly critique his own words and actions will repeat all of the errors of both that fill his past and create a future far more threatening and severe than is necessary. Of course, the same is true for an institution.

But self-introspection is as difficult as it is necessary. I am sure that I do not have to tell you how hard it is for us to look at ourselves honestly. All too often, we do not like what we see. We much prefer to judge other people than ourselves and to blame others for all that goes wrong in our lives rather than to accept responsibility. Following those defensive preferences and failing to do the difficult work of self-evaluation guarantee us a future that will mirror our past.

Profound theological truth is at stake here. But please do not relegate what I am saying exclusively to the realm of theology. The basest aspects of reality are present here – how we feel when we get up in the morning; how we face the complexities of relationships; whether or not we live with resentment in our heart, a scowl on our face, and a chip on our shoulder; how we shape the future; whether or not the days ahead of us will contain all of the mistakes and heartaches of the past.

Recently I spent a stretch of time with former Senator Bob Kerrey. We both addressed a forum at the University of California Santa Barbara. As you may know, Kerrey, a recipient of the Bronze Star for service in Vietnam in which he lost a leg and almost his life, has been the object of a media blitz of criticism because of revelations about his actions during a midnight raid in Thanh Phong, a tiny hamlet in the Mekong Delta.

Struggling with his past, Kerrey decided to talk openly about the horrors that haunt his memory. Kerrey told the *New York Times* that he could not be what he once was. He said that he could no longer enjoy a life free from nightmares, pain, remorse, and regrets. He spoke of no longer being able to go to church and feel like God was smiling warmly down upon him as if he were the most special thing on earth. Kerrey lamented that all of that was gone. I felt strongly that no system of justice could inflict more punishment on this man than he has inflicted upon himself.

Obviously Kerrey was struggling with the issue of forgiveness. Listening to Kerrey speak, I was struck by an observation that he made in a public setting, "We are not our memories!" Though I do not know Kerrey's religious convictions and affiliations, I know that his statement was Christian to the core. Kerrey went on to say that he could not wait for forgiveness from another person, he had to accept God's forgiveness and get on with his life. I thought of the tongues of fire and the rush of wind with which we speak of God's coming among us with power and forgiveness.

Sometime back, after addressing a national conference on preaching, I was detained by two ministers who wanted to talk about their troubled consciences. "How should we deal with this barbaric spectacle in our town?" they asked, referring to the execution of Timothy McVeigh, the perpetrator of the horrible bombing of the federal building in Oklahoma City. "We feel an obligation to preach the gospel of forgiveness. But people will turn on us," they explained. What would you say to these conscientious pastors?

Does God extend forgiveness even to a person like Timothy McVeigh? If the answer to that question is a negative one, then who decides which person is a candidate for God's forgiveness and which person lives beyond grace? Oh, I know the premeditated hatred vented by this man. By almost any standard, McVeigh deserved to die. The blood of 171 civilians was on his hands. But the question is should McVeigh's blood be on *our* hands? Will our future be better because we have done to McVeigh what this young man did to others? Are we changing the future or replicating the past?

Frankly, we cannot even think such thoughts apart from an assurance of forgiveness. Only forgiveness can help us deal with the past and change the future.

Retaliation and vindication promise us no more than that the future will look just like the past; neither brings any lasting satisfaction to our lives. Once we have repaid a hurt, exacted our revenge for something done to us, what happens? Once we have watched the killing of a man whose killing wounded our lives, are our wounds gone or are they, in some ways, made deeper? What if we refuse to forgive a neighbor? "I'll show them," we say to ourselves. Who is hurt most? Of course, the guilty neighbor may hurt from not receiving forgiveness, but any immediate surge of satisfaction in seeing the neighbor hurt is followed by the refusal to forgive eating away at the soul like a malignancy on a once-healthy cell.

Only forgiveness allows us to change the future – forgiving ourselves, forgiving other people, and, in some instances, working through what we perceive to be the need to forgive God. We can change the future only by appropriating for ourselves and extending to others forgiveness – forgiveness made possible by God.

Not long ago, I spoke to a press conference involving a man whose son was killed in a hate crime carried out against a Jewish community center. A few days later, I visited with members of the extended family of Matthew Shepherd, a victim of violence against gay men. Then, on another speaking trip, came conversations with some people in Oklahoma City. This I know: the people who cannot move beyond anger, resentment, and a desire for retaliation toward others, cannot get on with their lives. Bitterness takes up residence in their hearts and they live locked in the prison of a tragic, evil episode. The people who move on – the father who lost his son, the mother of Matthew Shepherd, the husband in Oklahoma City who said he didn't want to see vengeance on the killer of his loved one – are the people who practice forgiveness.

Please understand that forgiveness is so much more than saying, "Oh, it's all right" when hurt by someone, so much more than a simple "I'm sorry." Forgiveness that changes the future involves promises that, when kept, assure that the future will not be like the past, alterations in patterns of behavior which reflect alterations in attitudes.

Perhaps at no time will we feel the wind gusts and fiery compassion of God's Spirit more than when, recognizing that we cannot alter what has been but realizing that we can change the future, can we fully begin to embrace forgiveness for ourselves and to offer forgiveness to others. Who is most capable of such forgiveness? According to Jesus, the answer to that question is those people who have been forgiven most. That means us! Amen.

– C. Welton Gaddy
Northminster Church
Monroe, Louisiana

June 20, 2004

3rd Sunday after Pentecost (Proper 7)

RC/Pres: 12th Sunday in Ordinary Time

Lessons

RCL	1 Kgs 19:1-4 (5-7), 8-15a	Gal 3:23-29	Lk 8:26-39
Roman Catholic	Zech 12:10-11; 13:1	Gal 3:26-29	Lk 9:18-24
Episcopal (BCP)	Zech 12:8-10; 13:1	Gal 3:23-29	Lk 9:18-24
Lutheran	Isa 65:1-9	Gal 3:23-29	Lk 8:26-39

Introduction to the Lessons

Lesson 1

(1 *1 Kings 19:1-4 (5-7), 8-15a* (RCL)

When Jezebel informs Elijah that she will not rest until he is dead, the prophet's fear is followed by feelings of despondency. While Elijah feels sorry for himself and laments being alone, God speaks to the prophet and instructs him to get on with his ministry.

(2) *Zechariah 12:10-11; 13:1* (RC); *Zechariah 12:8-10; 13:1* (Epis)

God promises to show compassion when the people of Jerusalem are consumed by the great grief that will accompany their recognition of the severity of their sins. Amid intense and pervasive mourning, God will offer all involved the gifts of cleansing and forgiveness.

(3) *Isaiah 65:1-9* (Luth)

God reveals mercy as the essence of divine identity, seeking out even those not looking for God and offering assistance to people who had never even called the divine name. Despite the sins and shortcomings of people who were supposed to be living as servants of God, God reaches out to these people and provides for them an inheritance of goodness.

Lesson 2

***Galatians 3:23-29* (RCL/Epis/Luth); *Galatians 3:26-29* (RC)**

The ministry of Christ moves people out of subservience to law and into the freedom of faith. Within the freedom of faith, individuals learn to relate to God through Christ and to each other as a family of equals in which all are children of God.

Gospel

(1) *Luke 8:26-39* (RCL/Luth)

When Jesus heals a demented man, residents of the region become so fearful of the compassionate power of Jesus that they ask him to leave their land. As Jesus departs, he denies the healed man's request to go with him and sends the man home to share with others what he has learned of the goodness of God and the ministry of the one who healed him.

(2) *Luke 9:18-24* (RC/Epis)

After Jesus inquires of the disciples regarding popular perceptions of his identity, Peter declares Jesus to be the Messiah. Eager to avoid any misunderstanding of the nature of his Messianic ministry, Jesus tells the disciples that he must suffer and die, a fate not unlike that to be shared by all who follow him.

Theme

Christianity is an inclusive, not an exclusive, faith.

Thought for the Day

We should not reject any person whom God accepts.

Call to Worship

Leader: Let us form now a community of worship.
People: "How good it is to worship God together."
Leader: Let us become an answer to Christ's prayer for unity.
People: "We pray that the love with which God has loved us may be found in us and find expression through us."
All: Amen.

Pastoral Prayer

O God, people are killing other people and attributing the murders to faith. People are teaching hatred and pointing to the Bible as the source of their lessons. Because of an awful sense of superiority among some people of faith, fear saturates other people of faith, especially those who are condemned for wearing turbans on their heads or scarves that cover their faces like Christians wear crosses around their necks. O God, people are dividing communities, even the world, drawing lines in the sand, and choosing sides on the basis of who is good and who is evil. You must be so hurt, God; your heart must be breaking. Can we comfort you as you comfort us? That which you have given to us as a source of healing in life is being manipulated by people to inflict suffering and even death. We hurt with you, God. We long for the honesty, humility, and compassion of the Christ. Please help us, God. Amen.

Prayer of Confession

God, please listen to us even if you do not like what you hear. Can you hear us? Our prayers are not nearly as loud as our songs and litanies. We speak our prayers softly or maybe just breathe them lightly. But we need for you to hear us. We are troubled both by what we cannot understand and by insights that we would prefer to ignore. We ache over unfulfilled visions and drooping dreams. We hurt as we see mental and physical erosion in people we love. We think we are screaming for help when we are only sighing deeply. Can you hear us, God? We need your love. A realization that we are loved – unconditionally, unfathomably, incomprehensibly loved – by you stills our racing emotions and silences many of our pounding questions. Can you hear us, God? We want to be heard by you. O, great God, even more important than you hearing us is for us to hear you. Would you visit us with a word born in the heart of mystery? If we can hear you, we can know of your love. We long for the sense of your forgiveness. Please speak to us, God. Amen.

Prayer of Dedication of Gifts and Self

Loving God, we dedicate ourselves as agents of your ministry of reconciliation. Confronted by bigotry, we promise to challenge destructive stereotypes, prejudice, and discrimination. Blessed with the gift of diversity, we pledge to involve ourselves in the kind of communication that results in mutual understanding and cooperation. Disturbed by forces of divisiveness, we offer ourselves as facilitators of grace, peacemakers, and community builders. Please use us to build a world that fulfills the vision of the apostle Paul, a world in which there is neither male nor female, black nor white, rich nor poor; a world in which all persons are equal participants in a unity that is complementary to your divine nature. Amen.

Sermon Summary

Christianity is an inclusive, not an exclusive, faith.

Hymn of the Day

"One Bread, One Body"

This moving hymn by Jesuit priest John B. Foley is at the same time a rich communion text and a celebration of the diversity that makes up the body of Christ. Many biblical texts come to mind in the singing of this hymn, one of them being, of course, Galatians 3:26-29, one of todays readings.

The gentle melody is very easy to learn, and can be sung with minimal accompaniment, or with any one of a number of instruments.

Children's Time

All in the Family

How many here have black hair? How about you sit over there. And blonde? You sit opposite there. And brown? You sit in the middle. *(Give the children a minute to move around.)*

Have you ever wondered why God made us all so different? Some have curly hair, some have straight. Some are chubby, some are thin. And so often, we want to be what someone else is, not knowing that they want to be like us. So sometimes people with curly hair will spend a lot of time trying to get it to lie flat, while straight-haired people will spend time curling it. And people with light hair will dye it dark and dark-haired people will dye it light.

We're all different in so many ways. Some of us are good at sports while others excell at school. Some like to listen to music while others prefer to go for a walk.

Some people's families have lived here for many generations while others arrived only a short time ago from different parts of the world.

What's the one thing we all have in common? Our love of Jesus. We're all children of God, belonging to one big family, united through Jesus' love. We don't need to be divided by our differences. (Encourage the children to sit together again.) Instead, we can rejoice at all being part of the same family, the family of God.

The Sermon

Does Christianity Teach Exclusion and Hatred?

Hymns

Beginning of Worship: "God Reigns o'er All the Earth"
Sermon Hymn: "In Christ There Is No East or West"
End of Worship: "God, We Thank You for Our People"

Scripture

Galatians 3:23-29 (For additional sermon materials on this passage, see the 2003 May/June planning issue and the March 2004 issue of *The Clergy Journal.*)

Christian history does not sketch a very attractive caricature of Christians' abilities to relate gracefully to people who are different or, sometimes, even to relate to other Christians who seem to be out of step with the majority. What's more, media reports on contemporary Christian attitudes and actions do little to encourage us that the situation is much better in the present. In the minds of some popular spokespersons, people who resist evangelization by Christians deserve demonization.

Why? How possibly could people committed to the faith inspired by Jesus develop an attitude of exclusion toward anybody? What are the sources of dislike for others that appears to the world as sheer hatred? How did Christianity move from vigorous devotion to the God who is love to the practice of discrimination among those who call themselves "the people of God" (discrimination practiced in the name of God)?

Frankly, sometimes the Bible itself has been a problem. How do we explain one gospel writer quoting the inclusive invitation of Jesus – Come to me *all* you that are weary and are carrying heavy burdens – and another gospel writer citing Jesus' apparently embittered identification of Jews, the children of Abraham, as children of Satan?

Despite our stringent and energetic calisthenics of biblical interpretation – tracing word meanings, analyzing grammatical structures, and studying literary nuances – aimed at concluding the Bible does not mean what it says, sometimes certain troublesome texts obstinately continue to state a perspective or a principle that does not sound like the Christ or square with what we know of the nature of God. Occasionally, exclusion, discrimination, and even the seeds of hatred can be found in a passage of scripture. How can that be?

Please keep in mind the nature of the Bible; it is both a human book and a divine book. The Bible contains the words of God and the words of human beings. Writers of the scriptures were moved by God to convey a particular message from God. However, these writers did not for one moment shed their personal limitations, political situations, and cultural indoctrinations. Consequently, God's word comes to us through the words of people like us.

Reading the Bible responsibly requires shaking individual texts through the sifter of God's nature so as to separate the eternal word of the infinite God from the personal judgments or time-bound conclusions of imperfect individuals. In order to believe the Bible, you do not have to turn off your mind and disregard everything you ever learned to affirm an ancient Hebrew writer's description of the world as square and flat. Similarly, as a person of faith, you do not have to ignore what seem to be contradictions in the scriptures – God meeting Moses on Mount Sinai and commanding people not to kill each other and God meeting Joshua outside the promised land and instructing him to engage in military conquests that would not leave a single person alive, not even a child. Such seeming inconsistencies and contradictions stem not from a severe case of schizophrenia in God but from an incomplete understanding, or a complete misunderstanding, of the biblical writers.

Please hear and heed this warning: When we fail to recognize base human elements in the Bible and allow cultural and political biases to be equated with divine truth, the Bible becomes a lethal book – endorsing exclusion, justifying violence.

Look specifically at the relationship between Christians and Jews. Following the crucifixion and the resurrection of Jesus, followers of Jesus saw themselves in competition with the Jews for claiming the title "the true Israel." In the face of the Jewish community's continued rejection of Jesus' identity as the Messiah, members of the Christian community decided to "prove" that Jesus was the Messiah. Christian writers returned to familiar narratives about Jesus and added to those records various scriptural citations aimed at establishing Jesus as the fulfillment of the scriptures.

Well, trouble erupted. Because the early Christians considered anyone who rejected their proofs of Jesus as the Messiah as enemies of Jesus, the editing of the gospels led to statements that demonized the Jews, prompted a mentality of exclusion among believers, and laid a foundation for hatred.

Consider what happened. The gospels took form during one of the most violent periods in all of history. Jews and Gentiles alike hated Rome because of its oppressive government. But, Jews and Romans locked themselves into a bitter conflict. Remember, in the year 70 CE, Rome destroyed the temple in Jerusalem. One historian observed that to read the New Testament apart from the context of the Roman war against Jews would be like reading Anne Frank's *The Diary of a Young Girl* without reference to the Holocaust.

Now, here is the crucial question; and it *is* crucial. Did anti-Jewish sentiments, along with the exclusion and hatred that they produced immediately and attempts at an annihilation of the Jews that they prompted eventually, stem from the life and teachings of Jesus? The answer to that question is an unequivocal, "No!" Do the gospels contain passages that commend exclusion and inspire a disregard for Jews and other people? The answer to that question is "Yes. Yes, *but* these passages have their source in the politics of the time of the writer not in the ministry of Jesus or the mind of God."

Hatred toward Jews was not (and is not) a part of the essence of Christianity. No aspect of Jesus' teaching inspired hatred toward anybody. Why, the best known of the early followers of Jesus, the apostle Paul, wrote that in Christ there is neither Jew nor Greek. His vision of the inclusion at the heart of Christianity went beyond Judaism, however. Paul declared that we are *all* one in Christ Jesus.

Now, why is all of this discussion so important?

First, *the integrity of Christianity is at stake in this discussion.* Christianity, like its savior the Christ, rejects rather than commends exclusion and hatred. Christianity centers on inclusion and love even if the practice of inclusion and love requires the death of the lover.

Second, *religious rhetoric can lead to physical violence.* We must not preach and teach passages of the Bible that contradict the essential nature of Jesus and the revelation of God. To label a person an "enemy of God," an immoral person displeasing to God, or a "Christ killer" makes that person worthless enough to kill, and invites sick minds to facilitate such killing as a means of serving God.

June 20, 2004
3rd Sunday after Pentecost (Proper 7)
RC/Pres: 12th Sunday in Ordinary Time

When Christians began the First Crusade in the year 1096, they defined violence against infidels as a religious act. Indeed, Christians were told that death incurred while eliminating pagans from the earth was a sure promise of eternal salvation. Friends, that same sick mentality is rearing its ugly head today among individuals who advocate ridding the world of those whom they consider to be immoral people as an act of righteousness or "taking out" people who advance another religion. Let us be very clear. When killing another person because that person is different from us is viewed as an act of Christian ministry, God is cursed, Christianity is blasphemed, and all of us who follow the Christ are diminished. Christianity has been misunderstood when one thinks it is a source of hatred or an inspiration for violence.

God modeled the way to handle differences. God loved the world. We repeat that truth every time we recite John 3:16. But, nothing could have been more different from God than the world; nothing more reprehensible to God than the world. The world was everything that God did not want it to be. Yet, God loved the world. More than that, God sought to save the world – the very antithesis to what God favored.

Christianity is not about exclusion. I point you once again to the life and ministry of Jesus. Christianity is not about hatred. I point you to the love of God incarnate in Jesus.

As the people of God, *if* we are to be the people of God, we must not allow anyone or any text – whether claiming secular or sacred authority – to divert us from the practice of inclusion and the commitment to unconditional love evidenced in the ministry of Jesus and commended to us by Almighty God. Within inclusion and love we discover the glory and the responsibility, the promise and the peril, of serving the risen Savior. So let it be. Amen.

C. Welton Gaddy
Northminster Church
Monroe, Louisiana

June 27, 2004

4th Sunday after Pentecost (Proper 8)

RC/Pres: 13th Sunday in Ordinary Time

Lessons

RCL	2 Kgs 2:1-2, 6-14	Gal 5:1, 13-15	Lk 9:51-62
Roman Catholic	1 Kgs 19:15-16, 19-21	Gal 5:1, 13-18	Lk 9:51-62
Episcopal (BCP)	1 Kgs 19:15-16, 19-21	Gal 5:1, 13-25	Lk 9:51-62
Lutheran	1 Kgs 19:15-16, 19-21	Gal 5:1, 13-25	Lk 9:51-62

Introduction to the Lessons

Lesson 1

(1) ***2 Kings 2:1-2, 6-14*** **(RCL)**

Within the providence of God, just prior to Elijah departing from the earth, Elijah prepares Elisha to take up his ministry. The older prophet blesses the younger prophet as well as reassures him and places his mantle upon him. When Elijah has departed, Elisha takes up the mantle given to him, tests his power, and begins his ministry.

(2) ***1 Kings 19:15-16, 19-21*** **(RC/Epis/Luth)**

Guided by God, the prophet Elijah serves as the medium through which a young Elisha hears the divine call to be a prophet. After Elisha feels the weight of Elijah's mantle on his shoulders, he kisses his father and mother goodbye and commits himself to serving God with Elijah.

Lesson 2

Galatians 5:1, 13-25 **(RCL/Epis/Luth);**
Galatians 5:1, 13-18 **(RC)**

God calls people to freedom. Followers of Christ resist slavery of every kind. To live in God's Spirit is to live freely, lovingly, and morally.

Gospel

Luke 9:51-62 **(RCL/RC/Epis/Luth)**

As Jesus sets his face toward Jerusalem and his passion, he wants to be sure that his disciples, as fully as possible, understand the cost of discipleship.

He explains the urgency and intensity of discipleship as well as its radical nature, before warning his followers that they should not begin a journey of commitment that they cannot complete.

Theme

Fear is an enemy of freedom.

Thought for the Day

God calls us to and equips us for a life of freedom.

Call to Worship

Leader: God calls us to the discipline of worship even as to a devotion to freedom.

People: Let us worship God in the sanctuary and with both our words and our actions live freely in the world.

Leader: "If the Son makes you free, you will be free indeed."

People: As servants of God we will "proclaim liberty throughout the land."

– Based on Leviticus 25:10 and John 8:36

Pastoral Prayer

God, if you would just listen to us, things could be better. We don't mean any disrespect, but you don't seem to be doing very well running the world. Bombs are disrupting peace talks. Schism is ravaging families. Good people are hurting and the bad guys seem to be winning everything. Maybe it is time to try a new tactic – maybe it is time for you, God, to ignore our freedom, to take over everything from the moment when it rains to when, or if, one of us has a headache. That will work; will it not? No? You love us too much to compromise our freedom and control us? You know that we never will develop as persons unless we make difficult decisions and prioritize what is right? Alright, God, alright, we will continue in faith. We will stoke again the fires of hope. We will do the best we can with love. But, we need to hear from you. Please speak to us, even if but a whisper, that we might be assured of your loving presence with us and your grace-filled strength within us. Amen.

Prayer of Confession

O God, despite our profound gratitude for freedom and all of its benefits, we must confess that we sometimes distort the nature of freedom even as at other times we take freedom for granted. Forgive us when we separate freedom from responsibility, emphasizing all that we are free *from* and ignoring all that we are free *for*. You have freed us to live beyond the law, to love without conditions, and to maximize our service to others. Forgive us when we ignore the law altogether, fail to consider love, and minimize our service within society. Teach us the wisdom of wedding freedom and responsibility. Forgive also the insensitivity with which we take freedom for granted – failing to give thanks for freedom regularly, to act to preserve freedom constantly, and to seek liberation for people in bondage vigorously. Instill within us the urgency of "standing firm" in freedom, as Paul counseled, and "bringing release to captives," as Christ modeled. Amen.

Prayer of Dedication of Gifts and Self

Sovereign God, created in your image, we dedicate ourselves to freedom – freedom that embraces responsibility. Loving God, blessed by your revelation in Christ and gifted by salvation through Christ, we promise to resist all forms of bondage both in our lives and in the lives of others. God of the Universe, instructed by your words about the path to national greatness, we commit ourselves to a life of citizenship worthy of Christian discipleship and pledge to work for the practice of righteousness and the protection of freedom within this nation. As an act of worship, we dedicate our tithes and our talents, our discipleship and our citizenship, to you O Free and Freeing God. Amen.

Sermon Summary

Though freedom is faith's good friend, we often fear freedom. God calls us to live in freedom and to resist bondage of any kind.

Hymn of the Day

"Will You Come and Follow Me?"

Also known as "The Summons," this delightful hymn is one of many to come from the Wild Goose Resource Group or Iona Community in Scotland. The first four stanzas serve as questions to us from God, and the last stanza is our response. Thus, if eliminating stanzas in the singing of the hymn, it is important to include the last one.

The tune cries our for dancing, or at least accompaniment that suggests liveliness and movement.

Children's Time

Fruits of the Spirit

(Preparation: Bring in a bowl of fruit, enough for the children to have a piece each. Talk about how trees bear fruit when they are carefully tended. They need to be watered regularly and to get enough sunlight. They can't get too cold or too hot or too dry. They need to be harvested regularly, because if the fruit isn't taken off the tree, it goes bad or drops on the ground and rots there.)

Fruit is very good for us. It's an important part of our diet. *(Offer a piece to each of the children, being careful of any allergies.)* As well as being delicious, it contains many vitamins and nutrients to help us grow.

Our friend, the apostle Paul, talked about fruit in his letter to the churches in Galatia. But he wasn't talking about apples or pears or bananas, or even figs or dates or pomegranates, which would have been the fruits he was more familiar with.

Instead, he was talking about the fruits of God's Spirit. He says that when we let the Spirit work in us, these fruits are easily evident: love, joy, kindness, generosity, and gentleness.

How can we tend the Spirit in us, so that these fruits can grow best? *(Invite the children to come up with concrete ideas.)*

When we put these into practice, we can harvest the Spirit's fruits and share them with others, generously spreading our love and kindness around.

The Sermon

Fear of Freedom

Hymns

Beginning of Worship: "Sing Praise to God, Our Highest Good"
Sermon Hymn: "We Shall Overcome"
End of Worship: "O Jesus, I Have Promised"

Scripture

Galatians 5:1, 13-25 (For additional sermon materials on this passage, see the March 2004 issue of *The Clergy Journal* and on Luke 9:51-62, see the 2003 May/June planning issue of *The Clergy Journal.*)

Freedom is faith's good friend. In fact, freedom is as good a friend to faith as is truth. But the intimate friend of faith that Paul praised so profusely, many people now fear. That fact is just cause for no little concern spiritually as well as politically. Once freedom is lost, recovery is difficult and faith is left to suffer. Faith and freedom belong together.

Make no mistake about it, fear is an enemy of freedom that threatens first the possibility of freedom and then the stability of freedom. "Why?" you may ask, "Why would anyone fear the very liberty that is so basic to realizing the full potential of human experience – individually and socially? Why would any person fear that which God intends for all persons – that to which God calls us, that which Christ has given to us?"

Often it's a matter of security. Where there is liberty, there is uncertainty. Along with the freedom to travel a new path comes a degree of insecurity about what is around the corner or over the next hill. Inherent in the freedom to think is the possibility of changing one's mind, breaking with the past, discarding old doctrines, and embracing new values. Living with freedom opens the door to disappointment as well as fulfillment, to failure as well as success, to losing everything as well as gaining anything. Freedom makes no guarantees.

Frankly, the insecurity that accompanies liberty is more than many people can tolerate. They prefer predictability, in some instances even the predictability of tyranny to the insecurity of freedom. Fear of insecurity often breeds actions that threaten the continuation of liberty. Worried that adults who think for themselves may reject the traditions of the past, some ideologues tell people only *what* to think rather than instructing them in *how* to think and encouraging them to think. Old ways can be preserved if people never experience the freedom to pursue new ways. Fearful of the influence of individuals opposed to their particular biases, many religious and political leaders seek to use the government to legislate prohibitions against thoughts and actions with which they disagree.

Insecurity is often the womb from which a fear of freedom is born.

Sometimes, though, the fear of freedom grows out of *a resistance to responsibility.*

June 27, 2004
4th Sunday after Pentecost (Proper 8)
RC/Pres: 13th Sunday in Ordinary Time

Students of contemporary religion tell us that the fastest growing congregations in this nation consist of people who want to be told what to believe rather encouraged to work out their own beliefs. Taking responsibility for one's own spirituality is far more difficult than bowing to an authority whose directives can be followed faithfully even if mindlessly. Recently a woman told me how much she welcomed someone just telling her what to say and do so that she did not have to figure out for herself the beliefs, ethics, and behavior that should fill her days.

The very promise of freedom that induces excitement and propels growth in some people incites fear in other people and results in their submission to one authority or another. Liberty and responsibility hold hands; they are two sides of an experiential coin. That is the good news. But the bad news is that, as free people, if we don't think, learn, grow, act, influence, serve, deter evil, and promote good, we have no one to blame but ourselves. However, that is more responsibility than some people want to assume.

Fear attacks freedom to weaken it or to abolish it, often successfully.

Now, allow me to introduce into this discussion yet another influential companion of freedom and faith – a friend of both that, according to the New Testament, casts out fear. Of course, I speak of love – love of self, love of other people, love of the nation. Be duly warned, though, that the introduction of love into this discussion increases significantly an already high level of tension.

Love like faith requires freedom – the freedom to be honest, to be decisive, to be responsive. But the maintenance of freedom among lovers is not always easy. Here fear raises its protests against freedom once more.

A lover wants what is best for her or his beloved. But when the beloved is free, the lover realizes that bad decisions can be made and wrong actions taken. Fearing hurt in the life of the beloved or deterioration in the intimacy of their relationship because of the beloved's freedom, a lover may have to struggle with the temptation to disdain freedom and exert control. Such action can be easily rationalized but the detrimental nature of its consequences almost defies imagination. The control that compromises freedom in the name of love also diminishes the quality of love. So! We are left with a conclusion that stokes insecurities and makes responsibility look heavy: love within a lover must support a freedom for the beloved that creates the possibility of a rejection of love and the dissolution of the relationship.

The truth in this conclusion is as old as creation and as costly as Christ's ministry of redemption. The loving God willed good for all of humankind from the first moment of creation. But, in that first moment, God gave persons the gift of volition – the liberty and ability to make decisions. The God who wanted nothing more than an eternal relationship with members of the highest order of creation provided persons with the freedom to reject the very purpose of creation because only in such freedom do there reside the possibilities of being human, practicing faith, responding to love with love.

Only if we can make choices are our choices meaningful. The liberty to make bad decisions contributes to the glory of making good decisions. God desires not robot like slaves parroting a preprogrammed love, but free individuals willing and choosing to love and to live in love.

Oh, that is scary. Freedom is scary. A certain level of fear will always accompany freedom whether in the political, personal, relational, social, or spiritual realm. Freedom is risky; and very costly. Inevitably, freedom stirs a certain amount of insecurity as well as requires a lot of responsibility. But all of the alternatives to freedom are worse. Apart from freedom there is no integrity or love.

"Stand fast in freedom," the apostle Paul admonished us. "Don't ever again submit to slavery." He wrote the words knowing full well the power of the temptation that resides in fear. "Stand fast in freedom," he wrote. We are free! As the gospel writer instructed us, when Christ makes us free, we are really free. We *are* free! We sense the promise and feel the exhilaration of that realization. But, honestly, we also know fear – fear of freedom. The lure of that fear is also real. Listen further. Weighing the blessings of liberty as well as the fear that is close at hand, hear and heed instructions drawn from the heart of the gospel and the essence of love: "Live in freedom" and "Fear not!" Amen.

– C. Welton Gaddy
Northminster Church
Monroe, Louisiana

July 4, 2004

5th Sunday after Pentecost (Proper 9)

RC/Pres: 14th Sunday in Ordinary Time

Lessons

RCL	2 Kgs 5:1-14	Gal 6:(1-6) 7-16	Lk 10:1-11, 16-20
Roman Catholic	Isa 66:10-14c	Gal 6:14-18	Lk 10:1-12, 17-20 or 10:1-9
Episcopal (BCP)	Isa 66:10-16	Gal 6:(1-10) 14-18	Lk 10:1-12, 16-20
Lutheran	Isa 66:10-14	Gal 6:(1-6) 7-16	Lk 10:1-11, 16-20

Introduction to the Lessons

Lesson 1

(1) *2 Kings 5:1-14* (RCL)

Namaan, commander from Aram, is a leper. His Israelite slave girl tells his wife that the prophet Elisha can heal him. Elisha instructs him to wash seven times in the Jordan River, a command that Namaan thinks is insulting. His servants convince him otherwise, and he is healed.

(2) *Isaiah 66:10-14c* (RC); *Isaiah 66:10-16* (Epis); *Isaiah 66:10-14* (Luth)

This last chapter of Isaiah speaks of Jerusalem's restoration in peace and prosperity. Judgment will be executed on her enemies.

Lesson 2

***Galatians 6:(1-6) 7-16* (RCL/Luth); *Galatians 6:14-18* (RC); *Galatians 6:(1-10) 14-18* (Epis)**

Restore those who transgress; bear each other's burdens. You will reap what you sow, so do not grow weary of sowing good things. We cannot boast of anything we have done, but we are made new by the grace of God.

Gospel

***Luke 10:1-11, 16-20* (RCL/Luth); *Luke 10:1-12, 17-20* (RC); *Luke 10:1-12, 16-20* (Epis)**

Jesus appoints 70 disciples to go ahead of him, "like lambs into the midst of wolves." They are to bless those who bless them, and, when they are not welcomed, to shake the dust off their feet. They return with joy because they were able to cast out demons.

Theme

As we consider our basic liberties in a free country, we remember the freedom we have in Christ.

Thought for the Day

What we say and what we do have far-reaching consequences. Let us, then, pay attention to those things, so we may honor Christ with our actions and live in Christian freedom.

Call to Worship

Leader: Thus says the high and lofty one who inhabits eternity, whose name is Holy:

People I dwell in the high and holy place,

Leader And also with those who are contrite and humble in spirit,

People To revive the spirit of the humble, and to revive the heart of the contrite.

– Based on Isaiah 57:15

Pastoral Prayer

Gracious and holy God, we are grateful for your many gifts: for the beauty of green trees, dark earth, cleansing rain; for the delight of children and youth, friends and family; for freedom and liberty. Help us, O God, by renewing within us the power of your love. May it make us bold to do good things in your name, and strong to stand up to injustice and wrong-doing. We pray, O Lord, for those who feel weak in their bodies or spirits. Heal them, we ask. Make them strong. Renew their souls. Give them the ability to face what lies ahead. We pray for those who are bound by loneliness, depression, and doubt. Lead them to the help they need, and put them on a path that will lead to health. We pray for those whose relationships are in trouble. Wrap your loving arms around them and help them to know your love. We pray for freedom, peace, and justice wherever they do not exist – in homes, in families, in cities, and in countries. In Jesus we pray. Amen.

Prayer of Confession

God of liberty and freedom, forgive us when we try to create boundaries to your grace that you never intended. We refuse to treat others the way we would be treated; we fail to do the things we should; many of the things we do are hurtful to others. We decline to tame our tongues, and we let our anger control us. Free us from our sinful nature, and help us to live after the example of Jesus, who showed your love to those around him. Amen.

Prayer of Dedication of Gifts and Self

Giving God, we are grateful not only for what we have received, but also for the ability to give back. As we ponder your gifts, show us where those same gifts may be used for the good of others. Amen.

Sermon Summary

We have been blessed with great freedom, both in our country and in our faith. Let us remember God's new creation in us and in others.

Hymn of the Day

"Bring Many Names"

Another hymn by Brian Wren that explores images of God (see also June 6), this hymn stretches even further our awareness of God's presence in a variety of forms. Each stanza works well on its own – people may choose to use certain ones at certain times – although the whole hymn is a powerful reminder that, while we can image God in many ways, God is still beyond all of our knowing and all of our naming.

The tune by Carlton Young was written specifically for this text.

Children's Time

Plant Carefully!

(Preparation: Bring a packet of garden seeds.)

What kind of seed are these? *(Show packet of seeds.)* What will happen if I plant them in the ground and give them a drink of water? If I take good care of the plants, what will I harvest?

There's a saying, "you harvest what you plant" or "you reap what you sow." This is an important saying. If we sow green bean seeds, we'll harvest green beans. If we sow pumpkin seeds, we'll harvest pumpkins.

This isn't just true in the garden or on a farm. What would happen if I went around planting seeds of meanness – you know, saying mean things to people all the time? What do you think I would get back? What kind of harvest would I get? *(Invite responses.)*

Or, what would happen if I went around planting seeds of kindness – you know, being kind to other people? What kind of harvest would I get back?

Our friend, the apostle Paul, told the church in Galatia to be careful, because we harvest what we plant. Paul encourages us to think about the kinds of things we do and what kind of harvest these actions bring. Paul encourages us not to become tired of planting good seeds.

The Sermon

A New Creation Is Everything!

Hymns

Beginning of Worship: "God of the Ages, Whose Almighty Hand"
Sermon Hymn: "Though I May Speak"
Closing Hymn: "Lift Every Voice and Sing"

Scripture

Galatians 6:(1-6) 7-16 (For additional sermon materials on this passage, see the March 2004 issue of *The Clergy Journal* and on Luke 10:1-11, 16-20, see the 2003 May/June planning issue of *The Clergy Journal*.)

We live in a country that allows freedom of religion. No, that's not right. We live in a country that guarantees freedom of religion. Today we celebrate that freedom among many others, which are provided by our constitution. Because of our country's unique history, the word *freedom* has become a significant part of our political and social vocabulary. We are hardly able to understand other countries where people seem to live happily with much less personal liberty. Nearly every politician who runs for public office speaks of "liberty" or "freedom" in ads and debates.

Freedom seems to run in our veins and flow in and out of our lungs along with the air we breathe.

Maybe our hearts race a little, then, when we read the letter to the Galatians. Though the word *freedom* doesn't appear in our text for today, it is certainly the overriding text for the entire letter. Paul wrote this letter to the church in Galatia because there were people who were preaching a gospel that wasn't really good news. It wasn't good news because it tied these new Gentile Christians to the laws of the Old Testament, particularly to circumcision. This so-called gospel restricted the freedom of the new Christians and bound them to the past in such a way that Paul believed it could stifle their very faith. He feared they would worry more about trying to observe the Law than they would about serving Christ.

So Paul wrote to the Galatian church and encouraged them to live by the Spirit, not as people who have so much freedom it doesn't matter what they do, but as freed people whose lives were controlled by the Spirit of Christ. They were to avoid the works of the flesh and exhibit the fruit of the Spirit: love, joy, peace, patience, kindness, generosity, faithfulness, gentleness, and self-control (Gal 5:22-23). No law forbids such things, Paul said.

In today's text from chapter 6, Paul tells his readers, these uncircumcised Gentile Christians, not to be fooled by those who say they must be circumcised. It's just an outward sign of a law that even the outsiders don't keep as they say they do, he says.

It's not circumcision that counts for anything, nor even staying uncircumcised, for that matter, says Paul. The only thing that counts is being a new creation, and that creation comes from the Spirit. It is something that changes the heart, not the flesh. It helps us follow the way of Christ, not some external set of laws. It sets us free. The Spirit makes us new people, a new creation.

As Americans know, freedom comes with responsibility. Freedom is not the license to do whatever we want whenever we please to whomever we will. If you try that in this free country, you will at some point run afoul of the laws of the land, or at least the unwritten laws of your family or neighbors who will not put up with your selfish behavior forever.

For the Christian, freedom means, at least partly, that we are free to do the will of God. It is the Spirit who sets us free from the damning law, which requires more of us than we could ever possibly give. But it is also the Spirit who puts in our hearts the desire to conform our lives more and more to the kind of life a Spirit-filled person would live.

When I was in seminary, I had two friends – married to each other – who were extremely talented students in the education program. Both were excellent teachers. Their lesson plans were hands down the best in our group, and I'm sure their grades were stellar. When the professors needed to send someone into the local churches to lead programs, they turned first to these two. I knew they were headed for big things, tall steeple churches, and more money than the rest of us would ever think of making in church work.

After they graduated, I heard that this couple had stayed in the community. I figured they were working for a large church nearby. Another student and I decided to go visit them in their new setting. I didn't recognize the address they gave us, and as we drove from the seminary to their apartment, we began to get uneasy. We went from middle class to lower middle class to obviously poor neighborhoods. Their apartment was at the center of the most rundown section of the city. I couldn't imagine why they lived in such a place. Perhaps they couldn't afford anything better? Surely that wasn't the case, since they had such great talent, references, and connections.

This couple chose to live in the inner city because it was their calling. It wasn't that they didn't have enough money to live elsewhere. They were free to live in a much nicer neighborhood, but they were also free to choose a different kind of service from the rest of us. And that is just what they did. They had helped start a small Christian school in a church building in the inner city, where mostly poor students would have an alternative to the substandard public education of that area. They wrote some of their own curriculum, had very small classes, and tuition was subsidized by churches and private donors. I could see from the joy on their faces that they were doing exactly what they wanted to do. We heard story after story of how this little school in the inner city was helping students to grow and develop, working with their families in ways that would be impossible in a larger school, and making a difference in the community.

You see, as Paul says, a new creation is everything! It is amazing, and counterintuitive, to see how the Spirit of Christ can make people into something new and different. My seminary acquaintances were free to choose to work in an environment most of us would find frightening, restrictive, or beneath our abilities. In the same way, you and I are free, because of being new creations of the Spirit, to choose to serve Christ in ever new and creative ways.

How has God called you in the past? What does your freedom in Christ enable you to do that you wouldn't have the courage for otherwise? What difference does it make that you are a new creation by the Spirit?

This holiday weekend, as you celebrate the freedoms you have in this country, I challenge you to reflect also on the freedom given to you in Christ. Let yourself be moved by the Spirit who has made you a new creation into evermore free expressions of your faith and service to God and God's people.

– Melissa Bane Sevier
First Presbyterian Church
Aurora, Indiana

July 11, 2004

6th Sunday after Pentecost (Proper 10)
RC/Pres: 15th Sunday in Ordinary Time

Lessons

RCL	Amos 7:7-17	Col 1:1-14	Lk 10:25-37
Roman Catholic	Deut 30:10-14	Col 1:15-20	Lk 10:25-37
Episcopal (BCP)	Deut 30:9-14	Col 1:1-14	Lk 10:25-37
Lutheran	Deut 30:9-14	Col 1:1-14	Lk 10:25-37

Introduction to the Lessons

Lesson 1

(1) *Amos 7:7-17* (RCL)

The prophet Amos is given a vision of a plumb line in the midst of Israel, telling of destruction. Amaziah, a priest in Bethel, tries to send Amos away because he prophesies against Israel. Amos refuses to go, saying he was called by God to bring this message.

(2) *Deuteronomy 30:10-14* (RC);
***Deuteronomy 30:9-14* (Epis/Luth)**

Moses is telling the people what will happen when they come into the land that God has given them. God will make them prosperous in the new land when they obey the commandments of the book of the law.

Lesson 2

(1) *Colossians 1:1-14* (RCL/Epis/Luth)

The author gives thanks to God for the faith of the Colossians, and expresses the desire that the Colossians be filled with the knowledge of God's will and lead lives worthy of the Lord.

(2) *Colossians 1:15-20* (RC)

This great confession contains what many believe to be an early Christian hymn. Christ reigns supreme from his position as cocreator and head of the church.

Gospel

Luke 10:25-37 **(RCL/RC/Epis/Luth)**

In response to a question meant as a test, Jesus tells a story to answer "Who is my neighbor?"

Theme

Love expresses itself through action.

Thought for the Day

We may speak of loving God and loving others, but those words must be acted out if we are to truly live as God's people.

Call to Worship

Leader: God has told us what is good;
People: And what does God require of us,
Leader: But to do justice, and to love kindness,
People: And to walk humbly with our God?

– Based on Micah 6:8

Pastoral Prayer

Generous God, how grateful we are for your love toward us. You have given us so much, assured us of your care, delighted us with the varieties of nature, and moved us to expressions of thanks and praise. Help us, O God, to share your generous nature. When decisions are to be made, may we lean in the direction of your love, grace, and mercy. When we are confronted with those in need, may we remember whose we are and respond as we have learned from the example of Jesus. When we see injustice, may our thoughts turn toward the one who ate with tax collectors and sinners. Help us respond with strength and solidarity with persons who are treated wrongly. When we know those who are sick, may we put ourselves in their place and creatively imagine what might improve their lot or make them know they are not alone. When we listen to the news, may we listen with hearts and minds infused by your Spirit. When we see the grieving, may our hearts break with their hearts, as your heart breaks with ours. Amen.

Prayer of Confession

How often, O Lord, we have passed by those who are in need. We have turned our heads against their hunger or pain. We have walked away as they told us of their illness. We have refused to listen, and failed to offer our assistance. We have ignored their muted cries for help. Forgive us our selfishness and make us whole once more. Teach us what it means to love you with our whole being, and our neighbors as ourselves. Amen.

Prayer of Dedication of Gifts and Self

When we pause to think, O Lord, of the various ways in which you have demonstrated your love to us, we are nearly stunned by the extent of your goodness. What we can give to others seems so small in comparison. Yet you are the one who can take the small offerings we bring and transform them into something great for your kingdom. Receive our gifts, our minds and hearts, our whole selves, we pray. And by these things, may your work be done. Amen.

Sermon Summary

Jesus tells a story about the demonstration of love through action. In the story, two members of the religious establishment pass by a man who has been hurt. A third man, a Samaritan, stops to help. A Samaritan is the last person Jesus' listeners would have expected to offer assistance.

Hymn of the Day

"Let Justice Flow like Streams"

Jane Parker Huber is perhaps best known for providing fresh new lyrics to traditional hymn tunes. In this particular instance she combines two verses from the prophet Amos into a strong challenge to make our worship more than mere lip service, but part of our work for justice and godliness.

The anonymous tune, "St. Thomas," is one of the tunes sometimes used with "Come, We that Love the Lord" (see May 9).

Children's Time

Who Is My Neighbor?

Preparation: Bring in some cans of food that you can donate to your local food bank.

I brought these cans for the food bank. Some people wonder why they should give their food away. Jesus teaches us to love our neighbor as ourselves, and that means taking care of our neighbors who are hungry, just as we would want them to take care of us, if we were hungry.

Just who is our neighbor? One day, a man asked Jesus this very question. Jesus didn't answer him directly. Instead, he told a story about a man who was robbed and beaten up and left beside a road. Two men walked by and ignored him, but a third man took pity on him. This third man stopped to help the injured person and made sure that he got help. Who was the neighbor in this story? The man who asked Jesus the question said that the one who helped was neighbor. Jesus said, "You're right!"

All people are our neighbors, even when we don't know their names. Jesus calls each one of us to love our neighbors as we love ourselves. For example, when our neighbor is hungry, we love them with a gift of food.

The Sermon

The Compassionate Samaritan

Hymns

Beginning of Worship: "Come, Great God of All the Ages"
Sermon Hymn: "Spirit of God, Descend Upon My Heart"
Closing Hymn: "Though I May Speak"

Scripture

Luke 10:25-37 (For additional sermon materials on this passage, see the March 2004 issue of *The Clergy Journal* and on Colossians 1:1-14, see the 2003 May/June planning issue of *The Clergy Journal*.)

When an expert in religious law asked Jesus a question, it really was a test. "Teacher, what must I do to inherit eternal life?" Jesus asked the lawyer what he thought, and the man gave the stock answer of the day, quoting the Shema, a very important Hebrew text. "Hear, O Israel," it says, "The Lord is our God, the Lord alone. You shall love the Lord your God with all your heart, and with all your soul, and with all your might" (Deut 6:5). Then he added Leviticus 19:18: "You shall love your neighbor as yourself." When Jesus told him he had answered well, the man continued the test: "So just who is my neighbor?" he asked. And Jesus told a story.

For someone to be robbed going down the road between Jerusalem and Jericho is like saying somebody was mugged in Chicago yesterday. It's not really news. Jesus described the horrible aftermath of the robbery – the victim was left half dead, beaten, and stripped.

A priest happened by, and when he saw the man, he went around him, avoiding any contact. Why?

It helps to know that the man may have appeared dead or near death. If a priest were to touch a dead person, or if the victim died while the priest assisted him, the priest would have become defiled, "unclean," and thus prohibited from fulfilling his priestly duties for a time. Perhaps the priest was afraid the robbers might still be around. However, as Jesus' listeners heard the story, they would think that the priest should have given those reasonable excuses up, and just helped the guy. The common folk weren't always all that keen on priests, anyway, imagining that priests sometimes thought more highly of themselves than they ought.

The story continues with a Levite, who acted in just the same way as the priest. Levites served the temple community in many ways, from musicians to custodians to those who examined animals who were to be sacrificed. Again, we don't know his internal motivations, but he also would have been rendered unclean by contact with a dead person, and unable to perform his job. Was it the defilement he feared, or something else?

The third passerby in Jesus' story was a person no one expected. He was a Samaritan. It is almost impossible today for us to understand the tension and dislike between Jews and Samaritans of the first century. Jews saw Samaritans as racially impure, deeply flawed in their religious understanding, and unclean. If the victim had known his helper was a Samaritan, he likely would have refused the aid.

However, to the gasps of Jesus' audience, the Samaritan is the one who administered first aid. He poured his own wine to cleanse the man's wounds and his own oil to soothe them. He got dirty and messy with his helping, and he even spent his own money at the inn, leaving enough for the man to stay there a couple of weeks. Finally, love had its way.

When Jesus turned back to the lawyer who had asked the original question and said, "Who was the neighbor to the man who was hurt?" it must have galled the lawyer to say, "The one who showed him mercy." He was unable to say the word "Samaritan."

Interestingly, Jesus never told the end of the story. Did the victim recover? Did he find out who had helped him? What became of the Samaritan?

The answers to those questions really do not matter, in one sense. The man who gave aid simply did what a person should do. He acted. He didn't just pass on by. Whether the victim survived or not, this man had done the right thing.

Mother Teresa said that her goal on the streets of Calcutta was to see that no one died unloved and alone. She was not able to save most of the lives of the dying, because the people were so sick when she and her sisters found them. But they could give them a clean bed, a loving touch, and whatever comfort they could. We cannot always undo the effects of evil, but we can at least see that evil does not have the last word.

Several years ago I helped chaperone a group of high school youth on a mission trip to New York state. We spent a week at a camp, roofing cabins. One day, we packed bag lunches and rode the subway to New York City for a day of sightseeing. We had 18 young people and I spent my day at the back of the pack, counting over and over to 18, making sure nobody was lost. I'd only been to that city one other time, and I was amazed by the number of people who appeared to be living on the streets. The young people also were quite moved by those people. "Why don't they have jobs?" they would ask. "Where do they live?" "What should we do when they ask us for money?"

"Just keep walking," I said. "There's no way we can help them all. Just look straight ahead and keep walking."

But they were unable to do that. They had never seen street people in such numbers, and they looked at each one. They made eye contact. Something in those young, unhardened souls was moved by the economic and spiritual poverty they saw. One girl asked me, "Would it be okay if I gave my lunch to that man over there? He asked me for food." What could I say? "It's your lunch," I said. "Are you sure that's what you want to do with it?" Immediately, she walked over to him, and with great respect asked him if he would like a sandwich and an apple. He nodded and reached out for it. I never saw such a look as the one on her face as she walked away, shyly glancing back to see the man hungrily eating the sandwich.

One by one, the lunches changed hands, until 18 lunches had been given away. Make that 20; the other chaperone and I gave ours away, too. How could we not? It wasn't that we felt guilty. It was that we saw such joy in the giving that we knew we wanted to be part of it.

Though we had enough money, no one bought lunch that day. They said they were saving their money for souvenirs, but I was pretty sure those young people wanted to feel what it was like to miss a meal, just once.

I learned much from them that day. We didn't get anyone out of homelessness; we didn't change the city; we probably didn't even make much of a difference in the lives of the people who ate our lunches. However, I can say with certainty that there was a difference in us. That night, as we reflected on the day, we talked about homelessness in a new way. We were not suddenly experts, but we had seen it close-up and we had been moved by what we saw. We imagined going hungry for days at a time. We wondered what it would be like to have to beg for money and food, and to be at the mercy of the elements. Those young people taught me that sometimes God calls us to do something, large or small. And that sometimes, love has its way, in the midst of evil, even if only for a moment.

– Melissa Bane Sevier
First Presbyterian Church
Aurora, Indiana

July 18, 2004

7th Sunday after Pentecost (Proper 11)
RC/Pres: 16th Sunday in Ordinary Time

Lessons

RCL	Amos 8:1-12	Col 1:15-28	Lk 10:38-42
Roman Catholic	Gen 18:1-10	Col 1:24-28	Lk 10:38:42
Episcopal (BCP)	Gen 18:1-10a (10b-14)	Col 1:21-29	Lk 10:38:42
Lutheran	Gen 18:1-10a	Col 1:15-28	Lk 10:38:42

Introduction to the Lessons

Lesson 1

(1) *Amos 8:1-12* (RCL)

The vision of a basket of summer fruit comes to Amos, along with a condemnation for a community that cares more about money and profit than it does for the poor and needy among them.

(2) *Genesis 18:1-10* (RC); *Genesis 18:1-10a (10b-14)* (Epis); *Genesis 18:1-10a* (Luth)

The Lord appears to the aged Abraham and Sarah in the persons of three men. Abraham offers them hospitality, and the promise is made that Sarah will bear a son.

Lesson 2

***Colossians 1:15-28* (RCL/Luth); *Colossians 1:24-28* (RC); *Colossians 1:21-29* (Epis)**

This great confession of faith contains what many believe to be an early Christian hymn. Christ reigns supreme from his position as cocreator and head of the church.

Gospel

***Luke 10:38-42* (RCL/RC/Epis/Luth)**

Jesus visits the home of Martha and Mary. Instead of helping Martha with meal preparations, Martha chooses to sit with Jesus and his other disciples. Martha complains to Jesus, asking him to have Mary help, but Jesus refuses. Instead, he praises Mary's choice.

Theme

Let go of your obsession to achieve, and come sit at the feet of Jesus.

Thought for the Day

Though Jesus does not condemn Martha's meal preparation (indeed, someone has to make the meal), he does call her to think beyond the things she feels need to be done. He reminds her that little is really needed, and that the better place is to sit and reflect with Jesus.

Call to Worship

Leader: Teach me, O Lord, the way of your statutes, and I will observe it to the end.

People: Give me understanding, that I may keep your law and observe it with my whole heart.

– Based on Psalm 119:33-34

Pastoral Prayer

How we struggle, O God, with when we should act and when we should simply be still and listen. Each day we are tempted to over-schedule, overwork, and overdo, even as we long for more intimacy with you. Remind us that in our prayer and study we are also doing your will, and that resting in your presence is both a gift and a privilege. Help us to look for and find you in the faces of others, the laughter of children, the glory of a warm day, the smell of freshly cut hay, and the taste of summer fruit. As we are renewed in your presence, may we become evangelists, helping to show others that all of life is not about work, but also about rest and renewal. We pray, O God, for those who are no longer able to work because of disease, age, or unemployment. We pray for the hungry, the poor, the lonely, and the oppressed. Even as we work to help improve the conditions of others, may they also find solace in a sense of your presence, knowing they are never alone. Through Christ we make our prayers, Amen.

Prayer of Confession

As you long to meet us, O God, we confess that we have hidden from you. We have been so busy and occupied, we have avoided taking the time to be renewed at the feet of Jesus. We have forgotten to listen to you; we have not made time for other people in our lives; we have forgotten what is truly important and spent our time on the things that scream for our attention. Help us to turn from our busyness, to pay attention to others and their needs, and to listen for your voice in the silence. Amen.

Prayer of Dedication of Gifts and Self

Receive these our gifts, O Lord, and accept, we pray, the offering of our lives. You have given us so much in Christ. Now we return to you a portion of those gifts to be used to further your kingdom. Amen.

Sermon Summary

We are challenged, along with Martha, to consider the importance of the things we do. Jesus invites us to come and sit at his feet where we may learn to listen and simply rest in his presence.

Hymn of the Day

"The Servant Song"

Virtually every hymnal titles this hymn differently; it is known variously as "Will You (or Won't You) Let Me Be Your Servant?," "Brother (or Sister), Let Me Be Your Servant," "Brother, Sister, Let Me Serve You," or even "We Are Pilgrims on a Journey," which replaces the original first stanza with the second.

Regardless of the title, however, this text by New Zealand musician Richad Gillard is a powerful one, reminding us that we are not Christians in isolation, but that we live in covenant community with our brothers and sister.

Gillard, who prefers to play by ear, wrote the tune, which has been transcribed and arranged by Betty Pulkingham.

Children's Time

A Tale of Two Sisters

Preparation: Bring an apron and a broom or dust cloth. Tie the apron around your waist and start sweeping or dusting the area as you begin to tell the story of Mary and Martha.

One day, Jesus went to visit his two friends, Mary and Martha. Mary immediately dropped everything to sit and listen to what Jesus was teaching, but Martha had so many things to do, that she just couldn't stop. Martha was busy in the kitchen, fixing a meal for Jesus and the disciples who were with him.

Finally Martha got mad! She went up to Jesus and said, "Lord, don't you care that my sister has left me to do all the work by myself? Tell her to get to work."

But Jesus only looked at her and said. "Martha, Martha. You are busy with so many things. But don't you know there is only one important thing to do right now? Mary has chosen to do it." *(Stop sweeping, take off your apron and sit with the children.)*

Jesus didn't say that we should stop cooking and cleaning. Jesus was telling Martha that sometimes there are other things that we should choose to do. That day, listening to what Jesus was teaching was the most important thing to do.

The Sermon

The Most Important Thing

Hymns

Beginning of Worship: "I Greet Thee, Who My Sure Redeemer Art"
Sermon Hymn: "Be Thou My Vision"
Closing Hymn: "Near to the Heart of God"

Scripture

Luke 10:38-42 (For additional sermon materials on this passage, see the March 2004 issue of *The Clergy Joujrnal* and on Colossians 1:15-28, see the 2003 May/June planning issue of *The Clergy Journal.*)

July 18, 2004
7th Sunday after Pentecost (Proper 11)
RC/Pres: 16th Sunday in Ordinary Time

Martha was put out with Jesus and with her sister. She had invited Jesus into her home as a gesture of hospitality and faith. He had all these men with him and so she invited them, too. It was the right thing to do. She wished she had known he was coming to town, because she really would have liked to have gone all out to impress him. After all, he was now a very famous teacher; it was a privilege to have him in her home.

Even without advance notice, though, she felt pretty good about her ability to improvise, and she was highly flattered he had accepted her invitation. Probably he knew he could count on her to provide hospitality on short notice. She had hurriedly sent servants to the market to obtain some of the best meats and produce. She set to work immediately planning and working on the meal. She would prepare the most elaborate dishes she could manage with the limited time. The servants had returned quickly and now everything was coming together all at once. She was moving quickly back and forth, preparing parts of the meal herself and overseeing the rest of the preparations.

All of a sudden, Martha realized she hadn't seen Mary for a while. Had she slipped off somewhere to avoid work as Martha felt she often did? Martha began to look around for her sister. She was horrified when she realized Mary was with Jesus – listening to him teach, sitting with the men!

Surely Jesus was just being polite by not asking her to leave. It was unheard of that a woman should be there, sitting like a disciple at Jesus' feet. Martha thought she would do them all a favor by getting Mary out of there.

"Excuse me," she said, when Jesus took a breath. "I hate to interrupt, but, Jesus, would you mind sending Mary in to help with the preparations? I know you men would like to eat soon and I could certainly use some help."

Jesus' answer must have shocked them all (except Mary, I'd like to think). "Martha, Martha, you're doing too much. You don't have to go to all this trouble. It would have been much better if you had prepared something simple and then had come to sit with Mary and the others here. Mary has chosen the right thing, and it shouldn't be taken from her."

This story of Jesus and the two sisters has much to say to believers, both women and men. It has to do with how we devote ourselves to Jesus.

Before we get to the main message of the story, though, it's important to notice some things about the story itself that make it an amazing testimony to how Jesus dealt with women.

Women in the days of Jesus, even more than in our lifetimes, were not encouraged to enter into men's territory. And men's territory included worship and study of scripture – the Torah. Some rabbis taught that it was better to burn the Torah than to teach it to a woman.

Just as last week's parable of the good Samaritan destroys old ideas of neighbor, this story about Jesus destroys old ideas about gender. Jesus pays no attention to the social taboos of the day. He enters the home of a woman, and he encourages a woman to sit at his feet while he teaches. "Sitting at the feet of a teacher" is the common expression for learning from a rabbi. The rabbi was slightly elevated, and the pupils gathered around at his feet to hear and to ask questions. Those who studied regularly with a particular rabbi were called disciples. These were all male disciples. Women could hear the Torah read, but they were not allowed to read nor study it.

Jesus made it clear this was the culture's way, not God's way. Women didn't need men to explain the Torah. They could learn on their own. They could even sit at Jesus' feet and be his disciples.

This is not unrelated to what Jesus seemed to feel was distracting to Martha in our story. "There is only one thing," he said.

Obviously, Martha did not think she was being distracted. She thought Mary was the one distracted by learning that shouldn't even belong to a woman, distracted from her work on the meal. To Martha, it was the meal, the event, that was most important.

Martha, though, was not just about hospitality. She was about all she thought she had to do: preparing dishes, probably elaborate ones for their honored guest; fussing in the kitchen; dealing with the servants; making sure that the best of everything would be ready for the table in abundant quantity, at the right time, and at the right temperature. She was so caught up in entertaining and providing for her guest, she had forgotten the identity of the guest.

Luke has chosen to put this account right after Jesus' story of the good Samaritan. That story showed us that faith without service is not real faith. Priests and Levites don't have a lock on spirituality, especially when their words are not lived out in action. Now this account seems to say that it's devotion, not action, that is important. So which is it?

The two passages ought to be read as complementary, as two sides of the same coin. Just as we cannot have true faith without serving others, we cannot truly serve until we have sat at the feet of Jesus. We show our purest love when we know Christ best. Listening to Jesus helps us keep our motives honest.

The difficulty may come when we try to figure out just when we should act and when we should reflect. In our culture, we are obsessed with many things. Cell phones and pagers go off in restaurants, at home, in public or intimate moments, and we answer them. We are get-it-done people, who derive our sense of self-importance from what we accomplish in a day or a year. It is into this culture that the words of Jesus break through, if we let them.

There is need of only one thing. Mary has chosen the better part.

Jesus offered Martha the freedom not to conform to the social norms of the day. He offered her the delightful option of putting away her obsessive desire to do and grabbing hold of the opportunity just to be in the presence of God.

So, all you Marthas, put down your aprons, your planners, your schedules and calendars, your to-do list, your obsession with accomplishment. Come and rest. Sit at Jesus' feet for a while and see how that changes you. Know the freedom that comes from letting go of all that has to be done, and listening for the voice of God. Amen.

– Melissa Bane Sevier
First Presbyterian Church
Aurora, Indiana

July 25, 2004

8th Sunday after Pentecost (Proper 12)

RC/Pres: 17th Sunday in Ordinary Time

Lessons

RCL	Hos 1:2-10	Col 2:6-15 (16-19)	Lk 11:1-13
Roman Catholic	Gen 18:20-32	Col 2:12-14	Lk 11:1-13
Episcopal (BCP)	Gen 18:20-33	Col 2:6-15	Lk 11:1-13
Lutheran	Gen 18:20-32	Col 2:6-15 (16-19)	Lk 11:1-13

Introduction to the Lessons

Lesson 1

(1) *Hosea 1:2-10 (*RCL)

Hosea marries Gomer, a prostitute, and they have three children together. God instructs Hosea to give them names that have specific meanings in the relationship between God and God's people.

(2) *Genesis 18:20-32* (RC/Luth); *Genesis 18:20-33* (Epis)

God determines to destroy Sodom and Gomorrah and tells Abraham. Abraham asks God to spare the city of Sodom if some righteous people are still to be found there. God relents: if there are 10 righteous persons found in the city it will not be destroyed.

Lesson 2

***Colossians 2:6-15 (16-19)* (RCL/Luth);**
***Colossians 2:12-14* (RC); *Colossians 2:6-15* (Epis)**

Christians need no worldly mediator between them and God, because that role has been fulfilled by Christ. God has made us alive through Christ even when we were dead in our sin.

Gospel

***Luke 11:1-13* (RCL/RC/Epis/Luth)**

Jesus teaches the disciples to pray. In other teachings about prayer, Jesus tells of a friend who was persistent in asking for help. Jesus says that just as we are willing to give good things to our children, even more is God ready to give us the Holy Spirit.

July 25, 2004
8th Sunday after Pentecost (Proper 12)
RC/Pres: 17th Sunday in Ordinary Time

Theme

God listens to our prayers.

Thought for the Day

The character of God is what we can count on when we pray.

Call to Worship

Leader: Faithfulness will spring up from the ground, and righteousness will look down from the sky.

People: The Lord will give what is good, and our land will yield its increase.

– Based on Psalm 85:11-12

Pastoral Prayer

Lord of the universe, remind us of your good creation. Let us look to the stars and see your vastness. Let us look to the sea and meditate upon your depth. Let us see the animals and ponder the wideness of your imagination. Let us taste the produce of the fields and think on your generosity and provision. Let us hear the wind and remember that you are beyond our comprehension. Let us look to children and believe you are love, joy, and peace. How often we pray, O Lord, "Your kingdom come." Teach us to see your kingly reign everywhere we look. Bring your love, peace, and grace among us. Bring your love in such a way that we are overpowered by the desire to share the good news of the gospel. Bring your peace into every household and family, every classroom and boardroom, every country and every city. Bring your grace so we may understand how we have been forgiven, and be quick to forgive others. Amen.

Prayer of Confession

Forgiving God, help us to see our shortcomings and sin. Make us aware of our hurtful words, cruel acts, and dreadful failures to act. Forgive us when we do not care for ourselves, for those around us, or for the world you have made. Free us from the sometimes overwhelming sense of our inability to serve you as we would like. Restore us to wholeness, and let us serve you with hope and grace, through Christ our Lord. Amen.

Prayer of Dedication of Gifts and Self

We thank you, O God, for the gifts of this life. You have made us stewards of your creation and have blessed us with abundance. Now we commit to you our time, our abilities, our possessions, our whole selves. Use us, we pray, to further your kingdom on the earth. Amen.

Sermon Summary

Jesus, through example, parable, and illustration, shows how God loves to hear our prayers.

Hymn of the Day

"Seek Ye First"

Probably more people first heard this hymn sung around a campfire than in a church building. Writer and composer Karen Lafferty has described it as "a song in which people can put God's desire for their lives above their own."

Brilliant in its simplicity, the song is easily learned, and can be sung unaccompanied or with guitar. It makes a nice musical "backdrop" sung behind rituals, during the serving of communion, or softly as an accompaniment to a time of silent prayer.

Children's Time

Why Do We Need to Pray?

Prayer is a conversation with God. What do we tell God when we pray? *(Invite responses.)*

It's a chance to thank God for all God has given us. We pray to say we're sorry for things we've done wrong. We pray to ask for what we need and what others need. Prayer is also a time to listen to God.

Sometimes people wonder why we need to pray. It's important for us to take time to worship God, remembering that we are God's children. It's important to ask for God's love and forgiveness. It's important to ask for God's strength to help us help our neighbors. God knows what we need, and when we pray we take time to think about what is important and to talk with God about those things.

Jesus taught his disciples and us to pray in many different ways. One prayer Jesus taught is the Lord's Prayer, which we still say each Sunday. Jesus promises that God will hear our prayers and answer us. That's good to remember.

The Sermon

The God Who Hears

Hymns

Beginning of Worship: "Praise, My Soul, the King of Heaven"
Sermon Hymn: "Seek Ye First"
Closing Hymn: "Jesus, Thou Joy of Loving Hearts"

Scripture

Luke 11:1-13 (For additional sermon materials on this passage, see the March 2004 issue of *The Clergy Journal* and on Colossians 2:6-15 (16-19), see the 2003 May/June planning issue of *The Clergy Journal*.)

It's apparent everywhere you look – from television talk shows to school classrooms, from seminars to magazines. People want to be more spiritual. Many, including people in churches, say they want to know how to pray, but don't know how. Perhaps we in the church even contribute to the feeling of never being able to do it right. We pray certain types of prayers, leading folks to think they need to pray at a certain time of day or for a certain length of time.

Here's the question most people are afraid to ask: Is anyone on the other end of our prayers, anyhow? If there is a God, does God really care about my little life?

Jesus tells us that someone is on the other end of the line. The disciples had the same questions we have. How are we supposed to pray, Lord? And they take out their pencils and paper to take notes, to write down this new form of prayer. Jesus gives them a different kind of form. It arises naturally from real life. It is real life. Prayer is a response to what is going on right in front of us, a response to what is going on within us.

Our prayers come right out of the circumstances of real life, not divorced from it. Jesus gives them an example of a prayer composed of completely natural elements: thanksgiving, petition, request for forgiveness.

For instance, when something good happens, we are motivated to breathe a prayer of thanks: the beauty of a cool morning after a series of summer's hot and humid days; kids who make us laugh; a good grade on a test; a good friend; a kind word; a new job or joy in a current job; enough money to pay the bills; a glorious vacation; new life in a marriage; a good night's rest; forgiveness; healing from an illness; good results on a medical test; chocolate.

We don't have to wait until some set time to give thanks. What if we were moved to say a quick prayer of thanks each thankful moment? Wouldn't we learn to connect the giver of the gift with the gifts of life?

In the exact same way, we are motivated to pray when things don't go so well. When someone is sick; when the children misbehave so much we want to give them to the grandparents who think they are perfect; when things go badly at school; when there isn't enough money to pay all the bills; when the marriage is in trouble; when we can't sleep at night; when worry overcomes us; when we are grieving a loss; when we hate our job; when the medical tests don't turn out right.

Again, prayer at such a time draws us into the connection between faith and life. We cry out to God, wanting God's presence, hope, love, protection. And sometimes we feel those things immediately. Sometimes they come along slowly. Sometimes we don't feel them at all. That's when we wonder if God really hears.

Our own failings, too, lead us to think of praying. We realize it's probably not right to wish the children would move to live with their grandparents and to hope they would all be punished by having to live together all the time; we cheat to make our money stretch to pay the bills; we say something and the second it leaves our lips we wish we could take it back; our anger overcomes us and makes us do things we regret. When we have recovered from our lapse of good judgment, it often occurs to us to ask forgiveness and to hope we can keep from making the same errors in the future. That is when we turn to God, again in prayer.

Jesus' model prayer is a prayer that arises out of the ordinary acts of living: thanksgiving, petition, and forgiveness.

Luke then gives us two additional teachings about prayer, the first in the form of a parable that is based on a Middle Eastern understanding of the requirements of hospitality. Hearing with our 21st-century ears, we often misinterpret this parable, feeling sorry for the one who was awakened in the middle of the night by a rude neighbor who was too lazy to prepare something for his own houseguests. Jesus' listeners would have heard something quite different.

A traveler who came to the home of someone in the village was considered to be a guest of the entire town. Inasmuch as hospitality was (and still is) a tremendously important cultural value of that area of the world, anyone in town could be called upon to help make the visitor comfortable. An unexpected guest at night could be a cause of particular anxiety, if one has no leftover bread from the day. At night you do not build the fire for baking, but the woman of the home might be aware that the woman next door had baked a few extra loaves that morning. The neighbors would consider it an honor to help you out of your bind.

The neighbor in Jesus' story doesn't act according to the way the listeners would expect. He refuses even to get out of bed and answer the door, but shouts from within, "Leave us alone! The children are in bed. You can't expect me to get up and help you." Well, of course the friend could and did expect the neighbor to get out of bed and offer whatever he had to ease the discomfort of the other. Finally, when the friend continues knocking and calling out for help, the lazy and selfish neighbor forces himself out of bed and to the door, just to shut the guy up. How much more, said Jesus, is a good God willing to hear you than this awful neighbor? You may think your prayers are unheard, that no one is listening. Nevertheless, God hears. Always.

Okay, you say, suppose I buy the line that God hears my prayers, that there is someone on the other end when I raise my voice to God. Then what about when I ask for something good and receive something bad instead? What about the time I prayed for my friend to be healed and she wasn't? What does that say about God's character?

That is a good question, and it is one that has been asked as long as people have been able to conceive of a good God. It is not one that Jesus ever answers. But here is what he makes clear: God hears us even when we think no one is listening or paying attention, like that unhelpful neighbor. We may feel as though we are pounding on the doors of heaven, trying to awake a sleeping God to our desperate heartfelt need. So don't give up praying. Pray as people who know that God is listening, even if you feel that nothing comes of your prayers. Pray as people who are knocking on heaven's door, and imagine God leaping from bed, not even bothering to put on shoes, running to the door to see what it is that you need. Imagine God flinging open the door, putting an arm around you, and inviting you in to share your joy or your pain.

Ask, and it will be given you; search, and you will find; knock, and the door will be opened for you. For everyone who asks, receives, and everyone who searches, finds, and for everyone who knocks, the door will be opened.

– Melissa Bane Sevier
First Presbyterian Church
Aurora, Indiana

Appendices

Resources for Preparing to Preach

by David H. Schmidt

The following bibliography offers one person's review of commentaries and overviews that a pastor might consult as she or he prepares the sermon. The first sections cover books that can be used all three years of the Revised Common Lectionary. These are followed by comments about books for the portions of the lectionary covered in this manual. They are grouped by gospels, then epistles, and, finally, Old Testament. An effort is made to include some of the newer works arriving on the market as well as some standard volumes that time has shown to be helpful to pastors. A variety of theological perspectives are included. Some reference is made to computer software resources as well.

One-Volume Commentaries and Software

One-volume commentaries that can be used throughout the three-year cycle include: *Harper's Bible Commentary*, James L. Mays, gen. ed. (Harper & Row, 1988). Published in cooperation with the Society of Biblical Literature, this one-volume commentary provides good, brief information that reflects the current state of scholarship. There are good overview articles as well as comments on each book (including the Deuterocanonical Books). A second current one-volume work is that of Raymond E. Brown et al., *The New Jerome Biblical Commentary*, rev. ed. (Paulist Press, 1989). Both of these works are now available on a *Logos Bible Software* CD-ROM, along with *Matthew Henry's Commentary* and the *Bible Knowledge Commentary*.

Logos Research Systems also makes available the *Harper's Bible Dictionary* and Doubleday's *Anchor Bible Dictionary*. Several software companies provide the *Holman Bible Dictionary* and/or others with some of their packages.

Several commentary series are now available on CD-ROM. Zondervan has released *The Expositor's Bible Commentary*, Frank Gaebelein, ed. *Word Biblical Commentary* is on a disc with Greek and Hebrew Texts and numerous Bible translations. Abingdon now has the whole *New Interpreter's Bible* on disc. Biblesoft has packages that include such older series as *Matthew Henry's Commentaries*, *Wycliffe Commentaries*, *Keil & Delitzsch's Old Testament Commentary*, *Adam Clarke's Commentaries*, and *Jamieson-Fausset-Brown Commentaries*.

Study of the Psalter

Years A, B, and C

Overviews

H. J. Kraus' *Theology of the Psalms* (Augsburg, 1986) is a good discussion by a scholar who has also published a major commentary (below). A brief introductory work is Klaus Seybold's *Introducing the Psalms* (T & T Clark, 1990). For a work that invites looking at the psalms in a different way see J. David Pleius' *The Psalms: Songs of Tragedy, Hope, and Justice, The Bible & Liberation* (Orbis, 1993). Stanley L. Jaki's *Praying the Psalms* (Eerdmans, 2001) invites Christians to reflect on the psalms by one who has made a lifetime of praying them.

Commentaries

H. J. Kraus' *Psalms 1–59* and *Psalms 60–150* (Augsburg, 1987, 1989) are the standard works full of detail. J. Clinton McCann provides exegetical and expository reflection on the psalms in the *New Interpreter's Bible*, vol. 4 (Abingdon, 1996). K. Schaefer's *Psalms*, Berit Olam: Studies in Hebrew Narrative and Poetry (The Liturgical Press, 2001) is a recent Roman Catholic study. James L. May's *Psalms*, Interpretation Commentaries (John Knox, 1994) is a fine expository work that can be used alongside of the above commentaries.

Study of Acts

Years A, B, and C

Overviews

Mark Allen Powell's *What Are They Saying About Acts?* (Paulist Press, 1991) will provide a good introduction to the state of research on Acts. Jacob Jervell's *The Theology of the Acts of the Apostles* (Cambridge University Press, 1996) offers an up-to-date review of the theological issues.

Commentaries

W. H. Willimon's *Acts*, Interpretation Commentaries (John Knox, 1988) gives a sound expository start for the pastor. E. Haenchen's *The Acts of the Apostles: A Commentary* (Westminster, 1971) is a significant reference. Luke Timothy Johnson's *The Acts of the Apostles*, Sacra Pagina 5 (The Liturgical Press, 1992) is a recent Catholic study with a fresh translation, notes, and interpretation that provides a solid alternative that may be easier to use. Joseph A. Fitzmyer's *The Acts of the Apostles*, Anchor Bible (Doubleday, 1998) is a good replacement volume in that series. Robert W. Wall's "The Acts of the Apostles," *New Interpreter's Bible*, vol.10 (Abingdon, 2002) offers a Wesleyan exposition and exegesis. Ben Witherington III's *The Acts of the Apostles: A Socio-Rhetorical Commentary* (Eerdmans, 1998) provides an evangelical study using the foci of cultural anthropology and rhetorical criticism. C.K. Barrett's *Acts of the Apostles,* International Critical Commentary, 2 volumes (T & T Clark, 1993, 1998) is a significant new study on the Greek text.

Study of the Gospel Lessons

John (Years B and C)

Overviews

Gerald S. Sloyan's *What Are They Saying about John?* (Paulist, 1991) provides a fine overview of current scholarship. Robert Kysar's *John's Story of Jesus* (Fortress, 1984) will give one a good overall review of John' gospel. D. Moody Smith's *John*, Proclamation Commentary, 2nd ed. (Fortress, 1986) is an alternative. He also provides a theological overview in *The Theology of John* (Cambridge University Press, 1995).

Commentaries

Raymond E. Brown's *The Gospel According to John*, Anchor Bible 29, 29A (Doubleday, 1966, 1970) has become a standard two-volume work for exegetical study. Couple this with the expository effort of Gerald Sloyan's *John*, Interpretation Commentaries (John Knox, 1988) for a solid set of resources. On the other hand, exposition and exegesis are in one volume in Gail R. O'Day's "The Gospel of John," *The New Interpreter's Bible*, vol. 9 (Abingdon, 1995). Charles H. Talbert's *Reading John: A Literary and Theological Commentary on the Fourth Gospel and the Johannine Epistles* (Crossroad, 1992) is a study using the newer literary approach. Ben Witherington III's *John's Wisdom, A Commentary on the Fourth Gospel* (Westminster/John Knox, 1995) offers another perspective. Bruce J. Malina and Richard L. Rohrbaugh's *Social Science Commentary on the Gospel of John* (Fortress, 1998) is another study that can allow one to look at the text in a new way. Francis J. Moloney's *The Gospel of John*, Sacra Pagina (The Liturgical Press, 1998) is another recent study.

Mark (Year B)

Overviews

Paul Achtemeier's *Mark*, Proclamation Commentaries, 2nd rev. ed. (Fortress, 1986) is a good overview. Frank J. Matera's *What Are They Saying about Mark?* (Paulist Press, 1987) is a fine alternative. An interesting book that introduces the reader to a variety of modern approaches to Mark is Janice C. Anderson and Stephen D. Moore's *Mark and Method: New*

Approaches in Biblical Studies (Augsburg/Fortress, 1992). W. R. Telford's *The Theology of the Gospel of Mark* (Cambridge, 2000) will provide a theological overview.

Commentaries

A recent study by Morna D. Hooker, *The Gospel According to St. Mark*, Black's New Testament Commentary (Hendrickson, 1992) is very helpful. Pheme Perkins' "The Gospel of Mark," *The New Interpreter's Bible*, vol. 8 (Abingdon, 1995) is another possibility. Lamar Williamson Jr.'s *Mark*, Interpretation Commentaries (John Knox, 1983) provides an expository study. Eduard Schweizer's *The Good News According to Mark* (John Knox, 1970) continues to provide solid help for the preacher. Ched Myers offers a pair of socio-literary studies that challenge us to take a different look at Mark in *Binding the Strong Man* and *Who Will Roll Away the Stone?* (Orbis, 1988 & 1994). Bruce J. Malina and Richard L. Rohrbaugh's *Social Science Commentary on the Synoptic Gospels* (Fortress, 1992) also can provide one to look at the text in a different way.

Luke (Year C)

Overviews

Mark Alan Powell, *What Are They Saying About Luke?* (Paulist Press, 1989) offers an excellent overview of what's happening in Lukan studies. F. W. Danker's *Luke*, Proclamation Commentary, 2nd rev. ed. (Fortress, 1987) also provides a good background discussion. Jerome Neyrey, ed., *The Social World of Luke/Acts* (Hendrickson, 1991) gives additional insight into current discussion.

Commentaries

A detailed standard set is Joseph Fitzyer's *The Gospel According to Luke*, Anchor Bible 28, 28A (Doubleday, 1981, 1985). Supplement this with the expository insight of Fred Craddock's *Luke*, Interpretation Commentaries (John Knox, 1990) for good preaching help. Richard Anderson's *Preaching Luke's Gospel: A Narrative Approach* (C.S.S., 1997) is another preaching study. R. Alan Culpepper offers exegetical and expository study of Luke in the *New Interpreter's Bible*, vol. 9 (Abingdon, 1995). Frederick W. Danker's *Jesus and the New Age*, rev. & expanded (Fortress, 1988) is well regarded. Luke Timothy Johnson's *The Gospel of Luke*, Sacra Pagina 3 (Liturgical Press, 1991) is another option for additional material. Also see Malina and Rohrbaugh under "Mark ."

Studies
Raymond E. Brown's *The Birth of the Messiah* (Doubleday, 1979) offers a detailed study of the infancy narratives. Loretta Darnish's *A Woman Reads the Gospel of Luke* (Liturgical Press, 1996) also offers further insight.

Study of the Epistle Lessons
(in order used)

1 Corinthians
William A. Beardslee's *First Corinthians: A Commentary for Today* (Chalice Press, 1994) is a book aimed at the pastor and teacher. J. Paul Smalley offers exegetical and expository insight in "First Letter fo the Corinthians," *New Interpreters' Bible*, vol. 10 (Abingdon, 2002). Gordon D. Fee's *The First Epistle to the Corinthians,* New International Commentary on the New Testament (Eerdmans, 1987) is a good, detailed evangelical study. Ben Witherington III's *Conflict and Community in Corinth: A Socio-Rhetorical Commentary on 1 & 2 Corinthians* (Eerdmans, 1995) offers another good study by an evangelical. H. Conzelmann's *1 Corinthians,* Hermeneia (Fortress, 1977) is a scholarly work based on the Greek text. Raymond F. Collins' *First Corinthians,* Sacra Pagina 7 (The Liturgical Press, 1999) places the book in its cultural context. Richard A. Horsley's *1 Corinthians,* Abingdon New Testament Commentaries (Abingdon, 1997) can be helpful as well. Victor Furnish's *The Theology of the First Letter to the Corinthians* (Cambridge, 1999) offers a theological overview.

Galatians
Richard B. Hays' "Letter to the Galatians," *New Interpreters' Bible,* vol. 11 (Abingdon, 2000) may be a place to start. Charles Cousar's *Galatians,* Interpretation Commentaries (John Knox, 1982) provides a fine expository discussion. It can be supplemented with the exegetical work of Frank J. Matera's *Galatians,* Sacra Pagina 9 (Liturgical Press, 1992) or Sam K. Williams' *Galatians,* Abingdon New Testament Commentaries (Abingdon, 1996). Dieter Betz's *Galatians,* Hermenia (Fortress, 1979) has become a scholarly standard on the Greek text. James D. G. Dunn's *The Theology of Paul's Letter to the Galatians* (Cambridge, 1993) offers a valuable overview. He also has a good commentary, *The Epistle to the Galatians,* Black's New Testament Commentary (Hendrickson, 1993).

Philippians
Morna D. Hooker's "Letter to the Philippians," *New Interpreters' Bible,* vol. 11 (Abingdon, 2000) has both exegetical and expository material. Fred B.

Craddock's *Philippians*, Interpretation Commentaries (John Knox, 1985) offers a brief expository study. It would need to be supplemented by Gordon Fee's *Paul's Letter to the Philippians*, New International Commentary on the New Testament (Eerdmans, 1995) for a good evangelical study or Markus Bockmuehl's *The Epistle to the Philippians*, Black's New Testament Commentary (Hendrickson, 1998). A study on the Greek text is found in Peter T. O'Brien's *The Epistle to the Philippians*, New International Greek New Testament (Eerdmans, 1991). Mark J. Edwards edits *Galatians, Ephesians, Philippians*, Ancient Christian Commentary on Scripture (InterVarsity Press, 1998), which provides insights drawn from the early church writers.

Ephesians

Rudolf Schnackenburg's *Ephesians: A Commentary* (T & T Clark, 1991) is a good Roman Catholic study. Pheme Perkins' "Letter to the Ephesians," *New Interpreters' Bible*, vol. 11 (Abingdon, 2000) is a fine new work. Markus Barth's *Ephesians*, Anchor Bible 34 & 34A (Doubleday, 1974) provides a detailed discussion. And Ralph P. Martin's *Ephesians, Colossians, and Philemon*, Interpretation Commentaries (John Knox, 1991) offers a helpful expository addition. Ernest Best's *A Critical and Exegetical Commentary on Ephesians*, International Critical Commentary (T & T Clar, 1998) provies a new scholarly study on the Greek text. See Edwards under Philippians for a work from early Christian writers.

Colossians

Andrew T. Lincoln's "Letter to the Colossians," *New Interpreters' Bible*, vol. 11 (Abingdon, 2000) might be the place to begin. Ralph P. Martin (see "Ephesians") provides additional exposition. Markus Barth and Helmut Blanke's *Colossians*, Anchor Bible 34B (Doubleday, 1994) or Petr Pokorny's *Colossians: A Commentary* (Hendrickson, 1991) can add the exegetical support. James D. G. Dunn's *The Epistle to the Colossians and to Philemon*, New International Greek Testament Commentary (Eerdmans, 1996) is a fine study of the Greek text.

James

Luke T. Johnson offers two recent studies, *Letter to James* Anchor Bible 37A (Doubleday, 1995) or "James," *New Interpreters' Bible,* vol. 12 (Abingdon, 1998). Pheme Perkins' *First and Second Peter, James, and Jude*, Interpretation Commentaries (John Knox, 1995) provides an expository study. S. Laws' *A Commentary on the Epistle of James*, Black's New Testament Commentaries (Hendrickson, 1980) remains helpful. Robert W. Wall's *Community of the*

Wise: The Letter of James (Trinity Press International, 1997) is another view worth reading. Peter Davids' *Commentary on James,* New International Greek Testament Commentary (Eerdmans, 1982) offers a scholarly look at the Greek text.

Hebrews

Fred B. Craddock provies an exegetical and expository study in the *New Interpreters' Bible*, vol. 12 (Abingdon, 1998). Thomas G. Long's *Hebrews*, Interpretation Commentaries (John Knox, 1997) is a fresh expository study. Other solid works include F. F. Bruce's *The Epistle to the Hebrews*, rev. ed., The New International Commentary on the New Testament (Eerdmans, 1990) and Harold W. Attridge's *Hebrews*, Hermenia (Fortress, 1989). Although the latter is on the Greek text, it can be used by all. Barnabas Lindars' *The Theology of the Letter to the Hebrews*, New Testament Theology (Cambridge, 1991) offers a theological overview.

Revelation

Christopher C. Rowland provides the study in the *New Interpreters' Bible*, vol. 12 (Abingdon, 1998). M. Eugene Boring's *Revelation,* Interpretation Commentaries (John Knox, 1989) offers expository help. Other exegetical studies include Jurgen Roloff's *Revelation: A Continental Commentary* (Augsburg Fortress, 1993) or Wilfrid J. Harrington's *Revelation*, Sacra Pagina 16 (Liturgical Press, 1993). Malina's *On the Genre and Message of Revelation* Hendrickson, 1993) reviews a social anthropological perspective. David L. Barr's *Tales of the End: A Narrative Commentary on the Book of Revelation* Polebridge, 1998) provies us with another current approach to biblical study.

Study of Old Testament Texts

Isaiah

Gene M. Tucker's "The Book of Isaiah 1–39" and Christopher R. Seitz's "The Book of Isaiah 40–66" in *The New Interpreter's Bible*, vol. 6 (Abingdon, 2001) are part of a hefty recent work. Seitz also offers expository study in *Isaiah 1–39*, Interpretation Commentaries (John Knox, 1993). In addition, he edited *Reading and Preaching the Book of Isaiah* (Fortress, 1988) which can assist the pastor in thinking about the use of Isaiah during the year. Paul D. Hanson's *Isaiah 40–66*, Interpretation Commentaries (John Knox, 1995) provies expository work on the rest of Isaiah.
R. Clements's *Isaiah 1–39*, New Century Bible Commentary (Eerdmans, 1980) and R. N. Whybray's *Isaiah 40–66,* New Century Bible Commentary (Eerdmans, 1975) provide good, inexpensive commentaries. Joseph

Blenkinsopp's *Isaiah*, Anchor Bible 19 (Doubleday, 2000) is an interesting replacement volume in that series. Brever Childs' *Isaiah*, Old Testament Library (Westminister, 2001) is a stimulating addition to that series.

Jeremiah

Patrick D. Miller's "The Book of Jeremiah," *New Interpreters' Bible*, vol. 6 (Abingdon, 2001) now offers the place to start. Ronald Clements' *Jeremiah*, Interpretation Commentaries (John Knox, 1989) is another expository study. R. P. Carroll's *Jeremiah: A Commentary*, Old Testament Library (Westminster, 1986) is one of several solid exegetical works that can be used to compliment Clements. Jack R. Lundbom's *Jeremiah 1–20*, Anchor Bible 21A (Doubleday, 1999) begins his study of this prophet. Walter Brueggemann's *A Commentary on Jeremiah: Exile and Homecoming* (Eerdmans, 1998) is a rich study not to be overlooked.

1 & 2 Kings

Richard D. Nelson's *First and Second Kings*, Interpretation Commentaries (John Knox, 1987) provides a good expository assistance. Choon-Leong Seow offers a fresh study in the *New Interpreters' Bible*, vol. 3 (Abingdon, 1999). Other exegetical supplements include G. H. Jones' *1 and 2 Kings*, New Century Bible Commentary, 2 vols. (Eerdmans, 1984) or Donald J. Wiseman's *1 and 2 Kings*, Tyndale Old Testament Commentaries (InterVarsity Press, 1993).

Proverbs

Michael V. Fox's *Proverbs*, Anchor Bible 18A (Doubleday, 1997) or Raymond C. Van Leeuwen's "Proverbs," *New Interpreters' Bible*, vol. 5 (Abingdon, 1997) provides recent studies for the pastor. A fresh overview can be found in Kathleen A. Farmer's *Proverbs & Ecclesiastes*, International Theological Commentary (Eerdmans, 1991).

Job

Expository insights abound in J. Gerald Janzen's *Job*, Interpretation Commentaries (John Knox, 1985). Carol A. Newsom's "Job," *New Interpreters' Bible*, vol. 4 (Abingdon, 1996) or N. C. Habel's *The Book of Job: A Commentary*, Old Testament Library (Westminster, 1985) would make good companion studies. David J. A. Clines' *Job 1–20* and *Job 21–42*, Word Biblical Commentaries 17 (Word, 1989, 2002) and Gustavo Gutierez's *On Job: God Talk and the Suffering of the Innocent* (Orbig, 1987) can stir up additional thoughts. John C. Holbert's *Preaching Job* (Chalice Press, 1999) also merits a look.

2003–2004 Writers

Sermons and Prayers

LaVonne Althouse
(Lutheran – ELCA)
14 St. Mark Ave.
Lititz, PA 17643
May 16, 20, 23, 30, 2004

Andrea La Sonde Anastos
(United Church of Christ)
62A Laurel St.
Greenfield, MA 01301
Sept. 28, Oct. 5, 12, 19, 2003

John Bucka
(Lutheran – ELCA)
3994 Zealand Ave. No.
New Hope, MN 55427
Mar. 7, 14, 21, 28, 2004

Dennis Bushkofsky
(Lutheran – ELCA)
200 No. Arlington Hgts. Rd. #421
Arlington Heights, IL 60004-6049
Oct. 26, 31, Nov. 1, 2, 9, 2003

Katherine W. Ellison
(Presbyterian USA)
51 Oak Grove Ave.
Hasbrouck Heights, NJ 07604
Apr. 4, 8, 9, 11, 2004

C. Welton Gaddy
(Baptist)
1012 - 14th St. NW - Ste. 700
Washington, DC 20005
June 6, 13, 20, 27, 2004

Catherine Malotky
(Lutheran – ELCA)
5901 Rowland Rd.
Minnetonka, MN 55343-8923
Dec. 28, 2003
Jan. 4, 6, 11, 2004

David W. Reid
(Baptist)
45 Woburn St.
Reading, MA -1867
Nov. 16, 23, 27, 30, 2003

William Schwein
(United Methodist)
8222 Windhaven Cir.
Indiapolis, IN 46236
Jan. 18, 25, Feb. 1, 8, 2004

Melissa Bane Sevier
(Presbyterian USA)
13047 Knopf Rd.
Sunman, IN 47041
July 4, 11, 18, 25, 2004

David Sharp
(Presbyterian USA)
959 Catkin Ct.
San Jose, CA 95128
Apr. 18, 25, May 2, 9, 2004

Diane Strickland
(Presbyterian Church in Canada)
236 Ranchero Pl. NW
Calgary, Alberta, Canada T3G 1C7
Dec. 7, 14, 21, 24, 25, 2003

Nancy E. Topolewski
(United Methodist)
124 Sunset Ave.
Vestal, NY 13850-5830
Aug. 3, 10, 17, 24, 2003

Norman Wahl
(Lutheran – ELCA)
810 Third Ave. SE
Rochester, MN 55904
Feb. 15, 22, 25, 29, 2004

Gary Walling
(Disciples of Christ)
15905 Fernway Rd.
Shaker Heights, OH 44120
Aug. 31,
Sept. 7, 14, 21, 28, 2003

Children's Time

Gillian Wallace
(Anglican)
155 Hopewell Ave.
Ottawa, Ontario, Canada K1S 2Z4

Preaching Resources

David H. Schmidt
2813 No. 400 West
West Lafayette, IN 47906

Hymn of the Day Selections

Donald Schmidt
(United Church of Christ)
677 Luakini St.
Lahaina, HI 96767

Four-Year Church Year Calendar

	Series B **2002**	Series C **2003**	Series A **2004**	Series B **2005**
Advent begins	Dec. 1	Nov. 30	Nov. 28	Nov. 27
Christmas	Dec. 25	Dec. 25	Dec. 25	Dec. 25
	2003	**2004**	**2005**	**2006**
Epiphany	Jan. 6	Jan. 6	Jan. 6	Jan. 6
Ash Wednesday	Mar. 5	Feb, 25	Feb. 9	Mar. 1
Palm Sunday	Apr. 13	Apr. 4	Mar. 20	Apr. 9
Maundy Thursday	Apr. 17	Apr. 8	Mar. 24	Apr. 13
Good Friday	Apr. 18	Apr. 9	Mar. 25	Apr. 14
Easter Day	Apr. 20	Apr. 11	Mar. 27	Apr. 16
Ascension Day	May 29	May 20	May 5	May 25
Pentecost	June 8	May 30	May 15	June 4
Trinity Sunday	June 15	June 6	May 22	June 11
Reformation	Oct. 31	Oct. 31	Oct. 31	Oct. 31
All Saints' Day	Nov. 1	Nov. 1	Nov. 1	Nov. 1

Calendars for 2003 and 2004

2003

JANUARY 2003

S	M	T	W	T	F	S
			1	2	3	4
5	6	7	8	9	10	11
12	13	14	15	16	17	18
19	20	21	22	23	24	25
26	27	28	29	30	31	

FEBRUARY 2003

S	M	T	W	T	F	S
						1
2	3	4	5	6	7	8
9	10	11	12	13	14	15
16	17	18	19	20	21	22
23	24	25	26	27	28	

MARCH 2003

S	M	T	W	T	F	S
30	31					1
2	3	4	5	6	7	8
9	10	11	12	13	14	15
16	17	18	19	20	21	22
23	24	25	26	27	28	29

APRIL 2003

S	M	T	W	T	F	S
		1	2	3	4	5
6	7	8	9	10	11	12
13	14	15	16	17	18	19
20	21	22	23	24	25	26
27	28	29	30			

MAY 2003

S	M	T	W	T	F	S
				1	2	3
4	5	6	7	8	9	10
11	12	13	14	15	16	17
18	19	20	21	22	23	24
25	26	27	28	29	30	31

JUNE 2003

S	M	T	W	T	F	S
1	2	3	4	5	6	7
8	9	10	11	12	13	14
15	16	17	18	19	20	21
22	23	24	25	26	27	28
29	30					

JULY 2003

S	M	T	W	T	F	S
		1	2	3	4	5
6	7	8	9	10	11	12
13	14	15	16	17	18	19
20	21	22	23	24	25	26
27	28	29	30	31		

AUGUST 2003

S	M	T	W	T	F	S
31					1	2
3	4	5	6	7	8	9
10	11	12	13	14	15	16
17	18	19	20	21	22	23
24	25	26	27	28	29	30

SEPTEMBER 2003

S	M	T	W	T	F	S
	1	2	3	4	5	6
7	8	9	10	11	12	13
14	15	16	17	18	19	20
21	22	23	24	25	26	27
28	29	30				

OCTOBER 2003

S	M	T	W	T	F	S
			1	2	3	4
5	6	7	8	9	10	11
12	13	14	15	16	17	18
19	20	21	22	23	24	25
26	27	28	29	30	31	

NOVEMBER 2003

S	M	T	W	T	F	S
30						1
2	3	4	5	6	7	8
9	10	11	12	13	14	15
16	17	18	19	20	21	22
23	24	25	26	27	28	29

DECEMBER 2003

S	M	T	W	T	F	S
	1	2	3	4	5	6
7	8	9	10	11	12	13
14	15	16	17	18	19	20
21	22	23	24	25	26	27
28	29	30	31			

2004

JANUARY 2004

S	M	T	W	T	F	S
				1	2	3
4	5	6	7	8	9	10
11	12	13	14	15	16	17
18	19	20	21	22	23	24
25	26	27	28	29	30	31

FEBRUARY 2004

S	M	T	W	T	F	S
1	2	3	4	5	6	7
8	9	10	11	12	13	14
15	16	17	18	19	20	21
22	23	24	25	26	27	28
29						

MARCH 2004

S	M	T	W	T	F	S
	1	2	3	4	5	6
7	8	9	10	11	12	13
14	15	16	17	18	19	20
21	22	23	24	25	26	27
28	29	30	31			

APRIL 2004

S	M	T	W	T	F	S
				1	2	3
4	5	6	7	8	9	10
11	12	13	14	15	16	17
18	19	20	21	22	23	24
25	26	27	28	29	30	

MAY 2004

S	M	T	W	T	F	S
30	31					1
2	3	4	5	6	7	8
9	10	11	12	13	14	15
16	17	18	19	20	21	22
23	24	25	26	27	28	29

JUNE 2004

S	M	T	W	T	F	S
		1	2	3	4	5
6	7	8	9	10	11	12
13	14	15	16	17	18	19
20	21	22	23	24	25	26
27	28	29	30			

JULY 2004

S	M	T	W	T	F	S
				1	2	3
4	5	6	7	8	9	10
11	12	13	14	15	16	17
18	19	20	21	22	23	24
25	26	27	28	29	30	31

AUGUST 2004

S	M	T	W	T	F	S
1	2	3	4	5	6	7
8	9	10	11	12	13	14
15	16	17	18	19	20	21
22	23	24	25	26	27	28
29	30	31				

SEPTEMBER 2004

S	M	T	W	T	F	S
			1	2	3	4
5	6	7	8	9	10	11
12	13	14	15	16	17	18
19	20	21	22	23	24	25
26	27	28	29	30		

OCTOBER 2004

S	M	T	W	T	F	S
31					1	2
3	4	5	6	7	8	9
10	11	12	13	14	15	16
17	18	19	20	21	22	23
24	25	26	27	28	29	30

NOVEMBER 2004

S	M	T	W	T	F	S
	1	2	3	4	5	6
7	8	9	10	11	12	13
14	15	16	17	18	19	20
21	22	23	24	25	26	27
28	29	30				

DECEMBER 2004

S	M	T	W	T	F	S
			1	2	3	4
5	6	7	8	9	10	11
12	13	14	15	16	17	18
19	20	21	22	23	24	25
26	27	28	29	30	31	

Index of Sermon Texts

Dear *Annual Manual* subscriber,

In past editions of *The Minister's Annual Manual,* we included a prepublication order form on this page.

Annual Manual has now been converted to a subscription.

In April 2004 you will receive a renewal notice reminding you to order the 2004–2005 issue. If you do not receive one, please call Logos Productions Inc. at 1-800-328-0200.

Thank you for your continued support of *Annual Manual.*

Yours in Christ,

Logos Productions Inc.